PARLIAMENT'S SECRET WAR

The invasion of Iraq in 2003, and the Coalition Government's failure to win parliamentary approval for armed intervention in Syria in 2013, mark a period of increased scrutiny of the process by which the UK engages in armed conflict. For much of the media and civil society there now exists a constitutional convention which mandates that the Government consults Parliament before commencing hostilities. This is celebrated as representing a redistribution of power from the executive towards a more legitimate, democratic institution. This book offers a critical inquiry into Parliament's role in the war prerogative since the beginning of the twentieth century, evaluating whether the UK's decisions to engage in conflict meet the recognised standards of good governance: accountability, transparency and participation. The analysis reveals a number of persistent problems in the decision-making process, including Parliament's lack of access to relevant information, government 'legalisation' of parliamentary debates which frustrates broader discussions of political legitimacy, and the skewing of debates via the partial public disclosure of information based upon secret intelligence. The book offers solutions to these problems to reinvigorate parliamentary discourse and to address government withholding of classified information. It is essential reading for anyone interested in war powers, the relationship between international law and domestic politics, and the role of the Westminster Parliament in questions of national security.

Volume 2 in Hart Studies in Security and Justice

Hart Studies in Security and Justice

Series editor: Liora Lazarus

The interplay between security and justice has always featured prominently in legal scholarship, but it has taken on a particular urgency since the new Millennium. The new scholarly questions that arise are theoretical, doctrinal and empirical, cutting across a range of traditional sub-disciplines within the legal academy. They address some of the most pressing legal issues of our time, such as the legal status of the 'the war on terror', the nature of states of exception, targeted killing, preventive pre-trial detention, mass surveillance and the numerous other threats that security poses to human rights, the rule of law and liberal democracy.

The purpose of this series is to engage with security and justice scholarship broadly conceived, and to promote a sophisticated and complex understanding of the important challenges it faces. The series is inclusive, promoting new and established scholars from a range of disciplines. It covers doctrinal, empirical, historical and theoretical work, as well as studies which focus on domestic, comparative and international dimensions of emerging security and justice fields. The series also strives to promote the most inclusive range of politics and methodologies, scrutinizing received wisdom and established paradigmatic approaches, and promoting an intellectual dialogue between its authors and the wider field of law as a whole.

Recent titles in this series:

Surveillance, Privacy and Trans-Atlantic Relations
Edited by David Cole, Federico Fabbrini and Stephen Schulhofer

Parliament's Secret War

Veronika Fikfak and Hayley J Hooper

·HART·
PUBLISHING
OXFORD AND PORTLAND, OREGON
2018

Hart Publishing

An imprint of Bloomsbury Publishing Plc

Hart Publishing Ltd
Kemp House
Chawley Park
Cumnor Hill
Oxford OX2 9PH
UK

Bloomsbury Publishing Plc
50 Bedford Square
London
WC1B 3DP
UK

www.hartpub.co.uk
www.bloomsbury.com

Published in North America (US and Canada) by
Hart Publishing
c/o International Specialized Book Services
920 NE 58th Avenue, Suite 300
Portland, OR 97213-3786
USA

www.isbs.com

HART PUBLISHING, the Hart/Stag logo, BLOOMSBURY and the
Diana logo are trademarks of Bloomsbury Publishing Plc

First published 2018

British Library Cataloguing-in-Publication Data

A catalogue record for this book is available from the British Library.

ISBN: HB: 978-1-50990-287-3
      ePDF: 978-1-50990-289-7
      ePub: 978-1-50990-290-3

Library of Congress Cataloging-in-Publication Data

Names: Fikfak, Veronika, author. | Hooper, Hayley Jayne, 1984- author.

Title: Parliament's secret war / Veronika Fikfak and Hayley J Hooper.

Description: Oxford ; Portland, Oregon : Hart Publishing, an imprint of Bloomsbury Publishing Plc, 2018.

Identifiers: LCCN 2017051085 (print) | LCCN 2017051854 (ebook) |
ISBN 9781509902903 (Epub) | ISBN 9781509902873 (hardback : alk. paper)

Subjects: LCSH: War and emergency legislation—Great Britain. | War,
Declaration of—Great Britain. | Prerogative, Royal—Great Britain.

Classification: LCC KD6004 (ebook) | LCC KD6004 .F55 2018 (print) | DDC 342.41/0412—dc23

LC record available at https://lccn.loc.gov/2017051085

Typeset by Compuscript Ltd, Shannon
Printed and bound in Great Britain by TJ International Ltd, Padstow, Cornwall

To find out more about our authors and books visit www.hartpublishing.co.uk. Here you will find extracts,
author information, details of forthcoming events and the option to sign up for our newsletters.

PREFACE

This book is about how Britain constitutionally decides to go to war, and in particular how the House of Commons is and should be involved in the decision to send British troops into harm's way. After the Iraq War of 2003 a constitutional convention known as the War Powers Convention, which allowed parliamentarians the opportunity to debate and vote on some aspects of armed conflict, began to emerge. The convention was recognised in the 2011 Cabinet Manual, which described its content in the following terms: 'before troops were committed the House of Commons should have an opportunity to debate the matter ... except when there was an emergency and such action would not be appropriate'. This codification was a seemingly uncontroversial expression of the political practices which had occurred since the turn of the twenty-first century.

But in August 2013 the almost politically unthinkable occurred: in a debate and vote pursuant to the War Powers Convention the Conservative–Liberal Democrat Coalition Government failed to secure a majority in favour of airstrikes against the Assad regime in Syria. The Government acknowledged that military action was politically off the table, having lost an historic vote. It seemed as though the War Powers Convention had real teeth: for the first time Parliament's democratic credentials looked secure in the face of the hitherto untameable royal prerogative to make war.

As a matter of domestic law, the decision to go to war or to initiate armed conflict remains a matter for the Government exercising power derived from the Royal Prerogative. The War Powers Convention, then, is a purely political innovation which has been almost universally welcomed. But all that glitters is not gold. As authors, we are concerned that there has been little if any critical discussion of these innovations. This book seeks to fill that gap. We seek to contextualise these recent developments within the historical context of Parliament's role in the war prerogative since the beginning of the twentieth century. For the first time, this work reveals the limitations on parliamentary engagement with armed conflict decisions which persist in our contemporary arrangements. Like the cover image (*The Open Debate* by Philip Bouchard), the book describes the 'chess game' played between Parliament and the Government in the context of war powers. In the cover rendering, the throne sits slightly out of reach, representing the spectre of monarchical power which still holds sway. Debate may be more open, but significant power structures remain hidden from view. The purpose of the book is to identify these hidden power structures, and to proffer solutions which seek to better empower the House of Commons to scrutinise the decisions of government in relation to armed conflict. Our argument seeks to promote both a culture of challenge and ultimately a culture of justification between government, the House of Commons, and the people insofar as is possible in the context of deliberation over the exercise of war powers. We aim to achieve this by suggesting ways in which the relationship could be recalibrated to instantiate the widely recognised good governance values of accountability, transparency, and participation.

Writing this book together has been an unexpected and rewarding intellectual journey. It began as a rough sketch of an article based on Skype conversations which took place on Fridays between our locations at the time: Cambridge (Veronika) and Jerusalem (Hayley) in early 2015. After several weeks of back and forth it became apparent that the idea was weightier than a typical law review article. A book was needed to do justice to both the volume of information amassed and the nature of the argument advanced. We began an intellectual journey which took us across the country to discussion groups in Oxford and Cambridge, before parliamentarians and academics at the Study of Parliament Group in the House of Lords, into the national archives, and to a remote mansion in mid-Wales where we interacted with (alleged) members of the intelligence community from across the world. It was a strange time.

Over the course of around two years of working on this project, the global political landscape has shifted and fractured in a way that two people growing up in the (relative) optimism of the 1990s and the turn of the twenty-first century could not have predicted. As children we watched the collapse of the Berlin Wall from two very difference countries (Slovenia and the United Kingdom, respectively) and proceeded to grow up in an era of globalisation and general liberal progression. That cycle now seems to be coming to an end. Britain unexpectedly voted to leave the European Union in June 2016, and a shock victory meant that Donald Trump was elected to be the 45th President of the United States in November 2016. Both political campaigns signalled a paradigm shift in public discourse, so much so that the term 'post-truth' became the Oxford Dictionaries' 2016 word of the year, and the Western world seemed to be shifting away from liberal constitutionalism towards a dark breed of populism. Similarly, *The Economist* reported on 10 September 2016 that: 'politics should be based on evidence ... Strong democracies can draw on inbuilt defences against post-truth'. But we should not be complacent about our defences. The solutions we put forward in this monograph ask a lot of both governments and parliamentarians. In short, if this book serves only one purpose, we hope that it alerts the reader to the fact that our constitutional defences in respect of the ultimate use of state power are currently precarious, and should not be taken for granted.

Overall, this project also benefitted from both authors coming from very different scholarly traditions, namely, public international law (Veronika) and domestic constitutional and administrative law (Hayley). Usually, the concept of war is discussed from one of these perspectives; rarely does a work consider the interaction of both fields. The value of this work is that it brings together insights from both. We seek to use our different scholarly backgrounds to expose the full depth and breadth of issues surrounding parliamentary engagement with the war prerogative, including the impact of public international law on domestic political discourse, and the relationship between international institutions and the domestic legislature.

Of course, we did not undertake this journey alone. Support has come in many shapes and forms. Homerton College, Cambridge and the Centre for Public Law provided supportive and collegiate working environments. Several funding bodies including the Centre for Research in the Arts, Social Sciences and Humanities (CRASSH) and the Isaac Newton Trust facilitated research leave for Veronika, and Hayley was generously supported by a Junior Research Fellowship from Homerton College (and latterly a fellowship at Christ Church, Oxford). We owe a deep debt of gratitude to our colleagues who read and supported the initial book proposal and discussed the intellectual dilemmas we grappled with along the way: John Bell, Paul Craig, Mark Elliott, David Feldman, Asif Hameed, David Howarth, Murray Hunt, Liora Lazarus, Aileen McHarg, Greg Messenger and Carne Ross. Alison L Young was generous enough to read the entire manuscript and provide feedback, criticism and a huge amount of support in the final stages. Finally, the team at Hart Publishing have provided generous support and patience. To everyone, thanks.

Veronika Fikfak and Hayley J Hooper
Cambridge and Oxford
August 2017

CONTENTS

Society can give its young men almost any job and they'll figure how to do it. They'll suffer for it and die for it and watch their friends die for it, but in the end, it will get done. That only means that society should be careful about what it asks for ... Soldiers themselves are reluctant to evaluate the costs of war, but someone must. That evaluation, ongoing and unadulterated by politics, may be the one thing a country absolutely owes the soldiers who defend its borders.

Sebastian Junger, *War* (London, Harper Collins: Fourth Estate, 2011)

1

Parliament's Secret War

VERONIKA FIKFAK AND HAYLEY J HOOPER

Deciding to pursue war or armed conflict is arguably the most serious decision that any government can take. Profound suffering and the loss of human life inevitably ensues. Legally, British constitutional orthodoxy dictates that the exercise of the power to enter into armed conflict remains a matter for the Prime Minister, exercising the royal prerogative.[1] This constitutional fact has remained unchanged throughout the twentieth and twenty-first centuries. However, since 2003 the ability of Members of the House of Commons to debate and vote upon a substantive motion of support for various kinds of armed conflict has fuelled an impression of structural constitutional change. For many members of the public and media commentators the balance of power has shifted from government towards the Commons, to the extent that the decision now requires a conjoined effort between Parliament and government.

In practice, however, war decision-making in Britain has long been described as 'an intensely prime ministerial activity',[2] one which can in itself render our democratic and parliamentary structures vulnerable. Although parliamentary consent for 'any war for the defence of any dominions or territories which do not belong to the Crown of England'[3] has been required since 1700 (and remains good law), this statute has received only fleeting mention in the twenty-first century.[4] Until 2003, there was no serious commentary arguing that parliamentary consent was constitutionally required to wage war. When we look to possible legal controls there is a similar drought: domestic courts have been unwilling to adjudicate upon

---

[1] Deployment by means of the royal prerogative has long been a constitutional principle in respect of the regular forces. The power to deploy the reserve forces, however, is statutory in nature. See section 56(1) of the Reserve Forces Act 1996: 'The Secretary of State may make an order under this section authorising the calling out of members of a reserve force if it appears to the Secretary of State that it is necessary or desirable to use members of a reserve force for any purpose for which members of the regular services may be used'.

[2] P Hennessy, *The Prime Minister: The Office and Its Holders Since 1945* (London, Allen Lane, 2000) 103.

[3] Act of Settlement 1700, s 3.

[4] HC Deb 21 October 2005, vol 437, col 1087, Claire Short (Lab) in respect of the Armed Forces (Parliamentary Approval for Participation in Armed Conflict) Bill.

the legality of the war prerogative's exercise. When presented with the opportunity to rule on the legality of using the prerogative to wage war, courts have thus far opted to treat the issue as non-justiciable.[5] This was reiterated by Lord Reed in the Supreme Court, when he remarked obiter that decisions 'such as declarations of war' remain among the 'well established exceptions' to the principle that judicial review of the exercise of executive discretion is a requirement of the rule of law.[6] This point was reinforced in 2017 by the Supreme Court in *Miller*.[7] In addition to this, the English courts remain unwilling to issue declaratory opinions on the legality of conflicts according to the rules of public international law due to both lack of jurisdiction and the view that to do so would be contrary to the public interest.[8]

Parliamentary involvement appeared to be shifting towards filling this account-ability lacuna in the early twenty-first century. After 2003, when the House of Commons had for the first time been asked to provide its approval prior to the invasion of Iraq, the talk of a 'War Powers Convention' (a rule of political practice), which requires the consent of the Commons prior to armed conflict, began to appear in the media, official publications, and Hansard.[9] Since Iraq, this rule appears to have solidified in practice through a series of parliamentary debates and votes prior to (or at the outset of) armed conflicts in 2011, 2013, 2014 and 2015.[10] After the Commons vote in August 2013, when the Conservative Government failed to secure parliamentary support for action against the Assad regime, some commentators hailed the impact of the convention as 'historic'[11] in the sense that it represented a strengthening of democratic control of the state's ultimate power to wage war. Others called it a 'vote of shame',[12] demonstrating that the Government had failed to convince Parliament of the need for action because it had not sufficiently learned from the experiences of previous administrations.

We were drawn to this project by a common curiosity, namely, a desire to understand the exact role Parliament plays in relation to armed conflict under the

---

[5] *R (on the Application of Gentle and Clarke) v Prime Minister, the Secretary of State for Defence, and the Attorney General* [2007] QB 689 [26]: 'issues relating to the conduct of international relations and military operations outside the United Kingdom are not justiciable', and *Campaign for Nuclear Disarmament v Prime Minister, Defence Secretary, and Foreign Secretary* [2002] EWHC 2777 (Admin) [47].

[6] *Evans v Attorney General* [2015] UKSC 21, [2015] 1 AC 1787, [52].

[7] *R (Miller and Others) v Secretary of State for Exiting the European Union* [2017] UKSC 5 [53].

[8] *CND v Prime Minister* [2002] EWHC 2777 (Admin), [2003] ACD 36.

[9] C Mills, 'Parliamentary approval for military action' (House of Commons Library Briefing Paper No 7166, 12 May 2015); J Rozenberg, 'Syria intervention: is there a new constitutional convention?' *The Guardian* (2 September 2013).

[10] However, in ch 3 we critique the extent to which the War Powers Convention has been complied with in practice.

[11] T Stanley 'Syria vote: this historic night was a humiliation for David Cameron but a victory for Parliament' *The Telegraph* (29 August 2013); R Hutton and T Penny, 'Historic Vote Sees Cameron Defeated by Lawmakers on Syria' *Bloomberg Online* (20 August 2013); G Phillipson, '"Historic" Commons' Syria vote: the constitutional significance (Parts I and II)' *UK Constitutional Law Association* blog (19 September 2013 and 29 November 2013).

[12] MJS, 'The vote of shame' *The Economist* (30 August 2013) <www.economist.com/blogs/blighty/2013/08/britain-and-syria> accessed 8 March 2017.

War Powers Convention. For the last 14 years, we have watched the debates in the Commons from our different public law and international law vantage points, both noticing changes in the interaction between government officials and members of Parliament, and the negotiation and later renegotiation of that relationship. Our investigations reveal a complex picture of how the British political constitution works in practice, and how it is shaped and determined through relationships between different political actors. It is these relationships and their negotiations that we trace and evaluate over the forthcoming chapters.

In this chapter, we set out the contrast between the former and the current engagement of Parliament on issues of war. The traditional manner of engaging the Commons on issues of war was limited to procedural motions, preventing Members from registering their views through a vote. But since 2003 debates have only been held on substantive motions which require parliamentary approval prior to the start of hostilities. Motions of this nature allow MPs to vote clearly for or against armed conflict.[13] It has been argued that whilst the previous engagement allowed members of the House to be barely informed, the new shift—and the new convention—finally involves Parliament in a meaningful manner on issues of war.[14] MPs receive information about the conflict, often in the form of a legal opinion on the lawfulness of military intervention, and some insight into the Government's strategic long-term plans. At first sight, the emergence of the new convention appears to have improved the quality of both parliamentary involvement and parliamentary scrutiny. In particular, we note, the decision of subsequent governments to abide by the War Powers Convention and seek parliamentary approval prior to the deployment of troops appears to have replaced governmental discretion with accountability, MPs' exclusion with their participation, and ultimately a prima facie increase in the transparency of any decision to wage war. These three values—accountability, participation, and transparency—we believe are core values in a democracy and should thus guide the proper relationship between the Government and Parliament.

In this monograph, our aim is to unpack the precise nature of the evolving War Powers Convention and contextualise this against the values of accountability, participation, and transparency. We therefore evaluate questions surrounding the emergence, content and strength of the putative War Powers Convention. Our analysis considers a series of parliamentary debates and votes which seem to suggest that the ancient prerogative to make war in the monarch's name is being gradually democratised by an increasingly strong Parliament. Thereafter, we turn to consider the extent to which the convention in its present state represents a step forward for political accountability, participation, and transparency in respect of the exercise of war powers.

---

[13] M Jack (ed), *Erskine May: Parliamentary Practice*, 24th edn (London, Lexis Nexis, 2011) 330.

[14] J Strong, 'Why Parliament Now Decides on War: Tracing the Growth of the Parliamentary Prerogative through Syria, Libya and Iraq' (2015) 17 *The British Journal of Politics and International Relations* 604.

A. The Role of the House of Commons in War Powers Decisions: An Historical View

In view of the furore surrounding the consequences of the new convention, readers are to be forgiven for thinking that parliamentary engagement is an entirely novel constitutional development. But this is much mistaken. There is a tradition of the Executive engaging Parliament on aspects of war powers which pre-dates the War Powers Convention. This practice stems from the beginning of the twentieth century. What stands out in particular when we consider this history is the stark shift effected by the new convention in Parliament's favour. It is therefore important to track the changes and progress which the War Powers Convention instantiates in our constitutional arrangements when compared with past practice.

I. The Adjournment Motion: Procedural Marginalisation and Public Deception

Throughout the last century, MPs discussed wars in Europe in the 1940s, the Korean War and the Suez invasion in the 1950s, the Falklands in the 1980s, the Gulf War and Kosovo in the 1990s, Iraq at the beginning of the twenty-first century, and more recently Libya, Syria and others. Numerous debates have been held in relation to almost every military deployment, some before and most after the start of military action. However, one of the crucial changes imported by the convention is the change in the nature of the parliamentary procedure used to effect such debates. Before Iraq, debates in the Commons were traditionally held pursuant to an adjournment motion.[15] It was the Government, not Parliament, that initiated such debates. The purpose of doing so was to allow the Government to control both the content of debates in Parliament and their outcome. The motion—'That this House do now adjourn'—was moved by a Government Minister, and gave the House a chance to discuss matters without recording a substantive decision on the merits of the matter. Although called 'the adjournment motion', the Government actually had no wish for the House to adjourn or to bring the debate on the floor to an end. In the words of Robin Cook, the late Foreign Secretary, a debate on an adjournment motion 'enable[d] the Commons to hold a debate without any risk of a serious division [vote] at the end of it'.[16] During these debates, then, no substantive vote would take place, and as a result the concerns of the House of Commons could be easily ignored.

The second problem with adjournment debates is how they were interpreted by the media and the wider public. They have been known to obscure the messages expressed in the debates. Parliamentarians have expressed concerns to this end.

---

[15] Jack, *Erskine May* (n 13) 402–04.
[16] R Cook, *The Point of Departure* (London, Simon & Schuster Ltd, 2003) 187.

Harry Ewing noted that 'People outside simply do not understand the procedures that the House of Commons adopts on such great occasions. It would have been far better to debate a [substantive] motion ... We would then have known clearly where we stood'.[17] In the same vein Kenneth Clarke complained that adjournment motions are used 'to make sure that there was no substantive vote taking place at any stage. The whole thing was used more as a process of explanation and persuasion than it was of giving Parliament a real way to challenge the decision of Government in respect of war'.[18] Moreover, an adjournment debate did not guarantee a parliamentary vote. Indeed, in practice adjournment debates frequently concluded without a vote taking place. If, however, the Opposition wished to express concerns about government policy, then a vote could be forced. Yet, even this did not represent a real, clear challenge to government policy. The vote could not take place on a matter of substance under the procedure; instead it was merely a vote for or against adjournment. Needless to say, this was exceedingly confusing to the public. From a constituent's position, it was unclear whether an MP's vote in favour of adjournment supported or condemned government policy on armed conflict. As Tony Benn declared, votes on adjournment debates afford the House 'absolutely no power in the matter'.[19] They allowed for no amendments and no opportunity to provide (and put on record) the support for military personnel or (dis)approval of the Executive's policies. In effect, adjournment motions engage Parliament whilst they also simultaneously 'de-parliamentarise decision-making'.[20]

Specific examples are required to understand the twin concerns of bypassing substance and confusing the public. The 1956 Suez crisis, which occurred when Egypt nationalised the Suez Canal, provides a particularly concerning illustration. Parliament was recalled from summer recess on 12 September 1956 and the House of Commons was given a chance to debate potential military action. During the discussion, the Opposition insisted that Britain should not use military force without an additional parliamentary debate, nor should action be taken without the approval of the international community (by way of the UN Security Council). Yet, although the Opposition wanted to push for a vote, under an adjournment motion this would have ended the debate and sent the House back into recess.[21] The absurd effect of this would be to postpone further discussion of the issue to a time when it would become irrelevant (eg when the Government would have already sent the troops abroad).

So, through an adjournment debate, Parliament was effectively being 'held hostage'. Although MPs could discuss the Suez Crisis, they did so under the pressure of being sent back into recess and being prevented from being involved

---

[17] HC Deb 11 December 1990, vol 182, col 894 (Harry Ewing).

[18] House of Lords, Select Committee on Constitution, 'Waging War' (2006), citing Kenneth Clarke, [42].

[19] HC Deb 31 May 1995, vol 260, cols 1021–22 (Tony Benn). See also M White: 'Britain debates aim of intervention as: War divides parties and unites old political foes' *The Guardian* (31 May 1995) 8.

[20] 'Waging War' (n 18), citing evidence given by Katja Ziegler [43].

[21] The pro-Government majority would insist on adjournment and send the House back into recess through a vote in favour of the adjournment motion. HC Deb 12 September 1956, vol 558, cols 2–149.

in the matter further. As one MP put it, to adjourn at a time like this would be 'a negation of democracy'.[22] But despite such concerns the debate was adjourned when the Labour leader failed to secure a promise from the Government to wait before using military force. He forced a division on the motion to adjourn and the Government won the vote 300 to 232, sending Parliament back into recess.

It should come as no surprise, then, that in respect of the use of adjournment motions in response to Suez, Kosovo and other wars, MPs and Government Ministers alike have argued that: 'The question of whether British troops are committed to action ought to require the dignity of a more meaningful procedure'.[23] By the time the Iraq war was under discussion in 2002, the calls for procedural change had reached fever pitch. MPs insisted that although they had no 'legal or constitutional right to decide the matters [of military deployment]', they had a 'duty to represent people'.[24] If Parliament was to be involved on issues of war, then this had to be in a manner in which its members could perform their representative function. As the Iraq War would subsequently demonstrate, this could only be achieved if Parliament had a real opportunity to debate on a substantive question of war and if it was able to vote clearly for or against military action.

II. Debate and Vote on a Substantive Motion: Empowering the House of Commons

Before the War Powers Convention crystallised, the Iraq War represented a major turning point in parliamentary practice. By October 2002, MPs began to pose basic questions regarding the Prime Minister's perception of his royal prerogative power and, more specifically, about whether Parliament could and would have a say on the use of military force. MPs across party lines insisted that the Commons should be consulted *prior* to the decision to go to war.[25] But Blair stood firm on tradition, emphasising that in respect of Kosovo and of Afghanistan 'we gave the House ample opportunity not only to debate, but to declare and express its view. I am sure that we will do so again, in accordance with the normal tradition of the House'.[26] The Prime Minister did not specify whether this would involve a debate on an adjournment or substantive motion, or indeed whether the House would be allowed to debate and vote prior to the initiation of hostilities. Both the form of engagement of Parliament and its timing were therefore at stake.

---

[22] HC Deb 13 September 1956, vol 558, col 322, Leslie Hale.

[23] R Cook, *The Point of Departure* (London, Simon & Schuster Ltd, 2003) 187–88.

[24] HC Deb 6 September 1990, vol 177, cols 774–75 (Tony Benn). Similar statements were also made in 2002–03, see Jack Straw HC Deb 18 March 2003, vol 401, col 900: 'never before, prior to military action, has the House been asked on a substantive motion for its explicit support for the use of our armed forces. The House sought that, but, more important, it is constitutionally proper in a modern democracy'.

[25] Graham Allen, Tam Dalyell, Alice Mahon from Labour, as well as Norman Baker and Charles Kennedy from Lib Dems, asked questions about the Government's intentions and received inadequate answers.

[26] HC Deb 24 September 2002, vol 390, col 11.

In December 2002, the Conservative leader, Iain Duncan Smith, once again raised questions in respect of a role for Parliament in the making of the actual decision to deploy troops to the Middle East. Mr Duncan Smith urged the Prime Minister to permit a vote on troop deployment using a substantive motion. But the request was rejected for its potential to endanger troops, whilst deployment itself was labelled as a merely 'contingent' move.[27] Ultimately, troops were deployed without a vote in Parliament, but this fact did not escape criticism in the House.[28]

Although troops had been deployed to the region, one crucial element had still not been decided: the question of whether or not the British Government would start hostilities against Saddam Hussein's regime. In early 2003, parliamentary support for a debate and vote on a substantive motion before any commitment to hostilities grew louder still. On 22 January 2003, the House of Commons debated an adjournment motion titled 'Defence of the World', which focused on the policy towards Iraq. At the end of the debate there was an adjournment vote, and 53 MPs voted against the adjournment: this was a show of rebellion against the Government's Iraq policy, since 44 of those who voted against the adjournment were Labour MPs.[29] Tam Dalyell, who had forced the division, reminded the Government: 'If the House is not to be demeaned, it should have a vote before any commitment to action. I hope that the House authorities and those who control these things will take that seriously, otherwise the House of Commons will be greatly demeaned'.[30] Dalyell of course had a vote on a substantive motion in mind.

By the end of February, the support for Parliament to vote on a substantive motion had reached across party lines. In quick succession calls for action came from Alex Salmond (SNP), Richard Allan (Lib Dem), Menzies Campbell (Lib Dem), Douglas Hogg (Con), and even the Leader of the House and then Foreign Secretary, Robin Cook (Lab).[31] On 26 February 2003, 121 Labour MPs voted in support of a motion that 'the case for military action against Iraq [was] as yet unproven'.[32] Robin Cook commented that 'For the Government, the outcome was difficult and revealing'.[33] A further signal indicating how serious MPs were about their involvement came in respect of an Early Day Motion affirming that Parliament had not approved military action in Iraq, and calling for a debate and vote in the House of Commons prior to the deployment of troops. This motion was put forward by Tony Wright MP (Lab), and received 126 signatures, the majority of which came from Labour MPs.[34] Graham Allen (Lab) had gathered a large

---

[27] HC Deb 18 December 2002, vol 396, col 835.

[28] Gerald Howarth (Con, Aldershot) asked why the press had received this information a day before the House Commons (ibid, cols 846–47). Jeremy Corbyn suspected that the whole statement was something that 'softens us up for war', that the Government had no intention of seeking either UN or parliamentary approval for war (ibid, col 856).

[29] HC Deb 22 January 2003, vol 398, col 405.

[30] ibid, col 372–73 (Tam Dalyell).

[31] HC Deb 24 September 2002, vol 390, col 51 (Douglas Hogg and Tam Dalyell).

[32] HC Deb 26 February 2003, vol 400, col 363.

[33] HC Deb 6 March 2003, vol 400, col 970 (Robin Cook).

[34] House of Commons Early Day Motion 773 of 2002–2003 (12 February 2003), Tony Wright MP.

number of MPs in support of the view that Parliament should be both the final decision-maker and the ultimate source of legitimacy in this sphere. If approved, the motion would give Parliament the right of approval before any British troops were committed to hostilities abroad.[35] This mounting pressure, coupled with the failure to secure international legal backing contributed to unrest within government (notably the resignation of Robin Cook). These factors compelled the Prime Minister to permit a substantive debate and vote on 18 March 2003. The Government secured a majority (412:149), but many Labour MPs rebelled. On 20 March 2003 Britain went to war in Iraq.

For the first time in the history of the Westminster Parliament, the House of Commons was permitted by government to debate and vote on a *substantive* motion *prior* to the start of hostilities. According to the main protagonists, the goal of this new parliamentary involvement was manifold. First, for MPs, the substantive motion allowed them to represent the people and voice their views through a vote.[36] In addition to representing the people, MPs aimed to hold the Government to account by challenging its policies and strategies, and requiring more information and explanation.[37] It was clear the sands were shifting. Cook explained the potentially serious impact of these new developments in the following terms:

> It has been a favourite theme of commentators that this House no longer occupies a central role in British politics. Nothing could better demonstrate that they are wrong than for this House to stop the commitment of troops in a war that has neither international agreement nor domestic support. I intend to join those tomorrow night who will vote against military action now.[38]

In short, a vote on an adjournment motion could easily be disregarded,[39] but the same could not be said of a vote following a substantive debate. As one former MP put it: 'A vote cannot be ignored'.[40]

Regardless of the motivations of the actors involved in the Iraq saga (explored in chapter two), a profound shift occurred in the relationship between the House of Commons and the Government in respect of war powers. The House of Commons had shifted from a position where it was marginalised by procedural involvement, using a motion which risked the deception of the public, to the centre stage, as it was asked to provide the political backing necessary to legitimise military action. MPs had negotiated a position of real influence on questions of war. The events surrounding Iraq firmly impacted upon subsequent

---

[35] P Bowers, 'Parliament and the use of force', House of Commons Library, Standard Note, SN/IA/1218 (25 February 2003) 4–11.

[36] HC Deb 6 September 1990, vol 177, cols 774–75 (Tony Benn).

[37] We are grateful to David Howarth, former MP, for this comment, 17 February 2016.

[38] HC Deb 17 March 2003, vol 401, col 736 ff.

[39] Narvik Debate on 7 and 8 May 1940, which Chamberlain won, but with a greatly reduced majority and thus two days later he resigned. HC Deb 7 May 1940, vol 360, cols 1073–196 and HC Deb 8 May 1940, vol 360, cols 1251–366.

[40] David Howarth, former MP, 17 February 2016.

parliamentary practice. Since 2003, a consistent pattern has emerged: every time the Government contemplated the deployment of troops, MPs have been invited to discuss and support military action through a substantive motion. This is true of almost every occasion in the last 14 years.[41] The outcome of each of these votes has been respected by the Government as a binding expression of parliamentary (and in turn democratic) will.

B. From Discretion to Democratisation

I. The Recognition of the War Powers Convention and the Values of Parliamentary Involvement

Since the debates on the Iraq War in 2002 and 2003 there has been a steady increase in both the nature and the scope of parliamentary engagement with the war prerogative. The nature relates to the change in the procedure used to involve Parliament, discussed above, whereas the increase in the scope of the involvement describes the type and extent of information provided to Parliament by government. This new era of parliamentary control of governmental discretion was given a constitutional foothold by the 2011 Cabinet Manual, which stipulates that:

> In 2011, the Government acknowledged that a convention had developed in Parliament that before troops were committed the House of Commons should have an opportunity to debate the matter and said that it proposed to observe that convention except when there was an emergency and such action would not be appropriate.[42]

This written exposition of the convention purports to guarantee the House of Commons a debate prior to the deployment of troops, save in the event of an emergency or where such activity would prejudice the public interest. The recognition of the existence of the War Powers Convention as a constitutional convention in the Cabinet Manual is important. First, a constitutional convention is a constitutional rule with political (as opposed to legal) force and as such usually remains uncodified. Conventions apply between political actors in the political realm.[43] They cannot be enforced by courts, unlike legislation or common law rules. Yet, nevertheless, they are an important element of Britain's uncodified constitution—without studying them, we would get a misleading and incomplete picture of the constitution.[44] Although there is much academic disagreement

---

[41] The notable exception being Mali, where no consultation took place. In addition, the timing of the engagement has not always been respected.

[42] HM Government, *The Cabinet Manual: A guide to laws, conventions and rules on the operation of Government*, 1st edn (London, The Stationary Office, 2011) [5.38].

[43] *R (Miller and Others) v Secretary of State for Exiting the European Union* [2017] UKSC 5 [141]–[146].

[44] M Elliott and R Thomas, *Public Law*, 2nd edn (Oxford, OUP, 2014) ch 2.

about the precise nature of conventions,[45] for the purposes of this discussion we need only be familiar with the fundamental (and uncontroversial) aspects of conventions. The role of conventions in the political sphere is to give effect to the 'morality of the constitution'.[46] To that end, it is helpful to think of conventions as a form of 'role morality', ie as rules of 'constitutionally appropriate behaviour' which become binding when any actor occupying a relevant role considers himself or herself to be bound by that rule in the context of his or her duties.[47] In that context, the decision by Tony Blair in 2003 to put the Iraq invasion to a vote, and his subsequent statement to a Parliamentary Select Committee that 'no Government could engage in a conflict if Parliament was against it',[48] indicate essential steps towards the emergence of a new rule. Blair's actions and statement represents the recognition or belief by a political actor in the context of his role in public life that he is required to be politically accountable to Parliament.

Yet, as Sir Ivor Jennings and others argue, the recognition of being bound by certain conduct is not sufficient to generate a rule of constitutional behaviour in and of itself.[49] A constitutional convention must be established by precedents (ie consistent practice), the relevant actors must believe they are bound by the rule in question, and there must be a constitutional reason (ie a normative reason) for the rule.[50] In this sense, the position of Tony Blair and his decision to take the matter to a vote was not sufficient to create a convention. It is only once this initial precedent—that government has to turn to Parliament and respect its position—has been consistently referred to and the rule has been given effect to by subsequent practice that a constitutional convention is solidified. For 14 years since 2003, the requirement for Parliament to be involved has been recognised by subsequent governments. Every time a new conflict arises, the Government through the Prime Minister, Foreign or Defence Secretary usually declares that it is committed to abide by the convention.[51] More and more frequently, members of the Government refer to the wording of the Cabinet Manual to bolster their commitment to the convention. In this context, the Cabinet Manual both expresses the certainty of existence of a new rule and clarifies its content. It confirms that there is a rule, that there are precedents, and that the rule has been followed by the

---

[45] J Jaconelli, 'The nature of constitutional conventions' (1999) 19 *Legal Studies* 24; G Marshall, *Constitutional Conventions: The Rules and Forms of Political Accountability* (Oxford, Clarendon Press, 1984), A McHarg, 'Reforming the United Kingdom Constitution: Law, Convention, Soft Law' (2008) 71 *Modern Law Review* 853.

[46] AV Dicey 'Nature of Conventions of the Constitution' in Marshall, *Constitutional Conventions* (ibid) 10–12.

[47] McHarg, 'Reforming the United Kingdom Constitution' (n 45) 860.

[48] 'Waging War' (n 18), [86], quoting the 2003 proceedings of the Liaison Committee.

[49] Jaconelli, 'The nature of Constitutional conventions' (n 45) 29.

[50] ibid, 28–29.

[51] See, eg, Defence Secretary Michael Fallon's written statement (18 April 2016) HCWS678.

relevant actors (the Government and Parliament) as a standard of constitutionally appropriate behaviour.

Thirdly and finally, the recognition of the convention in the Cabinet Manual marks the successful end to a struggle to strengthen the position of Parliament in this realm of the constitution and to place it upon a more secure, codified footing.[52] Its codification is indicative of the importance and constitutional reason behind the political rule. This third and final element of the so-called Jennings' test is normative in nature.[53] There could be many reasons and justifications offered for the War Powers Convention, but our work focusses on the following over-arching justification, namely, that the Convention contributes to the democratisation of the war prerogative, and in turn, instantiates the values of 'good governance' (accountability, participation, and transparency) into the relationship between the Executive and Parliament in the context of the war prerogative.[54]

Although our chosen values have become ubiquitous in official[55] and academic literature[56] promoting good governance there are no agreed or exhaustive definitions of any or either of them. Choosing values by which to measure the worth of any constitutional process is always an inherently controversial venture. In recent years, there has been an academic movement to establish the existence of 'global values' in constitutionalism.[57] This can be seen as part of a wider move towards 'cosmopolitan constitutionalism' in Western liberal democracies.[58] However, it remains a widely held view that values in constitutions remain the subject of inherent political contestation in respect of both their internal definitions, and their order of priority in any one system.[59] This is as true of the United Kingdom's uncodified constitution as any other system. One possible framework is to distinguish between those values which are of 'intrinsic' value (ie are of value in and of themselves), and those which are of 'ultimate' value because they promote particular goods.[60] In respect of the British Constitution, Jowell and O'Cinneide identify the three core (or intrinsic) values as 'liberty', 'representative government', and the 'rule of law'. These authors consider that 'transparency', 'accountability',

---

[52] A Blick, *The Codes of the Constitution* (Oxford, Hart, 2016) 109, and House of Commons Political and Constitutional Reform Committee, 'Constitutional Implications of the Cabinet Manual, 6th Report of 2010–2011, HC 734, [61].

[53] WI Jennings, *The Law and the Constitution*, 5th edn (London, University of London Press, 1959) 81.

[54] B Kingsbury, N Krisch and RB Stewart, 'The emergence of global administrative law' (2005) 68 *Law and Contemporary Problems* 15–61.

[55] OECD, 'Accountability, Transparency, Participation: Key Elements of Good Governance' <www.oecd.org/governance/regulatory-policy/irrc.htm> accessed 21 June 2017; European Commission, 'Principles of Good Governance: A White Paper' COM (2001) 428 (25 July 2001) 10–11.

[56] Kingsbury, Krisch and Stewart, 'Global administrative law' (n 54) 15–61.

[57] D Davis, A Richter and C Saunders (eds), *An inquiry into the existence of global values* (Oxford, Hart, 2015).

[58] M Loughlin, 'The end of avoidance' (2016) 38 *London Review of Books* 12–13.

[59] Davis, Richter and Saunders, *Existence of global values* (n 57) 13.

[60] J Raz, *The Morality of Freedom* (Oxford, OUP/Clarendon Press, 1986) 200 quoted in *Existence of global values* (n 57) 12.

and 'participation' are secondary values 'which have not yet become embedded in the bedrock of the British constitution'.[61] By contrast, Cane considers our chosen values of accountability, transparency, and participation to be 'immanent' or background values which underpin public law.[62] Although we agree that our chosen values may not be 'core' or 'intrinsic' values in the British constitution, we believe that they are the central values which drive our evaluation. We have chosen to test the relationship between government and Parliament against the benchmarks of accountability, transparency, and participation because we believe that they are the goods that political deliberation over armed conflict should strive to realise. Since the Iraq War of 2003 successive governments have attempted to argue that the War Powers Convention makes the process of deciding on war more open, accountable, and democratic due to the input of elected politicians. We test these claims throughout the book.

In chapters two, three and four we look at the three values in turn. But the boundaries between individual values are necessarily artificial. For example, although no one would dispute the status of accountability as a 'golden concept' in governance, its 'evocative powers make it ... very elusive ... because it can mean many different things to different people'. In short, accountability is capable of encompassing notions of transparency, trust, and the requirement of participation by relevant actors, depending on the definition adopted.[63] In truth, the situations described in each chapter engage with all of the values in different ways. Each of the values are dependent on each other for their own existence. Their relationship mirrors the domino effect: where one value is undermined the others must also fall.

a. Accountability

Despite the above caveats, each of the values deserves preliminary attention on its own terms. Accountability can be conceptualised as the core value underpinning any democratic endeavour.[64] The nuts and bolts of the War Powers Convention, namely the requirement to have a debate and vote on a substantive motion prior to armed conflict, can be seen as an accountability process. If well executed, an accountability process can 'promote [the] efficient and effective performance of the required task' by encouraging 'the primary actor to gather information and to exchange ideas with those calling to account'.[65] The new trend favouring debates and substantive motions, which has crystallised into a constitutional convention, clearly denotes the construction of such an accountability process

---

[61] J Jowell and C O'Cinneide, 'Values in the UK Constitution' in *Existence of Global Values* (n 57) 360.
[62] P Cane, 'Theory and values in public law' in P Craig and R Rawlings, *Law and Administration in Europe: essays in honour of Carol Harlow* (Oxford, OUP, 2003) 14–16.
[63] M Bovens, 'Analysing and Assessing Accountability: A Conceptual Framework' (2007) 13 *European Law Journal* 447, 448.
[64] ACL Davies, *Accountability: A Public Law Analysis of Government by Contract* (Oxford, OUP, 2001) 76.
[65] ibid, 79.

which was previously unavailable in the British constitutional order. According to Tony Benn MP, 'If you tell young men in the Services that they have got to go under orders and kill, and may be killed, you are talking about the most important decision literally in their lives and that should not be taken other than by a democratic vote in the House of Commons, in Parliament'.[66] This sentiment was echoed by a former Attorney-General, who suggested that increased parliamentary involvement in the war prerogative was essential to restoring public confidence in its exercise: 'I do not think today that it is practicable to suppose that the public will be satisfied in terms of confidence in the commitment of our Armed Forces to what we might call an "armed conflict" situation solely on the exercise of the prerogative by the Prime Minister'.[67]

b. Participation

Citizen participation, whether directly or through elected representatives, imbues governmental decisions with legitimacy. Alongside accountability, participation acts to dilute corruption in decision-making.[68] In the broader context, participation involves consulting 'parliamentary' bodies across a range of national and international organisations which perform governance functions.[69] There is also an inextricable link between participation and the type of representative democracy which operates in Westminster. At the core of participation as a value, is the idea that decisions subject to citizen (or representative) participation can be made in a more deliberative manner, and that the outcome will be enhanced as a result.[70] Although all votes falling under the War Powers Convention have been subject to some form of party whip, Members of the Commons have shown sensitivity to the views of constituents in the course of debates. In 2015, in respect of air strikes against ISIS/ISIL in Syria, Labour party leader Jeremy Corbyn allowed members of the parliamentary party a free vote, despite maintaining an official 'anti-war' party line.[71] In respect of entirely whipped votes, significant numbers of MPs have rebelled in successive votes.[72] In the simplest terms, the advent of debates and votes under the War Powers Convention constitutes evidence of enhanced participation by democratic representatives.

One of the key contributions of parliamentary participation in this context, then, is to provide a process by which the dominance of any one figure in the

---

[66] 'Waging War' (n 18) [38].

[67] ibid, [39], quoting former Attorney-General, Lord Mayhew of Twysden.

[68] C Harlow, 'Global Administrative Law: The Quest for Principles and Values' (2006) 17 *The European Journal of International Law* 187, 199.

[69] ibid, 200.

[70] RA Irvin and J Stansbury, 'Citizen Participation in Decision Making: Is It worth the Effort?' (2004) 64 *Public Administration Review* 55–65.

[71] P Wintour and R Mason, 'Syria airstrikes: Jeremy Corbyn gives Labour MPs free vote' *The Guardian* (30 November 2015).

[72] The largest rebellion occurred in respect of the Iraq War against Toby Blair's Labour Government: J Ennis and J Grogan, 'The mother of all rebellions' in P Cowley (ed), *The Rebels: How Blair mislaid his majority* (Politico's, London, 2005).

decision-making process can be counteracted by publicly testing the Government's case for war. Participation by elected representatives can act to prevent executive dominance of any given policy area. Although the Iraq War was clearly the original catalyst for what the convention would become, history will not look kindly on the Blair Government's treatment of Parliament, nor will it look favourably on the actions of Blair towards his own Cabinet ministers and officials. After the completion of his inquiry, Sir John Chilcot remarked that within the Executive, Blair exhibited 'sheer psychological dominance' over key actors within the Cabinet.[73]

Other MPs have straightforwardly suggested that increased parliamentary participation would contribute to *better* decisions being made about armed conflict. Clare Short told the Lords' Constitution Committee in 2006 that the exercise of the royal prerogative power by the Prime Minister alone leads to decisions being taken in a 'vacuum'. She further highlighted that a requirement for parliamentary scrutiny may result in better considered and prepared decisions: 'If any Prime Minister knew that he had to bring before the House of Commons … a full statement of why and the analysis, I think that means the whole issue would have to be better scrutinised, better thought through, better prepared and the decision would be better made'.[74]

c. Transparency

Transparency is amongst the most pervasive values in the liberal democratic order. Its use cuts across fields and disciplines including the 'media, markets, democracy, regulation, and public administration'.[75] In its simplest form it connotes the idea that for a decision to be made visible, there must be a disclosure of the information or resources upon which the decision is based. As a value, its contribution to governance is that it allows the affected party (in our case, the citizen represented by Parliament) to avoid 'making shots in the dark, in circumstances where the light could so easily be switched on'.[76] Transparency is relevant in two senses in the context of the War Powers Convention; first, the mechanism of public voting on substantive motions (ie a vote directly 'for' or 'against' an armed conflict) allows members of the public to directly assess the views of their constituency MP, and the stance of political parties.[77] In comparison to the discussions and votes on adjournment motions, which used to be the traditional way of engaging the House, now debates are accessible and votes easily understandable. Secondly, we have

---

[73] Sir John Chilcot, Oral Evidence to the House of Commons Liaison Committee (2 November 2016), Question 48 <www.parliament.uk/documents/commons-committees/liaison/John-Chilcot-oral-evidence.pdf> accessed 2 November 2017.

[74] 'Waging War' (n 18), [44] and Volume II: Evidence, Q 2.

[75] EC Fisher, 'Transparency and Administrative Law: A Critical Evaluation' (2010) 63 *Current Legal Problems* 272, 272.

[76] *R (Eisai Ltd) v National Institute for Health and Clinical Excellence (NICE) and Others* [2008] EWCA Civ 438 [50].

[77] Mainstream news outlets have taken to publishing the voting roll. See BBC.

seen how the increased disclosure of intelligence, legal advice, and information in general by government to Parliament, fuels more informed decision-making by Members of the Commons. Although the information supplied to Parliament still depends 'on the goodwill of the Executive or the existence of a convention that Parliament should be informed',[78] there appears to be less of an effort to consciously 'marginalise [Parliament] by lack of information'.[79] In short, prerogative discretion has given way to democratic deliberation and control. The question remains, however, whether these new levels of transparency are sufficient to render Parliament an effective scrutineer of discretion in the use of the war prerogative.

II. Towards Balanced Political Deliberation

When placed in its broader context, the War Powers Convention itself, and its results, illustrate a trend away from hierarchical decision-making towards a form of representative participation mirrored across public administration.[80] In some ways, the convention has helped formalise the role of the Loyal Opposition in Parliament by importing the maxim of *audi alteram partum* (or the 'duty to hear the other side').[81] Although the legal decision to initiate war will always remain solely within the purview of the Government, one of the core purposes of the War Powers Convention is to permit prior political scrutiny of the Government's case for war. In further evidence that parliamentary involvement in the war prerogative had become a moral imperative, several key parliamentarians report that the developments of the twenty-first century rendered them 'much exercised'[82] and in favour of the 'generosity'[83] that government had shown to Parliament. This, in turn, truly meant that the prerogative (the residue of discretionary legal power stemming from the Crown) was being recognised as 'a relic of a past age'[84] and is being treated as such by the new convention-driven constitutional arrangement. As such, the convention was essential because 'Accountability and representative Government go together'.[85] The Convention, therefore, imports some sense of political balance into decision-making about armed conflict by enhancing Parliament's role. However, it cannot be said to put Parliament on an equal footing with government, as the Government retains the final power of decision-making.

---

[78] 'Waging War' (n 18) [43] and S Payne, Volume II: Evidence, 17.

[79] ibid, K Zeigler, Volume II: Evidence, 56 (s III).

[80] L Blomgren Bingham, T Nabatchi and R O'Leary, 'The New Governance: Practices and Processes for Stakeholder and Citizen Participation in the Work of Government' (2005) 65 *Public Administration Review* 547.

[81] G Webber, 'Loyal Opposition and the political constitution' (2017) 37 *Oxford Journal of Legal Studies* 357, 371.

[82] House of Commons Public Administration Select Committee, 'Taming the Prerogative: Strengthening Ministerial accountability to Parliament' 4th Report, 2003–04, HC 422, para [19]: '"much exercised" by the approach taken by the Government to the war in Iraq. He believed that modern conditions demanded that any major military action should have explicit parliamentary approval'.

[83] ibid, William Hague para [22].

[84] Per Lord Reid in *Burmah Oil Co (Burma Trading) Ltd v Lord Advocate* [1965] AC 75 at 101.

[85] C Harlow, *Accountability in the European Union* (Oxford, OUP, 2002) 190.

If there was any doubt as to democratic progress and the 'withering'[86] decline of the prerogative, the events of August 2013 provided clarification. For the first time in constitutional history, Parliament voted to prevent government from pursuing armed conflict in Syria. The Conservative–Liberal Democrat Coalition Government motion supporting intervention against the Bashar Al-Assad regime to prevent chemical weapons attacks against the Syrian people was defeated by 272 to 285 votes. The Deputy Prime Minister, Nick Clegg (Liberal Democrat), made clear that the Government would respect 'the will of Parliament'.[87] No military action was taken, and the press called the result of the vote 'historic'.[88] For one commentator the events of 2013 demonstrated that 'Votes such as last night's are no longer mere rubber stamps but a binding convention that can change the foreign policy of a government'.[89] In short, a sovereign Parliament had finally tamed the most primal exercise of the prerogative.

The constitutional convention, which came to be known as the 'War Powers Convention' had injected 'constitutional propriety'[90] into a previously unchecked area. The lacuna between law and politics into which the war prerogative had previously fallen was now imbued with the values of good governance, which prevented the exercise of arbitrary power. In some senses, the United Kingdom had finally made progress in eroding what is known as the 'double democratic-deficit' in relation to war powers, referring to the lack of democratisation in both international organisations and national constitutional arrangements for controlling deployment of the armed forces.[91] For the first time, the convention gave teeth to Parliament's democratic credentials.

There are of course a range of ways in which parliaments across democracies can be involved in the democratic control of war powers. The parliaments with the strongest form of democratic control are those which are legally empowered to conduct *ex ante* approval of military action and can compel debates and investigations into the use of war powers, regardless of Executive will. By contrast, the parliaments with the weakest form of democratic control are those which exist in constitutional arrangements requiring no parliamentary action for the use of military force; and where no specific control or debate could be initiated by Parliament relating to the use of military force.[92] Currently the German Constitution,

---

[86] A Blick, 'Emergency powers and the withering of the Royal Prerogative' (2014) 18 *The International Journal of Human Rights* 195.

[87] HC Deb 29 August 2013, vol 566, col 1545.

[88] T Stanley 'Syria vote': (n 11), R Hutton and T Penny 'Historic Vote' (n 11).

[89] J Hallwood, 'The Syria vote was a triumph of parliamentary sovereignty' *New Statesman* (30 August 2013).

[90] S Payne (2008) 'War Powers: The War Prerogative and Constitutional Change' (2008) 153 *The RUSI Journal* 28, 29.

[91] H Hanggi, 'The use of force under international auspices: parliamentary accountability and "democratic deficits"' in H Born and H Hanggi (eds), *The 'Double Democratic Deficit': Parliamentary Accountability and the use of Force Under International Auspices* (Geneva, DCAF, Ashgate, 2004).

[92] S Dieterich, H Hummell, and S Marschall, 'Strengthening Parliamentary "War Powers" in Europe: Lessons from 25 National Parliaments' Geneva Centre for the Democratic Control of Armed Forces (Policy Paper No 27, 2008), Ch 4.

considered to be amongst the strongest democratic arrangements, requires a vote of consent in the German Parliament (*Bundestag*) before military action is lawful in Germany. In a decision in 1994, the German Federal Constitutional Court (*Bundesverfassungsgericht*) confirmed that such a consenting vote was a legal requirement inherent in the background principles which inform interpretation of the German Constitution.[93] The *Bundesverfassungsgericht* ruled that:

> The provisions of the Basic Law that relate to the forces are designed not to leave the *Bundeswehr* (armed forces) as a potential source of power to the executive alone, but to integrate it as a "parliamentary army" into the constitutional system of a democratic state under the rule of law.[94]

Although the British constitution contains no legal arrangements compelling parliamentary involvement in war powers, let alone any rules permitting Parliament to initiate controls of its own motion as is the case in Germany, it would be misleading to argue that there are no constitutional limits on Executive power in the area. In fact, the War Powers Convention has significantly strengthened parliamentary control in this domain. Despite not being a legal rule, the convention appears capable of producing results to the same effect as the German arrangements. Given that the military action in Syria was voted down by Parliament in 2013, and the Government respected the outcome of that vote, we can see an emerging parallel between the normative force of the German and British constitutional rules.

C. Roadmap of the Book

The promised enhancement of Parliament's participation in the process of political deliberation over armed conflict implicit in the War Powers Convention raises questions of its real effect. Namely, the enthusiasm accompanying the changes in the relationship between Parliament and government assumes that in practice the convention has encouraged the values of accountability, transparency and participation to flourish. Both authors were drawn to the project by a common curiosity about how the War Powers Convention really works in practice and in the chapters that follow, we subject the assumption that the War Powers Convention facilitates the recognition of the three good governance values to scrutiny. To do this we examine the extent to which the current relationship between the Government and Parliament in the context of war powers actually vindicates these governance values. Our argument presents an outside perspective of what happens between Parliament and the Government.[95] At this juncture we should make clear the limitations on the scope of our argument. We do not claim that the

---

[93] German Federal Constitutional Court's 'Out of area' Judgment (BVerfGE 90, 286 of 12 July 1994).
[94] Judgment of the Second Senate of 7 May 2008 on the basis of the oral hearing of 12 February 2008—2 BvE 1/03—[57], <www.bundesverfassungsgericht.de> accessed 7 November 2016.
[95] We spoke informally with several MPs about various aspects of the book. However, this is not, nor is it intended to be, an empirical study which draws upon interviews or qualitative analysis.

involvement of the House of Commons in armed conflict decisions will render decisions to wage war or refrain from action inherently more strategic or morally better. Instead, we simply accept that the democratisation of certain aspects of armed conflict decisions has now reached a point of no return. That is to say, there are certain circumstances in which the House of Commons will expect to be politically and democratically involved in armed conflict decisions under the War Powers Convention. In light of this, we seek to uncover ways in which parliamentary engagement in these circumstances can be both constitutionally meaningful and useful.

Chapter two evaluates the relationship between Parliament and the UN Security Council in relation to armed conflict decisions. By mapping out both the international and the domestic avenues for securing support for the use of force, we reveal that there is a 'hierarchy of fora' in which decisions to go to war are discussed. This is driven by the Government's own perspective: first comes the need to build a case on the international political stage (usually before the UN Security Council), and subsequently, after having failed to secure legal backing for its action from the international community, comes the need to build a domestic political case for war in Parliament. The dynamics of these two-stage processes demonstrate that the War Powers Convention requiring parliamentary (and in turn democratic) approval was not born for reasons of constitutional 'good governance'. Instead, it was strategically designed to fill a lacuna in legitimacy created when the British Government has failed to secure explicit and unambiguous support from international institutions. It is then that Parliament has been used as a surrogate for the Security Council to compensate for the lack of an international legal basis. What is additionally worrying, however, is the extent to which international legal language dominates the discourse used by the Government and other participants both on the international and domestic level. The terminology used before the House of Commons is almost no different in kind to the discussion in the UN Security Council. In fact, the debates mirror Security Council discussions. The pervasiveness of the international legal language means that when the decision to go to war is 'brought home', international law acts as a trump card, effectively stifling political discourse. This prevents MPs from engaging on important policy questions, which we argue they are constitutionally mandated to ask. The current situation therefore prevents MPs from performing their duty and negates the purported reasons behind the birth of the War Powers Convention—accountability, transparency and participation.

In chapter three we consider the extent to which the relationship between the Government and Parliament as defined by the War Powers Convention fails to adequately promote the value of political accountability. We deepen our inquiry by showing in more detail how Parliament's role on questions of war depends entirely upon the extent to which the Government is willing to cooperate with Parliament and to share information. If the convention initially looked like it would level the playing field between Parliament and the Government, the analysis of practice since its codification in the Cabinet Manual reveals that this is simply not true.

The Government remains substantially in control of when the convention is used and the circumstances to which it applies. Precedent by precedent, dispute by dispute, successive governments have made use of both the timing and the 'emergency argument' to avoid prior debates or votes in Parliament. On occasions where Governments have allowed parliamentary debate and votes, this engagement has been timed so as to be 'too late to influence policy'.[96] We further reveal how additional exceptions to the operation of the convention have been created incrementally—first, by excluding the use of drones from parliamentary oversight and secondly, by exempting special forces embedded in other countries' military forces and their subsequent participation in military actions abroad under the public interest exception. The exceptions that have been carved out of the codified convention significantly reduce the number of occasions on which Parliament would be expected to be involved.

Chapter four digs deeper still into the process of parliamentary engagement to uncover the deficit in participation which has been present in armed conflict decisions throughout the twentieth and twenty-first century. This deficit is driven by an endemic information asymmetry that exists between government and Parliament in the context of war powers. Unsurprisingly, this asymmetry favours the Government. It has a corrosive effect on Parliament's ability to exercise its constitutional functions. The negative effects of secrecy begin with where decisions to go to war are taken within the internal machinery of the Government. Secrecy's ill-effects can be seen in the way that government uses secrecy as a justification for excluding Parliament altogether, or for releasing select amounts of sensitive information to a small number of parliamentarians who are subject to an oath of confidentiality. The chapter tracks the uses of classified information on a spectrum which ranges from a blanket ban on disclosure by government, to the carefully managed public disclosure of claims based on classified information (secret intelligence). It reveals that the unequal and asymmetric relationship between the Government and Parliament serves the former since it allows the twin evils of groupthink and information asymmetry to flourish. An information-starved or poorly informed Parliament is ultimately easier for a government to control and to persuade. In the end, 'unanimity override[s MPs'] motivation to realistically appraise alternative courses of action.'[97]

Chapters two through four of *Parliament's Secret War* therefore reveal how the emergence and operation of the constitutional convention requiring parliamentary approval prior to the deployment of troops masks the real reasons behind parliamentary involvement (one of convenience and strategy), the extent to which the convention is subject to arbitrary exceptions, and the information asymmetry that dictates the engagement between Parliament and government. Even more, the chapters demonstrate that overt reliance on the international legal

---

[96] HC Deb 24 September 2002, vol 390, cols 96–97, Edward Garnier (Con).
[97] P t'Hart, *Groupthink in Government: A study of small groups and policy failure* (Baltimore, The Johns Hopkins University Press, 1990) 7.

discourse actively stultifies domestic political discourse. In this sense, we argue that the convention is a distraction, and that focusing on it to describe the relationship between Parliament and government is misleading. In fact, to talk about a co-equal political relationship between Parliament and the Government is to remain blind to the inherent imbalance and asymmetry between the two institutions. The first three chapters of the book therefore uncover the real 'secret war' that Parliament has fought for meaningful involvement, accurate information, and to compel the Executive to present its case for armed conflict with integrity.

Given the gap between what the convention is seeking to achieve and the problems identified when examining the actual operation of the relationship between the Government and Parliament, in the final two chapters we propose possible solutions. In light of this, chapters five and six put forward a package of solutions intended to bolster the governance values by reinvigorating political discourse within Parliament.

In Chapter five, we first consider the proposals made by other scholars. We show how the efforts of 'formalising' Parliament's role—either by capturing the convention in a parliamentary resolution or in primary legislation—misunderstands the true nature of the deficit in the current relationship between the House of Commons and the Executive. We believe that these proposed solutions would not fundamentally address the problems identified in this book. It is not the locus of rules about the relationship that matter, but the nature of political activity that is important. In view of this, we put forward alternative solutions to foster political discourse and deliberation and to promote both a culture of challenge and ultimately a culture of justification in Parliament. In this context, we insist that whilst the Government may present military action to MPs in legal terms (ie as a 'legal' or potentially 'illegal' war), in the political sphere law has the effect of suffocating political discussion and politics.

We therefore look for solutions that can free MPs of the straitjacket that law and legalistic language imposes. In the first instance, we argue that MPs can divorce their understanding of their own function from international law and perceive interventions as *wars of choice*. In addition, we argue that from an MPs' perspective a discussion about military action has to start with an awareness and understanding of the available information. From our perspective, an informed Parliament and more particularly, informed MPs are the antidote to poor decision-making and groupthink.[98] By educating themselves about the situation on the ground, the international and domestic motivations for action, the long-term strategy and the economic investment as well as the capability of the British armed forces, MPs can ensure better transparency and accountability of governmental decision-making. In the end, the fuller the inclusion of the House of Commons, the higher the number and diversity of challengers of the 'case for war' and a potentially more nuanced decision. Ultimately, our aim is to reveal that although Parliament may be

---

[98] Sir John Chilcot, 'Sir John Chilcot's Public Statement' (6 July 2016), <www.iraqinquiry.org.uk/the-inquiry/sir-john-chilcots-public-statement> accessed 12 February 2017.

used strategically, MPs have a number of options available to them to expand their own influence over the final decision and to question government policy.

Finally, chapter six responds to the current misuse of secrecy in order to avoid the pitfalls of the public presentation of intelligence described in chapter four. The argument proposes a solution to ameliorate the issues to date with the public reliance by the Government on claims based upon classified intelligence. The solution uses secrecy. In short, it proposes that the whole House of Commons should scrutinise and debate reports of the Joint Intelligence Committee in closed sessions. This form of secrecy, which we might call *inclusive secrecy* works for the benefit, as opposed to the detriment, of the constitution. It recognises that our elected representatives must see classified information or secret intelligence in the context of war powers because the secrets kept therein are in some sense "'our" secrets".[99]

D. Methodology: The Political Constitution and Evidence-Based Public Law

In this book, we try and depict how our political constitution works in practice. As public lawyers, we often distinguish between political and legal constitutionalism. Whilst we regularly analyse how the legal part of the constitution operates and what the constitutional legal rules in this context are,[100] the political constitution often remains only an abstraction, dominated by theoretical debates among scholars.[101] We may talk of different sources—constitutional conventions and traditions— and reiterate provisions contained in Cabinet Manuals and Ministerial Codes, but we fail to really capture what type of behaviour these political rules require. Our interest in this monograph is therefore precisely that which usually escapes analysis—the political constitution in action. To understand the scope of these political rules—constitutional conventions—is to understand how they operate in practice. Because constitutional conventions are born out of and changed through political interaction and negotiation, studying this context is key to understanding the scope of the constitutional rule.[102]

The methodology adopted in this monograph is thus two-fold: first, our aim is to map out the scope and content of the convention from the ground up. In this context, we build on parliamentary materials, debates in the Commons, reports of

---

[99] J Chafetz, 'Whose Secrets?' (2013–2014) 127 *Harvard Law Review* 86, 87.
[100] Consider inter alia A Tomkins, 'In defence of the political constitution' (2002) 22 *Oxford Journal of Legal Studies* 157 and G Gee and G Weber, 'What is a political constitution?' (2010) 30 *Oxford Journal of Legal Studies* 273.
[101] See, for example, (2013) 12 *German Law Journal*: a special issue on 'political constitutions'.
[102] D Feldman, 'Constitutional Conventions' in M Qvortrup (ed), *The British Constitution: Continuity and Change* (Oxford, Hart, 2013) 94.

select committees and inquiries, as well as statements made by politicians to try to accurately depict the perception of the convention held by MPs,[103] ie those who 'operate the constitution' in this context.[104] In short, if the political constitution is 'no more and no less than what happens',[105] then, we seek to build an accurate picture of what is happening in the context of war powers. To do this, we adopt the same methodological approach we would take in relation to determining how legal rules work. We use the materials to understand how 'each institution builds up its own picture of the constitution as viewed from its own position within it'[106] and contrast these conflicting conceptions to establish the 'proper standard of behaviour'.[107] We look at political history and practice to determine 'what the political rule is' and how it has developed.

In a purely legal context, our approach would be called doctrinal, seeking to provide a 'systematic exposition of the rules governing a particular legal category, analysing the relationship between rules, explaining areas of difficulty and, perhaps, predicting future developments'.[108] But because our inquiry concerns the political dimension of the constitution, our work has to be informed by what happens in the political context. We need to understand how the War Powers Convention as a rule is 'implemented' and whether or not it is obeyed or departed from. In a legal context, a departure would suggest a violation of the law, but would not affect its *status* as the law. But in a political context, a breach or departure from a political rule is crucial because it undermines the existence of the rule, its scope or indeed the belief that a behaviour captured by the convention is binding.[109] In this sense, in the political context, understanding how the political rule—a constitutional convention—is obeyed is to understand what the rule is and what it requires. In this regard, our analysis of how the convention, as it is captured in the Cabinet Manual, fails to live up to its promise in practice is crucial in showing the extent, content, and true nature of the convention.

We call the approach we adopt to mapping out the constitutional convention *evidence-based public law*, because we feel this is an approach that allows us to achieve the goals set by doctrinal-style research in a political setting. We use it to determine the current political practice and also to build up an evidence base from which we can later construct more theoretical normative arguments. Both of these elements are typical of public law scholarship. As a consequence,

---

[103] ibid, 94.

[104] Jennings opined that: 'the short explanation of the constitutional conventions is that they provide the flesh that clothes the dry bones of the law' in Jennings, *The Law and the Constitution* (n 53) 81–82.

[105] JAG Griffith, 'The political constitution' (1979) 42 *Modern Law Review* 1, 19.

[106] Feldman, 'Constitutional Conventions' (n 102) 94.

[107] P Morton, 'Conventions of the British Constitution' (1991–1992) 15 *Holdsworth Law Review* 114, 138–44.

[108] E Pearce, E Campbell and D Harding, *Australian Law Schools: A Discipline Assessment for the Commonwealth Tertiary Education Commission* (Canberra, Australian Government Publication Service, 1987).

[109] Jaconelli, 'The nature of constitutional convention' (n 45) 42–45.

from chapter to chapter, the reader will notice a recurrent style of governmental behaviour. We depict this behaviour in relation to several military interventions to reveal the extent to which the repetitive behaviour is the norm in the relationship between government and Parliament. This repetition of examples also reinforces the extent to which government has through consistent practice determined or perhaps even cemented the presence of this troubling asymmetry. We believe strongly that such a case-by-case evidence based approach is beneficial for public lawyers, as it allows us to fully understand the operation of the constitution in context. This could not be achieved by simply focusing on abstract concepts or indeed only on written rules.

The second part of the book—chapters five and six—moves from an approach intended to establish 'what the rule is' to an approach that examines 'what the rule or appropriate standard of behaviour ought to be'. Here, we argue that the constitution as it applies to war powers would be best served by politics being liberated from the constraints imposed by public international law.[110] At this point we do introduce normative solutions, which some readers may see as theoretical. This is true to the extent that the future relationship between government and Parliament in the context of war powers is not readily predictable. If it is predictable, it perhaps cannot be predicted by public lawyers. However, our normative arguments sit atop the evidence base we have constructed in the previous chapters. This is what informs and strengthens their contribution: it offers solutions to problems we have directly identified. The solution is to map out a space in which the politics of the political constitution can be reinvigorated and permitted to flourish.

Finally, this book—and even its title—is focused on 'war', even though no formal declaration of war has been made since World War II.[111] Today, most military conflicts between nations are 'undeclared', with both sides failing to issue a formal declaration of war. Instead, warfare is referred to as 'military action', 'armed response' or in UN speak the 'use of force'. We use all of these terms— including war—interchangeably to refer to any deployment of troops or weapons (including drones and Special Forces) abroad. Although our definition of war or armed conflict is generous, as the analysis shows, governments seek to define conflicts and carve out exceptions to the convention based on equally generous interpretations.

---

[110] M Loughlin, *Sword and Scales: An examination of the relationship between law and politics* (Oxford, Hart, 2000), ch 1; H Arendt, 'Reflections on Little Rock' in P Baehr (ed) *The Portable Hannah Arendt* (London, Penguin Classics, 2003), C Schmitt and G Schwab (trans), *The Concept of the Political* (Chicago, University of Chicago Press, 1995), chs 7–8, B Crick, *In Defence of Politics*, 5th edn (London, Continuum, 2005), ch 7.

[111] The last formal declaration was made against Thailand (formerly Siam) in 1942; see 'Waging War' (n 18) [10].

2

A Legal War?

VERONIKA FIKFAK

The engagement of Parliament on questions of war has been welcomed as contributing to the democratic legitimacy of government's actions. Yet it is important to put this increased involvement of Parliament—and the development of the new constitutional convention—into context. Namely, going to war has never been an exclusively domestic issue. In fact, for most of this and the past century the issue has been one for the international community. After the experience of the two World Wars, the international community has insisted on regulating the use of force. Indeed, one of the main purposes of the United Nations has been to make decisions about the waging of war the business of the entire international community. The UN Charter clearly provides that in order to maintain international peace and security the United Nations should take effective collective measures for the prevention and removal of threats to the peace, and that it should also act to suppress acts of aggression. In this context, the Charter—as we will see later—clearly mandates that the use of force by UN Member States is allowed only when explicitly authorised by the Security Council or in a situation of self-defence. In all other situations, military action is prohibited under international law. The aim of the UN Charter was to bring to an end the times in which states attacked and conquered other states without regard for (or perhaps without the requirement to be held accountable to) the rest of the international community. As a consequence, for most of the last hundred years, the use of force has primarily been an issue of the international community, rather than one for national parliaments.

However, during the last 10 to 15 years, national parliaments have been increasingly asked to authorise or support the use of force against other states.[1] Their involvement has been triggered by a frustration at the Security Council's

---

[1] For example, in relation to the Gulf War, legislatures around the world insisted they had to authorise the deployment of their own forces. The US Congress, the British Parliament, the French *Assemblée nationale*, and the Canadian Parliament all adopted motions authorising or approving the Executive's decision to deploy national military forces to help Kuwait. More on parliamentary power to oversee the use of force: H Born and H Hanggi 'The Use of Force under International Auspices: Strengthening Parliamentary Accountability' Geneva Centre for the Democratic Control of Armed Forces, Policy paper No 7, August 2005, <dcaf.ch/content/download/34940/525097/file/pp07_use-of-force.pdf> accessed 17 September 2017.

inability to respond to threats that endanger lives, communities, and even countries. The veto power of the Security Council's permanent Member States blocks the action of the international community, often when it is most needed. The failure of the United Nations to respond to humanitarian crises and to prevent the abuse of civilians at the hands of dictators has led to increasing criticism and a search for new avenues through which action can be achieved. Both Samantha Power (former US representative to the UN) and the former British Prime Minister David Cameron have insisted that the Security Council cannot be 'the only way to have a legal basis for action'.[2] In this context, they have sought to reduce the relevance of securing the support or authorisation of the Security Council and have turned instead to national parliaments. It is these domestic legislatures that have gradually been entrusted a central role in debating, supporting and even authorising actions against ISIS, Al-Qaeda, Iraq and others.

Yet, the use of national parliaments has also been strategic. By going to their legislatures, governments are now able to send their own militaries into combat without a Security Council mandate, or even against the wishes of the international community. Whilst domestic legislatures are used to compensate for the inefficiency of international institutions, the revival of unilateralism and the shift of the decision-making process into the domestic arena means the Government also has more control and influence over the end result than it would have in the Security Council.[3] Paradoxically, therefore, the involvement of Parliament is convenient and welcomed not only by those who champion greater democratisation of war powers, but also by the Government itself. Instead of relying on the UN, governments can make their case for war at home. Today the ultimate last word rests with national legislatures, including the Westminster Parliament.

This chapter maps out the two avenues—the international and the domestic— through which the Government can secure support for the use of force; two arenas in which it can make its case for war. By looking at examples of conflicts since World War II, we reveal how the two options are used strategically by the Government—first and foremost, the international, via the Security Council, where the Government seeks to persuade the international community of the need for and legality of the military intervention; and second, the domestic, via Westminster Parliament, where the Government looks for political support.

When going to war, there is a 'hierarchy of fora' from the Government's perspective: first comes the need to build a case on the international stage, and subsequently, after having failed to secure legal backing for its action from the international community, comes the need to build a domestic political case in

---

[2] HC Deb 29 August 2013, vol 566, col 1429; Samantha Power on 'forum-shopping' in J Borger and B Inzaurralde, 'Russian vetoes hurt UN Security Council's legitimacy, says US' *The Guardian* (23 September 2015) <www.theguardian.com/world/2015/sep/23/russian-vetoes-putting-un-security-council-legitimacy-at-risk-says-us> accessed 17 September 2017.
[3] C Murray and A O'Donoghue, 'Towards Unilateralism? House of Commons Oversight of the Use of Force', (2016) 65 *International and Comparative Law Quarterly* 305, 311.

Parliament. As a result, this chapter will demonstrate that although the War Powers Convention requiring parliamentary approval contributes to 'good governance', it was not necessarily born for such reasons. Instead, it was strategically designed to fill a lacuna in legitimacy created when the British government has failed to secure explicit and unambiguous support from international institutions. It is then that Parliament has been used to compensate for the lack of an international legal basis.

In this sense, this chapter is about the value of transparency in the British Constitution. It seeks to shine a light[4] on how decisions to go to war are made and in particular, to show and make visible how governmental power is used and exercised in this context.[5] Although the process of involving Parliament in decisions to go to war has become more transparent, shifting from debates on adjournment motions to substantive debates, this chapter shows that the exercise of war powers nevertheless remains opaque.[6] The more Parliament is involved on decisions on military action, the bigger the need to understand how the Government operates and when and why it turns to the legislature. As Fisher argues, the key element of transparency is to understand the institutions and what they do.[7] In this chapter, we seek to show how the Government uses international institutions and Parliament to go to war.

The analysis is divided across three categories of situations where Parliament can be engaged by the Government: part A, where the international backing for military action is clear and unambiguous, having been authorised by an explicit Security Council Resolution under Article 42 of the UN Charter; part B, where states have relied on their inherent right to defend themselves under Article 51 of the UN Charter and have issued a notification to the Council in that regard, but have received only ambiguous support from the Council. Finally part C, where the international backing was not forthcoming and the domestic legislature remained the only alternative forum to provide political support for military intervention.

As Figure 2.1 below suggests, this chapter will show an inversely proportional relationship between the presence and clarity of the international authorisation and the Government's motivation and need to seek out Parliament's support. The clearer the international basis, the less parliamentary involvement is needed; the less forthcoming the Security Council, the more the Commons' support becomes crucial. Although Parliament may play a subsidiary role in (A) and even in (B), in situation (C) the debate in the House of Commons takes centre stage. In this situation Parliament's support appears crucial in determining whether military

---

[4] *Eisai Ltd, R (on the application of) v National Institute for Health and Clinical Excellence* [2008] EWCA Civ 438 at [50]. Or in the words of Justice Brandeis 'letting the sunlight in' as quoted in S Aftergood, 'Reducing Government Secrecy: Finding Out What Works' (2009) 27 *Yale Law and Policy Review* 399 at 399 and <data.gov.uk blog>, 'Drive for Transparency and new data released' (2 June 2010) <http://data.gov.uk /blog/drive-transparency-and-new-data-released> accessed 17 September 2017.

[5] E Fisher 'Transparency and Administrative Law' (2010) *Current Legal Problems* 272, 275.

[6] ibid, 281.

[7] ibid, 308.

action will take place or not. The close link between the existence and clarity of
the international authorisation and the quality (intensity) of involvement of the
Westminster Parliament will become apparent.

Clarity of international authorisation

Intensity of domestic involvement

**Figure 2.1: The link between the clarity of international authorisation and
the intensity of parliamentary involvement**

The discussion in part D analyses the impact of scenarios A, B, and C in terms
of constitutional politics. The discussion reveals that in spite of two different
'venues' in which decisions to go to war take place—the international and the
domestic—the discourse used by the Government and other participants is
surprisingly similar. For example, before the Security Council governments speak
of 'international threats', 'international legality', 'proportionality' and 'self-defence'.
When, in turn, they make their case for war before domestic legislatures, the
language used is almost no different in kind to the discussion in the Council. In
fact, the debates mirror Security Council discussions. This is highly problematic
because the Government is effectively using Parliament as an alternative forum
for adjudication on technical questions of international law. The pervasiveness
of the international legal language means that when the decision to go to war is
'brought home', international law seems to act as a trump. As we argue in chapter
five, this international legal discourse has the effect of stifling political discourse,
and (in our view) comes at the expense of policy questions, which Parliament
is constitutionally mandated to ask. The current situation therefore prevents
MPs from performing their constitutional duty.

   For us, the value of transparency lies at the heart of decisions to go to war. Yet,
for the Government 'control of information is a potent form of power. This is why
governments value secrecy.'[8] Traditionally, the decision-making process of going
to war has been inaccessible and shrouded in mystery. In this chapter, we seek to
lift this veil. We depict a recurrent style of governmental behaviour: a conditioning
of the domestic involvement of Parliament on the developments on the international level. This conditioning may not be apparent or even problematic in a single

---

[8] P Cane 'Freedom of Information' in P Cane, L McDonald and K Rundle, *Principles of
Administrative Law*, 3rd edn (Melbourne, OUP, 2018).

case of military intervention, but when this behaviour is consistently present in relation to several military interventions, a pattern emerges revealing the extent to which the behaviour is ingrained in the relationship between the Government and Parliament. By shining a light on what government does, how it uses Parliament strategically to secure approval for military action, and how it deploys international legal arguments to present war as an obligation or as a necessity and not as a complex moral choice, we reveal how MPs are robbed of an opportunity to be meaningfully engaged on issues of war. Transparency, meaningful participation, and accountability are regularly sacrificed by governments for pragmatism.

A. Use of Force as an International Legal Question

I. The Prominent Position of the Security Council

The 1945 United Nations Charter heralded the dawning of a new world order in terms of relations between states. Following the atrocities of the Second World War, the threat or use of force by states against other states was for the first time prohibited.[9] States were permitted to use force only in situations specifically defined by the Charter, such as self-defence contained in Article 51, or when sanctioned by the Security Council pursuant to Article 42. Although at first glance these two categories seem to encompass all situations in which force could be used, both terms are importantly limited by the text of the UN Charter. First, before the Security Council can authorise force, Article 39 of the Charter requires that the Council first establishes that a threat to international peace and security exists. Once such a threat is established, and only after having exhausted other available measures (ie economic and diplomatic sanctions), the Security Council can—pursuant to Article 42—call upon states to take 'such action by air, sea, or land as may be necessary to maintain or restore international peace and security'. The authorisation to states to 'use all necessary means' is usually code for states to respond to the threat using force.[10] It is important to underline that all 15 Member States of the Council have to agree to the use of force. If a veto is used by one of the permanent members—China, France, the Russian Federation, the United Kingdom and the United States—then the Resolution authorising force will not be adopted. Only this explicit authorisation to use force under Article 42 provides an unambiguous legal basis for action.

As far as self-defence is concerned, the situation is less clear. Under Article 51 defensive action by states is only permitted against an armed attack which has already

---

[9] Article 2(4) UN Charter.
[10] Articles 39, 42 and 53 UN Charter.

taken place.[11] The Charter requires that the Security Council be informed of the attack and that defensive action lasts only until the Council has decided to take actions on the international plane regarding the matter. This means that a state can claim to be acting in self-defence only when acting in response to an ongoing attack.[12] Any use of force (even if defensive) has to be proportionate and necessary. In these circumstances, the Security Council will acknowledge that the attack constitutes a threat to international peace and security and recognise the inherent right of a state to self-defence. If, however, military action falls short of Article 51 requirements or if an 'attack' is not considered a threat which requires a response, then such recognition will not be forthcoming. In turn, other states may dispute the invocation of Article 51 and the Security Council may refuse to recognise the state's legal basis for action. As far as Article 51 is concerned, therefore, whether the legal basis will be undisputed and therefore unambiguous depends on the assessment by other Member States of the threat and the need for defensive action.

UN Charter provision	Article 42—authorisation to use 'all means necessary'	Article 51—'self-defence'
Assessment of threat and use of force	*Member States* reach consensus in Council about threat and measure	*State* unilaterally assesses threat and need for response
Who triggers article and use of force?	Security Council issues authorisation for use of force	States unilaterally invoke article and go into action on their own
Prior or ex-post involvement of Council	Use of force on basis of *prior* authorisation by Council	Use of force *without* prior Council approval but Council may *later* recognise threat and right
Ambiguity of legal basis	Unambiguous legal basis	Potentially ambiguous or disputed legal basis

Figure 2.2: Legal bases for action under Chapter VII of the UN Charter

[11] Article 51 UN Charter, which provides for the right to self-defence, uses the following terms: 'if an armed attack *occurs*'. Under the strict-constructionist theory anticipatory self-defence is therefore not allowed. I Brownlie, *International Law and the Use of Force by States* (Oxford, OUP, 1963) 278; H Kelsen, *The Law of the United Nations: A Critical Analysis of Its Fundamental Problems* (New York, Stevens & Sons 1950) 797–98; L Oppenheim, *International Law*, Vol 2, 7th ed (London, Longmans, Green and Co, 1952) 156; H Wehberg, 'L'Interdiction du Recours á la Force: Le Principe et les Problèmes qui se Posent', (1951) 78 *RCADI* 1, 81; P Jessup, *A Modern Law of Nations* (New York, Archon Books, 1968) 166; L Henkin, *International Law: Politics, Values and Functionss, 216 Collected Courses of the Hague Academy of International Law* (Boston, Brill Njihoff, 1990) 156; Y Dinstein, *War, Aggression and Self-Defence*, 3rd edn (Cambridge, CUP, 2001) 1, 138, 167.

[12] See further C Gray, *International Law and the Use of Force*, 2nd edn (Oxford, OUP, 2008) and note the difference in practice before and after 9/11 at 195ff. On pre-emptive self-defence: SD Murphy, 'The Doctrine of Pre-emptive Self-Defence' (2005) 50 *Villanova Law Review* 699; AC Arend, 'International Law and the Pre-emptive Use of Military Force' (2003) 26 *Washington Quarterly* 89.

The framework provided by the UN Charter in Chapter VII is captured in Figure 2.2 above. It portrays the situations in which the use of force (as long as the strict limits imposed by the text are complied with) is legal. It shows that although the Charter allows states to act unilaterally, this applies only in exceptional circumstances, ie in specific situations of self-defence. Even in such circumstances, the existence of a threat may be disputed and the legal basis for action may be ambiguous. The decision to limit the use of defensive force in this way and to only permit military action when authorised by the Council under Article 42 stems from a demand after the Second World War to replace the classical situations of unilateral state action and ad hoc alliances with a new framework. As Woodrow Wilson argued, 'There must now be, not a balance of power, not one powerful group of nations set off against another, but a single overwhelming group of nations who shall be the trustee of the peace of the world'.[13] Within the UN, states have therefore agreed to replace the traditional self-interest and self-concern with a membership in a universal organisation which focuses on ensuring *international peace* and *collective security*. The legal language contained in Chapter VII is used to distinguish between permitted and prohibited behaviour in this international community, but what is crucial is that the response is collective; it is the combined force of all states that is used to thwart the unlawful use of force, not ad hoc or unilateral use of force.

This focus on the collective security was meant to change the perception of threats. No longer is the focus on how one single state understands the use of force. Instead, from the perspective of international law, the focus is on identifying and establishing the 'international' threat. In 2001, when the US was attacked on 9/11, the UN Security Council described the bombings as 'international terrorism' and therefore a threat to 'international peace and security'.[14] In Kosovo, although the conflict was a civil war and arguably concerned issues that were domestic in nature, the Security Council nevertheless defined the conflict as a threat to 'international peace and security'. In this regard, the concern was that the conflict would spread outside the Yugoslav borders and across the Balkan region. The threat to international peace and security was identified both prior to the intervention of NATO against Yugoslav forces in mid-1999 and afterwards.[15] Even when Argentina invaded the Falkland Islands in 1982—giving rise to a bilateral conflict—the President of the Security Council expressed his concern about the growing tension in the region and spoke of the need to maintain 'international peace and security'. In its Resolution the Security Council called the Argentinian invasion a 'breach of that peace'.[16] Even in intra-state conflicts or in traditional

---

[13] W Wilson, *War and Peace* (New York, Harper and Brothers, 1927) Vol I, 343.
[14] SC Resolution 1373 (2001).
[15] SC Resolutions 1203 (1998) and 1244 (1999).
[16] SC Resolution 502 (1982), including statement of President of the Security Council of 1 April 1982.

self-defence situations the focus is therefore on the *international* implications of these conflicts, as opposed to the domestic impacts on the states involved.[17]

The aim of the UN framework is to shift the thinking about war from the domestic, unilateral sphere to the international, communitarian sphere, where use of force is addressed collectively. This shift has effectively 'internationalised' the question of war. It has forced states to think about and present disputes in international terms and put aside domestic concerns about waging war. Internationalisation of this nature has also distanced the decision-making in respect of armed conflict from the domestic political communities where the ramifications of conflicts are most acutely felt. Instead of focusing on concerns over the risk of casualties, accountability to the national electorate, and the domestic consequences of military action, governments articulate their positions in terms of their concern for the international community or, more importantly, a concern about forming international commitments and alliances. In this multilateral context, states work together to present conflicts as requiring their intervention. Often alliances are formed within the Security Council to secure support for resolutions backing use of force or authorising a response to particular threatening situations.[18]

In order to secure unanimity (or at least avoid the Russian/Chinese veto), countries have to persuade each other about the necessity and legitimacy of their position. Obviously, this requires presenting their case in a common legal and most importantly 'international' language. This international focus or lens through which disputes and conflicts are viewed necessarily affects the manner in which states approach and present their own position when it comes to the use of force. War is about 'helping friends',[19] 'fulfilling commitments' or 'international obligations',[20] avoiding 'humanitarian catastrophe and disaster',[21] or 'genocide',[22] etc. Although these are noble goals, they neglect the domestic cost of such interventions. The result of this law-driven internationalisation is that in their domestic political presentation of the use of force, governments conceal the risk to military troops on the ground, the economic cost of waging a war, and sometimes completely neglect the opinion of the home public. As a consequence, it is often possible, even probable, that on the international level a commitment to the use of force is made without regard for national parliaments or accountability to the people of the home state.

---

[17] C Ku and H Jacobson, *Democratic Accountability and the Use of Force in International Law* (Cambridge, CUP, 2003) 17, where authors note that the doctrine and language of collective security has been used for several purposes that were not envisaged when the UN Charter was adopted such as preventing genocide, serious violations of human rights and restoring democratically elected governments.

[18] When the UK was considering going to war in Iraq in 2003, it 'co-sponsored' a resolution together with the US, giving a final opportunity to Iraq to address its complete disarmament: SC Resolution 1441 (2002).

[19] R Mason 'Chilcot under pressure to report after leaked Blair-Bush Iraq memo', *The Guardian*, 18 October 2015. The leaked memo revealed that the UK would follow the White House's lead in relation to the invasion of Iraq in 2003.

[20] HC Deb 3 August 1914, vol 65, col 1809 (Sir Grey).

[21] HC Deb 23 March 1999, vol 141, cols 169 (Blair), in relation to Kosovo.

[22] HL Deb 21 July 1994, vol 557, col 43WA (Avebury). AJ Kuperman, *The Limits of Humanitarian Intervention: Genocide in Rwanda* (Washington, DC, Brookings, 2001) 110.

II. Securing International Authorisation for Action Under Article 42 of the UN Charter

The 'internationalisation' of the question of using force or waging war has important consequences for domestic parliaments. In particular, the fact that the
determination of a 'threat' and the need for 'collective action' is taken by the international community appears to importantly decrease the need for involving the
Westminster Parliament. In this section, we show how focused both the Executive
and Parliament are on securing the international authorisation. Until the Security
Council has recognised force as necessary, Parliament is usually kept informed
of the Government's international efforts, and briefed on the situation on the
ground. Members of the House actively encourage the Government to obtain the
support of the UN, at times even making it clear that their own approval is conditional upon the widest possible international agreement being achieved.

Our analysis shows that once the international legal basis for action is provided pursuant to Article 42 of the Charter, the perception of the conflict and the
Government's confidence about deploying troops changes. An international legal
mandate appears to make the Government more confident of the legitimacy of
its decision to deploy troops, and in turn, this makes it less interested in seeking
a domestic political mandate for action via the national legislature. Often Parliament is merely advised of the international obligation and responsibility placed
upon the UK to join the international action. The House of Commons then plays
a minimal and mostly passive role. By looking at three examples—Korea, the
Gulf War and Libya (which was debated after the emergence of the War Powers
Convention), the highly limited role that Parliament has been given becomes self-
evident. Even when invited to debate and vote on military action, Parliament was
only symbolically allowed into that process.

a. Three Conflicts—Korea, the Gulf War, and Libya

Here we look at three examples. The first occurred in 25 June 1950, when North
Korea invaded South Korea. The Security Council reacted quickly, unanimously
condemning the invasion, calling it a breach of the peace and insisting that
North Korean forces withdraw from the area.[23] Two days later, on 27 June 1950,
the Security Council adopted Resolution 83 recommending Member States of
the United Nations to 'furnish such assistance to the Republic of Korea as may
be necessary to repel the armed attack and to restore international peace and
security in the area'.[24] This was an explicit, unambiguous authorisation to states
to use force.

---

[23] SC Resolution 82 (1950).
[24] SC Resolution 83 (1950).

The second example is the Gulf War. In August 1990, when Iraq invaded Kuwait, the international community condemned the invasion as a 'breach of peace'.[25] The Security Council recognised Kuwait's 'inherent right of individual or collective self-defence in response to the armed attack by Iraq against Kuwait', in accordance with Article 51 of the UN Charter and required Iraqi forces to leave.[26] When, four months into the invasion, Iraqi forces still refused to withdraw from Kuwait, the Security Council, acting on the basis of Article 42 of the UN Charter, adopted Resolution 678. The Resolution—passed in November 1990—authorised the Member States to 'cooperate with the Government of Kuwait'. It set a deadline of 15 January 1991 for Iraq to withdraw from Kuwait. In the same Resolution, the Council also authorised the Member States 'to use all means to uphold and implement Security Council resolutions … and to restore international peace and security in the area' after the 15 January 1991 deadline.[27] This therefore was a clear authorisation to use force to expel Iraq from Kuwait.

Military intervention in Libya in 2011 provides our third example. In February, the Libyan Revolution between forces loyal to Colonel Muammar Gadhafi and those seeking to oust his government led to clashes with security forces that fired on protestors in Benghazi. The protests escalated into a rebellion that spread across the country, with the forces opposing Gadhafi establishing an interim governing body, the National Transitional Council. Concerned by the development of the situation, the Security Council froze Gadhafi's financial assets and adopted Resolution 1973 on 17 March 2011. In the Resolution, the Security Council found that the Libyan Civil War represented a threat to international peace and security and demanded 'an immediate ceasefire' authorising the international community to establish a no-fly zone, and to use all means necessary short of foreign occupation to protect civilians.[28]

b. Wide International Consensus as Priority

In Korea, the Gulf, and Libya, the legitimacy of UK involvement in the three conflicts was perceived to be inextricably linked with the consensus of the international community. Debates in Parliament prior to authorisation show that MPs clearly saw their function as one of encouraging the Government to secure international consensus.

Before 27 June 1950, when the legal basis of any military intervention in Korea became indisputable, discussions were held in the Westminster Parliament as to whether the UK should assist South Korea in an action of 'collective self-defence' under Article 51 of the UN Charter. This provision of the Charter allows for states

---

[25] SC Resolution 660 (1990), followed by SC Resolution 661 (1990) imposing economic sanctions, and SC Resolution 665 (1990) authorizing naval blockade to enforce embargo against Iraq.
[26] SC Resolution 661 (1990).
[27] SC Resolution 678 (1990).
[28] SC Resolution 1973 (2011).

to call upon other states to assist them in defending themselves, and such calls for assistance do not require a special Security Council Resolution authorising such action. The Prime Minister was explicitly asked in Parliament whether the UK would join the US in coming to the assistance of South Korea. The response of the Prime Minister—just five years after the ending of the Second World War—was clear: the UK would wait for an explicit resolution which would authorise the use of force. The position of the Government was therefore that any measures taken by the UK would be made through the 'international machinery'.[29] Ultimately, on 27 June 1950, and only after the adoption of the Resolution, British forces were made available to the United States, which led the multinational force acting in support of South Korea.

The reluctance to act without international backing was evident also in the Gulf War. Due to the slow progression of the situation and the gradual response of the Security Council (first recognising self-defence then issuing an authorisation to use force after 15 January 1991), Parliament had sufficient time between August and November to debate whether British involvement in the dispute should be undertaken under or outwith UN authority. Shortly after the invasion, the US sent its own troops to Kuwait to help defend the country from Iraqi forces. The UK sent some troops to the region in September, without a final decision committing them to action. The question raised in Parliament was whether an explicit authorisation was necessary (under Article 42) or whether troops could be committed to help in 'collective self-defence' (under Article 51).[30] Without a clear Security Council resolution authorising force, the then-Prime Minister Margaret Thatcher main-tained that 'I am not willing to limit our freedom of action … We are not pre-cluded by reason of any of the SC Resolutions from exercising our inherent right of collective self-defence in accordance with the rules of international law'.[31] The opposition challenged this position,[32] arguing for a need to build 'the strongest international consensus'.[33] Liberal Democrat Leader Paddy Ashdown explained: 'I believe that the Government would find it extremely difficult to carry pub-lic opinion in this country—and international opinion abroad—if they were to embark on such an adventure without the backing of the United Nations'.[34] This sentiment was echoed by former Conservative Prime Minister Edward Heath, who argued that while the right of self-defence under Article 51 could not be ruled out if Iraq expanded its invasion, without such a move 'it [would be] difficult to imag-ine a position in which we would launch a deliberate attack without at least having the authority of the UN'.[35] The debates in Parliament therefore clearly focused on

---

[29] HC Deb 27 June 1950, vol 476, col 2159–60 (Attlee). There was no adjournment debate in the House. Instead, a statement was made by the Prime Minister both on 26 and 27 June 1950.
[30] HC Deb 6 September 1990, vol 177, col 737 (Thatcher).
[31] ibid.
[32] ibid, cols 746–49 (Kinnock).
[33] ibid, col 754 (Ashdown).
[34] ibid, col 756 (Ashdown).
[35] ibid, col 752 (Heath).

Article 51 and the scope of authority for the use of force. Throughout September MPs made it clear that their support was conditional upon the 'widest possible international agreement' being achieved if the use of force proved necessary.[36] By November 1990, when it became clear that a new resolution would most likely be passed by the Security Council, both parliamentarians and the Government insisted that a clear international mandate was necessary for the 'military option to be fully credible'.[37] Ultimately, the UK troops joined the operations in the Gulf on 17 January 1991, after an explicit resolution authorising force had been passed and two days after the deadline imposed by the Security Council had elapsed.

These debates reveal some concern over the extent of claims regarding the application of Article 51 (the self-defence argument) and the legitimacy of acting without an explicit UN authorisation under Article 42. By calling for international consensus, members of Parliament argued for patience. As MPs argue, to shatter the possibility of such consensus 'through impatience would be foolish, and even a successful military outcome could nevertheless represent a serious political failure'.[38] For both the Government and MPs, securing international authorisation therefore appears to be a priority.

c. An 'International' Military Action

The reluctance, patience or involvement of Parliament, however, are no longer needed once a resolution authorising force is adopted pursuant to Article 42 and its language is clear. In all three cases, we see that within (exactly two) days of the authorisation or the passing of internationally imposed deadlines, British troops are on the ground. This is the case in relation to Korea, the Gulf and indeed Libya.

These examples show that when force is used under the authority of the United Nations, this affects both the Government's perception of the conflict and its confidence when deploying troops, as well as the intensity of parliamentary involvement. An international legal mandate makes the Government more certain of the legitimacy of its decision to deploy troops and allows it to share responsibility for the decision with other states, thus protecting it from potential criticism. Although constitutionally the Government enjoys the prerogative power to send troops into battle regardless of the position of the international community or indeed that of Parliament, the moment of the adoption of the Resolution under Article 42 of the Charter appears crucial to how the conflict is presented to Parliament and the public. Once international backing is secured through the Security Council, all doubt as to the legal basis of military intervention is removed, and previous concerns about the potential lack of legitimacy for the use of force

---

[36] HC Deb 8 September 1990, vol 177, col 883 (Steel); vote on an adjournment motion 437:35.
[37] HC Deb 28 November 1990, vol 181, col 869 (Hurd).
[38] HC Deb 6 September 1990, vol 177, col 756 (Ashdown).

or uncertainty as to defensive involvement (collective self-defence) of British troops are all but silenced.[39] The perception of any given conflict is that the British Government is acting to fulfil its international legal obligations under the UN Charter and the basis for its action is to 'be found in [the] resolution.'[40] This impacts directly upon how Parliament is engaged by government. For example, in relation to Korea and the Gulf War, this is clearly seen from the phrasing of the motion in the House of Commons, which indicates that troops are acting 'in conformity with their obligations under the United Nations Charter, in helping to resist the unprovoked aggression against the Republic of Korea'[41], or pursuant to Resolution 678 in respect of the Gulf War. Winston Churchill, in opposition during the Korean conflict, emphasised the international nature of the action even further when he expressed his confidence that the Government would 'act up to [its] supreme international obligations'.[42] In relation to Libya, the Prime Minister remarked that the adoption of the Resolution 'marked the beginning of our involvement in an international operation ... to enforce the will of the United Nations' and UN Security Council Resolution 1973.[43] Military forces were acting pursuant to 'the full, unambiguous legal authority of the United Nations' and were 'backed by Arab countries and a broad international coalition'.[44]

An international legal mandate appears to give the Government the basis to define its action as 'international' and therefore present it before Parliament as already 'legal' and 'legitimate' as a direct consequence of this. As White argues, 'By taking their case for war to the Security Council and recognising the authority of that body, those states [governments] prosecuting the wars ... were able to present much more convincing cases to their parliaments and peoples'.[45] But often this international legal certainty has also meant a lesser political involvement for Parliament. The presence of a Security Council resolution affects the timing of parliamentary debates. Although members of the House are kept regularly informed and invited to debate the potential deployment of troops prior to international authorisation, the moment the Security Council issues a resolution authorising force, Parliament's involvement appears to be reduced.

In relation to Korea, a debate was held only on 5 July 1950, after the commitment of forces.[46] In relation to the Gulf crisis, Parliament's support was actively sought by the Government until the moment the SC Resolution was adopted. In this regard, Parliament was consulted as to whether it supported

---

[39] This is of course also the case with the most recent expansion of the intervention against ISIS into Syria in 2015. HC Deb 2 December 2015, vol 603, col 321, referring to SC Resolution 2249 (2015).

[40] HC Deb 5 July 1950, vol 477, col 493 (Attlee).

[41] ibid, cols 485–90, 492–93, 502, 596.

[42] HC Deb 28 June 1950, vol 476, cols 2292 (Churchill).

[43] HC Deb 21 March 2011, vol 525, col 700 (Cameron).

[44] HC Deb 21 March 2011, vol 525, col 709 (Cameron), dismissing the abstention of India, Russia and China.

[45] N White, *Democracy goes to War* (Oxford, OUP, 2009) 112.

[46] HC Deb 5 July 1950, vol 477, col 485 (Attlee).

the provisional sending of troops to the region and in relation to timing. The Government kept the House of Commons abreast of developments in the Security Council and on the eve of the adoption of Resolution 678 advised Parliament of the change in its policy, namely that the adoption of the Resolution was necessary for the 'military option to be fully credible.'[47] After the adoption of the Resolution, the Government successfully defeated an adjournment vote opposing the use of force against Iraq[48] and proceeded to send troops abroad, committing the UK fully to war. It was only after these decisions were made—after the UK's participation in the Gulf War was effectively a *'fait accompli'*[49]—that the Government in a substantive motion asked for Parliament's support of its action.[50] On 21 January 1991, after the commitment of troops, the House expressed its full support for British forces in the Gulf, and their contribution to the implementation of the UN Resolutions. A clear UN mandate therefore appears to have reduced the need for explicit domestic support of the action prior to the sending of troops abroad.

Finally, we turn to Libya. In the first conflict to arise after the recognition of the constitutional convention requiring for Parliament to be consulted prior to the deployment of troops, the House of Commons did not get to debate the issue until after troops had already been sent into action, on 17 March 2011. MPs were only advised of the Government's decision two days after troops had been deployed, and four days after the adoption of the resolution in the Security Council. On 21 March 2011, Members of the Commons were asked to vote on a substantive motion welcoming the Resolution, deploring use of violence by the Libyan regime, and supporting the Government's decision to implement Resolution 1973. The House was also invited to offer its wholehearted support to the men and women of the armed forces. Therefore, Parliament's support for action was not sought prior to deployment, but only after fundamental strategic decisions had already been made and military action had already been taken. In this regard, the international authorisation appears to act as a tool to empower the Government to act on its own, sending troops on combat missions without prior parliamentary involvement or consent.

This belated timing of the debate or the apparent departure from the convention is not per se problematic. But because the engagement of the House comes after the start of hostilities, the discussion in the House is limited to the issue of the operation of the conflict, to the terms of the resolution, and the implications of a long-term intervention, as opposed to its initiation. In October 2011 the Cabinet Manual recognised the constitutional convention as requiring an

---

[47] HC Deb 28 November 1990, vol 181, col 869 (Hurd).
[48] HC Deb 15 January 1991, vol 183, cols 734–36; vote 435: 57.
[49] R Joseph, *The War Prerogative: History, Reform, and Constitutional Design* (Oxford, OUP, 2013) 69.
[50] A debate on a substantive motion differs considerably from one on a motion to adjourn (see ch 1 A1). In the case of the Gulf, only adjournment debates were allowed prior to the adoption of the SC Resolution authorising force. A substantive debate follows after and once troops have already been deployed.

opportunity to debate before troops were committed to a conflict.[51] However, it would be misleading to argue that Parliament's involvement (such as in relation to Libya) strengthens the operation of the War Powers Convention. Voting on an issue after troops were already involved in battle is merely the task of rubber-stamping a decision that has already been made.[52]

The international legal mandate therefore changes the content of parliamentary discourse, and crucially, the perceived need (from a governmental perspective) of whether parliamentary legitimation is in fact necessary. The issue of legality is resolved. For the rest, the issues Parliament can discuss appear to be substantially limited. This directly detracts from the democratic primacy of Parliament, and diverts deliberations in the Commons away from domestic political issues engaged by the conflict.

B. Bringing the War Question Home

I. Playing Both Sides—the Self-Defence Argument at Home and Internationally

Whilst a resolution of the Security Council provides a legal basis upon which a state can use force, until such authorisation is forthcoming, there is often uncertainty as to the international legality of any proposed armed conflict. Most frequently, this international silence is filled by the argument that the need to use force without a Security Council mandate arises out of self-defence. According to Article 51 of the UN Charter, a state has an 'inherent right' to defend itself against an armed attack and has to inform the Council of its intention to exercise this right. Once the Security Council is informed, it will most often proceed to describe the situation as a 'threat to peace' and recognise the state's right to defend itself.

As stated above, a claim to self-defence is the only situation in which a state can use force without a prior approval of the international community. And yet, when we look at the examples of the Falkland Islands and the UK intervention in Afghanistan, it is clear that the sole reliance on self-defence (ie Article 51 of the UN Charter) was often not considered sufficient by the Government to proceed with the use of force. As a rule, Prime Ministers were concerned about how the international community perceived the conflicts and how willing it was to recognise the state's right to self-defence. When international acknowledgment or political support was ultimately lacking or ambiguous, the Government sought to persuade

---

[51] HM Government, 'The Cabinet Manual: A guide to laws, conventions and rules on the operation of government (1st edn)' (London, The Stationary Office, 2011), para [5.38].

[52] In the end, the majority of the MPs voted in favour of the motion to support the Government's action and armed troops. HC Deb 21 March 2011, vol 525, cols 700 ff; vote 557:13.

Parliament to support its action. The two examples that follow seek to show how in face of an ambiguous legal position, the Government is trying to play a double game—by generating sufficient international consensus and by rallying the support of the Commons.

a. Falklands

The Falklands dispute was a conflict over the Malvinas Islands, which had been occupied by Britain since 1833, but to which Argentina claimed title, arguing that said title to the islands succeeded from the Spanish. The inhabitants clearly wanted to remain in association with the UK, and a negotiated solution was sought 'in which the Argentine claims for sovereignty would be met and the desire for islanders to retain a British way of life safeguarded'.[53] When Argentina invaded the Islands in 1982, however, these discussions were suspended. The UK responded by sending its own navy to the area and by invoking its inherent right of self-defence under Article 51.[54] The decision to send troops abroad was immediate: as soon as the invasion occurred the Government announced that the decision had been taken to send troops to the Falklands, and that it would take weeks for them to arrive to the area.[55]

This intermediate period (between the sending of troops and their arrival) was therefore an ideal moment for the UK to persuade the international community politically that the Argentine action represented a threat to peace, and to secure the necessary support to legitimise its response to this threat. On the day following the invasion, the UK secured Security Council Resolution 502 which labelled the invasion of the Falklands Islands as a 'breach of peace' in the region and called for a complete withdrawal by Argentine forces. Yet, the Council remained silent about Article 51 and did not recognise the UK's right to self-defence. Instead, it called upon both governments for immediate cessation of hostilities; and it also urged both states to seek a diplomatic solution to the situation and refrain from further military action.

Although the UK had managed to rally some European partners to its side and persuade them to impose non-military measures against Argentina,[56] the lack of recognition of the UK's 'inherent right to self-defence' by the Security Council gave rise to several domestic political issues. First, the failure of the Security Council to explicitly authorise a military response to the Argentine invasion, or indeed to describe the action in familiar terms as constituting 'a threat to international

---

[53] W Little, 'Anglo-Argentine Relations and the Management of the Falklands Question' in P Byrd (ed) *British Foreign Policy under Thatcher* (Oxford, Philip Allan, 1988) 137. One proposed solution was to formally transfer sovereignty to Argentina with a lease-back of territory to Britain for a long period.

[54] 1982 UN Yearbook 1320.

[55] The indication was that it would be a few months up to a year before an invasion. M Hastings and S Jenkins *The Battle for the Falklands* (London, Book Club Associates, 1982) 57.

[56] EC Regulation 877/82 of 16 April 1982, OJ L102/1.

peace and security' rather than a more geographically limited 'breach of peace in the *region*' meant that as a matter of international law, the legal basis for the use force against Argentine forces was shaky. This compelled the Government to seek domestic *political* support for the planned military response. Thus, the Prime Minister turned to Parliament for its support of 'those who are now embarked in defence of British territory and to protect the rights we and the Falklands islanders hold equally dear'.[57] Five different adjournment debates were held prior to the arrival of troops at their destination.[58]

Secondly, although the Government had failed to persuade the Security Council to recognise its right to self-defence, before Parliament the Government consistently phrased its position in international legal terms—by emphasising the 'illegal' and 'unprovoked' attack of Argentine forces and the need and responsibility to recover the islands in accordance with the wishes of the islanders and Article 51 of the UN Charter.[59] When the issue arose, for example, about the effect of Resolution 502—which called upon both states to cease hostilities and seek a diplomatic solution[60]—Prime Minister Thatcher made it very clear to the Members of Parliament that the Resolution did not affect Britain's right to self-defence.[61] In that sense, the Government insisted that regardless of the position of the Security Council, the basis for its response was Article 51 of the UN Charter. In other words, it presented its own interpretation of international law before a domestic political institution (the Westminster Parliament) to secure legitimacy for its actions. In accordance with that, it made consistent use of the terms 'defence of British territory', 'response', 'protect[ion] of' the rights and the people of the Falkland Islands.[62]

b. Afghanistan

The Falklands example shows how self-defence situations trigger two parallel actions by the Government. On one side, the Government seeks international acknowledgement and recognition of its right to self-defence and on the other, it also turns to the domestic legislature not only to inform its members of the progress made on the international plane, but often to obtain additional domestic legitimacy for its action. The same type of behaviour was repeated decades later in the aftermath of 9/11. Days after the attacks, the US relied on the right to self-defence to mount an operation against the Taliban in Afghanistan.[63]

---

[57] HC Deb 7 April 1982, vol 21, col 962 (Pym).

[58] HC Deb 3 April 1982, vol 21, cols 629ff; HC Deb 7 April 1982, vol 21, cols 959ff; HC Deb 14 April 1982, vol 21, cols 1146ff; HC Deb 19 April 1982, vol 22, cols 21ff (no adjournment motion put); HC Deb 29 April 1982, vol 22, col 1045.

[59] HC Deb 3 April 1982, vol 21, cols 633, 635, 642 (Thatcher).

[60] SC Resolution 502 (1982).

[61] HC Deb 29 April 1982, vol 22, col 982 (Thatcher).

[62] HC Deb 14 April 1982, vol 21, col 1146 (Thatcher). The motion was agreed without a vote.

[63] Letter from Ambassador John Negroponte, Permanent Representative of the USA to the UN in New York, to the President of the Security Council, S/2001/946, 7 October 2001.

The UK wished to join the coalition, relying on the right to collective self-defence. In truth, however, the UK's main aim was to help an ally in need (the United States).

Although before Parliament, Blair spoke of the need to respond to 9/11 'to protect our country, our people, our economy, our way of life',[64] the defensive intervention against Afghanistan raised important legal questions. The Afghanistan situation was unlike any before. In comparison to the invasion of the Gulf or even the Falkland Islands, where military intervention was launched against an ongoing armed attack, the problem with Afghanistan was that the response was planned a month after 9/11 attacks. The argument for self-defence was therefore wider than on previous occasions.[65] Both the US and UK Governments were therefore eager to secure the legitimacy for their defensive action before the Security Council.

Once both the US and later the UK notified the Security Council of the attacks and their intention to exercise their right to (individual and collective) self-defence, the Council affirmed their positions. Although the Council never agreed that the terrorist atrocities of 9/11 constituted an 'armed attack' within the meaning of the Charter or indeed a 'breach of peace' or an 'act of aggression', it found that there was a 'threat to peace' and condemned the action of terrorists. The Security Council also generally recognised the inherent right of self-defence of the involved states (UK and US). Whilst the Council therefore did not authorise use of force, its recognition of both the 'threat' and the right to self-defence was enough under Article 51 of the UN Charter for international defensive action.[66]

During the time between the events of 9/11 and the adoption of the Resolution, Parliament was kept informed both of the plans 'of our allies'[67] and of the Government's international efforts to secure a resolution recognising the right to self-defence. The concern on the part of MPs was that the UK had to ensure the complete legality of its action. In this respect, for example, MPs worried about the Government's decision to insist that it did not need to issue a separate notification to the Security Council of its decision to exercise the right to self-defence. Such notification was required under Article 51 and was a key element in making the exercise of self-defence legal. Yet, the Government claimed that since it was helping the US, it was already covered by the notification of the USA. As Hoon stated: 'This is a coalition operation and I have no doubt that for technical legal purposes, we are covered by the notification that the US has given'.[68] This position was challenged by Members of Parliament who insisted that the Government had to consult with the Foreign and Commonwealth Office and if necessary issue a

---

[64] HC Deb 8 October 2001, vol 372, col 815 (Blair).

[65] N White, *Democracy* (n 45) 197; G Wilson, 'The Impact of 9/11 on the Use of Force in International Law' in R Utley (ed) *9/11 Ten Years After: Perspectives and Problems* (London, Routledge, 2012) 179, 193; N White 'Self-defence, Security Council authority and Iraq' in R Burchill, ND White, J Morris (eds) *International Conflict and Security Law: Essays in Memory of Hilaire McCoubrey* (Cambridge, CUP, 2005) 235, 253.

[66] SC Resolution 1368 (2001).

[67] HC Deb 4 October 2001, vol 372, col 672 (Blair).

[68] ibid, col 832 (Hoon).

notification to the Security Council to legalise its position in international law. The House of Commons was clearly concerned that the state's international position should not come into question. In the end, the UK Representative to the UN did inform the Security Council accordingly.[69]

Although the Security Council backing seemingly reduces the need for parliamentary involvement, before the legality of military action became clear, both the Government and MPs were clearly focused on securing international authorisation. The role of the domestic legislature, however, became more prominent as the Afghanistan conflict progressed. As the Afghan defensive response grew in length and scope, questions arose in Parliament about whether action remained within the scope of the initial Security Council Resolution, which allowed the United States and Britain to exercise self-defence.[70] The length and scope of the response raised issues of proportionality and necessity, putting the legality of the whole intervention in question. To redress these uncertainties, the UK Government sought MPs' support for its continuing action through an adjournment debate in the Commons in 2009[71], and a 'take-note' debate in the Lords in 2013.[72] On 9 September 2010—nine years into the war—the House of Commons was given the opportunity to debate and vote on the continued deployment to Afghanistan. MPs voted overwhelmingly in favour of the motion 'That this House supports the *continued* deployment of UK Armed Forces in Afghanistan'.[73] Parliament was used therefore to provide further legitimacy to an intervention that had expanded beyond the initial authorisation.

This analysis of the Falklands and the Afghanistan episodes reaffirms the argument that governments give the international legal case for war priority over domestic political considerations. Support for conflict is pursued aggressively in international venues (such as the UNSC and the wider international community) until those institutions provide a clear basis for military action. When, however, the Security Council's position is ambiguous or when the international community starts raising questions about the continued right to self-defence, the Government presents its legal and political case for war to Parliament.

One would expect that this shift from the international to the domestic sphere would require the Government to change or adapt its 'case for war' to domestic circumstances. Yet, although domestic arguments about protecting territory and ensuring support for citizens are mentioned, the main points of the case for war remain the international arguments about 'inherent self-defence', 'proportionality'

---

[69] ibid, col 851 (Short).

[70] HC Deb 9 September 2010, vol 515, col 499 (Flynn); col 523 (Winnick), and others.

[71] HC Deb 8 December 2009, vol 502, col 1WH (Flynn).

[72] HL Deb 14 March 2013, vol 744, col 354 (Warsi). In the House of Lords, debates may take place on a motion 'That this House takes note of …' This formula enables the House to debate a situation or a document without coming to any positive decision and is regularly used for select committee reports. Motions to take note are also used when a Minister wishes to put down a neutral motion. Such motions are usually agreed to.

[73] HC Deb 9 September 2010, vol 515, cols 494. Vote was 310:14 in support of the motion.

and 'necessity'.[74] The Government is therefore using Parliament to reinterpret international law in the Government's favour, and to compensate for a potentially unclear or ambiguous position of the international community.[75] Whilst relying upon the domestic legislature for support, governments continue to speak using primarily international legal terms. In the final blow to Parliament's political function, this allows domestic political concerns about war to be pushed off the agenda. The focus is almost exclusively on (international) law.

C. Use of Force as a Domestic Question

I. Reducing the Importance of International Institutions

When the Security Council passes a Resolution authorising the use of force, this creates a mandate to act under international law. There is no doubt as to the legality of the armed conflict, and the British Government is quick to offer its assistance in the international military action. But consensus in the Security Council is not always easy to secure. In particular, the use of the veto power by the permanent members has importantly limited the ability of the Council to address humanitarian and human rights crises around the world.[76] Most recently in 2017, the Council has failed to agree upon concerted action in relation to Syria, even after more than 220,000 Syrians have died, and more than 11 million have been forced from their homes. The adoption of resolutions authorising force against the Syrian leader Bashar Al-Assad were blocked by Russia's threats or actual use of its veto power.[77]

In response, the US has warned that this blanket use of the veto would 'jeopardise the Security Council's long-term legitimacy and could lead the US and like-minded countries to bypass it as a decision-making body'.[78] In 2013, Samantha Power, the US permanent representative to the UN, said that the US and other

[74] Taking as example the 2010 debate on Afghanistan (ibid): on necessity—cols 496, 501, 523, 525, etc from both the opposition and the backbenchers; on proportionality—col 543, 548, etc; on self-defence or presence of threat—496, 497, 501, 506, 508, 510, 547, etc.

[75] In doing this the Government is also using Parliament to provide evidence of state practice and *opinio juris* that fits with the case the Government is making. With time such self-constituting evidence can create a customary international law exception to the UN Charter's prohibition of force. We return to this in ch 5.

[76] The veto power originates from Article 27 of the UN Charter, which provides in part that decisions of the Security Council on non-procedural matters shall be made by an affirmative vote of nine members including the *concurring votes* of the permanent members. Whilst permanent members may abstain, a resolution will not be adopted if they vote against it.

[77] Russia had vetoed multiple SC resolutions in relation to Syria: 4 October 2011, 4 February 2012, 19 July 2012 and most recently 12 April 2017. Russia has adopted a similar attitude to the situation in Ukraine, having annexed Crimea on 18 March 2014.

[78] Borger and Inzaurralde, 'Russian vetoes' (n 2).

countries had increasingly been going elsewhere to have atrocities investigated, and that a 'forum-shopping' trend was likely to continue. 'It's a Darwinian universe here. If a particular body reveals itself to be dysfunctional, then people are going to go elsewhere,' Power told the *Guardian*. '[I]f that happened for more than Syria ... and you started to see across the board paralysis ... it would certainly jeopardise the Security Council's status and credibility and its function as a go-to international security arbiter. It would definitely jeopardise that over time.'[79] The British ambassador to the United Nations, Matthew Rycroft, agreed: 'Syria is a stain on the conscience of the Security Council. I think it is the biggest failure in recent years, and it undoubtedly has consequences for the standing of the Security Council and indeed the United Nations as a whole.'[80]

These statements are important because they reveal the inability of the Security Council to act when blocked by one or two permanent members, whilst revealing the frustration on the part of other states like the UK, the US, and France, who wish to use an armed response to address serious humanitarian crises through the international machinery. Of course, these frustrations are expressed not only in relation to Russia, but anytime a veto in the Council hampers states from taking action. The UK and US similarly lamented France's threats to use its veto powers in relation to Iraq in 2003 when France was un-persuaded by the evidence regarding the presence of chemical weapons in Iraq. At the time, the UK argued that France's threat to use its veto power (a so-called pocket veto) was holding the whole of the UN hostage.[81]

At different times, all of the Security Council's permanent members have been accused of prioritising their 'national interest' or political deals and alliances with other powers, thus blocking proposals for the use of force. For example, there was a lot of 'unhappiness' when the United States and Britain systematically blocked Security Council action to impose economic sanctions on South Africa during the 1980s.[82] Members of the Security Council also lamented the fact that they had been prevented from exercising their responsibility for the maintenance of international peace and security in relation to the Suez crisis in 1956 when France and Britain blocked its action.[83] Similar frustration was expressed at the UN's failure to take action in relation to Vietnam in the 1960s and 1970s due to the US veto;[84]

---

[79] ibid.

[80] ibid.

[81] See intervention of H Bayley in Parliament: 'Does my right hon. friend agree that France's decision to use the veto against any further Security Council resolution has, in effect, disarmed the UN instead of disarming Iraq?' HC Deb 18 March 2003, vol 401, col 764 (Bayley). The Prime Minister agreed with the statement.

[82] Vetos used on 31 October 1977 at Security Council meeting no 2045 and on 30 April 1981 at meeting no 2277.

[83] Vetos used on 30 October 1956 at Security Council meetings nos 749 and 750.

[84] Vetos used on 11 August 1975 at Security Council meeting no 1836 and on 30 September 1975 at Security Council meeting no 1846 and others. See Report of the Open-ended Working Group on the Question of Equitable Representation on and Increase in the Membership of the Security Council and Other Matters related to the Security Council, A/58/47, Annex 1.

or when the Soviet Union prevented action on Afghanistan in the 1980s.[85] Today, concerns are increasingly raised about the Council acting in line with the geopolitical interests of major powers.[86] In the past decade, the US has used its veto on three occasions to protect Israel from criticism for its actions in the Palestinian territories. China has used seven vetoes, in tandem with Russia, while Moscow has used its veto 12 times over the same period.[87]

These examples demonstrate that the UN is often unable to take action because of one or two permanent members. But these frustrations about the veto (and the corresponding allegations that the dominant and exclusive role of the permanent members render the Security Council increasingly undemocratic and non-representative of the rest of the world)[88] are also strategic. They serve to reduce the relevance of securing the support or authorisation of the Security Council and make way for more unilateral arguments. In relation to Iraq, for example, when the UK was unable to secure a resolution through the Security Council, the Government condemned the international community for failing to 'meet its clear responsibilities'.[89] The British Government argued that because the UN had failed to act, unilateral action was necessary. In short, Britain should act alone, and 'must uphold the authority of the United Nations'.[90] In relation to Syria in 2013, the Prime Minister similarly argued that: 'We could have a situation where a country's Government were literally annihilating half the people in that country, but because of one veto on the Security Council we would be hampered in taking any action'. He continued, 'it cannot be the case that that is the only way to have a legal basis for action, and we should consider for a moment what the consequences would be if that were the case.'[91] Joining the Prime Minister, Defence Secretary Liam Fox insisted that:

> We cannot allow a situation whereby the international community's ability to implement international law is thwarted by a constant veto by Russia and China … If we do nothing

---

[85] Veto on 11 January 1980 at meeting no 2191.

[86] D Mahapatra, 'The Mandate and the (In)Effectiveness of the United Nations Security Council and International Peace and Security: The Contexts of Syria and Mali' (2016) 21 *Geopolitcs* 43; R Murphy 'Is the UN Security Council fit for purpose' (2015) 24 *Politics Review* 1; J Paul 'Security Council Reform: Arguments about the Future of the United Nations System' February 1995, <www.globalpolicy.org/security-council/security-council-reform/41128-veto-analysis.html> accessed 17 September 2017.

[87] A nice graphic showing permanent members' vetos decade by decade in 'Russian vetoes' (n 2). Information was generated from the Veto List maintained by the Dag Hammarskjöld Library at <http://research.un.org/en/docs/sc/quick> accessed 17 September 2017.

[88] In 2005, the then-UN Secretary General Kofi Annan called on the UN to expand the Security Council to 24 members and argued that both Asia and Africa were inadequately represented, a fact which posed a serious threat to the UN's legitimacy. 'In Larger Freedom: Towards Security, Development and Human Rights for all' Report of the Secretary General A/59/2005; <www.un.org/en/ga/search/view_doc.asp?symbol=A/59/2005> accessed 17 September 2017. A number of other proposals have also been suggested, eg a proposal by Italy, Argentina, Canada, Colombia and Pakistan 'Uniting for Consensus', etc.

[89] HC Deb 5 November 2002, vol 392, col 127 (Straw).

[90] HC Deb 18 March 2003, vol 401, col 760 (Blair).

[91] HC Deb 29 August 2013, vol 566, col 1429 (Cameron).

I believe it would be an abdication of our international legal and moral obligations, which we should take extremely seriously.[92]

The failure of the international institutions to reach a decision authorising action has led to different responses by states seeking to achieve military goals. First, the UK (along with the US) has placed a stronger reliance on the argument of self-defence as a matter of international legality, because it can be invoked unilaterally under the UN Charter without the need for Security Council approval. During the last decade in particular, the concept of 'self-defence' has allegedly been expanded through UK and US practice from individual to collective self-defence, as well as to pre-emptive self-defence and targeted killings, as will be seen below.

Secondly, states have placed more emphasis on action within NATO to avoid gridlock in the Council. In relation to Kosovo, for example, the bombing was undertaken under the authority of the NATO Treaty rather than through the UN.[93] Before Parliament, the UK Government insisted that support of the international community in this manner gave the action legitimacy. The Prime Minister stated that it was a war fought for a 'just cause'.[94] The UN Charter does not recognise NATO as an organ capable of legalising force.

This quest for new international venues for legalising/legitimising use of force has also been mirrored by a greater involvement of national legislatures. On the domestic level, government has sought to address the ambiguous and often lacking international legal basis by involving Parliament to secure domestic political legitimacy. The House of Commons—as well as legislatures in other states—is therefore the institution that appears to have most benefited from the failure of the United Nations to secure consensus, and from the increasingly unilateral actions of the UK and the US. In fact, as some scholars argue, the extension of Parliament's role has been intentional 'in an effort to shift the locus for legitimating uses of force away from UN institutions, where the UK cannot control the actions of other states, and towards domestic processes which are more susceptible to the Government's influence'.[95]

II. Using Parliament to Compensate for the Lack of an International Basis

Where international support is unlikely, there is evidence of a complete shift by governments towards the national legislature as the locus of authorisation.

---

[92] ibid, col 1454 (Fox).

[93] Article 5 NATO Treaty: 'The Parties agree that an armed attack against one or more of them in Europe or North America shall be considered an attack against them all'.

[94] T Blair at the NATO Press Conference given by Javier Solana and him, (20 April 1999) <www.nato.int/docu/speech/1999/s990420a.htm> accessed 17 September 2017.

[95] Murray and O'Donoghue, 'Towards Unilateralism? (n 3) 306.

This can be noticed in situations that extend beyond the traditional forms of individual and collective self-defence, such as pre-emptive action and other more creative uses of force. For example, in the cases of Iraq and Syria, in which international legal authorisation was conspicuous by its absence, Parliament emerged as the key actor in legitimising governmental action. The involvement of Parliament—and the emergence of the so-called War Powers Convention—has been strategic, as opposed to driven by the ideals of 'good governance' explored in this monograph. In the hope to compensate for the international lacuna—ie lack of a clear international legal basis—Parliament has been involved instead of the international community to provide support for action. Paradoxically, as the examples show, this 'domestication' of decision-making on the use of force has not resulted in a more domestically focused discourse. Instead, the discussions in the House have focused precisely on those questions which the international community should have resolved—questions of the legality of the use of force. As we argue later, we find such internationalisation and legalisation of parliamentary discourse problematic.

a. *Iraq 2003*

Following the Gulf war, there was growing concern that Saddam Hussein was developing a chemical weapons programme. Suspicions grew after Saddam expelled UN weapons inspectors from Iraq in August 1997. Concerns intensified after 9/11, which US President George W Bush sought to tie to Saddam. Thereafter, the US and the UK adopted a more aggressive policy towards Iraq. A formal case to the international community for an invasion of Iraq began in September 2002 with an address to the UN Security Council. But France and Russia, acting in their capacity as permanent members in possession of a veto, made clear that they did not consider the situation as warranting the use of force to overthrow the Iraqi Government. Instead, they argued for continued diplomacy and weapons inspections. A compromise—Resolution 1441—was adopted, which authorised the resumption of weapons inspections and gave Iraq 'a final opportunity to comply with its disarmament obligations'.[96] Both the UK and the USA agreed that although the Resolution promised 'serious consequences' for non-compliance, there was no 'automaticity' or 'trigger' in the Resolution for an invasion without further consultation with the Security Council.

Despite these assurances and the lack of proof that Iraq possessed weapons of mass destruction,[97] the US pushed forward with its plans. In February 2003, US Secretary of State Colin Powell addressed the Security Council, where he showed

---

[96] SC Resolution 1441 (2003).

[97] The inspections 'found no evidence or plausible indication of the revival of a nuclear weapons program in Iraq'. Security Council Press Release, 7 March 2003, SC/7682, citing Mr ElBaradei, Director-General of the International Atomic Energy Agency.

a computer-generated image of 'a mobile biological weapons laboratory'.[98]
Afterwards, the United States, the United Kingdom, Poland, Italy, Australia, Denmark, Japan and Spain proposed a Resolution authorising the use of force in Iraq, but NATO members including Canada, France and Germany, together with Russia, strongly urged continued diplomacy. Facing a losing vote as well as a likely veto from France and Russia, the Resolution was eventually withdrawn. The failure to secure international backing for the invasion meant that from an international law perspective, any use of force against Iraq would be illegal. There was no explicit authorisation from the Security Council and it was becoming more apparent that with time the position of France and Russia would not change. The situation was also not one of self-defence—neither the US nor the UK made any notifications to the Council about an imminent attack, and therefore Article 51—at least before the Council—was not applicable. The then-Secretary General stated that 'if the US and others were to go outside the Council and take military action, it would not be in conformity with the Charter'.[99]

This is precisely what happened. National legislatures became the alternative source of legitimation of this action. The US sought authorisation from Congress for military action. President Bush argued that the US had to attack pre-emptively before Saddam had a chance to use the weapons of mass destruction. In the UK, the Government pursued a similar course of action by seeking parliamentary support for military intervention in Iraq. However, following the resignation of three Government Ministers, including the then-Leader of the House of Commons and Foreign Secretary, Robin Cook, the Blair Government was forced to seek a vote on a substantive motion to support its decision 'that the United Kingdom should use all means necessary to ensure the disarmament of Iraq's weapons of mass destruction [and] offers wholehearted support to the men and women of Her Majesty's Armed Forced now on duty in the Middle East'.[100] This debate and vote was the first of its kind in British constitutional history. Even prior to the Cabinet resignations, members of the ruling Labour party insisted that both an international legal authorisation had to be provided, and a motion in the House of Commons would have to follow before any action was taken.[101] Tam Dalyell MP (Labour, Linlithgow) unsuccessfully proposed a motion 'that this House declines to support a war against Iraq using the royal prerogative unless it has been authorised by both the United Nations Security Council and a motion carried in this House'.[102]

---

[98] Remarks of Colin Powell at the UN Security Council (5 February 2003) <www.state.gov/secretary/former/powell/remarks/2003/17300.htm> accessed 17 September 2017.

[99] UN Secretary General Kofi Annan, Press Conference, The Hague, The Netherlands (10 March 2003) <www.hri.org/news/world/undh/2003/03-03-10.undh.html> accessed 17 September 2017.

[100] HC Deb 18 March 2003, vol 401, cols 760–858.

[101] HC Deb 24 September 2002, vol 390, col 24 (Dalyell).

[102] ibid.

Regardless of a lack of an explicit international authorisation, the Government asserted that the invasion was legal and that it was supported by the international community. The Prime Minister produced a briefing, known as the September Dossier, based upon the work of the Cabinet Joint Intelligence Committee (made available for the first time to the full House) regarding Iraq's possession of weapons of mass destruction. Aside from this, however, the case made to Parliament was almost entirely a legal one. Tony Blair did not follow Bush's doctrine on pre-emptive self-defence. Instead, the Government went to great lengths to construct new legal arguments from existing law. The Attorney-General produced a report (since discredited), which argued for a revival of the old Resolution 678 of 1990 in relation to the Gulf War, which authorised 'all necessary means' to be taken if Iraq did not comply with international demands in previous resolutions. Read together with Resolution 1441, the report argued that the two sources allowed for the use of force. In his speech to the House, Tony Blair relied on these two separate Security Council Resolutions, and underlined Iraq's 'continuing non-compliance with Security Council Resolutions' and the fact that its failure to comply 'pose[d] a threat to international peace and security'. In the motion, the Government further condemned the international community for failing to 'meet its clear responsibilities'.[103] It lamented France's veto power, arguing effectively that the UN was being held hostage, and insisting that in such circumstances the UK 'must uphold the authority of the United Nations' and act on its own. Finally, it asked for Parliament's support of the Government's decision to 'use all means necessary to ensure the disarmament of Iraq's weapons of mass destruction'.[104]

International law scholars objected to the Attorney-General's revival theory contained in the legal memorandum on the use of force in Iraq.[105] Its detractors included the then-deputy legal adviser at the Foreign & Commonwealth Office, Elizabeth Wilmhurst, who resigned in protest.[106] Numerous sources within the Labour Party criticised the Government, arguing that its reference to 'international peace' was reducing the 'international community' to two sovereign states (the UK and the USA). Glenda Jackson MP (Labour), in a pointed intervention, asked the Defence Minister whether:

> On the issue of a strike against Saddam Hussein, it would seem that the international community has reduced to two sovereign states, namely the United Kingdom and the United States. Is he saying that this now constitutes the international community and

---

[103] HC Deb 5 November 2002, vol 392, col 127 (Straw).

[104] HC Deb 18 March 2003, vol 401, col 760 (Blair).

[105] At the time a letter drafted by 16 academics was published objecting to the construction of the resolutions and insisting that the war was illegal, <news.bbc.co.uk/1/hi/uk_politics/2829717.stm>; two practicing barristers issued a similar legal opinion at <www.cnduk.org/campaigns/item/495-rabinder-singh-qc-and-charlotte-kilroy-iraq-war-legality-opinion> accessed 17 September 2017.

[106] Letter of resignation, 18 March 2003, released under the Freedom of Information Act: <news.bbc.co.uk/2/hi/uk_news/politics/4377605.stm> accessed 17 September 2017.

that we will engage against Iraq if the rest of what I understood to be the international community stays where it is, firmly saying no to a pre-emptive strike?[107]

Over a decade after the dust has settled on the Iraq conflict, there is a 'shared understanding' that Resolution 1441 did not amount to the legal authority to use force against Iraq.[108] In short, as a matter of international law, the war in Iraq was illegal. As the British Government was proceeding on such shaky legal ground, the timing of the vote in Parliament (and political support) was therefore crucial to provide legitimacy prior to the commencement of hostilities. Despite all of the objections, on 18 March 2003, the vote in Parliament succeeded 412 to 149. On the very same day, the bombing of Iraq by the United States, the United Kingdom, Australia, Poland, Spain, Italy and Denmark began.

From a constitutional standpoint, many scholars noted the enhanced role of Parliament on Iraq and today many refer to this precedent as the trigger in the development of the new constitutional convention.[109] For the first time in the history of the Westminster Parliament, Members of the House were asked in a substantive motion and *prior* to the start of hostilities to support the Government and troops on the ground. Writing later about this new approach, the Foreign Affairs Committee said: 'unlike previous conflicts, the war in Iraq took place only after a substantive vote in Parliament, a development which we welcome'.[110]

But such engagement may have been first and foremost strategic. The new constitutional convention may not have been primarily created to democratise the ancient prerogative of war for the overall good of the British Constitution.[111] Rather, the redefined relationship between the Government and Parliament appears to have been prompted by the reluctance of the international community to provide authorisation for any military action. The new approach reflected the sentiment of the US and UK Executives that the Security Council cannot be 'the only way to have

---

[107] HC Deb 17 October 2002, vol 390, col 495–96 (Jackson).

[108] I Johnstone, 'Security Council Deliberations: The Power of Better Argument' (2003) 14 *EJIL* 437, 456. Since then a number of scholars have rejected the revival theory: S Murphy, 'Assessing the legality of invading Iraq' (2004) 92 *Georgia Law Journal* 173; C Warbrick, 'The Legal Justification for the Use of Armed Force by the United Kingdom against Iraq in March 2003' Submission to the Iraq inquiry, <www.iraqinquiry.org.uk/media/184873/submission-international-law-warbrick-2010-09-01.pdf> accessed 17 September 2017; G Simpson, 'Memorandum on the Legality of the War and on the Interpretation of United Nations Security Council Resolution 1441', Submission to the Iraq inquiry, <www.iraqinquiry.org.uk/media/184861/submission-international-law-simpson-2010-09-13.pdf> accessed 17 September 2017.

[109] J Strong, 'The accidental prerogative: why Parliament now decides on war' (2015) 17 *British Journal of Politics and International Relations* 604.

[110] House of Commons Foreign Affairs Committee 'The Decision to go to War in Iraq', 9th Report of Session 2002–03, 7 July 2003 (HC 813-I), [1].

[111] Prior to the March vote, 121 Labour MPs voted in support of a motion that 'the case for military action against Iraq (was) as yet unproven.' (HC Deb 26 February 2003, vol 400, col 363). As some commentators described the situation, 'For the Government, the outcome was difficult and revealing, and it showed that the Government needed to uphold the Commons' role as the source of legitimacy simply in order to keep the Labour Party as united as possible'. HC Deb 06 March 2003, vol 400, col 970 (Robin Cook).

a legal basis for action'.[112] If the Security Council failed to act and support action, then this international lacuna could be filled by domestic legislatures carrying out a similar function to the Security Council, by authorising military action. A new convention requiring the involvement of the domestic Parliament therefore emerged first and foremost because the British Government sought an alternative form of legitimacy. By turning away from the international sphere and looking inwards, subsequent governments have placed the debate in Parliament centre stage.

b. Humanitarian Interventions—Kosovo 1999 and Syria 2013

Although in relation to Iraq the Government did not argue about self-defence, in the eyes of MPs the discussion of intelligence and possibility of triggering WMDs in 45 minutes clearly created a feeling that they were deciding on a question of self-preservation.[113] When a country is said to be under attack, whether from terrorists or dictators and whether directly or implicitly, it is more likely that Parliament will act to 'rally behind the Crown', ie politicians will be predisposed to support the Government's case for armed conflict.[114] By contrast, in cases where the use of force appears to be a matter of choice, ie where military action is not needed for reasons of self-preservation, but to protect civilian populations in other countries, domestic political support is not necessarily guaranteed. Moreover, humanitarian interventions of this nature cannot be fought unilaterally on the basis of Article 51 of the UN Charter. They also usually do not generate enough support in the UN Security Council to secure an explicit authorisation under Article 42 of Chapter VII (the exception being Libya in 2011). In situations of this type, the British Government has sought support from the House of Commons. This can be illustrated by the contrasting examples of Kosovo 1999 and Syria 2013.

The humanitarian intervention argument had been first made by Tony Blair and Bill Clinton in relation to Kosovo. In the late 1990s, the former Yugoslav autonomous entity had seen its rights stripped away and its government dissolved by the Serbian Leader Slobodan Milošević. In response, Kosovo proclaimed itself a republic, a move which was met with a brutal assault by the Serb forces. Civilians were driven from their homes and a war began between the Kosovo Albanian fighters and the Serbian forces. In the UN, the situation was discussed as *not merely* 'an internal affair of the Former Yugoslavia'.[115] Yet, in spite of the 'grave concern' about the displacement of large numbers of people from their

---

[112] HC Deb 29 August 2013, vol 566, col 1429; Samantha Power on 'forum-shopping' in J Borger and B Inzaurralde, 'Russian vetoes hurt UN Security Council's legitimacy, says US' *The Guardian* (23 September 2015) <www.theguardian.com/world/2015/sep/23/russian-vetoes-putting-un-security-council-legitimacy-at-risk-says-us> accessed 17 September 2017.

[113] HC Deb 18 March 2003, vol 401, col 848 (Jackson), referring to 'defence against international terrorism' and 855 (Bradley) speaking of 'defence of freedom'.

[114] Joseph, *The War Prerogative* (n 49).

[115] Security Council Provisional Verbatim Record, 9 August 1993, (S/PV.3262) 341 ff. Chinese delegation asserting it was an 'internal affair' and Madeleine Albright for the United States disagreeing.

homes and the 'excessive and indiscriminate use of force by Serbian security forces and the Yugoslav Army,'[116] the Security Council had—due to a Russian veto— failed to authorise force to stop Serbian forces.[117] Frustrated by the Council, the then-Prime Minister Tony Blair insisted 'we have to act now to avert the humanitarian disaster'.[118] The Government presented 'the legal basis for our action' as 'that the international community [of] states do have the right to use force in the case of overwhelming humanitarian necessity'.[119] Once NATO backing was secured and the NATO Secretary General authorised air strikes,[120] the Government argued that it was enforcing the 'will of the international community'.[121]

Most interestingly, in the example of Kosovo, the Government avoided taking the issue to a vote in Parliament. Without a clear UN backing serious questions of legality arose in relation to the intervention, and MPs' support was not guaranteed. Labour MP Tony Benn was amongst those who questioned the legal basis of the proposed military intervention, pointing out that it lacked any express mandate from the UN. He further criticised the Government for not allowing a proper debate in Parliament, lamenting that 'to treat the House as though it were just an audience for "Newsnight" on so grave a matter is simply below the standard that we are entitled to expect'.[122] Other MPs seriously questioned the legal basis in spite of NATO's backing.[123] Yet although MPs were clearly sceptical, they never got a chance to vote on the issue. The House was sidelined completely. The Government rejected calls to put the issue to a debate and a vote[124] and airstrikes began without parliamentary approval.

In relation to Syria in 2013, Cameron faced a similar situation to Kosovo. After reports surfaced that Syrian President Assad had used chemical weapons against his own people, Western countries sought to secure a Security Council Resolution authorising military action against Syrian government forces. Their attempt was unsuccessful and due to a threatened veto from Russia, the Security Council was politically deadlocked.[125] No authorisation would be forthcoming. However, instead of sidelining Parliament in the manner of the Blair Government in relation

---

[116] SC Resolution 1199 (1998).

[117] SC Resolution 1203 (1998).

[118] HC Deb 23 March 1999, vol 141, col 169 (Blair).

[119] House of Commons Foreign Affairs Committee, Minutes of evidence for 'Kosovo: Interim Report', 7th Report of Session 1998–99, Evidence given 14 April 1999 (HC 188-ii) Q152.

[120] Statement of the North Atlantic Council on Kosovo, Press Release (99) 12 (30 January 1999) [5], <www.nato.int/docu/pr/1999/p99-012e.htm> accessed 17 September 2017.

[121] HC Deb 18 May 1999, vol 331, col 882 (Cook).

[122] HC Deb 23 March 1999, vol 328, col 169 (Benn).

[123] HC Deb 24 February 1999, vol 326, cols 409 (Benn) and 412 (Dalyell). HC Deb 23 March 1999, vol 328, cols 167 (Tapsell), 168 (Benn), 169 (Salmond).

[124] Benn's efforts to secure a debate and a vote were unsuccessful, though there were several adjournment debates held after the beginning of airstrikes: HC Deb 25 March 1999, vol 328, col 536; HC Deb 19 April 1999, vol 329, col 573; HC Deb 18 May 1999, vol 331, col 882.

[125] Russia had vetoed three Security Council resolutions in relation to Syria and it was only at the end of September 2013 that Russia had agreed to a resolution requiring destruction of all chemical weapons (SC Resolution 2118).

to Kosovo, the Prime Minister turned to the Westminster Parliament for prior approval for action.[126] He condemned the use of chemical weapons by the Assad regime, which had killed hundreds and injured thousands of civilians, and argued that by making use of these weapons, President Assad had violated the world-wide prohibition on the use of chemical weapons under international law, and thus had committed both a war crime and a crime against humanity. He insisted that a strong humanitarian response was necessary and that this required military action that was proportionate and focused on saving lives by preventing and deterring further use of Syria's chemical weapons. Since the only aim of the intervention would be 'to alleviate humanitarian suffering by deterring use of chemical weapons',[127] Cameron insisted he had a 'sound legal basis' for taking military action.

His decision not to rely on the legal powers inherent in the royal prerogative without political input from Parliament is unsurprising when read in light of the Kosovo example. The questionable legal basis on which Blair relied in 1999 was ultimately rejected by the House of Commons Foreign Affairs Committee, which issued a report contradicting some of the positions taken by the Government during the bombings. In reviewing the legality of Operation Allied Force, the Committee concluded that the operation was contrary to the UN Charter, having received no UN authorisation from either the Security Council or from the General Assembly. It further held that, 'at the very least, the doctrine of humanitarian intervention has a tenuous basis in current customary international law, and that this renders NATO action legally questionable'.[128] As White astutely remarked, their critique came 'too late to affect the military operation in question.'[129]

Moreover, between the events in Kosovo and Syria, an important clarification of international law had taken place. Military action to address a possible humanitarian crisis could no longer be undertaken unilaterally,[130] but had to be explicitly authorised by the Security Council under Article 42 of Chapter VII of the UN Charter.[131] Post-Kosovo the use of force to prevent a humanitarian disaster was legally permitted only if authorised by the Security Council under the

---

[126] Note that Cameron acted after the convention had been recognised in the Cabinet Manual.

[127] HC Deb 29 August 2013, vol 566, col 1426 (Cameron).

[128] House of Commons Foreign Affairs Committee, 'Kosovo', 4th Report of Session 1999–2000, 23 May 2000, [132]. The report also dismissed an earlier report by the House of Commons Defence Select Committee, 'The Future of NATO: The Washington Summit', 3rd Report of Session 1998–99, 13 April 1999 (HC 39) [176], which found that 'insistence on a UN SC mandate for such [humanitarian] operations would be unnecessary as well as covertly giving Russia a veto over Alliance action. All 19 Allies act in accordance with the principles of international law and we are secure in our assertion that the necessity of unanimous agreement for any action will ensure its legality'.

[129] White, *Democracy* (n 45) 234.

[130] Blair's action in relation to Kosovo, which took place outside of the Charter was questioned (though not condemned) as a violation of international law. SC Resolution 1244.

[131] On responsibility to protect: General Assembly, Resolution of 24 October 2005, Outcome Document of the 2005 United Nations World Summit (A/RES/60/1, paras 138–40); UN Secretary General, Secretary-General's 2009 Report on Implementing the Responsibility to Protect (A/63/677).

'responsibility to protect' principle. A sufficient international consensus therefore had to be reached within the Security Council before a humanitarian intervention in Syria could be legal under international law.

Both the domestic implications of Kosovo and the developments in international law left an impact on Cameron, but not in the way an international lawyer would expect. For example, he did not stop and accept that without a Security Council Resolution his hands were tied. Instead, Cameron took the view that the UN was not 'the only way to have a legal basis for action'. In accordance with the new constitutional convention—developed in part to provide legitimacy to the Government when it needed to go to war—he would take the issue to Parliament.

The lack of an international legal basis meant that during the 2013 Syria debate, MPs queried the legality of the intervention and criticised the Government for trying to act too hastily. The Leader of the Opposition pressed the Prime Minister to delay any use of force until compelling evidence was produced to confirm that the Syrian regime was responsible for the use of chemical weapons, and until the Security Council had considered and voted on the matter. This clearly indicated that some MPs wanted to wait and defer their decision until sufficient international consensus had been generated on the international plane. They were concerned further about the scope of the action, its proportionality and duration, and the wider implications of attacking Syria. Others, for example, expressed disquiet about the motives behind the intervention, arguing that support for military action was sought not out of self-defence, deterrence, or protection, but punishment: 'The conversations that have been had with the media over the past few days have talked about Syria not having impunity for the use of chemical weapons'.[132] But if 'impunity' was driving the action, then this 'new doctrine' needed 'considerably wider international consensus than currently exists'.[133]

Legality was at the heart of the parliamentary debate on Syria. The Prime Minister had insisted that international law had been violated by the Assad regime's use of chemical weapons and that action was required because Assad had crossed a red line. In turn, MPs asked why—if the case was so clear—the Government was rushing into action without a clear authorisation from the UN.[134] What is, however, most striking about Parliament's involvement is that the lack of authorisation from the UN unsettled both the Government and MPs, and that as a consequence MPs felt a need to step into the shoes of the UN. They treated the issue of international legality as a pre-condition for their support. Both front and back benchers saw the legality gap and refused to fill it with their own interpretation of the law. It is against this background that the Government was defeated in the House in 2013 in relation to Syria. For the first time in history, Parliament had refused to 'rally behind the Crown' and support a motion on military action. The Government

---

[132] HC Deb 29 August 2013, vol 566, col 1462 (Arbuthnot).
[133] ibid.
[134] ibid, col 1447 (Miliband), 1461 (McDonnell).

lost the vote by 282 to 271, prompting the Prime Minister to give an assurance that military action would not take place.[135] There was no military action in Syria. The Government had failed to secure domestic political legitimacy and fill the lacuna left by international law.

D. The Implications of Linking International Legality to Parliament's Constitutional Role on War

I. Turning a Political Discourse into a Legal Discourse

The constitutional role of the legislature on the question of war appears to be inextricably linked with the international legality of the action. But the impact of the international legality is twofold: on one side, the lack of international authorisation enables Parliament to become involved; on the other, it puts one idea centre stage: the law. When the Government presents its case to Parliament, the language—the argument of trying to persuade Parliament to provide its backing—is almost entirely legal.

The pervasiveness of legal language in the debate is striking. As demonstrated above, there are a number of ways in which the Government presents its case to Parliament as legal. Readers will recall from Figure 2.1 (above) that when international authorisation is forthcoming (part A), most often the Government will talk about the need to fulfil its international obligation under the UN Charter. In the case of Korea, before the Security Council authorised the use of force, the issue was 'essentially a United Nations problem'.[136] Some MPs noted that 'the outcome of the war will have an important effect on the authority and prestige of the United Nations'. In this regard, it was 'vital' and supremely 'important … that any settlement should be arrived at under United Nations auspices'.[137] Once the Security Council passed the Resolution, the use of force became an international, UN action. In the debate, the Government's motion emphasised that action had to be taken 'in conformity with their obligations under the United Nations Charter, in helping to resist the unprovoked aggression against the Republic of Korea'.[138] Winston Churchill, then in opposition, expressed his confidence that the Government would 'act up to [its] supreme international obligations'.[139] Not only was the deployment of troops done under the auspices of the UN Charter, statements in Parliament supported

---

[135] ibid, col 1556 (Cameron).
[136] HC Deb 14 December 1950, vol 481, col 1353 (Attlee).
[137] ibid.
[138] HC Deb 5 July 1950, vol 477, cols 485–90, 492–93, 502, 596.
[139] HC Deb 28 June 1950, vol 476, col 2292 (Churchill).

the idea that the UK *must* use force if 'the rule of law' is to prevail. Even as recently as Libya, the use of force under a Security Council Resolution has been described as taking part 'in an international operation ... to enforce the will of the United Nations'.[140] These international authorisations have therefore been treated as 'the law'.

When the UK acts in self-defence (collective or individual), and when no international authorisation to use force is forthcoming (part B), the need to rely on 'the law' is equally pressing. In the Falklands, the UK invoked Article 51, the right to inherent self-defence. Although this right was not recognised before the Security Council, the then-Prime Minister Margaret Thatcher invoked Article 51 and the right to self-defence before Parliament. In making the case for war, the Government followed the wording of Article 51 of the UN Charter to the letter: first, it insisted that Argentine intervention constituted an 'illegal and unprovoked attack'; second, it argued that it had an 'inherent right of self-defence', which included the right to 'defend the British territory', 'respond', or act to 'protect' the rights and the people of the Falkland Islands; third, the Government had notified the Security Council of its actions under Article 51 as required by the Charter. Even when the Security Council passed Resolution 502 which called upon both states to cease hostilities and seek a diplomatic solution, Thatcher made it very clear to Parliament that the Resolution did not affect Britain's right to self-defence.[141] Although the Government was pursuing a combination of diplomatic, military, and economic solutions in accordance with the Resolution,[142] it would continue its action to recover the Falkland Islands in accordance with Article 51 UN Charter criteria. Finally, the Thatcher Government's concern about the law and the image of a 'legal' response extended also to the issue of proportionality of the response to the Argentine invasion. In this regard, the Government sought and provided Parliament with the advice of the Attorney-General, who emphasised that the use of force had to be restricted to the Falkland Islands alone, since an attack beyond this area would be considered disproportionate and therefore illegal under the UN Charter.[143]

In situations when the international situation is not 'clear' or when the international legal basis is uncertain (part C), the Government makes an entirely legal case to Parliament, rather than focusing on a broader range of issues pertaining to the legitimacy of any given armed conflict. In Iraq, the reliance upon existing Security Council Resolutions was used by the British Government to construct new legal arguments from existing law which were in turn presented to Parliament.

---

[140] HC Deb 21 March 2011, vol 525, col 700 (Cameron).

[141] HC Deb 29 April 1982, vol 22, col 982 (Thatcher).

[142] HC Deb 14 April 1982, vol 21, col 1146 (Thatcher).

[143] M Hastings and S Jenkings, *Battle for the Falklands* (New York, Pan Military Classics, 2010) 162. On proportionality and necessity in international law, *Oil Platforms (Iran v United States)* [1996] ICJ Rep 803; Gray, *International Law* (n 12) 148.

Similarly, in Kosovo, a purportedly new legal basis was constructed to support the intervention. An equation of previous Security Council Resolutions establishing a 'threat to international peace', coupled with the will of the international community, and the necessity to intervene to prevent a humanitarian disaster were used to provide the Government with an arguable legal basis for intervention. Although Kosovo and Iraq were labelled as examples of 'just war[s], based not on any territorial ambitions but on values',[144] both interventions were self-authorised: the will of the international community was determined and enforced unilaterally by the British Government.[145]

II. Law as a Trump

The discussion above reveals the pervasiveness of international legal language in debates on the issue of war. The British Government uses international legal jargon within the United Nations and in its relations with other states. When support from international institutions and the international community is not forthcoming, it then turns to Parliament and speaks to it in similar language and phrases. In effect, therefore, Parliament acts as a quasi-replacement of the Security Council, as it becomes a forum where international claims can be made. Members of Parliament appear happy to use legal propositions, and to adopt the role of an adjudicator on questions of international legality. When the Government argues before Parliament that military action is required to fulfil an international obligation or to act in self-defence, support is generally forthcoming. When the international legal basis is somewhat more ambiguous, Members of the House of Commons query the interpretation and construction of international law arguments.

The role of this common language—shared between the Government and Parliament—is as fascinating as it is constitutionally misguided. First, it is striking that the Government makes precisely the same types of arguments before the UN Security Council as it does before the domestic Parliament. This appears to imply that the case for war is the same whether it is made in the international sphere or on the domestic plane. But surely, there are good constitutional reasons for discourse in these institutions to take different forms. In the Security Council, the UK acts as a member of the United Nations and is concerned with entirely different, international concerns (eg international peace and security). By contrast, concerns on the domestic plane should be informed by the respective constitutional roles

---

[144] T Blair, 'Doctrine of the International Community' Speech in Economic Club, (Chicago, 24 April 1999) <http://webarchive.nationalarchives.gov.uk/+/www.number10.gov.uk/Page1297> accessed 17 September 201).

[145] N Krisch, 'Unilateral Enforcement of the Collective Will: Kosovo, Iraq, and the Security Council' (1999) 3 *Max Planck Yearbook of United Nations Law* 59; although in Iraq fewer states sided with the UK.

of government and Parliament in a representative democracy. Under our domestic constitutional arrangements the Government acts as a power governing its citizens, whilst Parliament acts as the citizens' representative. Discussion of these responsibilities cannot be conducted entirely on the same linguistic register; they are simply too different. In this regard, domestic rather than international preoccupations should take centre stage in any discussion of the national legislature (ie risk to troops, economic and budgetary concerns, public opinion, long-term strategy and implications). As we argue in chapter five, in addition to the legality of armed conflict, MPs should consider whether the state *should* intervene militarily. In this context, Parliament and government should prioritise domestic concerns.

Secondly, there is an important distinction between making international law arguments on the international level and the domestic level; a distinction driven by relative institutional competence. In the Security Council, the meaning of international law is rightly at the centre of all discussions. The idea of whether something is an 'international threat', whether the situation is one of 'self-defence', and whether 'all means necessary' (code for the authorisation of force) ought to be authorised is debated by legal experts and ambassadors each representing their own state. The forum in which they are debated—the Security Council—provides balance by allowing states to express different views upon issues of international law; views which can compete with the perspective of the British Government. In this forum, other states also have access to a veto to block the UK's efforts (and vice versa).

This is not the case with the Westminster Parliament: the House of Commons has no such institutional competence. It is not staffed by the lawyers, nor is it a forum for international legal actors. The real institutional competence of the House of Commons is to provide a forum for the airing domestic political concerns, using political discourse. In this system, in which the Government holds simultaneous positions in both Parliament and the Executive, ie where power is 'fused' as opposed to 'separated',[146] the Crown has the first and the last word. As argued above, if the Security Council has authorised action and its legality is uncontested, the Government can exclude Parliament from meaningful discussion. History demonstrates that at best it will inform Parliament of its intention to fulfil its international obligations, either because it feels bound by these commitments or because it no longer needs to justify its actions to MPs. The Government appears uninterested in discussing domestic questions.

In the opposite situation, when the legal basis is lacking, the Government will use its own interpretation of international law to persuade Parliament of its position. The focus will be on concepts of authorisation and self-defence, the possibility of future resolutions, and the ideas of international consensus and international community. Most often interventions by Members of the House will mirror those

---

[146] W Bagehot, *The English Constitution* (Oxford, OUP: Oxford World's Classics, 2009) 11; H Phillips 'A Constitutional Myth: Separation of Powers' (1977) 93 *LQR* 11; De Smith, 'The Separation of Powers in New Dress' (1966–67) 12 *McGill Law Journal* 491.

of the Government. Articles of the UN Charter will be referred to by both sides of the political spectrum. Where the Government introduces a legal opinion from the Advocate General or the Foreign and Commonwealth Office, this material will be debated thoroughly. In both situations, therefore, the question on what basis force is lawful appears to be the main question both the Government and Parliament will focus on. It is used as a tool to exclude Parliament from discussion or to include it; it is employed to shape the Government's case for war and to dictate debate in Parliament; and ultimately, it is interpreted to lend legitimacy to military action whether it is taken unilaterally by the Government (hopefully acting under international authority) or with Parliament's support. In effect, therefore, international law is used and acts as a trump. It is a tool which the Government uses to shape parliamentary discourse.

The 'legalisation' of political and especially parliamentary discourse in relation to war poses significant problems. The first relates to expertise. Given the pervasiveness of legal language in discussions on war, one would assume that the majority of the members of the House are lawyers, and international lawyers at that. However, as David Howarth reveals in his work, the number of lawyers in the House of Commons has decreased in the last few elections. In 2005, only 11.7 per cent of members had practiced as barristers or solicitors. The number was slightly higher in 2010 (13.8 per cent) but it still remains considerably under the 40 per cent that populates the US Congress. As Howarth says: 'the brute fact of the matter is that, far from being a majority, lawyers are outnumbered in Britain's primary legislative chamber by more than five to one'.[147] Howarth further shows that lawyers are increasingly being replaced by media and political professionals and that, in turn, 'political authority rests less on formal structures [which lawyers like] and more on the ephemera of media reputation and on fame itself'.[148] This is marked by a 'declining respect for law' alongside a tendency 'to treat legislation itself as a form of press release'.[149] He concludes: 'the decline of lawyers in Parliament, and the accompanying lack of people with political experience in the legal system, is a seriously disturbing development'.[150]

Whilst MPs as representatives of the people do not have to be lawyers to perform their legislative function, recourse to legal language without having a legal background is concerning particularly because politicians, by the very nature of their function, are likely to misconstrue and distort legal arguments. The problem with accepting legal language in a political context is that both the Government and MPs are likely to shy away from the normal, qualified language that is part and parcel

---

[147] D Howarth, 'Lawyers in the House of Commons' in D Feldman (ed) *Law in Politics, Politics in Law* (Oxford, Hart, 2014) 41, 42.

[148] D Howarth, 'In the Theatre State' *Times Literary Supplement* 23, 11 March 2011. See also HC Deb 20 October 2009, vol 497, col 828 (Howarth).

[149] Howarth, 'Lawyers' (n 147) 61, mentioning The Warm Homes and Energy Conservation Act 2000, Fiscal Responsibility Act 2010, and the Child Poverty Act 2010.

[150] ibid. On distinguishing political vs legal questions see also R Cranston 'Lawyers, MPs and Judges' in D Feldman (ed), *Law in Politics, Politics in Law* (Oxford, Hart, 2014) 17.

of any legal advice provided by the Attorney-General (the official responsible for giving legal advice to the Government on the legality of armed conflict). A lawyer's job is to make conditional arguments and to qualify their advice depending on the circumstances. But whilst a lawyer has to be careful, a politician using legal language is prone to avoid qualifications that are an inherent part of the legal world. A politician cannot accept the vagueness and conditionality of legal language. Instead, he will speak of war in binary terms as 'legal' or 'illegal'. These options— often used by governments and usually also adopted by parliamentarians— give the impression that there is only one alternative: if faced with a choice between a legal and an illegal war, obviously only the former is acceptable. It is in this context that the need to show that the war is *legal* arises.

Part of the qualification a legal adviser would make in relation to international law on the use of force is that certainty as to the legality of an intervention is often lacking. When the Security Council has not explicitly authorised military action, or has not been sufficiently unambiguous, the question often arises whether a certain intervention is permitted. Since the Charter prohibits the use of force generally in Article 2(4), in principle any action outside of the Charter is prohibited. For states who wish to proceed unilaterally, the Security Council does not pass resolutions prohibiting action in advance of their act. Instead, condemnation of a particular use of force by the Security Council (or the General Assembly) or express findings of aggression which are 'conclusive or at least persuasive as to illegality' are issued ex post facto.[151] Prior to a vote Parliament is therefore unlikely to know for certain whether an intervention is clearly illegal.

The Government and MPs appear to be unaware of (or unwilling to recognise) this inherent uncertainty in international law. Instead, they reach for all available legal grounds on which they can show that the intervention is legal. During the last debate on Syria in 2015, then Prime Minister Cameron and then Shadow Foreign Secretary Hilary Benn, in opposition, relied on all legal bases available to support military action: a self-defence argument and separately on a Security Council Resolution.[152] Interestingly, such accumulation of different legal bases is not accepted in international law. The legal basis for the use of force is either self-defence or an express authorisation by the Security Council. Yet, the Resolution Cameron, Benn, and others relied on did not authorise force explicitly; it also did not recognise the UK's inherent right to self-defence.[153] But the obviously questionable nature of their use of international law did not stop politicians from both ends of the spectrum from accepting the legal argument and supporting the military intervention.

---

[151] C Gray, *International Law and the Use of Force* (OUP, Oxford, 2008) 20 ff.

[152] HC Deb 2 December 2015, vol 603, cols 323 (Cameron) and 484–85 (Benn).

[153] D Akande and M Milanović, 'The Constructive Ambiguity of the Security Council's ISIS Resolution', EJIL Talk (21 November 2015) <www.ejiltalk.org/the-constructive-ambiguity-of-the-security-councils-isis-resolution> accessed 17 September 2017; V Fikfak, UK Constitutional Law Association blog (28 November 2015) <ukconstitutionallaw.org/2015/11/28/veronika-fikfak-voting-on-military-action-in-syria> accessed 17 September 2017.

In addition to relying upon two separate legal bases to present a more persuasive case for war, the traditional interpretation of self-defence was stretched to near breaking point. In relation to Syria, there had been no 'armed attack' as required by Article 51 of the UN Charter, nor had the UK issued a notification to the Security Council advising it of its intention to exercise self-defence. Yet, before the House of Commons, the position of the Government was explained using international legal concepts such as 'international threat', 'self-defence', 'necessity' and 'proportionality' and the same terms were used by MPs who supported the interventions. Amongst international lawyers the discussion raised serious concerns about MPs' understanding of legal regime like 'self-defence'.[154] Why in a House with so few lawyers is the language that pervades throughout the debate on war so overtly legal? If as Howarth argues, law is frowned upon as polluting politics, then why do non-lawyers put so much emphasis on concepts of international law, and why do they appear to give them so much weight? The lack of expertise amongst MPs contributes to parliamentarians mirroring the Government's position and—whether in opposition or not—framing their interventions in international legal language.

Perhaps it is precisely because of what the law can offer that international rules are invoked so strongly. A decision to go to war is the result of a complex combination of moral values and political strategy. There are hardly any right or wrong answers. Yet international law provides structure and form, it provides a clear process through which decisions about war are to be made or notified, and language with which interventions and use of force can be made to look 'just' and 'legitimate'.[155] In this context, the label 'legal' is often shorthand for 'moral' and 'legitimate'. Through the Security Council or on their own, the international rules provide the ingredients which have to be fulfilled and the roadmap of what is 'permitted' and what is not. For those making the case for war, these international norms therefore provide a process through which they can explain or support the decision to go to war. Even more, the legal discourse appears to have the effect of legitimising (and perhaps even legalising) war.[156] As Howarth argues, from the point of view of law the political discourse infused with legal terms could act as a means of achieving legality.[157] By presenting the proposed military actions in 'superficially impressive legalese',[158] the members of the Government and indeed

---

[154] 'Towards Unilateralism?' (n 3).

[155] Legitimacy is easier to sell, since it is a 'combination of legal, political and moral considerations which do not necessarily align'. 'Towards Unilateralism?' (n 2) 309. See also C Thomas, 'The Use and Abuses of Legitimacy within International Law' (2014) 34 *OJLS* 729, 733.

[156] A Roberts, 'Legality vs Legitimacy: Can Uses of Force Be Illegal but Justified?' in P Alston and E MacDonald (eds), *Human Rights, Intervention, and the Use of Force* (Oxford, OUP, 2008) 179, 207.

[157] Howarth, 'Lawyers' (n 147) 42.

[158] Murray and O'Donoghue, 'Towards Unilateralism?' (n 3) 306.

Parliament could be perceived as acting within the law or indeed as being almost constrained by the law to allow action. In this regard, the law acts both as a trump and a distancing device for the Government and Members of Parliament. As well as motivating and facilitating action, legal norms also provide the distance and the objectivity that MPs are looking for when voting on a politically charged decision which is likely to endanger British lives. In this context, the legal language therefore serves to present war as an obligation or as a necessity and not as a complex moral choice.

This pervasive misuse of legal language also detracts from and conceals other issues that could be discussed in Parliament, issues that are more relevant and issues on which MPs may have more experience or more of a say, such as economic consequences, the implications for British troops, and the opinions of their constituents. These political questions appear to be enclosed within the 'straitjacket of law',[159] a move that some argue can have a corrosive effect on social life.[160] The focus on the legality of intervention is so pervasive that it gives the impression that 'law, in modern thought, is treated as an activity which is not only distinct from, but also manifestly superior to, politics'.[161] It is precisely this myth that we seek to debunk: that by sticking a label of 'legality' on an intervention, the decision reached is correct or *a priori* more legitimate than one achieved through political discourse. In practice, this is far from being the case, and by allowing international *law* to have fundamentally shifted the discourse of domestic politics, the Government and parliamentarians have permitted this legal language to act as a means of stultifying political debate. In chapter five we discuss how politics can be 'freed' from law and how political discussion in Parliament can be fostered.

Ultimately, the pervasiveness of legal language in political debates can also have unintended (or perhaps intended) consequences in international law. The practice of using international legal arguments such as self-defence in domestic contexts 'complicate[s] the question of whether a use of force complies with international law'.[162] International scholars have rejected domestic behaviour which labels military action as defensive and does so without involving the Security Council as 'unilateralism'.[163] They argue that when governments bypass the Security Council and make their case for the use of force before national

---

[159] M Loughlin, *Sword and Scales* (London, Hart, 2000) 11.

[160] J Gray, *Enlightenment's Wake: Politics and Culture at the Close of Modern Age* (London, Routledge, 1995) 76.

[161] Loughlin, *Sword and Scales* (n 159) 11.

[162] 'Towards Unilateralism?' (n 3) 307.

[163] ibid. Also WM Reisman, 'Unilateral Actions and the Transformations of the World Constitutive Process: The Special Problem of Humanitarian Intervention' (2000) 11 *EJIL* 3, 12; KR Mayer, 'Executive Power in the Obama Administration and the Decision to Seek Congressional Authorization for a Military Attack against Syria: Implications for Theories of Unilateral Action' [2014] *Utah LR* 821, 821; H Koh, 'Syria and the Law of Humanitarian Intervention Part II: International Law and the Way Forward' *Just Security* (2 October 2013) http://justsecurity.org/2013/10/02/koh-syria-part2 accessed 17 September 2017; C Stahn, 'Between Law-Breaking and Law-Making: Syria, Humanitarian Intervention and "What the Law Ought to Be"' (2014) 19 *JCSL* 25, 46.

legislatures, the claims to self-defence have been stretched far beyond what international law envisages. Self-defence cases have been made not only in cases of individual but also collective self-defence (Afghanistan), and have been expanded to situations where no 'attack' has taken place. Most famously, the Bush Administration argued for pre-emptive self-defence against Iraq, and arguments to the same effect have been used to support the use of targeted killings (use of unmanned aerial vehicles or 'drones') against individuals and terrorist groups.[164] Through internal processes and by seizing national legislatures, governments in the US, UK, and elsewhere have sought to use state practice to effectuate an incremental change in international law. If in the 2000s, the then-US President George W Bush was criticised for circumventing international law by adopting the doctrine of pre-emptive self-defence,[165] his doctrine has subsequently become accepted as the new status quo, and forms part of the current practice of a number of countries, including the UK. Following Bush, subsequent governments have combined domestic parliamentary support with novel legal bases for action to facilitate the use of military force. Their arguments of what international law *should allow* have changed into what international law *does allow*. They have, in the words of Hans Blix, become the 'global policeman' and act as such without a UN mandate.[166] The victim in this process of domesticating decisions on war has been international law, and in particular the UN Charter. In addition, the institutions set up after the Second World War to protect us from the misuse of power are being increasingly marginalised. As former Labour Leader Ed Miliband asserted in the debate in which MPs rejected the Government's motion to support action in Syria in 2013, 'The UN is not some inconvenient sideshow, and we do not want to engineer a "[United Nations] moment". Instead, we want to adhere to the principles of international law.'[167]

By acting instead of the UN and by using international law language, governments have sought to sideline the international community and invited MPs to—step by step—aid them in redefining what is acceptable in the international law on the use of force. The ultimate question is whether members of the House of Commons are aware of how strategically they are being used and how actively they are participating in this process of changing the law on war.

E. Shining a Light on the Subjugation of Politics

This chapter shines a light on the real reasons behind governmental decisions to shift the legitimisation of armed conflict decision from the international fora to

---

[164] HC Deb 7 September 2015, vol 599, col 26 (Cameron).
[165] Murphy, 'Pre-emptive Self-Defence' (n 12).
[166] HC Deb 29 August 2013, vol 566, col 1464 (Llwyd).
[167] ibid, col 1442 (Miliband).

the domestic Parliament. The above analysis mapped out a pattern whereby armed conflict decisions become progressively more domesticated as clear legal authorisation from the UN Security Council declines. This strategic domestication of the decision-making may be understandable, though from the perspective of the writers of the UN Charter, who sought to prevent unilateral use of force, and to limit military action to those exceptional circumstances in which the world community thought it necessary, such behaviour clearly steps outside of the Charter's legal framework. Moreover, the involvement of Parliament gives the impression that by being seized of the opportunity to debate military action, parliamentarians give the decision to send troops into battle the appearance of hitherto unavailable democratic legitimacy. The bare image of Parliament playing a part in the process suggests that armed conflict decisions are more democratic because they are subject to debate and disagreements: discussions which are profoundly political in nature. Yet, the reality is different. Parliament is only symbolically part of the decision-making process. In these instances Parliament is not used as a true forum for political discussion, but more covertly as a surrogate Security Council. Technical legalese is used to make the case for war before the House of Commons. In this context, parliamentarians have little if any opportunity to raise domestic issues relating to war. A fully transparent inquiry demonstrates that the effect of the Government's use of Parliament as an alternative forum for international law subjugates the core constitutional function of the House of Commons: to question and disagree with the Government on the political consequences of armed conflict. This is not obvious to even the keenest observers in the electorate: the deception of the public is profound.

3

The Convention as a Battlefield

VERONIKA FIKFAK

Ever since the Iraq War of 2003, commentators and scholars have argued that a constitutional convention has developed which requires that the House of Commons should have an opportunity to debate and vote before troops are deployed.[1] In 2011, the Government explicitly recognised the existence of this convention through statements in Parliament and by referring to the new practice as a 'convention' in the Cabinet Manual. The Manual stated that 'before troops were committed the House of Commons should have an opportunity to debate the matter'.[2] The Government said that it 'proposed to observe that convention except when there was an emergency and such action would not be appropriate'.[3] The inclusion of the convention in the Manual provides more certainty about 'its exact character' but it also makes 'adherence to it more plausible'.[4] Indeed, looking at deployments subsequent to the Cabinet Manual's publication, the House of Commons has been given the opportunity to debate and vote upon military deployments in relation to Syria, against Islamic State (IS) in Iraq, and most recently against IS in Syria. After the defeat of the Government's motion to deploy troops to Syria in 2013, some commentators went as far as to argue that the decision of Prime Minister Cameron to comply with the vote in the House suggested that this so-called 'War Powers Convention' has solidified into a binding constitutional convention; a convention regulating the relationship between government and Parliament in the context of war.[5]

The recognition of and the commitment to observe the War Powers Convention has been welcomed by commentators and scholars as addressing the democratic

---

[1] J Strong, 'The accidental prerogative: why Parliament now decides on war' (2015) 17 *British Journal of Politics and International Relations* 604; G Phillipson, '"Historic" Commons' Syria vote: the constitutional significance (Part I)', UK Constitutional Law Association blog (19 September 2013) <https://ukconstitutionallaw.org/2013/09/19/gavin-phillipson-historic-commons-syria-vote-the-constitutional-significance-part-i> accessed 17 September 2017.

[2] Cabinet Manual, Cabinet Office, 2011, 1st edn, para [5.38].

[3] ibid.

[4] A Blick, *The Codes of the Constitution* (Oxford, Hart, 2016) 109.

[5] T Stanley 'Syria vote: this historic night was a humiliation for David Cameron but a victory for Parliament' *The Telegraph* (29 August 2013); R Hutton and T Penny 'Historic Vote Sees Cameron Defeated by Lawmakers on Syria' *Bloomberg Online* (20 August 2013).

deficit and dangers exposed by the Iraq invasion in 2003. Although historically the monarch's power to make war and deploy forces was counter-balanced by Parliament's control of the resources necessary for the exercise of power,[6] in the recent constitutional environment 'the Government of the day not only exercises the royal prerogative but also generally controls the House of Commons and therefore its power over finance—through parliamentary majorities, use of the Whips and control over the parliamentary timetable—thereby undermining this historical brake on executive power'.[7] This renders accountability measures ineffective because debates are used 'more as a process of explanation and persuasion than [for] giving Parliament a real way to challenge … decision[s]'.[8] Air Marshal Lord Garden pointed out that

> When we keep on saying Parliament is informed, we all know how Parliament is informed: we get a statement, if we are lucky we get it ten minutes before it is given and we debate it for under an hour. That does not seem to me to be a democratic process.[9]

The recognition of the convention in the 2011 Cabinet Manual seeks to address these accountability concerns. On one side, it is argued that the convention allows the representatives of the people to have a say as to the engagement of British forces abroad, and thus represents a wresting of power from the Executive by a more legitimate, democratic institution.[10] The War Powers Convention ensures accountability of the Government in an area which has consistently escaped judicial oversight.[11] In addition to this, it may be that MPs' insistence on additional information, and upon Government's articulation of long-term military strategy, might prevent a repeat of the wars in Afghanistan and Iraq. Defenders of the War Powers Convention may claim that the Prime Minister is unlikely to take decisions in a 'vacuum', and in turn the Government's strategy will be better prepared and considered.[12] In this regard, Parliament's role is seen as one of facilitating and encouraging good governance in the area of war powers.

In the previous chapter, we demonstrated that in decisions to go to war the domestic involvement of Parliament is directly contingent upon the developments on the international plane. If the Government is unable to get authorisation from the Security Council for the use of force, then Parliament is used to fill the lacuna and provide the Government with the legitimacy it needs for military action. In this regard, the soliciting of international support always takes priority: the Government will concentrate most of its efforts towards persuading international partners of its plans. Our analysis revealed that it is only when this fails that the

---

[6] R Joseph, *The War Prerogative: History, Reform, and Constitutional Design* (Oxford, OUP, 2013) ch 3.

[7] House of Lords, Select Committee on Constitution, 'Waging War' (2006), [40].

[8] ibid, [42] Kenneth Clarke MP.

[9] ibid, [42].

[10] Phillipson, '"Historic" Commons' Syria vote' (n 1).

[11] *R (on the application of Campaign for Nuclear Disarmament) v Prime Minister* [2002] EWHC 2777; *R (Gentle) v The Prime Minister* [2007] QB 689, 710–24; *R v Jones* [2006] UKHL 16.

[12] 'Waging War' (n 7), citing Clare Short.

domestic story takes centre stage. This clear hierarchy of institutions led us to question whether the genesis of the War Powers Convention was really motivated by the demand for greater democratisation of war powers.

In this chapter, we give government the benefit of doubt and accept that the convention may have been motivated by good governance values, in particular by the need to ensure greater accountability of decisions to go to war. By involving Parliament, government has perhaps sought to address the 'double democratic deficit' from which most multilateral military operations suffer.[13] Whilst military interventions can involve 'many thousands of personnel, from all the armed services, down to a handful from a single service', as a rule there is 'inadequate accountability at the domestic level', a gap that is 'not compensated for at the international level of decision-making'.[14] In situations where military action has been authorised by the Security Council, the regular involvement of Parliament could thus address the democratic deficit on the international level, whilst giving the national legislature a chance to examine separately whether—from the domestic perspective—the reasons for war were sufficient. In other situations, for example where the Security Council remains silent, the domestic Parliament would inspect the legitimacy of war regardless of the position of the Security Council.

Our focus in this chapter is on the quality of parliamentary engagement. In particular we focus upon assessing whether the current operation of the convention enables Parliament to hold government adequately to account. We understand accountability to be defined as 'a relationship between an actor and a forum, in which the actor has an obligation to explain and to justify his or her conduct, the forum can pose questions and pass judgment, and the actor may face consequences'.[15] In a political context, accountability is crucial because it provides 'a democratic means to monitor and control government conduct'.[16] A proper accountability relationship should also have the capacity to prevent 'the development of concentrations of power, and to enhance the learning capacity and effectiveness of public administration'.[17] In essence, accountability is therefore a form of control—a power to monitor and control, to question and pass judgement, and a power to impose sanctions. This chapter seeks to uncover whether or not the constitutional convention has given Parliament any real control over the Government in relation to initiating armed conflict. As some commentators argue, the process of codifying the convention in the Manual could on its own 'potentially reduce the discretion available to the executive'.[18] Yet, the analysis herein finds that in

---

[13] H Born and H Hanggi, 'The Use of Force under International Auspices: Strengthening Parliamentary Accountability', Geneva Centre for the Democratic Control of the Armed Forces, Policy Paper No 7, 2005.

[14] 'Waging War' (n 7) [17].

[15] M Bovens, 'Analysing and Assessing Accountability: A Conceptual Framework' (2007) *European Law Journal* 447, 450.

[16] ibid.

[17] ibid, 462.

[18] Blick, *Codes* (n 4) 116.

the context of war powers a transfer of control from the Government to Parliament has not been effected. The Government continues to hold the balance of power, even where the benefit of the doubt about enhancing good governance is conceded.

In the sections that follow, we show how the need to secure the legitimacy for military action at home determines the manner in which the Government uses the convention. More specifically, it is the Government's perceived need for legitimacy which *still* determines how it involves Parliament on questions of war. For example, although the Cabinet Manual requires that the House be given an opportunity to debate the issue of deployment of troops *before* these are committed, in relation to Libya in 2011, this condition was not respected. Instead, Parliament was presented with a fait accompli—once troops were already on the ground in Libya, engaged by air and sea in an offensive action, MPs were asked to support the decision of the Government.

In spite of the enthusiasm expressed over an historic change in constitutional practice, we therefore find that the developments since 2011 call into question the precise scope and content of the War Powers Convention, and thus the role of Parliament in relation to military action.[19] In part B, we reveal how instead of being used as an accountability arrangement, the convention has been used tactically so as to sideline Parliament or even demean its role on questions of war.

In part C, we focus on the extent to which the War Powers Convention is binding on the Government and Parliament. On the last occasion the House was asked to consider the use of force—in November 2015 in relation to the extension of military action against IS from Iraq into Syria—another question arose giving cause for concern about the control the Government maintains over the involvement of Parliament in this area. The Prime Minister David Cameron insisted that he would not take the issue to a vote in the House until he was sure he would get a majority. 'Let me be clear,' he said, 'there will not be a vote in this House unless there is a clear majority for action, because we will not hand a publicity coup to ISIL.'[20] Some academics have argued that this refusal to put the matter to a vote has recognised that Parliament holds a veto over government decisions, and that the convention has thus been recognised as a binding political rule maintaining the appropriate relationship between Parliament and the Government. In contrast, we show that such claims are greatly exaggerated and that conditioning the involvement of the House on a positive outcome raises concerns about the Government's intention to abide by the convention.

As this chapter demonstrates, Parliament's role of holding the Government to account depends entirely upon the extent to which the Executive is willing to cooperate with it and to share information. If initially the convention looked like

---

[19] Constitutional and Political Reform Committee, 8th Report of 2010–12, para 6; House of Lords, Constitution Committee, 'Constitutional arrangements for the use of armed force', 2nd Report 2013–04, HL Paper 46, [1].

[20] HC Deb 26 November 2015, vol 602, col 1494.

it would 'level the playing field' between Parliament and the Executive, our analysis of practice since the codification of the convention shows that this is simply not true. The Government remains substantially in control of the engagement and the operation of the convention. It has taken advantage of conventions' inherent malleability to incrementally reduce its own obligations in relation to Parliament. Precedent by precedent, dispute by dispute, successive governments have made use of both the timing and the 'emergency argument' to avoid prior debate or vote in Parliament. On occasions where governments have allowed parliamentary debate and votes, this engagement has been timed so as to be 'too late to influence policy'.[21] Additional exceptions to the operation of the convention have been created incrementally—first, by excluding the use of drones from parliamentary oversight; and secondly, by exempting special forces embedded in other countries' military forces and their subsequent participation in military actions abroad under the national security exception. These exceptions (discussed in part D) coupled with the extensive secrecy, which we turn to in chapter four, show that successive governments have consistently failed to keep the House of Commons informed or have even provided parliamentarians with misleading information. The 'holy grail' of ensuring governmental accountability through parliamentary engagement has proved—and still appears—elusive.

As Figure 3.1 shows, today the convention applies in extremely limited circumstances and its scope is significantly smaller than is initially suggested on the face of the Cabinet Manual. The exceptions which have been carved out of the codified convention reduce the number of occasions on which Parliament would be expected to be involved.

In and of itself, the convention fails to alter the quality of parliamentary discourse in any meaningful sense. Focusing on it to discuss and assess parliamentary engagement diverts attention from the fact that government has maintained its upper hand and has used the different modes of engagement tactically to prevent Parliament from being able to clearly express its position, or to effectively question

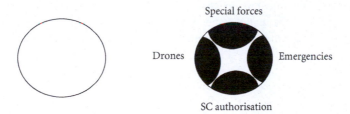

Figure 3.1: Perceived scope of convention as codified in the Manual (left) and the exceptions imposed by practice (right)

---

[21] HC Deb 24 September 2002, vol 390, cols 96–97, Edward Garnier.

government's policies. In short, the Government's continuing de facto monopoly over elements of the war prerogative could potentially render any participation by parliamentarians or their efforts towards ensuring governmental accountability meaningless. In this sense, the convention is merely a *distraction*.

A. The Role of Conventions in the UK Constitutional Sphere

I. The Flexibility of Constitutional Conventions

Conventions are not legal rules. Instead, they have been described as 'understandings, habits or practices'[22] operating alongside law in the British Constitution.[23] What makes these principles or traditions constitutional is that they both shape the constitution and govern the relationships between constitutional institutions.[24] According to Morton, constitutional conventions are instruments of dispute settlement; they emerge and develop to manage disagreements and tensions between different institutions of the constitution.[25] As he argues, 'each institution builds up its own picture of the constitution as viewed from its own position within it'.[26] In this context, each institution puts itself centre-stage and ultimately, a number of conflicting conceptions of the constitution and its fundamental values arise. Conventions, as rules of dispute settlement, help institutions 'cooperate', by 'encapsulating right behaviour'[27], and guide institutions as to the proper standard of behaviour.[28] They are born out of a need for institutions of the constitution to cohabit and work together.

In principle, when considering the scope and extent of a constitutional convention which operates between any two institutions, the perspectives of both institutions on the constitution are important.[29] As a binding rule of political behaviour, a constitutional convention can develop only when a practice emerges from the managing of a relationship between two audiences, in which one feels bound to behave in a specific manner and the other expects that behaviour as a matter of obligation rather than courtesy. In this sense, a convention 'can come about,

---

[22] AV Dicey, *Lecture Introductory to the Study of the Law of the Constitution* (London, Macmillan, 1885) 25.

[23] ibid.

[24] P Morton, 'Conventions of the British Constitution' (1991–92) 15 *Holdsworth Law Review* 114, 156–58.

[25] ibid, 163.

[26] D Feldman, 'Constitutional Conventions' in M Qvortrup, *The British Constitution: Continuity and Change* (Oxford, Hart, 2013) 94.

[27] ibid, 95.

[28] Morton, 'Conventions' (n 24) 138–44.

[29] ibid, 204, speaking of 'institutions beyond the executive, such as Parliament, having a full role to play'.

persist or change to a significant extent because of views held about [it]'.[30] Once a certain 'degree of social consensus' or a 'special agreement' has been established about the norm in question,[31] a convention 'cannot be changed unilaterally and must be complied with if in force until changed by agreement'.[32] In this sense, constitutional conventions as rules of political behaviour are 'exceptionally dependent upon what people think'.[33] They operate as binding rules once those concerned in the working of the constitution have accepted to be bound by them regardless of their political orientation.[34]

The constitutional convention allowing for consultation of Parliament in relation to armed conflict is a political rule intended to manage the relationship between two institutional actors: the Government and Parliament. It is intended to provide an opportunity to Members of Parliament to engage on questions of the deployment of troops and to hold the Government to account. In principle, the convention is born and takes shape on the basis of views of those in power as well as the reactions of the beneficiary (the Members of the House of Commons). For the convention to work effectively, then, both institutions should contribute to its scope and content. MPs as the beneficiaries have to accept, agree, or acquiesce to the behaviour suggested or offered by the Government. The belief of the beneficiaries, and specifically their perception that the practice encompassed by the convention is binding, will therefore be crucial.

Yet, as this chapter shows, it is striking the extent to which the scope and operation of a rule that is intended to regulate and control governmental behaviour is in fact utterly dependent on the Government. The Government unilaterally controls the timing of parliamentary engagement, and conditions the involvement of Parliament on the active support of government policy. The Government has also carved out other exceptions to the convention of its own volition. Since the publication of the convention in the Cabinet Manual, governments have used the inherent flexibility and malleability of conventions, and the process in which they are changed and renegotiated, to fundamentally change the scope of the War Powers Convention.

There is a further dimension which fuels the lack of accountability of the Government to Parliament in the context of the convention. The Government may have been aided by concessions made by MPs about the scope and extent of the War Powers Convention post-2011. MPs' reactions are important because breaches or departures from conventions as political rules will not be punished in courts: 'the very nature of a convention, as political in inception and as depending

---

[30] A Blick, 'The Cabinet Manual and the Codification of Conventions' (2014) *Parliamentary Affairs* 191, 197.

[31] ibid, 204.

[32] G Marshall, *Constitutional Conventions* (Oxford, OUP, 1987) 216–17.

[33] Blick, 'The Cabinet Manual' (n 30) 196.

[34] K Wheare, *Modern Constitutions* (London, OUP, 1966) 102, 137–48. Along similar lines see P Hood, 'Constitutional Conventions: Dicey's Predecessors' (1966) *MLR* 29; Marshall, *Constitutional Conventions* (n 32).

on a consistent course of political recognition by those for whose benefit ... the convention developed over a considerable period of time is inconsistent with its legal enforcement'.[35] Instead, breaches or departures from the convention may at best be condemned in the area of public opinion: 'The observance of constitutional conventions depends upon the acceptance of the obligation of conformance by the actors deemed to be bound thereby'.[36] Whilst those who are bound by the convention will seek to explain their actions, the breach 'is liable to bring political trouble in one form or another',[37] or in Jaconelli's terms, 'criticism and pressure to conform'.[38] However, if the behaviour inconsistent with the convention is repeatedly ignored or acquiesced to, departures from conventions can enable the carving out of exceptions to the main rule. This is precisely what we argue has happened in the context of the War Powers Convention. In putting side by side the views and reactions of the Government, and from those who benefit from binding behaviour (MPs), this chapter seeks to establish the extent to which the agreement about the content of the rule as expressed in the Cabinet Manual has changed since it was first published in 2011. Once we establish a clear picture, we can then assess the extent to which the War Powers Convention fulfils its core purpose of ensuring the accountability of the Government to the House of Commons in the context of war powers.

II. The Importance of the Cabinet Manual

In establishing the existence and scope of constitutional conventions, commentators have relied on the test proposed by Sir Ivor Jennings, which asks three questions: 'First, what are the precedents; secondly, did the actors in the precedents believe that they were bound by a rule; and thirdly, is there a reason for the rule?'[39] Jennings' test appears to be favoured because it was singled out by the Supreme Court of Canada in the *Patriation Reference* case, in which the Court used Jennings' work to identify the existence of a constitutional convention.[40] Looking closely, all three elements of the test are contestable. What are the legitimate precedents that one should look to in order to establish the existence and scope of a convention? What is a good enough reason for a convention to develop? And how can one be satisfied that the actors genuinely believed they were bound by a rule rather than following an established practice out of convenience, economic or political calculation

---

[35] *Re Resolution to Amend the Constitution* [1981] 1 SCR 753, 774–75 (Laskin CJ, writing for the majority); reiterated in *Miller* [2017] UKSC 5, [141].

[36] *Re Resolution to Amend the Constitution* [1981] 1 SCR 753, 853.

[37] Lord Wilson of Dinton 'The Robustness of Conventions in a Time of Modernisation and Change' (2004) *Public Law* 407; I Jennings, *The Law and the Constitution*, 5th edn (London, University of London Press, 1959) 134.

[38] J Jaconelli, 'The Nature of Constitutional Convention' (1999) *Legal Studies* 24.

[39] Jennings, *The Law and the Constitution* (n 37) 119–20.

[40] *Re Resolution to amend the Constitution* [1981] 1 SCR 753.

or rational choice, or even mistaken belief?[41] There is therefore often an inherent uncertainty about the existence, content, and scope of any given constitutional convention.

Yet Jennings insisted that the most important element in determining whether a practice amounted to a convention was whether there was good constitutional reason for it. Jennings appeared to see this as a binary matter: either the reason was or was not good enough to warrant characterising the practice as a convention. But, as Mark Elliott argues, 'a better approach is to view matters in less starkly binary terms, such that the extent (if any) of a convention's prescriptiveness will turn upon the strength of the underlying normative justification. On this view, not all conventions are equal'.[42] For us, the main question is not whether a convention exists, but instead how its underlying rationale—holding the Government to account—has been undermined through practice.

In the context of the War Powers Convention, the Cabinet Manual provides that before troops are committed, the House of Commons should have an opportunity to debate the matter, save in situations of emergency when such engagement may not be appropriate. There is therefore no doubt that a convention exists. The War Powers Convention is recognised and acknowledged by the Government in the Cabinet Manual. The Manual sets out the internal rules and procedures under which the Government operates. For the first time the conventions determining how the Government operates are transparently set out in one place. Codifying and publishing these sheds welcome light on how the Government interacts with the other parts of our democratic system. The Cabinet Manual 'expresses not the will of the Prime Minister but a collection of norms ... which are said to be accepted by actors in the constitutional machinery'.[43] It was negotiated with different actors, including several parliamentary select committees, and ultimately 'considerable care was ... taken to secure wide agreement to the formulation of the norms'.[44] In this regard, the Cabinet Manual reflects the state of the constitution at the time of its publication and specifically, the agreement of 'members of or participants in institutions with a principled interest in the operation of a non-legal norm'.[45]

The Cabinet Manual explicitly refers to the practice of prior parliamentary consultation as a 'constitutional convention'. Evidently, at the time of the publication the Government intended for the Manual to encapsulate the correct constitutional behaviour. As Blick argues, the act of having codified the convention is

---

[41] B Galligan and S Brenton 'Constitutional conventions' in B Galligan and S Brenton (eds) *Constitutional Conventions in Westminster Systems Controversies, Changes and Challenges* (Cambridge, CUP, 2015) 20.

[42] M Elliott, 'Does the Salisbury convention apply during hung Parliament?' (10 June 2017) <https://publiclawforeveryone.com/2017/06/10/does-the-salisbury-convention-apply-during-a-hung-parliament> accessed 17 September 2017.

[43] Feldman, 'Constitutional Conventions' (n 26) 102.

[44] ibid.

[45] Morton, 'Conventions' (n 24), 163; 'Constitutional Conventions' (n 26), 97.

important because the 'inclusion of a convention in a code can establish more certainty regarding its exact character …'.[46] Yet, although the Cabinet Manual is important, it is neither binding nor does it create the rule in question. Whilst the process of transmuting a previously unwritten War Powers Convention into a written document may encapsulate previous practice, the precedents relating to the development of the convention do not suddenly become irrelevant.[47] Instead, looking to prior practice is still required to uncover the precise scope and content of the War Powers Convention at the time of publication of the Cabinet Manual.[48] We have, for example, already mentioned the important progress made by the Government in changing the traditional engagement of Parliament from using adjournment motions to using both substantive motions and voting. The enhanced role of Parliament after the Iraq War of 2003 is self-evident. For the first time in the history of the Westminster Parliament, members of the House were asked *prior* to the start of hostilities using a *substantive* motion to support the Government and troops on the ground.

The requirement that Parliament be seized through a substantive motion is not contained in the text of the Cabinet Manual. Nonetheless, this important shift in practice has solidified into an important and long-term shift in relations between the House of Commons and the Government. Ever since 2003, the practice of those in power has been consistent: every time the Government has contemplated the deployment of troops, MPs have been invited to discuss and support military action through a substantive motion. This was the case at every occasion during the last 13 years both in relation to actions that had international backing or where assistance was explicitly sought (Libya, expansion of action against IS to Syria in 2015 and IS in Iraq 2014) and to actions which lacked a clear legal basis (Syria 2013). This new approach appears to have been universally welcomed across party lines, with former Prime Minister Cameron (who was in Opposition during Iraq 2003) turning to Parliament with a substantive motion in every conflict during his tenure. Equally, MPs have subsequently expected and requested to be involved in such a manner.

The House of Commons has transitioned from a House marginalised by procedural involvement and risking deception of the public, towards the centre stage. It is now asked to provide the backing necessary for military action, as MPs have negotiated for themselves a new manner of being involved on questions of war. Ultimately, this shift in practice remains an essential element of the constitutional convention because it reveals clearly the intended reason behind the birth of the new convention; the reason which is essential, according to Jennings, to turn a mere practice into a constitutional and binding convention. That reason is to allow MPs

---

[46] *Codes* (n 4) 109.

[47] R Rawlings, 'Concordats of the Constitution' (2000) *LQR* 257, 263.

[48] Blick, 'The Cabinet Manual' (n 30) 195, though note the Joint Committee on Conventions stated that since conventions are prone to development, establishing their exact nature at any given moment in time might be difficult. Joint Committee on Conventions, 'Conventions of the UK Parliament', HL 265-I (2006).

to hold the Government to account[49] whilst being able to represent the interests of the electorate and giving them a voice through their vote on the motion.[50] In view of this, the debate cannot be a mere theatre performance, with Parliament allowed to discuss legal and strategy issues whilst having its hands tied behind its back. Instead, Parliament has to be involved in a meaningful manner, so that MPs can fulfil their functions.

Prior practice is therefore an essential element of interpreting and determining the scope of the convention contained in the Cabinet Manual. However, practice occurring after 2011 is equally important. This is because the convention as captured in the Cabinet Manual 'might not long remain an accurate encapsulation' of the constitutional rule. 'In light of practice, disagreement and continued discussion and negotiation, the accepted norm is likely to move away from the written version.'[51] In this context, 'settlements between institutions are always temporary ... Both legal and non-legal norms are always subject to, and are usually in a continual process of, renegotiation and adjustment as circumstances and institutional priorities change'.[52] The subsequent practice that is considered in the sections below will show to what extent the written norm contained in the Cabinet Manual still commands consensus, and to what extent that norm has grown or shrunk through disagreement and renegotiation.[53] Although, therefore, the Cabinet Manual's recognition of the convention captures the image of constitutional relations at a moment in time (October 2011), this chapter will show that these relationships have changed with subsequent practice. Because conventions—even when acknowledged and recognised—are fluid and flexible, they adapt to different circumstances and situations. It is this subsequent practice that we turn to now.

B. The Timing of the Engagement

I. The Importance of Prior Engagement

The precise point in time at which Parliament is seized of the issue of armed conflict has a decisive impact upon its ability to exercise its scrutiny and accountability functions. In the early phase of any international crisis the Government

---

[49] House of Commons Political and Constitutional Reform Committee, 'Revisiting the Cabinet Manual', 5th Report of Session 2014–2015, HC 233. I am grateful to David Howarth, a former MP, for this comment, 17 February 2016.

[50] HC Deb 6 September 1990, vol 177, cols 774–75 (Tony Benn).

[51] Feldman, 'Constitutional Conventions' (n 26) 103. See also A McHarg, 'Reforming the United Kingdom Constitution: Law, Convention, Soft Law' (2008) 71 *MLR* 853; A Young, 'Constitutional Implications of Brexit' (2017) *European Public Law* (forthcoming).

[52] Feldman, 'Constitutional Conventions' (n 26) 97, citing P Morton, 'Conventions of the British Constitution' (1991–92) 15 *Holdsworth Law Review* 114, 162–63, 166–73.

[53] A Blick, 'Constitutional reform' in Galligan and Brenton, *Constitutional Conventions in Westminster Systems* (n 41) 249, 258.

and Parliament may still have 'a variety of options available'[54] in terms of military or non-military strategy. Commentators have thus described this early stage of the conflict as 'the most important one'[55] as once war has broken out, 'the possible political options are limited because the idea of stopping the fighting and retreating from the theatre of war is much more difficult to implement than before the outbreak of actual hostilities'.[56] The timing, in turn, affects *how* Parliament is involved. If decisions at the earlier stages have already been made and step-by-step the situation appears to be turning into a full-scale armed conflict ('war creep'), then Parliament is asked merely to act as a legitimising organ, providing support for Government decisions—which are already a *fait accompli*—and to provide moral support to deployed troops. Therefore, the reduction of possible 'strategic' options will importantly limit the role and constrain the power of Parliament. If Parliament is to perform its role fully and unconstrained, it is therefore crucial that the timing of its engagement on issues of war pre-dates the beginning of hostilities.

Prior to the codification of the convention, the normal tradition of the House of Commons required that Parliament be informed of the Government's decision to begin a military intervention or be given an opportunity to debate only once armed forces had already been deployed or after commitments to allies had already been made.[57] This manner of engagement importantly restricted the capacity of Parliament to perform its scrutinising function and to hold the Government to account.[58] In a number of conflicts—from the Gulf War to Kosovo—Members were only advised of the Government's plans after these were already in place and 'the options for different [strategic] alternatives were reduced greatly'.[59] Some MPs 'deeply resent[ed]' this fact.[60]

The first occasion on which Parliament got to debate and vote on a substantive motion *prior* to the beginning of hostilities was the Iraq War.[61] MPs welcomed this opportunity, insisting that if Parliament was involved prior to the start of

---

[54] T Häkkinen, *The Royal Prerogative Redefined: Parliamentary Debate on the Role of the British Parliament in Large-scale military Deployments, 1982–2003* (Helsinki, Jyväskylä Studies in Humanities 224) 14.

[55] ibid.

[56] ibid.

[57] In early days of Iraq, Blair reminded the House: 'In relation to the House of Commons, let me say to Members in all parts of the House … that in the cases of Kosovo and of Afghanistan we gave the House ample opportunity not only to debate, but to declare and express its view. I am sure that we will do so again, in accordance with the *normal tradition* of the House.' HC Deb 24 September 2002, vol 390, col 11 [emphasis added].

[58] The traditional manner included both a debate on an adjournment motion, which took place only after deployment of forces or indeed after the start of hostilities. On Falklands: L Freedman, *The Official History of the Falklands Campaign, Volume I* (London, Government Official History Series, Routledge, 2004) 15–16, 206–10; M Thatcher, *The Downing Street Years* (London, HarperCollins, 1995) 179–11; on the Gulf War: HC Hansard 21 January 1991, vol 184, cols 23–113. As Benn argued: 'We have had three debates on the Adjournment without substance. Today, we are having a debate without choice' (col 24); HC Deb 11 December 1990, vol 182, col 894.

[59] Häkkinen, 'The Royal Prerogative Redefined' (n 54) 82, summarising GM Dillon, *The Falklands, Politics and War* (London, Palgrave MacMillan, 1989) 122.

[60] HC Deb 21 January 1991, vol 184, cols 23–113, Alice Mahon (col 49).

[61] We underline here the distinction between substantive and adjournment motions. Although Parliament did get to debate the issue of deployment of troops in relation to the Falkland Islands *prior* to the deployment of the navy to the islands, this was done in an adjournment debate only.

hostilities, it could play an important part in ensuring the Government explored all available options, and by querying its short-term and long-term strategy.[62] In effect, the timing of the engagement could potentially facilitate better decision-making. Although the timing of the vote prior to the use of force was crucial in order for Parliament to provide legitimacy to the Government's action, in the absence of explicit legal authorisation by the United Nations, Parliament was in fact seized at a moment when all strategic options were no longer open. When the vote took place on 18 March 2003, more than 40,000 British troops had already been mobilised into the region in December 2002[63] and they could not have been withdrawn, according to MPs speaking in the debate, 'without undermining our own credibility'[64] and 'damag[ing] immensely, if not terminally, our alliance with the United States ... [and] a great many countries in Europe'.[65] In the end, although important progress had been made to give Parliament a relevant say on war, even in a *prior* debate on a substantive motion, the Commons' input was reduced to 'essentially a rubber stamp of a fait accompli'.[66] As the Chilcot report revealed, Blair had committed to making British troops available to Bush even before the debate in Parliament by saying: 'I will be with you, whatever'.[67]

The 2011 Cabinet Manual, which sought to capture the convention that had been triggered by Iraq, puts the prior involvement of Parliament front and centre. It seeks to address the problems raised by the timing in Iraq and requires that before troops are committed the House of Commons should have an opportunity to debate the matter save in situations of emergency and/or when such engagement may not be appropriate. It therefore moves the consultation to a point even earlier than the Iraq precedent—prior to deployment of troops. At least on paper, the Cabinet Manual appears to give MPs a meaningful say on military action. Yet, as subsequent practice shows, the Government has circumvented the timing requirement twice since 2011. In this way, it has limited the situations in which the convention seems applicable, and has cast significant doubt on its effectiveness as a tool of accountability.

II. Compromising on Timing

On the first occasion after Iraq, the Government failed to turn to Parliament before the start of hostilities in Libya in 2011. Although the Government acknowledged that a constitutional convention had developed,[68] it failed to comply with the timing requirement supposedly mandated by that convention. Once the Security

---

[62] R Cook, *The Point of Departure* (London, Simon & Schuster Ltd, 2003) 187–88.
[63] HC Deb 18 December 2002, vol 396, cols 845–46, Statement by Defence Minister Geoff Hoon.
[64] HC Deb 21 January 1991, vol 184, col 829.
[65] ibid, cols 840–41.
[66] Joseph, *The War Prerogative* (n 6) 105.
[67] Prime Minister's note to George W Bush of 28 July 2002, 'Declassified Note on Iraq' 198/02.
[68] Sir George Young for the Government stated in the House of Commons on 10 March 2011 that 'a convention has developed in the House that before troops are committed, the House should have an opportunity to debate the matter ... As with the Iraq war and other events, we propose to give the

Council Resolution 1973 was adopted on 17 March 2011, British forces were promptly sent into action. On 19 March 2011 Royal Navy submarines and Royal Air Force Tornado fighter jets had fired cruise missiles at Libya whilst Tornados flew over Libya on 20 March 2011, in an offensive mission. In the words of the Prime Minister, 'this marked the beginning of our involvement in an international operation ... to enforce the will of the United Nations'.[69] The House of Commons was not advised of the Government's decision or allowed to debate the issue until two days later—on Monday 21 March 2011. During these proceedings MPs were asked to debate and vote on a substantive motion welcoming the UN Security Council Resolution, deploring the use of violence by the Libyan regime, and supporting the Government's decision to implement Resolution 1973. In the end, an overwhelming majority of MPs voted in favour of the motion to support the Government decision to use force.[70]

In 2013, the Government again failed to consult Parliament on the deployment of troops to Mali. Neither a debate nor a vote took place. No reason (emergency or otherwise) was provided for such a decision, although the Under-Secretary of State for Foreign and Commonwealth Affairs specified that British troops would assist only for training and would have 'no combat role'.[71] The drafters of the Manual may have intended that the requirement of parliamentary involvement should apply only in situations when troops are deployed into battle, yet the wording in the Manual clearly suggests otherwise: it requires that 'before troops are committed' Parliament should have an opportunity to debate their deployment.[72] Moreover, even if it is assumed that the War Powers Convention applies only to the deployment of troops with the intention to use of force, successive governments should have taken the opportunity to clarify the wording of the Cabinet Manual to this effect.[73] Yet, this has not happened. On the face of the convention, therefore,

---

House the opportunity to debate the matter *before* troops are committed.' HC Deb 10 March 2011, vol 524, col 1066, emphasis added.

[69] ibid, vol 525, col 677.

[70] The result was 557:13.

[71] HC Deb 14 January 2013, vol 556, col 622. The initial involvement of the UK was limited to planes and advisors, about 330 troops were deployed to the region to support French troops. BBC News, 'Mali Crisis: 330 UK military personnel sent to West Africa', 29 January 2013, <www.bbc.co.uk/news/uk-21240676> accessed 17 September 2017.

[72] Note that the drafters would have been aware of the Sierra Leone precedent, in which Tony Blair sent British troops to the region to provide logistical and technical support. The initial engagement was approved by the Security Council (UN Security Council Resolution 1313 to increase UNAMSIL operation), but there was no debate or vote in Parliament (a statement was made by Secretary of Defence, HC Deb 15 May 2000, vol 350, col 23). Given the opposition in the Commons to the initial deployment to Sierra Leone, there was reluctance to commit British troops to an open-ended peacekeeping operation. However, gradually British troops were in charge of evacuation, providing support to the Sierra Leone Army and humanitarian assistance. Eventually, they were also involved in combat. E MacAskill and R Norton-Taylor 'Flawed evidence led to "mission creep"', *The Guardian*, 16 May 2000.

[73] Though note that since the Mali example, the House was given a full opportunity for a prior debate in the case of military action against ISIS in Iraq in 2014. The legal basis of intervention was similar—a request from the Iraqi government to the US to strike ISIL sites with the express consent of Iraq.

Parliament should have been consulted before the deployment of 330 troops to Mali. But no such engagement occurred and British troops were sent to the region without a debate and vote.

These two examples—Libya and Mali, which depart from the literal wording of the Manual—cannot be disregarded. They represent important subsequent practice interpreting the existence and scope of the War Powers Convention. The codification of the convention in the Manual 'might not long remain an accurate encapsulation ... In light of practice, disagreement and continued discussion and negotiation, the accepted norm is likely to move away from the written version'.[74] Although the Cabinet Manual captures the image of constitutional relations at a moment in time, these relationships may have changed with subsequent practice. In this regard, it is important to establish how the Government presented the timing to the House and how MPs responded, whether there was disagreement between the two institutions about the use of the convention, and the reasons for such departure.

The 2011 debate on Libya opened with a Point of Order, during which David Winnick MP (Labour) raised the issue of the timing of the debate and noted that the 'convention whereby the House debates military action before such action takes place has not been followed'.[75] The Speaker insisted that the 'arrangement of business is a matter for the Government, not the Chair' and suggested that Winnick could return to the point 'later in the afternoon'. Aside from this initial Point of Order, however, the timing was not really central to the discussion in the House. The debate began at 3.30pm and the issue of 'when' the House had been engaged was first raised at 5.47pm, more than two hours into discussion, and indeed after over 60 MPs had intervened on the issue of military action.[76] At that point, Graham Allen MP (Labour) argued that because the House of Commons was seized only after troops had been deployed 'This House is not taking any decisions: the Government have already taken a decision and have graciously allowed us a debate today. ... we need to resolve the question of the House's rights in respect of when this country goes to war.'[77] An hour later David Winnick also argued that the convention required for a meeting prior to the start of military action, and suggested that Parliament could have met on the day of the start of hostilities, a Saturday.[78] Edward Leigh, who raised the issue again insisted that 'when we go to war, the House of Commons should vote *first*.'[79]

---

[74] Feldman, 'Constitutional Conventions' (n 26), 103.

[75] HC Deb 21 March 2011, vol 525, col 699.

[76] When MPs will intervene depends on the Speaker of the House and the order in which they intervene in principle is not indicative of how important the issue is/is not. Yet, the number of interventions reveals how important the majority of intervenors thought the point was.

[77] HC Deb 21 March 2011, vol 525, col 739, Graham Allen.

[78] ibid, col 752, David Winnick. Katy Clark remarked that she would have 'preferred a vote to have taken place before troops were deployed, even if it meant the House convening on a Saturday'. ibid, col 749.

[79] ibid, col 771, Edward Leigh, with agreement from David Winnick and Graham Allen, emphasis added.

These three MPs were the only ones to raise the issue of timing, amongst more than 100 MPs who spoke during the debate. The Prime Minister did not address the issue at all, and the Foreign Secretary William Hague said that the Government had involved Parliament as soon as possible. Notably, the Government did not argue that it had to act quickly and made no reference to the emergency exception inbuilt into the War Powers Convention as a reason for delayed parliamentary involvement. Yet, other MPs came to the rescue of the Government, arguing in response to Allen that the statements made to the House prior to the intervention allowed MPs a 'lengthy discussion' and 'an opportunity to put their views before we went into the conflict in Libya'. One MP responded to criticisms of the Government even more strongly, by suggesting that 'the commitment of the Government in allowing us this debate takes us a further step along that road, and the Prime Minister has given a commitment to keep the House informed of further developments, so at least there are those indications that the Government are taking the House and the views expressed in it seriously'.[80]

It is evident from this discussion that most of the MPs did not notice the timing issue or that, if they did, they chose to ignore it. Given that the issue was raised as a Point of Order before the debate began, there were plenty of opportunities to protest, label the departure as a breach of the convention, and to require that in future a debate takes place before any military deployments are undertaken. Yet, aside from the concerns raised by the three MPs, no such interventions took place and the Government did not choose to address the issue. The central question raised by the Libya episode is why no real protest occurred in Parliament over the departure from the timing requirement. It might be that MPs clearly did not consider the timing of the engagement a breach of the convention that required condemnation in strongest terms possible. It is also possible that MPs are happy to compromise on timing as long as Parliament is involved at some point. In private, for example, MPs have admitted that the question of timing should not be 'fetishised'.[81] In relation to Libya, Graham Allen, the MP who was arguably the driving force behind the emergence of the War Powers Convention—and one of the three who raised the issue of timing in relation to Libya—accepted that consultation either 'before or after an action takes place' would be sufficient.[82] Other parliamentarians appeared to have accepted a similar approach along the lines of 'before or as soon as possible after' deployment of troops.[83] An alternative interpretation of MPs' behaviour in this context might be that the timing of parliamentary engagement becomes irrelevant once international authorisation has been provided for military action, and the focus of MPs is instead on how the country's international commitments will be implemented.

---

[80] ibid, col 739, Donaldson.
[81] Comments at Parliamentary Studies Group and UKCLA Presentation 'Debating Parliament's Role in Conflict Decisions after Syria' 22 February 2016 by MPs and experts.
[82] HC Deb 21 March 2011, vol 525, col 739.
[83] David Howarth, 17 February 2016.

In the next two sections, we respond to these questions and show how MPs' relaxed attitude to this facet of the War Powers Convention has allowed the Government to use timing strategically by linking it to the success of the international processes. This accepted practice reveals that the War Powers Convention applies in fewer situations than the literal wording of the Cabinet Manual initially suggests. We begin, however, with an outline of how crucial the timing of engagement is for the quality of parliamentary engagement.

a. The Rally Behind the Crown Effect

The most problematic aspect of the ex post facto engagement of Parliament is that it triggers the 'rally behind the Crown effect'[84] and a need for 'unity of purpose'.[85] Once the Government has made its international commitments or has sent troops abroad, Parliament can hardly criticise its decision. As military generals testified during the consultation on British war powers, parliamentary criticism at this stage would seriously damage the morale of military personnel.[86] In the build-up to the 2003 Iraq War, Jack Straw, the then-Foreign Secretary, frequently reminded Parliament that the opportunity for scrutiny had to take second place to military strategy and the safety of British servicemen and women:

> We, in Government, have no difficulty at all about the idea of a substantive motion at the appropriate time, I make that clear, with one condition about the exact timing and that is that we, and no one would expect us to, we cannot undertake to put down a motion immediately, shortly before military action commenced if the effect of that would be to give the enemy advance notice of our military activities ...[87]

In order to preserve the element of surprise and so as not to compromise the task of the armed forces on the ground, Straw proposed that a motion be taken after hostilities commenced. His position relied on a long line of precedents (including the Falklands, the Gulf War, and Kosovo) in which Parliament was allowed to debate only after initial military decisions had already been made and after troops had already been deployed on the ground.[88] In these cases, the respective Prime

---

[84] HC Deb 31 March 1854, vol 132, col 281, Benjamin Disraeli.

[85] HC Deb 5 August 1914, vol 65, cols 1963–2093; HC Deb 20 August 1940, vol 364, cols 1132–274; and P Towle, *Going to War: British Debates from Wilberforce to Blair* (Basingstoke, Palgrave MacMillan, 2009) 9.

[86] Ministry of Justice, Foreign and Commonwealth Office & Ministry of Defence, 'War powers and treaties: Limiting Executive Powers' (Governance of Britain CP No 26/07, 25 October 2007) 23 [39].

[87] Jack Straw, Uncorrected Evidence presented by the Rt Hon Jack Straw, Foreign Secretary on 25 September 2002 in respect of Foreign Affairs Select Committee, 'Foreign Policy Aspects of the War Against Terrorism' 2nd Report (2002–2003) HC 196 (19 December 2002) <www.publications.parliament.uk/pa/cm200203/cmselect/cmfaff/196/196.pdf> accessed 17 September 2017.

[88] HC Deb 13 April 1999, vol 329, col 25, Tony Blair; the Falklands is also an example of ex post facto involvement of the House of Commons. The day after the decision had been made the Prime Minister advised the House of Commons that Britain *would be* responding to the invasion and was sending its troops towards the islands. L Freedman, *The Official History of The Falklands Campaign, Volume I* (London, Government Official History Series, Routledge, 2004) 15–16, 206–10; Thatcher, *The Downing Street Years* (n 58) 179–81.

Ministers insisted that a 'full debate on military options with the House making a decision' was not possible. In short: 'Nothing would be more helpful to the enemy or more damaging to our boys'.[89]

The ex post facto timing means that instead of performing its functions without restriction, Parliament ends up being politically compelled to support the Government. The "rally behind the Crown" principle dictates that if the Government unilaterally informs Parliament that it is necessary to engage in war, then Parliament ought to accept the 'wisdom of the policy' and withhold from unnecessarily pressing the issue.[90] In this context, there is little room for argument between the Government and the Opposition. Although Parliament retains the right to enquire into the reasons and information basis behind the Government's decision to go to war, those questions should not be asked whilst war is on-going because: 'it would be imprudent, as well as improper for us, to enter upon any such enquiry, until peace has been some way or other restored.'[91] Instead, MPs 'must render the Executive influential, powerful, and capable of rapid and certain action.'[92] To avoid causing embarrassment to the country at a time of crisis, the House needs to give the appearance of support and unity in the national interest.

Those are 'the responsibilities placed on [MPs]'.[93] The uncritical support of the House of Commons was clearly visible in respect of the Falklands campaign in 1982, in relation to the Gulf War in 1990, and even in relation to Afghanistan in 2010. Even when the UK's entry into armed conflict was controversial, MPs considered it proper to express support for the war effort. This is evident in relation to the military deployment to Kosovo in the late 1990s[94] as well as in relation to the Iraq War:

> There are matters at stake that rise above party politics. It is the duty of the Government to act in the national interest, and it is the duty of the Opposition to support them when they do so. The Prime Minister is acting in the national interest today. That is why he is entitled to our support in doing the right thing.[95]

After strategic decisions have already been made, armed conflict is presented as being legitimately excluded from the arena of active political debate and scrutiny. Because of their significance, wars already begun lie above and beyond politics.

---

[89] HC Deb 13 May 1982, vol 23, cols 943–44, Michael Foot and Margaret Thatcher.

[90] HC Deb 17 July 1857, vol 144, col 1617.

[91] HC Deb 2 December 1755, vol 15, col 557.

[92] HC Deb 5 February 1900, vol 78, cols 627–28, during the Boer War.

[93] ibid.

[94] In the absence of international authorisation for the use of force, there were serious reservations about the deployment to Kosovo. But the general sentiment was that the Commons should express its support for the action and the armed forces: 'The right hon. Gentleman and the Government will have the support of the House because the credibility of NATO has been put at issue and because our service men are in action, but we should not have been brought to this pass.' HC Deb 24 March 1999, vol 328, col 489, Douglas Hogg.

[95] HC Deb 18 March 2003, vol 401, col 779, the leader of the Opposition Iain Duncan Smith.

The Opposition does not challenge the Government and instead seeks to show 'bi-partisan consensus'.[96]

Whilst taking precautions to protect troops from unnecessary risk is understandable and even desirable, the fact that the timing of a debate can compromise the quality of engagement remains highly problematic for MPs:

> If the House is not to be demeaned, it should have a *vote before any commitment to action*. I hope that the House authorities and those who control these things will take that seriously, otherwise the House of Commons will be greatly demeaned.[97]

Clearly, concerns about revealing operational strategy and putting the troops at risk materially affect *when* Parliament is allowed to scrutinise the Government's decision to go to war. As a result, this directly impacts upon the quality of engagement and the extent of scrutiny the House of Commons is able to perform. If troops are already on the ground (as was the case in the Falklands, Gulf, Iraq and Afghanistan wars) or if other important commitments have already been undertaken, then the timing of after-the-fact engagement effectively renders the Government immune from meaningful criticism.[98] This, in turn, means that Parliament is stripped of its power to perform either its representative or scrutinising function effectively or to hold the Government to account. Even worse, in contravention of the idea of democracy, Parliament becomes a rubber stamp, as it uncritically legitimises perhaps the most important decision any government can take: risking the lives of its own citizens by sending them to war. In doing so, Parliament neglects its constitutional duties. Under these conditions Parliament cannot be an effective scrutineer of the Government's decision to wage war.

b. The Narrow Application of the Convention

Whilst the Government determines the timing of the involvement of Parliament strategically, we argue that MPs' willingness to acquiesce to compromises on timing further reduces the quality of parliamentary scrutiny of decisions to go to war. Allowing ex post facto engagement to pass relatively unchallenged in the House of Commons means that the convention applies much more narrowly than initially thought.

In respect of Libya, MPs were willing to sacrifice timing because their first and foremost concern was the issue of international legality. Almost everyone who intervened in the debate in the House of Commons raised the fact that the Government had secured UN Security Council backing for the intervention and that as

---

[96] A Barnett, *Iron Britannia: Why Parliament Wages its Falklands War* (London, Allison and Busby, 1982) 19. The House divided in an adjournment vote that ended with a clear majority (296:33) in support of the Government. The anti-war lobby pushed for an adjournment, but the supporters of the Government voted against this. HC Deb 20 May 1982, vol 24, col 560.

[97] HC Deb 22 January 2003, vol 398, col 373, Tam Dalyell, emphasis added.

[98] S Low, 'The Foreign Office Autocracy' (1912) 91 *Fortnightly Review* 1, 5.

a consequence, the legality of the military action was undisputed and the intervention would be done as part of an international coalition. MPs congratulated the Government for managing to secure widespread support and for turning to them in a different situation than Iraq: 'this case is different as it does have the backing of the United Nations'.[99] Even further, Sir Menzies Campbell MP (Liberal Democrat) insisted that when compared with Kosovo, the House was 'on much stronger ground because the Security Council has said expressly in the provision that "all necessary measures" may be taken'.[100] MPs were therefore reassured by the UN Resolution (or as some put it 'pleased')[101] and readily recognised that British troops were needed to protect civilians of Libya 'from a regime that shows no appetite to stop'.[102] They encouraged the Prime Minister to further 'internationalise' the mission as far as possible to cement support across the international community.[103]

MPs appear willing to accept a secondary role for themselves in the presence of a clear Security Council Resolution. Once the UN provides the legal basis for action, the role of the House of Commons appears to be substantially reduced.[104] In the case of Libya, this meant that a debate and vote came after the start of hostilities. In the case of Mali, two years later, no engagement of Parliament whatsoever took place. MPs were merely informed of troop deployment; and although it was perhaps assumed that the convention did not apply, neither the emergency exception nor other reasons were invoked to explain why parliamentary involvement was unnecessary.[105] Instead, the Security Council Resolution and an explicit request from the Mali Government was cited as a sufficient basis for the deployment of troops.[106] This close link between the international authorisation and the secondary role of the domestic legislature was explored in chapter two. Yet, in both Mali and Libya, the international legality also directly affected the operation of the War Powers Convention and in particular, the timing. The subsidiary role of the domestic legislature was expressed in two ways: in Mali, the international legal

---

[99] HC Deb 21 March 2011, vol 525, col 701, Angus Robertson (SNP) intervened first.

[100] ibid, col 717, Sir Menzies Campbell (LD).

[101] ibid, col 703, Elfyn Llwyd (PC).

[102] ibid, col 730, Ben Wallace (Con), also Sir Menzies Campbell (LD).

[103] ibid, col 732, Martin Horwood (LD).

[104] This is confirmed in discussions with MPs who assert that the most important element of holding the Government to account is the question of the legality of the intervention, along with long term strategy. Again, I am grateful to David Howarth for this suggestion. The legality issue is effectively 'the only constraint' on government and thus gives MPs something tangible to discuss.

[105] HC Deb 14 January 2013, vol 556, col 628.

[106] In addition to the specific request from the Government of Mali for intervention, the Under-Secretary cited United Nations Security Council resolution 2085, which had authorised the deployment of the African-led International Support Mission to Mali. Previous resolutions of the Council had called for military intervention in Mali to be considered and a plan to be developed by the Economic Community of West African States (ECOWAS) and the African Union. ECOWAS released a statement that they considered intervention to be necessary in resolving the Mali conflict and authorised a ground force. Although the Security Council did not authorise action prior to the intervention, the legal basis was firmed up on 25 April 2013, when the Security Council 'welcomed the swift action by the French forces, at the request of the transitional authorities of Mali'. See UN Security Council Resolution 2100.

	War of neccessity (self-defence)	War of choice
No UN backing	Prior Parliamentary involvement is key *Iraq, Syria, IS Syria*	Potential prior parliamentary involvement *Falklands, Gulf War (initially)*
Clear UN backing	Posterior involvement, if any *Korea, Libya, Mali*	Posterior involvement, if any *Gulf War, Afghanistan*

Figure 3.2: The narrow use of prior timing in the context of the War Powers Convention[107]

basis was used to render the involvement of Parliament (apparently) meaningless, whilst in Libya, its involvement took place only ex post facto.

The discussion in chapter two therefore reveals not only how Parliament is used strategically to fill the gap left by the international institutions, but in addition, how the international legality—and the presence of international authorisation—directly affects the domestic constitutional question of how the War Powers Convention is used. Figure 3.2 (above) depicts the current situation.

In contrast to Mali and Libya,[108] where Parliament appears sidelined, the support of Parliament emerges as crucial when the UN provides no backing. In these situations, the support of MPs needs to be expressed as clearly as possible. As is visible from the figure above, Iraq 2003, Syria 2013, and IS in Syria 2015 were such examples requiring *substantive* and *prior* involvement of Parliament.[109] In these situations, the Government needed support for its action before it entered the theatre of war, whilst MPs wanted to make their views known and to query

---

[107] The only example that does not fit the division in this table is the intervention against ISIS in Iraq 2014, when Iraq had requested the assistance of the USA to lead international efforts to strike ISIL sites with Iraq's express consent. See Letter from the Permanent Representative of Iraq to the UN, 20 September 2014; UN Doc S/2014/691, 22 September 2014. Although the intervention is widely accepted as an example of collective self-defence, David Cameron sought prior approval from Parliament. HC Deb 26 September 2014, vol 585, col 1255.

[108] Libya's practice mirrors that adopted in relation to Korea, with the start of hostilities on 27 June 1950 and a substantive vote eight days later. HC Deb 5 July 1950, vol 477, col 493.

[109] In this regard, the last vote in November 2015 is also a reaffirmation of the convention, since although the Security Council had adopted a Resolution referring to 'all necessary measures', the international legal basis and specifically lack of reference to Chapter VII of the UN Charter was unclear and dubious. D Akande and M Milanovic, 'The Constructive Ambiguity of the Security Council's ISIS Resolution', EJIL Talk (21 November 2015) <www.ejiltalk.org/the-constructive-ambiguity-of-the-security-councils-isis-resolution>; V Fikfak, UK Constitutional Law Association blog (28 November 2015) <https://ukconstitutionallaw.org/2015/11/28/veronika-fikfak-voting-on-military-action-in-syria>; both accessed 17 September 2017.

the Government's motivations for action which had not secured United Nations backing. Parliamentarians wanted to perform their function of holding the Government to account before any major decisions were taken. In all of these examples, no international authorisation was forthcoming and Parliament was needed to provide the domestic political approval necessary for the Government to intervene. MPs were presented with explanations justifying the need for military action, they were provided with legal opinions making a case for war, and with information showing the dangers faced by the people on the ground and to the international community as a whole. In a substantive motion MPs were asked to support military action. When in relation to Syria in 2013, they rejected the Government's motion and refused—in the absence of an international legal backing—to give support for military action against Assad, the Government complied with the vote and took no further action. Without an international backing and having risked going to Parliament for support and lost, the Government therefore did not dare engage in military action. The political fallout would simply have been too great.[110]

The pattern of needing Parliament when the UN Security Council fails to provide a legal basis and proceeding without its prior support when international authorisation is clear, is striking, but it is also reflected in precedents that predate the recognition of the War Powers Convention in the Cabinet Manual. In emergency or self-defence situations (Figure 3.2, second column), governments have pursued both domestic and international routes to secure support for military action. Although arguably the convention excludes such emergency situations from the requirements of prior engagement to allow for a rapid response to an attack, these precedents suggest that governments may seek to keep Parliament informed and allow it to debate the appropriateness of the planned response if enough time is available between the invasion and the start of hostilities. This was the case in the Falklands and the Gulf War in which Parliament was asked to debate on adjournment motions whilst the United Nations worked to agree on providing a clear legal basis for action (Figure 3.2, top row). In both situations, Parliament was involved *before* major strategic decisions were taken. Yet, once the right to self-defence was recognised by the UN (which was the case only in relation to the Gulf War), further parliamentary involvement was limited and deferred until only after the start of military action.[111] On the first day of the Gulf War, an adjournment debate against the war was defeated, whilst a substantive motion supporting the

---

[110] Tony Blair statement: 'I mean, can you honestly imagine a set of circumstances in which the Government is defeated by Parliament over a conflict and says, "Well, I'm just ignoring that"?' The House of Commons Liaison Committee. Session 2002–03. Minutes of Evidence 21 January 2003, Q126, <www.publications.parliament.uk/pa/cm200203/cmselect/cmliaisn/334-i/3012108.htm> accessed 17 September 2017.

[111] Note that both on the Falklands and the Gulf War, the debates were on adjournment motions, which we criticise in ch 1. The vote on a substantive motion regarding the Gulf War was on 21 January 1991. See ch 2 for details.

troops was put to a vote only six days after the start of UN authorised hostilities. In relation to military action in Afghanistan, which had been authorised by the UN and initiated in coalition with the US, no prior debates took place. The approval of military action came many, many years later.[112]

In these examples, the timing of the involvement of Parliament therefore depended on the ability of the Government to guarantee international backing for military action. Yet, the interplay between the international and domestic paths for securing legitimacy for military action also influenced the quality of parliamentary engagement. In the above situations, before the start of hostilities Parliament was involved only on adjournment motions and through statements, an engagement that limits the ability of MPs to criticise or hold the Government to account and to clearly voice their position in relation to war. Only after the UN had authorised action and after military action had already started were MPs invited to debate a substantive motion and vote clearly to support government's plans or to reject them. Timing and the type of involvement were used to reduce or enhance Parliament's significance in proceedings.

All of the precedents mentioned pre-date the recognition of the War Powers Convention in the Manual. In fact, they also fall squarely within the 'self-defence' or 'emergency' situation, which are arguably not covered by the convention.[113] Yet, they follow the same pattern that is still clearly visible after the recognition of the convention: The only situations in which the Parliament will have a chance to debate prior to deployment of troops are those in which there is no UN backing. Whilst today the expectation is that Parliament will be involved through a substantive motion and vote rather than adjournment motions, this expectation only speaks further to reinforce the Government's desire to delay parliamentary involvement unless its support is absolutely crucial.

On its face, the Cabinet Manual does not limit the application of the War Powers Convention to specific situations. The only limit it imposes are 'emergencies', which are neither articulated nor defined. Yet, looking at both prior and subsequent practice, it has become apparent that MPs are used to fill the shoes of the Security Council and to replace its role in the process of legitimising military action. Although in relation to self-defence situations such involvement may not be key, it is often necessary and strategic to secure widespread cross-party support for military action. In contrast, in non-self-defence situations, when the UN remains silent, the substantive involvement of Parliament and a prior vote are essential. As a consequence, the convention as captured in the Cabinet Manual (ie requiring engagement before deployment of troops) applies only when there is no international backing for military action. Although the Cabinet Manual

---

[112] The debates on continued military action in Afghanistan took place in 2009 and 2010. See ch 2 for details.

[113] There have been no self-defence situations since 2011 under which the application of the convention or potential exceptions under the 'emergency' heading could be tested.

gives the impression of a broad unqualified convention, our analysis reveals that the convention applies very rarely. Its scope of application—and our expectation that Parliament will get approval prior to the deployment of troops—is therefore extremely narrow (amounting to the highlighted square in Figure 3.2).

These precedents clearly map out a very specific view of the War Powers Convention. The precise timing of the involvement of Parliament has depended on the presence of a clear international legal basis for action. In turn, the constitutional role of the legislature on the question of war appears to be inextricably linked with the presence or absence of an international legal basis for military action. As a result, the Government has adopted different types of behaviour depending on the clarity and certainty of that legal basis. In this regard, the timing appears not to be a core element of the convention, despite the text of the convention explicitly indicating a requirement of 'prior' parliamentary engagement. It is neither an element the Government feels 'bound' by, nor—looking at the reactions of MPs—is it thought to be so. Rather, the convention (and specifically the timing) is used strategically by the Government to facilitate military action. Accountability takes second place.

C. Parliament's Hollow Veto Power

Further concerns about the operation of the constitutional convention were raised by the Syrian conflict in 2015. Prime Minister David Cameron insisted that a vote in the House of Commons in respect of air strikes against ISIS/ISIL in Syria would only take place if a clear majority of parliamentarians supported military action. This statement by Cameron came against the backdrop of the Coalition Government's 2013 defeat in relation to Syria. Then, instead of supporting the Government as they had done on every single previous occasion,[114] MPs rebelled. Since the Prime Minister was unable to secure sufficient support for a UN-backed international response against the alleged use of chemical weapons by Syrian President Assad, MPs queried the legality of the intervention absent a clear UN Security Council Resolution, and criticised the Government for trying to act too hastily. This was the first ever defeat for a ruling party on a question of war since 1782, when Lord North, then Prime Minister, lost a vote of confidence in relation to the British military defeat at the battle of Yorktown, Virginia.

The 2013 Coalition Government had failed to secure support for a 'strong humanitarian response ... and military action'.[115] Many Conservative MPs rebelled (as did Liberal Democrats, who were at the time part of the Coalition

---

[114] Even in the Narvik Debate on the vote of confidence in 1940, Chamberlain enjoyed a narrow victory.
[115] HC Deb 29 August 2013, vol 566, col 1425.

Government) and voted against the motion. In light of this loss, the Prime Minister gave his assurance that:

> I ... believe in respecting the will of this House of Commons. It is very clear tonight that, while the House has not passed a motion, the British Parliament, reflecting the views of the British people, does not want to see British military action. I get that, and the Government will act accordingly.[116]

There was no military action in Syria. Therefore, when the issue of military action arose again two years later in 2015 (this time in the context of expanding action against ISIS/ISIL in Iraq to Syria), the Prime Minister was clear that the issue would go to a vote in the House only if a clear majority of MPs supported the action: 'Let me be clear: there will not be a vote in this House unless there is a clear majority for action, because we will not hand a publicity coup to ISIL'.[117] The Prime Minister, therefore, was prepared to condition the engagement of the House of Commons so as to secure majority support. Without an assurance of support there would be no vote.

The statement is evidently a strong response to the Syria 2013 precedent. Having been previously unsuccessful in securing backing for military action against the Assad regime, Cameron stated that such involvement would only come if 'there was a clear majority for action' against ISIL in Syria, as opposed to coming immediately before the Commons and risking further political embarrassment.[118] From the perspective of the traditional, normal parliamentary engagement in which the House regularly provides the backing the Government needs, this statement is an open call to Parliament to 'rally behind the Crown' or risk exclusion from the process altogether. It is both an ultimatum to Parliament, and an important reminder of where the power lies in the unequal relationship between the Government and Parliament. In short, the War Powers Convention does not secure the 'free will' of Parliament. In fact, depending on how willing MPs are to support the action, engagement can be timed to take place before or after troops are sent abroad.

Yet, some scholars have argued that the refusal of MPs to support military action in 2013 amounts to a veto power over military action on the part of the House of Commons. Professor Gavin Phillipson, for example, argues that the statement by Cameron suggests: 'if the Government believes it will not get approval for a proposal to use military action, it will not put the matter to a vote, and without a vote the military action will not happen. Thus Parliament has an effective veto ...'[119] The statement should therefore be interpreted as 'further evidence of the existence of the Convention'. Philipson continues: 'If the Government took the view that it was free, constitutionally, to disregard the view of the Commons, that would surely make it more likely to risk defeat in the Commons, embarrassing as it would be, since it would not then be bound to alter its policy.'[120] According to

---

[116] ibid, col 1556.
[117] HC Deb 26 November 2015, vol 602, col 1494.
[118] Phillipson, '"Historic" Commons' Syria vote' (n 1).
[119] ibid.
[120] ibid.

Phillipson, the vote is avoided due to the obligation that would kick in if the assent were refused, as was the case in Syria 2013.

Professor Phillipson speaks of 'bindingness', ie of the governmental belief that it was constitutionally required to follow the will of Parliament. However, there are several problems with this interpretation. On one side, there is the pressing issue of whether sufficient evidence exists (in the form of practice and statements) to prove that the Syria situation demonstrates the existence of a parliamentary veto. On the other side, Philipson's proposed reading of the convention makes two important, yet questionable leaps in making the case that a parliamentary veto exists under the War Powers Convention.

Philipson argues that the War Powers Convention constitutionally requires 'the *assent* of the Commons ... before the government takes military action'.[121] He also refers to the need for parliamentary 'approval' and discusses the 2013 precedent as an example of 'disapproval' by Parliament of military action. He is not alone in this exercise. The media regularly report that consent or approval is necessary before the country goes to war. The suggestion proffered by some is that the decision of the Prime Minister to accept the result of the Syria 2013 vote, was actually bolstered by his statement in 2015 to the effect that he would not take the issue to a vote unless the Government motion would be successful. In turn, it is suggested that these events changed the convention from allowing Parliament an 'opportunity to debate' to imposing upon Parliament 'an obligation to assent'.

When we revisit the text of the Cabinet Manual, we can see that it clearly states that the convention entails 'the opportunity to debate' before troops are committed. Moreover, the wording does not mention assent or approval.[122] Nor does it mention a requirement that the House of Commons is permitted to vote. However, the Cabinet Manual is merely a statement of the 'constitution' of 2011. It is perfectly possible that the constitution has subsequently changed. There is some evidence that would support this proposition. In 2013, whilst debating whether the House of Commons would be afforded an opportunity to discuss airstrikes on Syria, the Speaker, John Bercow MP, reminded MPs of 'an explicit commitment by the Foreign Secretary that there will be no implementation of such a decision without the prior *assent* in the form of a vote on a substantive motion in this House'.[123] At the same time, the House of Lords Constitution Committee acknowledged that 'It is now widely accepted that Parliament should have a role in debating and approving the Government's decisions to deploy Her Majesty's armed forces overseas.'[124] Others have similarly spoken of government's duty to seek 'the express *approval*

---

[121] ibid.

[122] This is the case both in relation to motion in 2013 and in 2015. HC Deb 2 December 2015, vol 603, col 323.

[123] HC Deb 18 June 2013, vol 564, col 761. Note, however, that there was no statement from the Government backing Bercow's interpretation of the motion.

[124] House of Lords, Constitution Committee, 2nd Report 2013, [37].

of the Commons in advance of the deployment of the armed forces on operations overseas that actually or potentially involve hostilities'.[125] Yet, although the use of the term 'approval' is widespread, Government motions are always presented to the House using the term 'support' rather than 'approval'.

Furthermore, the motives which may have influenced both the 2013 and 2015 statements by Cameron appear to be contestable. Cameron stated publicly that he was unwilling to 'hand a publicity coup to ISIL'.[126] There is perhaps an implicit recognition or acquiescence that he would be compelled to follow the result of a Commons' vote,[127] but most importantly there is an overwhelming concern about jeopardising any military action through an unsuccessful vote in Parliament. The statement clearly indicates that the parliamentary vote will be withheld in a situation where a cost–benefit calculation on the part of the Government mitigates against parliamentary involvement. We must then consider this together with the 2013 statement in which Cameron accepted the result of the Commons' vote, and agreed to 'act accordingly.' For Phillipson, the decision of Cameron to abide by this result, coupled with a lack of any stipulation that the Government could wage war without a vote or in the face of a negative vote in 2013, leads to the conclusion that the Government considers itself bound by any vote in Parliament. Although this appears an attractive argument, the reasons for government compliance with parliamentary will remain open to question. In a BBC discussion Sir Malcom Rifkind, a Conservative politician who served in both the Thatcher and Major governments, insisted that 'it is a political, not constitutional necessity which makes a government abide by the will of the Commons in such situations'.[128] In Rifkind's opinion, the decision to obey the will of MPs over Syria in 2013 was not due to a belief that the Government was constitutionally bound to do so, but instead motivated by embarrassment at the defeat and the desire to move on quickly. Other authors have made similar suggestions, indicating that 'in theory the Prime Minister could have pressed on anyway, since he was under no legal obligation to abide by the will of the Commons in the area, … he judge[d] such a course of action *politically* impractical'.[129] These statements would appear to suggest that Cameron's decision was strategically rather than constitutionally motivated.

To some extent Rifkind and others' distinctions between political and constitutional or legal and political are artificial. The convention that the Government cannot commit troops without the assent of Parliament may still exist and may

---

[125] Blick, 'Constitutional reform' (n 53) 255.

[126] HC Deb 26 November 2015, vol 602, col 1494.

[127] Many have acknowledged that it would be difficult to imagine circumstances in which a vote of the House would be disregarded by the Government. House of Lords, Constitution Committee, 2nd Report 2013, [59]. As Lord Gurthrie of Craigiebank put it, any Government who did this would be 'mad'.

[128] As reported by Phillipson (n 1), who appeared with him on air.

[129] A Blick, 'Emergency powers and the withering of the Royal Prerogative' (2014) *International Journal of Human Rights* 195, 204, emphasis added.

have exclusively political consequences. In this sense, there may be a blurring between the political and the constitutional when it comes to conventions. We would not argue that there is no convention of individual ministerial responsibility, despite the fact that this is enforced predominantly for political or strategic reasons.[130] There are still good constitutional reasons for the convention, even if it is mostly enforced when it is politically expedient.

The most fundamental misconception inherent in the idea that the Syria debates have given rise to a parliamentary veto over military action relates to the notion that there is an automatic link to be drawn between assent, vote, and action. This argument is expressed in the following terms: 'if the Government believes it will not get approval for a proposal to use military action, it will not put the matter to a vote, and without a vote the military action will not happen'.[131] The most problematic part of the proposition is the myth that if there is no vote in Parliament, no governmental action will follow. The assumption is that under the War Powers Convention the vote has to come before any deployment of troops or the start of hostilities. This argument disregards the Libya and Mali precedents (and those preceding 2011) in which the Government went ahead with military action without a vote (especially where it had a sufficient international legal basis), and only allowed a debate after the start of hostilities.[132] The fact that the Government has the power to 'decide whether there is a conflict decision', and whether and when parliamentary involvement is necessary,[133] fundamentally changes the nature and quality of that involvement. In the 'assent-vote-action' equation the argument assumes (or perhaps implies) an equal relationship between the two institutions on issues of military action but, as is clear, such a relationship is far from an accurate account of the actual interaction between the two branches. The Government can and does go to war without parliamentary approval. In 2015, this was especially the case since the Conservative party enjoyed full majority in Parliament (compared to the Coalition Government during the 2013 Syrian vote). It could therefore very easily send troops into action 'on its own'.

Nevertheless, the importance of the historic parliamentary triumph in 2013 over Syria cannot be underestimated. Since that August, MPs appear 'empowered' or almost 'freed' of the need to automatically support the Government on military action. They argue that the result of voting down the Government's proposal in relation to Syria means they could in the future similarly refuse to support a motion on a military action already in progress.[134] The extent to which this is

---

[130] M Elliott and R Thomas, *Public Law* (Oxford, OUP, 2017) 409 ff; A Tomkins, *Public Law* (Oxford, OUP: Clarendon Press, 2003) 131–69.

[131] Phillipson, '"Historic" Commons' Syria vote' (n 1).

[132] Note that in relation to Syria 2015, the Government invoked the Security Council Resolution as a basis for action. Although this reliance is legally problematic, based on the analysis in the previous section in international legality, the vote was therefore technically not a necessary requirement for military action to take place.

[133] Blick, 'Emergency powers' (n 129) 206.

[134] D Howarth, 17 February 2016. Also the Constitution Committee asks 'what happens if approval is denied'. House of Lords, Constitution Committee, 2nd Report 2013, [52].

truly a realistic prospect still remains debatable, however. The Syria 2013 vote took place before any deployment of troops and prior to the start of hostilities. Therefore, at the time of the vote, all options were still available in terms of military or non-military strategy. The situation would have been different if the debate took place after key decisions had already been made, and if step-by-step the situation had turned into a full-scale armed conflict. If the Government, for example, had sidestepped Parliament, sent troops to Syria and only afterwards asked Parliament for its support, it is unlikely that the decision would have been condemned by MPs. Although Parliament would have retained a theoretical right to enquire into the broad reasons behind the Government's decision to go to war, as we saw earlier, war is treated as a matter 'that rise[s] above party politics. It is the duty of the Government to act in the national interest, and it is the duty of the Opposition to support them when they do so'.[135] Those are 'the responsibilities placed on [MPs]', responsibilities which they often willingly accept[136] and in turn avoid criticising the Government's decision.[137] If the Government had made strategic use of the timing—as Cameron suggested in his 2015 statement— one would expect MPs to 'rally behind the throne'.[138] The fusion of power between Government and Parliament, the control the Government enjoys in the House of Commons, and the work of party Whips all lead to the conclusion that the Government's decision would likely have been upheld by the Commons. Claims about the existence of a veto power therefore appear to have been greatly exaggerated.

D. Emergencies, Drones and Special Forces

The convention states that in an event of an emergency, the Commons may not have to be provided with an opportunity to debate the matter *prior* to the deployment of troops if such action would be inappropriate. This 'emergency' exception appears to allow the Government the flexibility to avoid a prior debate in the House if there were 'a critical British national interest at stake';[139] 'the need to act to prevent a humanitarian catastrophe';[140] or 'considerations of secrecy make it impossible'.[141] In such exceptional cases the convention allows for the Government to use force immediately and to explain its actions to the House of Commons afterwards, at the earliest opportunity. As the Prime Minister put it in September 2014: 'If there was the need to take urgent action to prevent, for

---

[135] HC Deb 18 March 2003, vol 401, col 779 (Duncan Smith).
[136] ibid, col 901.
[137] S Low 'The Foreign Office Autocracy' (1912) 91 *Fortnightly Review* 1, 5.
[138] Joseph, *The War Prerogative* (n 6).
[139] HC Deb 26 September 2014, vol 585, col 1265 (Prime Minister, David Cameron MP).
[140] ibid.
[141] HC Deb, 23 February 2016, vol 606, col 149 (Foreign Secretary, Philip Hammond).

instance, the massacre of a minority community or a Christian community, and Britain could act to prevent that humanitarian catastrophe … I would order that and come straight to the House and explain afterwards.'[142]

The emergency exception was tested for the first time in autumn 2015. On 21 August 2015 Reyaad Khan, a 21-year-old British citizen from Cardiff, was killed by an Royal Air Force Unmanned Aerial Vehicle (commonly known as a 'drone') strike in Raqqa, Syria. He had appeared in a recruitment video for ISIL/ Da'esh and was suspected of being involved in plotting and directing terrorist attacks in the UK and elsewhere. The targeted killing of this suspected terrorist took place without a debate in Parliament. In fact, the Commons were only informed of the use of force after they had returned from summer recess, on 7 September 2015. Then, the Prime Minister stated: 'I want to be clear that the strike was not part of coalition military action against ISIL in Syria: it was a targeted strike to deal with a clear, credible and specific terrorist threat to our country at home.'[143]

It is important to put the use of drones in this manner into the overall context of the scope and operation of the War Powers Convention. The targeted killing took place on Syrian territory in 2015, after the Commons had voted against the use of military force in Syria in 2013 and even more importantly, after Parliament had explicitly excluded the use of airstrikes in Syria as part of military action against ISIL in Iraq.[144] On two occasions the Commons had therefore made it clear that it did not support the use of force on Syrian territory. Yet, in August 2015, the Government disregarded this position and allowed the strike without involving Parliament. In September, it then sought to clarify its position by labelling the strike as a 'new departure'.[145] Until then Britain had used remotely piloted aircraft in Iraq and Afghanistan (both approved by Parliament), but for the first time, the former Prime Minister argued it had used military force outside an area of armed conflict. The decision to qualify the intervention as a 'new departure' and to refer to it as 'outside an area of armed conflict' indicated that the targeted killing had taken place outside of other conflicts that had been debated and approved by Parliament. This, therefore, was not an extension of the action approved by Parliament in relation to ISIL in Iraq, it was also not an expansion of the intervention in Libya.

Instead, the clarification provided by the Secretary of State for Defence and by the Prime Minister was that the intervention was altogether new and responded to a 'new' threat wherever the threat came from:

> As part of this counter-terrorism strategy, … if there is a direct threat to the British people and we are able to stop it by taking immediate action, then, as Prime Minister, I will always be prepared to take that action. That is the case whether the threat is emanating from Libya, from Syria or from anywhere else.[146]

---

[142] HC Deb 26 September 2014, vol 585, col 1265.
[143] HC Deb 7 September 2015, vol 599, col 26.
[144] HC Deb 26 September 2014, vol 585, col 1255.
[145] HC Deb 7 September 2015, vol 599, col 30.
[146] ibid, col 25.

In its report on the Government's policy on the use of drones for targeted killing, the Joint Committee on Human Rights (JCHR) concluded that:

> The Prime Minister's statements … about a new departure in UK policy … were made in the context of the constitutional convention and should be read in that light … The nature of the operation was such that it was not appropriate for the House of Commons to debate the use of force in advance.[147]

The Prime Minister had therefore defined the action as 'new' for the purposes of the constitutional convention, a move that allowed him to avoid the previous defeat (2013), and the decision of Parliament prohibiting action in Syria (2014). The Joint Committee on Human Rights concluded that this was the 'first time since the establishment of [the] convention that the Government had invoked the exception recognised by the convention'.[148] This allowed the Government to act unilaterally and only later turn to the House of Commons to explain the action taken:

> Because of the importance attached to that convention, [the Prime Minister] was keen to establish that the Government had not ignored the will of the Commons, but rather had acted in accordance with the convention, by taking urgent military action and then coming to the Commons at the earliest opportunity to explain the justification for that action. His remarks about the strike not being part of armed conflict were part of his explanation as to why the Government had in fact acted in accordance with the domestic constitutional convention rather than ignored it.[149]

The Joint Committee on Human Rights was generous in its interpretation of the Government's action. The Prime Minister never defined the action against Khan as an 'emergency'. He did speak in terms of a 'direct threat' to the British people and the opportunity to respond 'immediately'. He also used terms like 'necessity' and 'proportionality'.[150] Although his statement before the Commons could therefore be interpreted as relating to an 'emergency', the Prime Minister never explicitly referenced the term 'emergency' nor did he directly state that the Government had chosen to invoke the exception to the War Powers Convention.

More disconcerting, however, is the fact that the Government did not offer the same interpretation of its action on the international level as it had on the domestic level. In a letter dated 7 September 2015 to the UN Security Council, the UK Permanent Representative to the UN said that the strike in Syria was not only in self-defence of the UK but was also an exercise of the right of collective self-defence of Iraq. The letter stated that 'ISIL is engaged in an ongoing armed attack against Iraq, and therefore action against ISIL in Syria is lawful in the collective self-defence of Iraq'.[151] The argument was that the targeted killing was a part of the international authorised action against ISIL in Iraq, although the killing

---

[147] Joint Committee on Human Rights, *The Government's policy on the use of drones for targeted killing*, 2nd Report 2015–2016, HC574, [2.23].

[148] ibid, [2.24].

[149] ibid, [2.25].

[150] HC Deb 7 September 2015, vol 599, col 26.

[151] Professor Sir David Omand testifying before the Joint Committee on Human Rights (n 147), [2.10].

took place in Syria. In effect, therefore, on the international level, the Government argued that it had expanded its military engagement in Iraq across the border into Syria. On the domestic level, this argument would not have held—Parliament had explicitly prohibited such involvement of the British military.

Although the JCHR Report sought to reconcile the 'contradictions and inconsistencies in the Government's account of its policy',[152] between the narrative presented by the Government to the House of Commons on the one hand, and the UN Security Council on the other, the targeted killing of Khan explicitly demonstrates that different stories are presented on the domestic level and the international level. By defining the intervention as a 'new departure' in the House of Commons, the Government can apparently (though not expressly) rely on the exception to the War Powers Convention and thus use force outside recognised areas of conflict without prior parliamentary involvement. This allows the Government to maintain that it is still committed to upholding the convention and respecting the will of Parliament[153] whilst avoiding its prior positions. Such manipulation of the convention (or indeed of the exception) is clearly problematic and raises serious questions about ignoring 'the will of the Commons.'[154]

The JCHR Report concludes that Khan's targeted killing is an exception to the War Powers Convention, and insists that far from undermining the convention the practice adopted by the Government reinforces the 'remarkable normative strength already acquired' by the convention.[155] Yet, it is unclear from this one example whether the use of drones outside of an existing armed conflict[156] will in the future be considered as falling under the War Powers Convention (ie whether the Government is expected to consult Parliament in the future prior to using drones), or whether drones may altogether be excluded from parliamentary oversight as an exception to the convention. This is possible for two reasons; first because the use of drones is often done in an emergency or, secondly due to the fact that drones are not troops and are therefore excluded from the operation of the convention, which focuses explicitly on the deployment of troops.

The second of these arguments appears to be confirmed in a statement of the Defence Secretary David Fallon MP, who when asked whether 'a debate in Parliament should be held before troops are committed in military action applies to the lethal use of armed drones', avoided the question by repeating the words of the convention as articulated in the Cabinet Manual.[157] However, a few months later, in October 2016, Mike Penning, the new Minister for the Armed Forces,

---

[152] ibid, [2.2].
[153] ibid, [2.25].
[154] ibid, [2.25].
[155] ibid, [2.25].
[156] Use of drones within a conflict is de facto authorised when Parliament approves military action.
[157] Written question 42596, 'Armed Forces: Deployment' <www.parliament.uk/business/publications/written-questions-answers-statements/written-question/Commons/2016-07-13/42596> accessed 17 September 2017.

responded to the same question in the following terms: 'Whether the Convention applies would depend on the circumstances in which [a] Reaper [drone] was to be used. Unmanned aerial systems are subject to the same operational accountability and oversight to that of manned aircraft, including the application of the War Powers Convention.'[158] His statement is somewhat more nuanced, allowing drones to be used in an emergency and thus escape the prior accountability requirements of the convention, but also to fall under the convention if no emergency exists. Whilst the picture is still unclear, it is more than likely that in the future the use of drones for targeted killings outside recognised armed conflicts will escape parliamentary oversight. This will occur either because they are used in an 'emergency', providing the Government the flexibility it needs to 'surprise' the unexpected targets, or because the Government will claim that they do not involve the deployment of British troops in the literal sense. Although the exemption of drones could be understandable within the strict wording of the Cabinet Manual, the involvement of Parliament in decisions relating to armed conflict is important for reasons beyond the operational safety of British troops. In light of this, we argue in chapter five that holding the Government to account extends to the legitimacy and necessity of military action in and of itself, and to the reputation of Britain in the international community. These questions arise both in the context of the deployment of conventional human troops and the use of drones.

An additional exception to the application of the War Powers Convention has been carved out for special forces[159] missions, which are currently not subject to parliamentary scrutiny. The UK Special Forces are the Special Air Service, the Special Boat Service and the Special Reconnaissance Regiment. The former Defence Minister Michael Fallon clearly stated in a response to a written question that 'The convention does not apply to British military personnel embedded in the armed forces of other nations'.[160] As with drones, special forces can—and have been— sent to conflicts which Parliament has not approved. In summer 2015, newspapers reported that member of the Special Air Service 'dressed in US uniforms joined special forces on an overnight raid in Syria'.[161] Although it is accepted that there

---

[158] Written question 49992, 'Middle East: Military Intervention' <www.parliament.uk/business/publications/written-questions-answers-statements/written-question/Commons/2016-10-24/49992> accessed 17 September 2017.

[159] P Rogers, 'Accountability in Shadow War', Oxford Research Group blog (30 March 2016) <www.oxfordresearchgroup.org.uk/publications/paul_rogers_monthly_briefing/uk_special_forces_accountability_shadow_war> accessed 17 September 2017.

[160] Written question—42596 (n 157). Fallon also recently stated, 'We do not, as the right hon. Gentleman knows, comment in this House on the deployment of our special forces in any country in the world.' HC Deb 12 September 2016, vol 614, col 580.

[161] L-M Eleftheriou-Smith, 'SAS troops "dressed in US uniforms and joined special forces on Isis Abu Sayyaf overnight raid in Syria"' *The Independent* (10 August 2015) <www.independent.co.uk/news/uk/home-news/sas-troops-dressed-in-us-uniforms-and-joined-special-forces-on-isis-abu-sayyaf-overnight-raid-in-10448018.html> accessed 17 September 2017.

is no accountability to Parliament in respect of United States' Special Forces operations because the UK is not in charge of the day-to-day operation of such missions, the Foreign Affairs Committee recently expressed concerns that the lack of 'parliamentary or public scrutiny ... increases the danger that such operations can become detached from political objectives'. Whilst the Committee did not wish to hinder the UK Government's ability to use its own special forces personnel 'without sanction from or scrutiny by Parliament' it underlined that 'this latitude should not be abused to circumvent the normal parliamentary authorisation for military deployments, especially when Special Forces are used in a role more usually performed by Regular Forces'.[162] Although the use of Special Forces for emergencies can be understood, again the question arises as to how far their use can and should be exempted from the convention in non-emergency situations.

E. Unrealised Accountability

The aim of the War Powers Convention was to provide a more democratic process through which military troops are deployed into battle. The idea was to strengthen the position of Parliament vis-à-vis the Government and to give the House of Commons an active role in compelling the Government to articulate its motives and formulate long-term strategy. In this regard, the codification of the War Powers Convention in the Cabinet Manual sought to 'establish more certainty regarding its exact character' and make 'adherence to it more plausible'.[163] Yet, despite Blick's suggestion that codification may reduce Executive discretion and potentially strengthen the position of a convention, we have found little evidence that this is so in respect of the War Powers Convention. As this chapter shows, both the exact character of the convention and the adherence to the convention have been undermined by subsequent practice, to the extent that the ability of Parliament to hold the Government to account has been called into question.

If accountability requires 'a relationship between an actor and a forum', (a) the actor has an obligation to explain and to justify his or her conduct, (b) the forum can pose questions and pass judgement, and (c) the actor may face consequences,[164] the War Powers Convention as observed in this analysis only partially achieves these three aims. First, Bovens argues, 'The actor must feel obliged to come forward—instead of being at liberty to provide any account whatsoever'.[165] The Cabinet Manual extends the Government's obligation to enable

---

[162] Foreign Affairs Committee, 'Libya: Examination of intervention and collapse and the UK's future policy options' 3rd Report 2016–2017, HC 119 [124], emphasis added.
[163] Blick, *Codes* (n 4), 109.
[164] Bovens, 'Analysing and Assessing Accountability' (n 15) 450.
[165] ibid, 452.

a parliamentary debate prior to deployment of troops. Although the Government frequently turns to Parliament to provide information and statements, the opportunity to debate is complied with only when an international legal basis for military action is lacking. In other examples—such as Libya and Mali—Parliament is involved only after hostilities have started or it is excluded from discussion altogether. Even when an explicit promise is made that engagement will take place before deployment (Libya), the Government failed to respect this commitment and did not provide an explanation as to why the obligation was not fulfilled.

Second, 'There must be a possibility for debate and judgement by the forum, and an optional imposition of (informal) sanctions or rewards—and not a monologue without engagement'.[166] Although MPs can ask questions when given the opportunity to debate, at a certain point their interventions become less effective because they have very little room to hold the Government to account due to the 'rally behind the Crown' effect. Parliamentary power to compel the Government to provide information or explain its motives is crucial because it provides 'a democratic means to monitor and control government conduct'.[167] Yet, once the troops are already on the ground, Parliament's power is importantly limited. MPs can hardly question the decision of the Government and risk embarrassing the state on the international level. In times of crisis, a proper accountability relationship through which the concentration of power could be prevented gives way to bi-partisan consensus. In Bovens' terms, the debate in the House can become 'a monologue without engagement'.

This leads to the third element: the consequences and sanctions inherent in a proper accountability relationship. In 2013, the Government faced the ultimate consequence of allowing the Commons to have a say on military action—it lost the vote in Parliament and as a consequence, the Prime Minister decided not to deploy troops to Syria. Yet, in spite of the rare rebellion from the House[168] a couple of years later, the same Prime Minister circumvented the Commons refusal on military action in Syria and allowed drones and special forces to be used on the territory without further consultation of Parliament. As the Constitution Committee concluded, 'there comes a point at which the number of exceptions is so great that it effectively negates the purpose of formalizing Parliament's role'.[169]

This picture reveals that the current accountability arrangements are ineffective and fail the Bovens test. It is the Government that still enjoys all control in the relationship between itself and Parliament. It is the Government that 'decides whether there is a conflict decision', whether parliamentary involvement is necessary,[170]

---

[166] ibid.

[167] ibid, 450.

[168] Fiona De Londras and Fergal Davis argue that rebellions are rare and are only likely to occur when doing so increases the chances of MPs' re-election. F de Londras and FF Davis, 'Controlling the Executive in Times of Emergency: Competing perspectives on Effective Oversight Mechanisms' (2010) 30 *Oxford Journal of Legal Studies* 19, 32.

[169] House of Lords, Constitution Committee, 2nd Report 2013, [58].

[170] Blick, 'Emergency powers' (n 129) 206.

and even when a consultation should take place.[171] Parliament's ability to ask questions and pass judgement is curtailed by complicit subsequent practice in which MPs have—either because of the timing of engagement or because of lack of information—had to accept a reduced function for themselves. Finally, the Government's monopoly over the development of the convention,[172] and the ability to carve out exceptions has 'limit[ed] the effectiveness of a formalised process in enhancing Parliament's control over deployment decisions'.[173] If an unwilling House of Commons refuses to provide its approval and support to the Government, then it can be easily sidelined through exceptions to the convention. The impact of any sanctions the forum (Parliament) may have against the actor (the Government) can thus be minimised.

Although the War Powers Convention is celebrated for creating greater account-ability, in practice there is a great degree of variance in the tools that can be used to hold the Government to account. Most crucially, the Executive still enjoys great flexibility in the arena of war powers.[174] Although some might argue that this power exists in spite of the convention, we believe that it is precisely because the rules are contained in a convention that they remain so malleable. 'The formation, adaptation and deletion of conventions is a continuing process which allows the Executive to determine what the constitution is.'[175] The inherent adaptability of conventions not only preserves the flexibility in this area, but also makes it impos-sible to conclude whether and when the Government may be engaged in uncon-stitutional behaviour. As Taylor argues:

> [D]espite the presence of conventions regulating the powers of the Crown, ... a gap in accountability nevertheless remains. Given the lack of clear rules governing the exercise of the prerogative, as well as the government's traditional dominance over the House of Commons, any appearance of political accountability or control as a consequence of ... conventions is purely illusionary.

In the end, 'dependency upon ... conventions is meaningless, where it is ineffective at controlling governmental behaviour'.[176]

Figure 3.3 (below) shows what remains of the War Powers Convention after the analysis of practice in this chapter. Looking at the exceptions, it is unsurprising that conventions have been described by scholars as 'profoundly undemocratic elements' in the constitution.[177] If the underlying reason for the adoption of the

---

[171] House of Lords (n 169), [52].

[172] R Hazell, 'The United Kingdom' in *Constitutional Conventions in Westminster Systems* (n 41) 186; Blick n 30, 203; Blick n 53, 259.

[173] House of Lords (n 169) [58].

[174] This concerned the Committee somewhat and it therefore recommended that the Government amend the Manual to include a detailed description of the internal arrangements in making decisions on the use of armed force. ibid, [35].

[175] B Hough, 'Conventions and Democracy' (2000) 29 *Anglo-American Law Review* 368, 370.

[176] RB Taylor 'Foundational and regulatory conventions: exploring the constitutional significance of Britain's dependency upon conventions' (2015) *Public Law* 614, 617.

[177] Hough, 'Conventions and Democracy' (n 175).

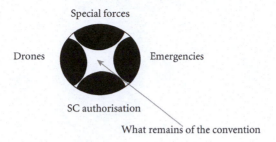

Figure 3.3: The remains of the convention

War Powers Convention was to maximise parliamentary accountability for decisions on military action, then this chapter has shown how successive governments have used the inherent malleability of the convention to reduce its usefulness as an accountability tool. From this perspective, the War Powers Convention is an inappropriate and ineffective tool to deliver on what it promised. For us, it is therefore merely a distraction.

4

The Deployment of Secrecy

HAYLEY J HOOPER[1]

Chapter three exposed the myriad of exceptions to which the War Powers Convention is subject, to the extent that focus upon its creation and application masks the realities of the relationship between government and Parliament in the context of war powers. But these exceptions to the application of the War Powers Convention form only part of the story. There is another problematic dimension to the relationship between government and Parliament which deserves standalone examination: the role of secrecy. In fact, secrecy hides in plain sight in our Constitution. It has done so throughout history, and continues to do so in our contemporary arrangements. This chapter explores how four forms of secrecy in the British Constitution actively impede the participation of our democratic representatives in armed conflict decision-making. Even after the genesis and crystallisation of the War Powers Convention, secrecy continues to vex the relationship between the Government and Parliament in the context of debates prior to the deployment of troops.

Despite playing host to the so-called 'mother of parliaments', Britain has a long history of enacting broadly drawn Official Secrets legislation.[2] Parliamentary select committees can debate and vote in secret,[3] and local government assemblies can enter closed sessions at the discretion of their Executive.[4] Some level of secrecy is of course to be expected in relation to war powers. After all, wars are partly fought and won on the basis of superior classified intelligence. There will always be a need for a core of 'genuine national security secrecy' which 'works to protect information that would pose an identifiable threat to the security of the nation by compromising its defence or the conduct of its foreign affairs'.[5] The following analysis reveals that the nature of secrecy in the context of war powers is far

---

[1] Initial drafts of part B were written by Veronika Fikfak and the final draft of part B partly relies on her text.

[2] JAG Griffith, 'The Official Secrets Act 1989' (1989) 16 *Modern Law Review* 273.

[3] Cabinet Office, 'Giving Evidence to Select Committees: Guidance for Civil Servants' aka 'The Osmotherly Rules' (London, Cabinet Office, 2014) para [37].

[4] Local Government Act 2000, s 22(2) and The Local Authorities (Executive Arrangements) (Meetings and Access to Information) (England) Regulations 2012 (SI 2089/2012).

[5] S Aftergood, 'Reducing Government Secrecy' (2009) 27 *Yale Law and Policy Review* 399, 402.

from monolithic. Misuse of secrecy by government has and continues to have a corrosive effect on Parliament's ability to exercise its constitutional functions. This chapter argues that secrecy is endemic in the relationship between government and Parliament, in both historical and contemporary practice. The negative effects of secrecy begin where decisions to go to war are taken within the internal machinery of the Government. Secrecy's ill-effects can be seen in the way government uses secrecy as a justification for excluding Parliament altogether, or releasing select amounts of sensitive information to a small number of parliamentarians who are subject to an oath of confidentiality. Secrecy is also used to justify the public presentation of information based upon classified sources to Parliament in a selective, acontextual manner.

The end result of the deployment of secrecy by governments relation to war powers is that it allows the twin evils of groupthink and information asymmetry to flourish. Decisions to go to war have always been made by a handful of individuals within government. Minimising the number of people has been encouraged because cohesive groups more easily and more quickly reach decisions and can react to different situations. Yet, this type of decision-making also encourages groupthink. Groupthink describes a 'mode of thinking that people engage in when they are deeply involved in a cohesive in-group'. This impacts negatively upon the quality of decision-making because the members' desire for 'unanimity override[s] their motivation to realistically appraise alternative courses of action'.[6] Governmental control of the flow of information to Parliament also perpetuates and unequal, and asymmetric, relationship between the Government and Parliament. The term 'information asymmetry' describes a situation where one constitutional actor possesses a greater or better degree of information relating to a decision than the other, and in turn gains an unfair advantage, such as a capacity to manipulate the flow of information, or predetermine the outcome of a particular discussion. This is a particular problem in respect of sensitive information, such as classified material or diplomatic negotiations, both of which feature heavily in armed conflict decisions.

This chapter tracks the uses of classified information (or secret intelligence as it is also known) on a spectrum which ranges from a blanket ban on disclosure by government, to the carefully managed public disclosure of claims based on classified information. This is not an historical trajectory per se, but there has been a generally marked increase in disclosure from the advent of the First World War up to the present day. In part A the phenomenon of groupthink will be set out and explained. As the decision to enter (or refrain from) armed conflict is amongst the most serious a country can take, it is vital that decisions are informed by a panoply of views, and that they stand up to scrutiny. The chief evils of groupthink are the suffocation of effective scrutiny and dissent. Secrecy in its various forms explored in each of the subsequent parts of this chapter creates information asymmetries

---

[6] P T'Hart, *Groupthink in Government: A study of small groups and policy failure* (Baltimore, The Johns Hopkins University Press, 1990) 7.

which help perpetuate the risk (and the reality) that groupthink will continue to flourish in the context of war powers.

In part A, the phenomena of groupthink and information asymmetry are explained in order to illustrate the defects they cause in decision-making processes. Part B then moves to explain how secrecy is used to insulate governmental decision-making processes and perpetuate maximum information asymmetry in the context of blanket bans on disclosure of sensitive information to Parliament, and the formation of secret diplomatic agreements before engaging Parliament on the question of war. Part C then explains how secret information is selectively shared with parliamentarians, either by making confidential disclosures to small groups of MPs, or by publishing selective digests of information based upon secret intelligence. These practices have generated well-documented problems. Part D sets out the various internal reforms made to the intelligence machinery by the incoming Coalition Government in 2010, in an attempt to undo the damage to public confidence caused by the Iraq War intelligence fiasco. It also explains how intelligence continued to be presented publicly to Parliament post-2010. Finally, part E argues that the foregoing examples compel us to understand the impact of secrecy in a new light: ie to see it as a tool for exclusion of participants in the decision-making process.

When viewed at a glance, this trajectory described in part A to E looks like progress from blanket secrecy of classified information towards at least partial (and welcome) publicity. But as we shall see, even in the face of public disclosure government deploys secrecy to control the messages Parliament receives. This is a trend (which varies only by degree as opposed to kind) that can be found in the journey from blanket refusal of disclosure through to the public presentation of claims based upon classified information in recent years. Secrecy in one form or another continues to play a pivotal role in insulating core government claims about the desirability of armed conflicts from meaningful scrutiny. The effect of this, in short, is that groupthink or the personal dispositions of the Prime Minister towards conflict can remain largely unchallenged. This is because information asymmetries remain present in every aspect of government interaction with Parliament over the war prerogative.

A. Groupthink and Information Asymmetry

Chapter three explained that the purpose of the War Powers Convention, as expressed in the Cabinet Manual, is to allow the House of Commons to debate on the deployment of troops prior to the initiation of armed conflict. It is trite to state that any informed debate requires all sides to have access to adequate information about the decision at hand. But throughout the twentieth century and up until the present day, the relationship between government and Parliament in the context of the war prerogative has been far from a level playing field.

The Government monopolises information, and uses the need for secrecy to protect the national interest as a justification for insulating decisions from the full force of the democratic process. The worst potential consequence of this (which has proven very real in the context of the Iraq War and the Libyan intervention) is that groupthink has infected and distorted the governmental decision-making process.

Groupthink is a pervasive phenomenon in armed conflict and national security decision-making. The basic premise behind the groupthink theory is that policy failures can be attributed to faulty decision-making procedures amongst small, secretive, informal groups of officials.[7] The core problem with the presence of groupthink is that it exacerbates concurrence seeking within the group, consequently leading to the loss of adversarial interrogation of policy choices. The presence of groupthink makes actors blind to alternative courses of action, and results in '*flaws in the operation of small, high level decision groups at the helm of major projects or policies that become fiascos*'.[8] Moreover, the chances of groupthink are markedly increased in a crisis situation, such as the build-up to an armed conflict.[9] The creation of the September Dossier on Weapons of Mass Destruction in Saddam Hussein's regime by the Blair Government (discussed below) has been described as the 'nadir' of 'sofa government'.[10] The term 'sofa government' was coined to describe Tony Blair's informal style of prime ministerialism whereby crucial decisions were taken within a small, informal circle of trusted individuals. This is the type of scenario which is emblematic of groupthink. Sir John Chilcot's Report on the Iraq Inquiry noted that in respect of Iraq the majority of key decisions were made: 'bilaterally between Mr Blair and the relevant Secretary of State … Some of those meetings were minuted; some were not'.[11] This culminated in the publication of a controversial dossier, which was alleged to be the work of the Cabinet Joint Intelligence Committee (JIC). It contained allegations about Iraq's capability to use weapons of mass destruction (WMDs), which later proved to be unfounded.

Although none of the subsequent inquiries into the approach to the Iraq War of 2003 found any evidence of embellishment by the Government of the relevant intelligence information, several reports pointed out shortcomings in the way in which intelligence officials and policy-makers interacted. For example, The Butler Inquiry reviewed the intelligence in relation to WMDs in Iraq, subsequently concluding that 'we are concerned that the informality and circumscribed character of the Government's procedures which we saw in the context of policy-making towards Iraq risks reducing the scope for informed collective political judgement'.[12] This is a classic example of the stifling of informed deliberation

---

[7] ibid, 22.
[8] ibid, 4, emphasis added.
[9] ibid, 7.
[10] J Richards, *A Guide to National Security* (Oxford, OUP, 2012) 31.
[11] J Chilcot, 'Report of the Iraq Inquiry' 6 July 2016, HC 264, Executive Summary, para 399.
[12] The Rt Hon Lord Butler of Brockwell KG GCB CVO, 'Review of Intelligence on Weapons of Mass Destruction: Report of a Committee of Privy Counsellors' 14 July 2014, HC 898, para [611], emphasis added.

which takes place when groupthink sets in. If groupthink flourishes, and a leaders' perceptions or pre-commitments go unchecked, then, the opportunity for parliamentary engagement and meaningful influence is profoundly weakened. This can have the result of making both governments and legislatures blind to any alternative to military action. The pursuit of unchecked small-group policies can lead to the wider misrepresentation of facts, and long-term strategic errors.

Groupthink theory reveals that membership of the group and secrecy become ends in and of themselves. If small-group secrecy is rigidly maintained it logically leads to the insulation of the decision-making group. This prevents outsiders from critiquing the groups' decisions, or offering advice. This results in a 'psychological impact upon the individual members of being part of a small group acting out a secret policy initiative ... the group in itself becomes a value, and the preservation of secrecy is held essential for the success of the group'.[13] This sense of belonging also discourages members from risking their membership by challenging the wisdom of the group's perspective.[14]

Groupthink has been used to explain the faulty decision-making process which resulted in the Iran-Contra Affair in the United States. Officials and agencies in the Reagan Administration sold arms to Iranian-backed extremists in an attempt to secure the release of American hostages. Afterwards they proceeded to use the funds from these transactions to fund the Contra rebels in Nicaragua. It was noted that during the critical phase of Iran-Contra 'evidence suggests that the key strategic decisions were, indeed, taken by a small, basically informal group of officials'.[15] Moreover, the obsession with secrecy became so great that Congress was kept in the dark, despite the legal obligation to keep it informed of national security activities.[16] The conclusion of the Tower Review Board (established to investigate the affair) was that:

> Because of the obsession with secrecy, interagency consideration of the initiative was limited to the cabinet level ... This deprived those responsible for the initiative of considerable expertise—on the situation on Iran, on the difficulties of dealing with terrorists, on the mechanics of conducting a diplomatic opening. *It also kept the plan from receiving a tough, critical review.*[17]

Groupthink flourishes in small, secretive groups, severely limiting the extent to which policies are tested and exacerbates poor decision-making on critical issues. Groupthink can also allow the personal philosophies of the leader of the Executive to remain unchallenged, which can result in a predetermination of the goals of the conflict, and in turn influence how the case for armed conflict is made before democratic institutions.[18]

---

[13] *Groupthink in Government* (n 6) 153–54.
[14] ibid, 153–54.
[15] ibid, 235.
[16] ibid, 238.
[17] ibid, 238.
[18] EN Saunders, *Leaders at War: How Presidents Shape Military Interventions* (Ithaca NY, Cornell University Press, 2011) ch 7.

B. Complete Asymmetry: Refusing Debates and Making Secret Pre-commitments

I. Justifying Secrecy: Protecting Classified Information

The practice of starving Parliament of information in relation to war powers has a long history.[19] Often, the presence of any sensitive information (be it secret intelligence or diplomatic material) in the context of the case for war compelled successive governments to claim that Parliament was simply an inappropriate forum for discussion of such issues. The risks to diplomatic relations, strategy, or troops on the ground was perceived to outweigh the potential benefits to be derived from disclosure and democratic scrutiny. In the approach to the Falklands War in the early 1980s, the Thatcher Government insisted that there were limits to what Parliament could scrutinise at a time when the Government was engaged in critical diplomatic negotiations. Although Parliament would be provided with enough information (by the Government's own definition), the Government had to ensure that it did not reveal too much.[20] In this context, the Prime Minister insisted: 'We really cannot have a full debate on military options with the House making a decision. Nothing would be more helpful to the enemy or more damaging to our boys'.[21] Thatcher's concern was that the Argentinians should be prevented from accessing information sensitive to national security which might have been revealed openly on the Floor of the House.

Similar justifications for secrecy were relied upon in subsequent situations. In respect of Kosovo (on which Parliament was permitted a debate, but not a vote), Tony Blair insisted that 'It is not possible for us—nor should it be expected of us—to go into every last detail of military tactics, strategy and capability when we are trying to conduct a campaign'.[22] On the same note, the Defence Secretary argued that 'there are many questions to which enormously detailed answers would be of more advantage to the opponents of the alliance than to the House'.[23] Later, in respect of conflict with the Taliban in Afghanistan, Blair told the House of Commons that he would share information setting out the essence of the reasons for concluding that Osama Bin Laden and Al-Qaeda were allied to the Taliban. However, he also maintained that 'much of the evidence that we have is intelligence and highly sensitive. It is not possible without compromising people or security to release precise details and fresh information that is daily coming in'.[24]

---

[19] R Joseph, *The War Prerogative: History, Reform, and Constitutional Design* (Oxford, OUP, 2013) 69–75.

[20] In fact the Government was concerned that it had already revealed too much information. See, for example, HL Deb 4 May 1982, vol 429, col 1078, Lord Shackleton.

[21] HC Deb 13 May 1982, vol 23, cols 943–44, Michael Foot and Margaret Thatcher.

[22] HC Deb 13 April 1999, vol 329, col 25, Tony Blair.

[23] HC Deb 26 May 1999, vol 332, col 359, George Robertson.

[24] HC Deb 4 October 2001, vol 372, col 672.

Alongside strategic reasons, the volume or complexity of relevant information held by Ministers is also used to justify near total secrecy. In fact, if a Minister wishes to avoid giving information, they can easily do so.[25] In 2004 the Public Administration Select Committee took the view that the Government's approach to answering questions 'has been characterised as minimising the opportunity for scrutiny of its actions through careful and skilful crafting of answers'.[26] Previously, this craft

> had been refined to the point where it was said of civil servants preparing answers for their Ministers that they followed a simple rule, 'Nothing may be said which is not true: but it is as unnecessary as it is sometimes undesirable, even in the public interest, to say everything relevant which is true; and the facts may be arranged in any convenient order. It is wonderful what can be done within these limits by a skilful draftsman'.[27]

Statements to Parliament on the subject of war are usually kept as general as possible. During the Suez crisis of 1956, Prime Minister Eden told MPs that he had been compelled 'to take certain precautionary measures of a military nature', including the movement of the navy, army and the Royal Air Force.[28] Responses of Government Ministers to questions posed in Parliament were carefully crafted along the following vague lines: 'In the opinion of His Majesty's Government any statement or discussion on the subject at the present moment would be inexpedient'.[29] Responses of this nature were found to be an endemic barrier to parliamentary accountability in the context of national security and armed conflict. As Sir Richard Scott concluded in his inquiry into the export of defence equipment to Iraq in contravention of stated Government policy: 'In circumstances where disclosure might be politically or administratively inconvenient the balance struck by the Government comes down, time and time again, against full disclosure'.[30] This trend has persisted into the twenty-first century. A 2016 letter to the Foreign Secretary from the Foreign Affairs Committee (FAC) expressed significant frustration regarding the Government's unwillingness to provide information on military activity in Libya. The letter, authored by Crispin Blunt MP, bemoaned that Government briefings were 'so narrow as to be wholly and deliberately misleading to the uninformed reader'.[31]

---

[25] DC Watt, 'Foreign Affairs, the Public Interest and the Right to Know' (1963) 34 *The Political Quarterly* 124.

[26] House of Commons Public Administration Select Committee, 'Ministerial Accountability and Parliamentary Questions' 3rd Report 2003–04, HC 355, [2].

[27] ibid, citing HE Dale, *The Higher Civil Service of Great Britain* (Oxford, OUP, 1941) 104–05, quoted in DN Chester and N Bowring, *Questions in Parliament* (Oxford, OUP, 1962) 239.

[28] HC Deb 2 August 1956, vol 557, col 1606.

[29] HC Deb 4 March 1901, vol 90, cols 377–78. See also DL Keir, *The Constitutional History of Modern Britain 1485–1937* (Adam and Charles Black, 1938) 231, 244 and ZS Steiner, *Britain and the Origins of the First World War* (London, MacMillan, 1977) 195.

[30] Lord Justice Scott, 'Report of the Inquiry into the Export of Defence Equipment and Dual-Use Goods to Iraq and Related Prosecutions' HC Deb 1996, 115, D1.165, and quoted further in HC Deb 1995–96, 313, [47].

[31] C Blunt MP, 'Letter from the Foreign Affairs Committee to the Foreign Secretary' (12 April 2016) <www.parliament.uk/documents/commons-committees/foreign-affairs/Correspondence/2015-20-Parliament/160412-Letter-to-Foreign-Secretary-on-Libya.pdf> accessed 17 September 2017.

This phenomenon of blanket non-disclosure extends beyond the protection of specific matters of detail, however. Often, the Government is hesitant to provide information even when the MPs seek its commitment as to how it intends to engage Parliament in the future.[32] In relation to the Iraq War of 2003, when Graham Allen MP asked whether the Government would 'bring forward proposals to make it a requirement for Parliament to be consulted on the use of [its] power under [the] Royal Prerogative to take the country to war',[33] Tony Blair refused to make a formal commitment, insisting that it was already possible for the House to be given opportunities for such debates.[34] The follow-up question of what precisely the words 'given opportunities' meant also remained unanswered.[35] The most representative vignette, however, comes from the Suez Crisis. So poor was the quality of information provided to Parliament that when asked whether Britain was at war or not, the Prime Minister simply refused to provide an answer.[36]

II. Secret Arrangements and Pre-commitments

Total secrecy can also be used to reduce the discourse in Parliament to near redundancy. The role of secret diplomatic arrangements and international pre-commitments by governments before parliamentary engagement results in the pre-determination of policy. This practice truly speaks to the nature of Parliament's secret war. Parliamentary support was frequently sought without disclosing secret international arrangements with other states. On other occasions, Parliament was asked to approve military action on the basis of misleading and inaccurate information; and when information was provided, this was done in order to guarantee approval of forthcoming action. The Government would allow Parliament to engage on the matter, but withhold any information relating to prior diplomatic activities. Parliament would thus be unaware that government policy had been pre-determined, and that any chance of meaningful scrutiny had effectively been eviscerated. The recent innovation of the War Powers Convention does nothing to erase this history. Ultimately, the capacity of Parliament to properly exercise its function of scrutinising the Government's proposals and holding government to account depends upon the nature of the information the Government willingly provides.

Before the start of World War One, the then Foreign Secretary, Sir Edward Grey, sought Parliament's support for the Government's decision to wage war.

---

[32] HC Deb 18 November 2002, vol 394, col 19W, Graham Allen; HC Deb 28 January 1991, vol 184, cols 374–5W, Graham Allen.

[33] HC Deb 21 October 2002, vol 391, col 78W; later posed again HC Deb 27 November 2002, vol 395, col 289W, Norman Bake.

[34] ibid.

[35] HC Deb 07 November 2002, vol 392, col 452W.

[36] HC Deb 31 October 1956, vol 558, col 1453; Kyle, Suez, 377–78. Another vote on adjournment took place after Britain had already used force against Egypt. Then the support for the Government was overwhelming 320 votes to 262. HC Deb 8 November 1956, vol. 560, col 404. K Kyle, *Suez: Britain's end of Empire in the Middle East* (London, IB Tauris, 2011) 471–73, 489–90.

However, the House of Commons was unaware of pre-existing secret engagements made on behalf of the country and entered into by the Government on the international plane. Although the Ministers in the debates leading up to the war assured Parliament that no secret agreements or arrangement had committed the British military forces to join military operations on the Continent,[37] this claim was entirely untrue. Secret arrangements, from which Parliament was entirely insulated were in place. On the eve of the War, Sir Edward spoke of the agreement that the UK had secretly entered into with France and Russia, in which it promised to provide support in the case of hostilities. Therefore, when France was attacked, the Government would be embarrassed if it did not help its ally and declare war on Germany. Parliament had clearly been misled, which is generally regarded as an unconstitutional act in the political as opposed to the legal sense. Despite the prevailing wisdom that integrity in representations before Parliament is part of the constitutional bedrock, it appears to also be the subject of informal exceptions. The Cabinet Manual mandates that Ministers shall not knowingly mislead Parliament.[38] However, this rule has been made the subject of a number of exceptions over the years. Matters involving armed conflict and national security, and the emergency devaluation of currency are potentially among the list of exceptions to the rule which prohibits misleading Parliament if the benefits of secrecy are reasonably judged by the Minister to outweigh disclosure of relevant information in public.[39]

Secret arrangements were also made during the Suez Crisis of 1956. Due to a strong polarisation between the Government and the Opposition regarding policy matters, Parliament was not advised of secret arrangements and commitments between the British Government and Israel that were made prior to the deployment of troops. Namely, the British Government secretly promised Israel that if it initiated hostilities with Egypt, Britain and France would issue an ultimatum to both Egypt and Israel to withdraw from the region. Thereafter Britain would launch an intervention to regain control and restore Western ownership of the Suez Canal. Since its inception in 1948 Israel had been in a longstanding dispute with Egypt and so was ready to commit to the plan.[40] When Israel therefore launched its attack in October, the UK Parliament was only informed a day later when the majority had

---

[37] Government Ministers made several statements to the House between 1911 and 1914, in which they denied the existence of any secret agreements or arrangements; see HC Deb 8 March 1911, vol 32, cols 1120, 1191; HC Deb 30 March 1911, vol 33, col 107.

[38] HM Government, *The Ministerial Code* (London, Cabinet Office, 2016) para 1.2(c): 'It is of paramount importance that Ministers give accurate and truthful information to Parliament, correcting any inadvertent error at the earliest opportunity. Ministers who knowingly mislead Parliament will be expected to offer their resignation to the Prime Minister'.

[39] See Treasury and Civil Service Committee, *The Role of the Civil Service*, 5th Report of 1993–94, HC 27, paras 124–26, and the Minutes of Evidence (Sir Robin Butler). For further discussion see A Tomkins, 'A right to mislead Parliament?' (1996) 16 *Legal Studies* 63.

[40] Since the creation of Israel in 1948, cargo shipments to and from Israel had been subject to Egyptian authorisation. This interference continued even after Security Council issued a Resolution in 1951 (UNSC Res 95/1951, *The Palestine Question*). The situation increasingly escalated when Egypt sponsored raids into Israel, killing many civilians. These raids in turn proved military reprisals from Israel.

no choice but to support the Government.[41] Parliament was completely unaware of these arrangements, and could therefore provide no meaningful scrutiny of Government policy, let alone achieve accountability.

Evidence of secret pre-commitments persists into the twenty-first century. In respect of the Iraq War Tony Blair had promised Parliament that there would be a debate and vote on a substantive motion of support for military action prior to conflict for the first time in history. However, the Chilcot Report reveals that the Cabinet may not have been fully committed to respecting the will of Parliament had the vote been lost. The US campaign, to which Mr Blair had already secretly pledged support, was scheduled to begin the day following the vote, and Mr Straw made clear in a minute to Mr Blair that 'We also need to start working up a Plan B for our armed forces if we cannot be sure of Commons' approval for their inclusion in the initial invasion of Iraq'.[42] Another declassified letter from Mr Blair to US President George W Bush written on 7 July 2002 stated that 'I will be with you, whatever'.[43] It has subsequently become clear from the Chilcot Report that at this time Mr Blair was personally committed to military intervention in Iraq.[44]

The practice of limiting Parliament's access to information is partly connected to the 'old feudal anachronism' that the decision to go to war resides exclusively with the Executive.[45] Within the Government, political power is concentrated in the Cabinet and in times of war the real power usually lies with an even smaller group: the War Cabinet. This practice is thought to be justifiable because it allows Governments to respond quickly to developing conflict situations. But the downside is that it shrouds war in secrecy by preventing any democratic engagement with armed conflict decisions. The legacy of this practice has led some Prime Ministers to take the view that Parliament 'should act as an approver of the policy already initiated' in the context of war.[46] Requests to share information with Parliament, then, are not necessarily welcomed. The Government often regards such requests for materials or for relevant information as troublesome, because they expose sources and have the potential to anger foreign powers.[47] This can lead to an attitude of

---

[41] Though, readers will recall that what an adjournment motion amounts to in substance (ie military action, support of troops on the ground, or decision to send the House back into recess) is often unclear.

[42] Chilcot Report (n 11) vol 3.8, [150], PM 03/022 (Declassified) Minute from Mr Straw to Mr Blair, 'Iraq: What if we cannot win the second resolution?', <www.iraqinquiry.org.uk/media/213911/2003-03-11-minute-straw-to-prime-minister-iraq-wha-t-if-we-cannot-win-the-second-resolution.pdf> accessed 1 October 2016.

[43] 'Note on Iraq' Prime Minister Blair's Letter to President George W Bush 28 July 2002 Ref 198/02 <www.iraqinquiry.org.uk/media/243761/2002-07-28-note-blair-to-bush-note-on-iraq.pdf> accessed 10 February 2017.

[44] Chilcot Report (n 11) Executive Summary, para 94.

[45] HC Deb 15 January 1991, vol 183, col 777, Tony Benn.

[46] T Häkkinen, *The Royal Prerogative Redefined: Parliamentary Debate on the Role of the British Parliament in Large-scale Military Deployments, 1982–2003* (Jyväskylä Studies in Humanities 224), 149, referring to Margaret Thatcher. Tony Benn strongly criticised this position, arguing that it had placed too much power in the hands of one individual, and he described the system as an 'elected monarchy'; see T Benn, 'The Case for Constitutional Premiership' (1980) 33 *Parliamentary Affairs* 7–13, 19–22.

[47] J Black, *A System of Ambition? British Foreign Policy 1660–1793* (London, Longman, 1991) 47–49. J Black, 'Parliament, the Press, and Foreign Policy' (2006) 25 *Parliamentary History* 9, 14.

contempt towards Parliament on the part of Foreign and Commonwealth Office Officials. One such official commented: 'What a nuisance they are with their ill-timed questions! They know nothing about foreign affairs: it is our business not theirs'.[48] Thus governments do not always accede to parliamentary requests for information. Instead, history demonstrates that when information is provided it is either redacted or delayed when the interests of security, political expediency, or international diplomacy so require.[49]

Parliamentarians unsurprisingly complain about the presence of 'secret diplomacy' of the nature described above. Molteno argued that such activities represented

a continuation of that old and disastrous system where a few men in charge of the State, wielding the whole force of the State, make secret engagements and secret arrangements, carefully veiled from the knowledge of the people, who are as dumb as driven cattle without a voice on the question.[50]

This sidelining of Parliament causes frustration and anger among MPs who feel ignored.[51] The end result is that Parliament has no other choice but to support the Government (as troops have potentially already committed to the hostilities). The only alternative option, suggested by the Solicitor General in 1743, in which Parliament would collectively refrain from exercising its right to advise the Crown 'except in cases where we have full information, and are perfectly masters of the affair'[52] has yet to be utilised.

C. Partial Asymmetry: Selective Disclosures

As shown above, the restriction of decisions to small, concurring groups of individuals promotes secrecy, as keeping the decision-making process insulated becomes an end in itself. Pozen has suggested that there is a dichotomy between deep and shallow secrets which influences the extent to which the publicity is realised in governance. Deep secrets are normatively undesirable because they: 'block out all sunlight from the decisional process beyond the small-circle of secret-keepers ... In addition to corruption and abuse, ideological amplification, bias, and groupthink will be more likely to flourish.'[53] A secret is 'deep' when

---

[48] Quoted in ZS Steiner, *The Foreign Office and Foreign Policy 1898–1914* (Cambridge, CUP, 1969) 197.

[49] GC Gibbs, 'Parliament and Foreign Policy in the Age of Stanhope and Walpole' (1962) 77 *The English Historical Review* 18, 32–33.

[50] HC Deb 3 August 1914, vol 65, col 1851. See also HC Deb 3 August 1914, vol 65, cols 2089–90, Percy Molteno (L Dem).

[51] HC Deb 24 September 2002, vol 390, col 97, Edward Garnier.

[52] Solicitor General Murray, during debate in the Commons on continuing the Hanoverian troops' British pay: HC Deb 6 December 1743, vol 13, col 252.

[53] DE Pozen, 'Deep Secrecy' (2010) 62 *Stanford Law Review* 257, 280.

'a small group of similarly situated officials conceals its existence from the public and from other officials'. By contrast, a secret is 'shallow' when 'ordinary citizens understand they are being denied relevant information and have some ability to estimate its content'.[54] This analysis implies that deep secrets are incompatible with democratic governance, but shallow secrets are tolerable.[55] However, this distinction only takes us so far in the context of parliamentary control of the war prerogative. The journey from blanket non-disclosure and secret diplomatic agreements towards the partial disclosure of intelligence information represents a journey from deep to shallow secrecy. This remains unsatisfactory because shallow secrets still permit damaging information asymmetries, and potentially permit groupthink to go unchecked.

I. Sharing Information on 'Privy Council Terms'

Whilst the policies of blanket non-disclosure and secret pre-commitments create an extreme information asymmetry and perpetuate 'deep secrets', the following policies of partial disclosure are equally problematic in their own way. Disclosure can be used selectively and tactically, to keep certain classes of parliamentarians informed of the Government's perspective without permitting public scrutiny, or public dissent about the chosen policy perspective. The most concrete example of a method of selective disclosure which perpetuates information asymmetry is found in the practice of sharing sensitive intelligence-based information on 'Privy Council terms'. The Privy Council has been described in Parliament as one of 'the shadier part(s) of our constitution'.[56] Its origin dates back to the middle ages. The present-day incarnation comprises all Cabinet Ministers (including the serving and former Prime Ministers), some Junior Ministers, and holders of senior appointments in Parliament, the Anglican Church, or the judiciary. Membership is for life. The Prime Minister is not required to be a Privy Councillor, but by 'unavoidable convention'[57] he or she will be. The Prime Minister may unilaterally appoint Privy Councillors, without any prior vetting of appointees.

All Privy Counsellors swear the Privy Councillor's Oath, first made public by Tony Blair in a Written Parliamentary answer in 2009.[58] The Oath, which has remained essentially unchanged since the Tudor era,[59] includes an obligation to 'keep secret all Matters committed and revealed unto you, or that shall be treated

---

[54] ibid, 274.
[55] A similar argument about the nature of deep and shallow secrets is made in A Gutmann and D Thomson, *Democracy and Disagreement: Why moral conflict cannot be avoided in politics and what should be done about it* (Cambridge MA, Harvard University Press, 1996) ch 3.
[56] HL Deb 12 May 2009, vol 710 col 1004, Lord McNally.
[57] R Brazier, *Ministers of the Crown* (Oxford, Clarendon Press, 1997) 83.
[58] HC Deb 28 July 2009, vol 317, col 182.
[59] O Stone-Lee, 'So what is the Privy Council?' BBC News Online (18 February 2003) <news.bbc.co.uk/1/hi/uk_politics/2589087.stm> accessed 17 September 2017.

of secretly in Council' in the course of duties as a Privy Councillor. Therefore, if classified information is revealed to Privy Councillors in this context, they are not notified under the Official Secrets Act 1989. All members of the Intelligence and Security Committee, and its successor the Parliamentary Intelligence and Security Committee, are also Privy Counsellors.[60] As of 2009 there were an estimated 550 members of the Privy Council, only some of whom played an active part in day-to-day governmental affairs. Privy Counsellors are entrusted with site of confidential information thought unsuitable for discussion in the public domain. This creates three distinct but related problems for the quality of parliamentary engagement in respect of armed conflict decisions. First, the system of sharing information on Privy Council terms creates a disparity in the level of information between Government and Parliament. The second problem is related but distinct: the sharing of information on Privy Council terms creates a privileged class of parliamentarians who can see certain sensitive information chosen by the Government for disclosure to this select group. Thirdly and finally, this mechanism of sharing intelligence-based information has the potential to artificially inflate the worth of classified information in the minds of parliamentarians without the privileged access provided by Privy Council membership.[61]

Whilst some defenders of the Privy Council dismiss it merely as a shorthand way of referring (albeit inaccurately) to government 'Ministers collectively',[62] the Privy Council remains an institution with a broad membership which wields considerable power. One phenomenon that may explain the willingness of parliamentarians to accept the longstanding government refusal to answer questions on the floor of either House concerning intelligence and national security is the ability to make intelligence and national security information available on 'Privy Council terms' to Leaders of the Opposition. Hennessy lists the rather large scope of matters which have been considered 'on Privy Council terms' since 1945, which includes: the Middle East in the 1950s, and MacMillan's conversations with President Kennedy during the Cuban Missile Crisis, Whitehall defensive measures against subversion by the Soviet Union, Ministry of Defence restructuring, the Profumo Affair and the creation of the Security Commission, the future of the nuclear deterrent and the pound sterling.[63]

It has been suggested that making use of Privy Council terms is a method for the avoidance of political opprobrium. For example, there is a 'clear advantage for the Government sharing intelligence information with the Opposition parliamentarians on Privy Council terms in that [it] prevents Opposition

---

[60] H Bochel, A Defty and J Kirkpatrick, *Watching the Watchers: Parliament and the Intelligence Services* (New York, NY, Palgrave MacMillan, 2014) 78; Justice and Security Act 2013, Part 1.

[61] M Travers, L Van Boven and C Judd, 'The secrecy heuristic: inferring quality from secrecy in foreign policy contexts' (2014) 35 *Political Psychology* 97.

[62] HL Deb 12 May 2009, vol 710, col 1010, The Lord President of the Council (Baroness Royall of Blaisdon).

[63] P Hennessy, *The Prime Minister: The Office and its Holders Since 1945* (London, Allen Lane: The Penguin Press, 2000) 61–62.

members from making political capital out of what they have been told'.[64] In the context of the suspected infiltration by Soviet agents in Whitehall in 1963 it was suggested that 'MacMillan was only too grateful that the Labour Party had offered him a degree of protection on the floor of the House of Commons'.[65] It is therefore unsurprising that parliamentarians do not always welcome the sharing of information on such terms, as it is undoubtedly insulated from the normal cut and thrust of parliamentary politics.[66]

More recently, in respect of both the Iraq War of 2003, and prior to the debate on military action against the Assad regime in August 2013, the Leader of the Opposition had access to sensitive information on Privy Council terms. Prior to the Commons Debate on the Iraq War, the Leader of the Opposition was also given access to the so-called 'Dodgy Dossier' (the September Dossier). It remains unclear what information Opposition Leader Ed Miliband was shown prior to the Syria Debate in August 2013. When asked by Angus Robertson if he had been briefed on 'Privy Council terms' Mr Miliband affirmed that this was the case.[67] These briefings do not involve the same level of detail or access to classified information as would be revealed in intelligence sessions to members of the Cabinet. Briefings on Privy Council terms will 'not be the same as a Cabinet sitting round the table, fully briefed with all the relevant military intelligence'.[68] Sharing information in this way creates two unequal classes of parliamentarian: those who are informed, and those who are left in the dark. It should also be remembered that the Leaders of the Opposition amounts to only a handful of members of the Commons. This sharing of information is problematic because the group of parliamentarians who are given access to sensitive information are unable to publicly question the wisdom of what they have learned in the Government briefing. Opposition leaders are forced to accept or reject the information, and cannot explain why during open debate. Furthermore, this method of selective disclosure means that government still controls the decision: the small group of trusted parliamentarians who are Privy Councillors cannot effectively debate the wisdom of the classified information; so opportunities for groupthink to set in remain manifold. In short, the present arrangements inhibit Parliament from working effectively in the war powers context.

II. Selective Disclosure of Intelligence in Parliamentary Debates

Arguments based upon intelligence have been a feature of several (but not all) open parliamentary debates on armed conflict since 2003, and their presentation has been the subject of controversy. There is no agreed definition of intelligence,

---

[64] Bochel, Defty and Kirkpatrick, *Watching the Watchers* (n 60) 35.
[65] D Rodgers, *By Royal Appointment: Tales from the Privy Council—The Unknown Arm of Government* (London, Biteback Publishing, 2015) ch 25.
[66] Bochel et al, *Watching the Watchers* (n 60) 35–36.
[67] HC Deb 12 August 2013, vol 566, col 1446.
[68] HL Deb 8 July 2016, vol 773, col 2266, Baroness Smith of Newnham (LD).

but in this book we take it to mean classified information which is held by the Government for the purposes of protecting national security or conducting foreign relations.[69] Intelligence of this nature will be classified by government, as its public dissemination is considered harmful to the public interest. Therefore, intelligence is a shorthand for 'secret intelligence'. This is a composite definition, which some readers well versed in intelligence studies may find overly simplistic. However, it is sufficient for the discussions in this book.

It still remains a convention that 'Government does not comment upon intelligence matters', and there is no compulsion for government to make a public intelligence-based case in support of military action.[70] The presentation of intelligence-based claims (ie a case for war based upon classified or partially classified information) has proven as controversial a policy as the blanket ban on parliamentary engagement which dominated the twentieth century. The nadir of the public presentation of intelligence occurred in September 2002 when the New Labour Government published a dossier known as the 'September Dossier' which was endorsed by the JIC. It claimed to outline the case for war against Saddam Hussein's Iraq by drawing upon classified information in a manner suitable for public presentation. A highly controversial war followed. When the Chilcot Inquiry finally reported on 6 July 2016, the report was highly critical of the manner in which intelligence had been publicly presented as making the case for war in Iraq because it was done so in a way which made assessments seem like certainties. This was done by starving Parliament of the nuances or contingencies which are crucial components of any intelligence report. The result was that the foreword to the Dossier may have misled some parliamentarians as to the strength of the case for taking military action against Saddam Hussein's regime.

Tony Blair's decision to rely openly upon intelligence to make the case for the 2003 invasion of Iraq via the publication of the Dossier entitled 'Iraq's Weapons of Mass Destruction: The Assessment of the British Government' (the 'September Dossier') was what appeared to be a hitherto unprecedented step in open government. It was the first time a British Prime Minister had openly sought to rely upon intelligence to justify military action to the British public.[71] However, the WMDs which the foreword to the dossier categorically stated existed and could 'be ready within 45 minutes of an order to use them'[72] were never found. This led to fervent speculation about both the legality of the war and the Government's presentation of intelligence to Parliament, as the dossier was based 'in large part,

---

[69] See for example, M Warner, 'Wanted: A definition of "intelligence"' (2002) *Central Intelligence Agency* (Defence Technical Information Centre: Washington DC, 2002), and Written Security Briefing for Members of European Parliament, <www.guengl.eu/uploads/publications-documents/ERNST2. doc> accessed 24 February 2017, 1.

[70] HC Deb 15 October 2002, vol 390, cols 527–530WA.

[71] RJ Aldrich, R Cormac and MS Goodman, *Spying on the World: The Declassified Documents of the Joint Intelligence Committee 1936–2013* (Edinburgh, Edinburgh University Press, 2014) 391.

[72] HM Government, 'Iraq's Weapons of Mass Destruction: The Assessment of the British Government' (2003) *Comparative Strategy* 63, 64 ('the September Dossier').

on the work of the Joint Intelligence Committee'.[73] The foreword to the September Dossier, written by Prime Minister Tony Blair, stated: 'What I believe the assessed intelligence has *established beyond doubt* is that Saddam has continued to produce chemical and biological weapons'.[74]

By contrast, the actual report of the JIC itself (which has subsequently been declassified) expressed the intelligence relating to WMDs in the following terms: 'Intelligence *remains limited* and Saddam's own unpredictability complicates judgements ... Much of this paper is *necessarily based on judgement and assessment*.'[75] Such measured and balanced language is to be expected of the JIC, which is a Cabinet committee composed of some intelligence professionals and some senior civil servants without an intelligence background. The purpose of the JIC is to give professional (as opposed to politicised or partisan) advice to government on intelligence matters. JIC reports draw upon open and secret information in order to present the collective judgement of the British intelligence community (MI5, MI6, GCHQ and military intelligence) on any given issue.[76] Sir David Omand, the former Permanent Secretary and Intelligence and Security Coordinator at the Cabinet Office, explains that JIC Reports 'include statements about the depth and adequacy of the intelligence base behind the paper, and will start with a set of key judgments ... drawing out for the policy maker the conclusions reached by the JIC, usually with a predictive flavour ("It is *likely* that ..." etc)'.[77] Such qualified language is typical of intelligence reports. According to one former senior member of the Army Intelligence Corps: 'To the constant frustration of many of their readers in both Whitehall and Washington, JIC assessments are models of carefully weighed language. [To] interfere with the wording of a JIC assessment *runs the very real risk of altering its meaning*.'[78] The interference with the JIC report language in the foreword to the Dossier starved Parliament of the crucial nuances of the report, and thus skewed the public presentation of intelligence in favour of the case for war against Iraq.

The impact of this interference with the report's language for the purpose of public disclosure is all the more damaging because JIC Reports are finely balanced models of consensus. The reports themselves reflect that 'the JIC system is also defined by a quest for consensus. The JIC does not rely on dissenting footnotes (as the Americans do), but instead aims to issue reports expressing an agreed interdepartmental viewpoint'.[79] In this respect they may not always reflect the

---

[73] ibid, 63.

[74] ibid, 64, emphasis added.

[75] Joint Intelligence Committee, 'Declassified 2004: Assessment 9 September 2002: Iraqi use of chemical and biological weapons—possible scenarios' in Aldrich, Cormac, and Goodman, *Spying on the World* (n 71) 394, emphasis added.

[76] D Omand, *Securing the State* (London, Hurst, 2010) 36–40.

[77] ibid, 38–39; emphasis added.

[78] J Hughes-Wilson, 'Pre-war intelligence and Iraq's WMD threat: Intelligence blundering or intelligence laundering? (2004) 149 *Defence and International Security (The RUSI Journal)* 10, 12–13, emphasis added.

[79] Alrich et al, *Spying on the World* (n 71), 3.

full universe of available intelligence. If agreement is unable to be reached on the credibility of certain information by key stakeholders, then the JIC report will be limited to that which has been agreed. In this context, therefore, the JIC's assessment that intelligence remained limited on Saddam's WMDs contains hardly any categorical language. Yet the foreword to the September Dossier drafted by Tony Blair's office conveyed the impression that the evidence was certain. The fact that the Prime Minister's office changed the September 2002 assessment disseminated by the JIC in order 'to strengthen the document', is now a matter of public record.[80] This slight alteration of emphasis substantially altered its meaning. The case for war was made stronger by the misrepresentation and artificial inflation of the worth of certain classified information.

The handling of the Iraq War intelligence was made the subject of an Inquiry chaired by Lord Butler. The report opened with a quotation from Clausewitz's *On War*, reminding readers, and indeed the New Labour Government that:

> Much of the intelligence that we receive in war is contradictory, even more of it is plain wrong, and most of it is fairly dubious. What one can require ... under these circumstances, is a certain degree of discrimination, which can only be gained from knowledge of men and affairs and from good judgement. *The law of probability* must be his guide.[81]

The central criticism of both the reports of the FAC and the (then) Intelligence and Security Committee (ISC) shared a similar theme, namely, that the provision of information based upon intelligence sources to Parliament *without proper regard to the context* was counterproductive. The FAC concluded that 'the process of compiling the February dossier should have been more openly disclosed to Parliament'.[82] Moreover, 'the 45 minutes claim did not warrant the prominence given to it in the dossier, because it was based on intelligence from a single, uncorroborated source'.[83] Similarly, the ISC concluded that:

> The dossier was for public consumption and not for experienced readers of intelligence material. The 45 minutes claim, included four times, was always likely to attract attention ... As the 45 minutes claim was new to its readers, the context of the intelligence and any assessment needed to be explained.[84]

At the end of the day, and by former Prime Minister David Cameron's own admission, intelligence assessment is a 'judgement'.[85] A judgement call is by its very nature a subjective assignation of value to information: it is not a categorical

---

[80] Hughes-Wilson, 'Pre-war intelligence and Iraq's WMD threat' (n 78) 10, 12–13.

[81] C Von Clausewitz, *On War*, Vol I, Bk I, ch VI quoted in 'Review of Intelligence on Weapons of Mass Destruction' (n 12) 7, emphasis added.

[82] House of Commons Foreign Affairs Committee, 'The Decision to go to War in Iraq' 9th Report 2002–2003, HC 813, para 123.

[83] ibid, para 70.

[84] Intelligence and Security Committee, 'Iraqi Weapons of Mass Destruction—Intelligence and Assessments' Cm 5972 (2003), para 86.

[85] HC Deb 29 August 2013, vol 566, cols 1426, 1429, 1432, 1433.

statement of truth, and there is significant room for error and unreasonableness. This means that the damage done by partial or a-contextual disclosures of information can severely hamper the making of accurate judgements, with potentially disastrous consequences.

The September Dossier was also the foundation of a Privy Council terms briefing for the Leaders of the Opposition prior to its publication. It was then debated publicly on the floor of the House of Commons pursuant to an adjournment motion on 24 September 2002.[86] The problems with the debate were manifold, on both the part of the Government and of parliamentarians themselves. When the Prime Minister spoke in support of the adjournment motion (on which the House divided ayes 6, noes 64), the September Dossier was presented in the following terms:

> The dossier that we publish gives the answer … [Saddam Hussein's] weapons of mass destruction programme is active, detailed and growing … The dossier is based on the work of the British Joint Intelligence Committee … I am aware, of course, that people will have to take elements of this on the good faith of our intelligence services, but this is what they are telling me, the British Prime Minister, and my senior colleagues.[87]

The statement presented the Dossier as being the work of the JIC exclusively. Moreover, it described the conclusions as hard facts, as opposed to contingent estimations of a rapidly developing situation. The claim that the September Dossier was the work of the JIC was repeated by the Prime Minister in the course of parliamentary debate.[88]

What followed by way of debate was the general acceptance of parliamentarians over the claims put forward by the Government related to the classified intelligence. There were very few sceptical interventions on this issue. This may have been driven by the fact that the Blair Government's disclosure was a novel step, and parliamentarians were therefore unsure as to how to handle such information, given the previous historical trend of almost blanket non-disclosure. For example, the then Leader of the Opposition, Iain Duncan Smith, uncritically accepted that: 'The Government dossier confirms that Iraq is self-sufficient in biological weapons and that the Iraqi military is ready to deploy those, and chemical weapons, at some 45 minutes' notice'.[89] Others in the Opposition agreed that: 'the Government should not give us raw intelligence—their most secret intelligence—but they must tell the British people enough to gain their trust. I believe that the Government have achieved that'.[90] Bernard Jenkin MP, in summing up the debate, noted that a 'broad consensus has emerged on the dossier and the evidence, which is broadly accepted by Members on both sides of the House'.[91] Only a handful of

---

[86] HC Deb 24 September 2002, vol 390, cols 1–155.
[87] ibid, col 3, Tony Blair (PM, Labour).
[88] ibid, col 11.
[89] ibid, col 7.
[90] ibid, col 83, Robert Key (Salisbury, Conservative).
[91] ibid, col 146.

parliamentarians actually asked substantive questions which went to the integrity of the claims made in the Dossier over the course of a debate, which lasted from 11:30am until 10:14pm. Substantive questions or criticisms can be traced to only seven MPs in a debate where 72 participated and voted.[92] The majority were Labour backbenchers and the remaining two were Alex Salmond of the SNP and George Galloway, who was subsequently expelled from the Labour party over comments he made about Tony Blair in relation to Iraq, and for making statements encouraging British troops to disobey orders relating to the conflict.[93]

There were, however, several further criticisms that related to the notice and timing of the debate. George Galloway revealed that 'The biggest pity of all is that the dossier—the dance of the seven veils—finally came to light just a couple of hours before this debate began'.[94] As argued earlier in this book, it is clear that control of timing of such debates by governments to gain a strategic advantage has been a pervasive feature of the last 100 years of parliamentary engagement with the war prerogative. However, in respect of the mere handful of hours parliamentarians had to engage with 50 pages of intelligence-based source material for the first time in parliamentary history, it cannot help bring to mind the treatment of Labour politicians prior to the public release of the Scott Report. The Scott Report on the inquiry into the export of arms to Iraq, published in 1996, revealed that the Major Government had been exporting machine tools for armaments to Iraq in contravention of their stated policy. The conclusions of the Report were so damning to the Conservative Government, that Members of the Opposition were given mere hours to digest its several thousand pages before its results were made public in a press conference. There is, of course, a numerical difference between 55 pages (the September Dossier) and 2000 pages (the Scott Report), but if the aim of Parliament is critical scrutiny, this still amounts to a 'farcical test of [MP's] ability to speed read'.[95]

In the debate on the substantive motion on Iraq which followed on 18 March 2003[96] the Resolution which the House of Commons approved by 396:217 votes opened as follows: 'this House notes its decisions of 25th November 2002 and 26th February 2003 to endorse UN Security Council Resolution 1441; recognises that Iraq's weapons of mass destruction and long range missiles ... pose a threat to international peace and security'.[97] The previous acceptance and endorsement of the intelligence-based claims was therefore central to securing parliamentary support for war in Iraq. Although the Chilcot Inquiry found that there was no improper

---

[92] ibid, col 56 (Alex Salmond, SNP, Banff and Buchan), col 81 (Alan Simpson, Labour, Nottingham South), col 100 (Alice Mahon, Labour, Halifax), col 108 (Peter Kilfoyle, Labour Liverpool Walton), col 112 (Doug Henderson, Labour, Newcastle upon Tyne North), col 131 (Roger Godsiff, Labour, Birmingham, Sparkbrook and Small Heath).

[93] M Tempest, 'George Galloway expelled from Labour' *The Guardian* (23 October 2003).

[94] HC Deb 24 September 2002, vol 390, col 60.

[95] A Tomkins, *The Constitution after Scott: Government Unwrapped* (Oxford, Clarendon, 1998) 9.

[96] HC Deb 18 March 2003, vol 401, col 761.

[97] ibid.

political influence on the text of the September Dossier (dubbed by the press as the 'Dodgy Dossier') it stated that there were issues with 'the judgements made by the JIC and how they and the intelligence were presented, including in Mr Blair's Foreword and in his statement to Parliament on 24 September 2002'.[98] The Report went on to criticise Mr Blair's foreword in the Dossier, which blurred the lines between the 'assessments' of the JIC and overall policy, and stated the case for war to Parliament and the public in categorical terms:

> It is unlikely that Parliament and the public would have distinguished between the ownership and therefore the authority of the judgements in the Foreword and those in the Executive Summary and the main body of the dossier. [The] deliberate selection of a formulation which grounded the statement in what Mr Blair believed, rather than in the judgements which the JIC had actually reached in its assessment of the intelligence, indicates a distinction between his beliefs and the JIC's actual judgements ... The assessed intelligence had <u>not</u> established beyond doubt that Saddam Hussein had continued to produce chemical and biological weapons.[99]

The Report emphasised that Parliament would continue to make demands for factual evidence when faced with controversial policy decisions. Such demands would inevitably include demands for intelligence, including 'where appropriate, *the explicit and public use of assessed intelligence*'.[100] In this event the Report recommended that intelligence should be subjected to scrutiny by an independent body, such as the Intelligence and Security Committee of Parliament.[101] This suggestion is revisited in detail in chapter six.

Since the Iraq War of 2003 there has been a move by government towards partially disclosing intelligence in public sittings of the House of Commons and to the public at large. Unlike sharing on Privy Council terms, this means that every Member of the Commons gets equal access to some information, although Privy Councillors may still receive more in-depth briefings. On its face, this may seem to be a welcome move. However, it is problematic in three respects. First, it brings claims based upon classified intelligence to the forefront of parliamentary debates. This requires parliamentarians to assign weight to the claims without essential contextual information which is required to make a proper evaluation of such claims. Secondly, this practice can lead parliamentarians to artificially inflate or diminish the worth of such claims when balancing them alongside other 'open source' or publicly available information on the situation under consideration. Finally, this 'selective publication' of intelligence-based claims by Government results in a perpetuation of the information asymmetry which plagues the relationship between government and Parliament. Whilst the policy of reporting on the conclusions of intelligence professionals on armed conflict situations may give Parliament the impression that they are being taken into government's

---

[98] Chilcot Report (n 11), Vol 4.2: 'Iraq WMD Assessments, July to September 2002', para 877.
[99] ibid, paras 877–901, emphasis original.
[100] ibid, emphasis added.
[101] ibid.

confidence, there is still ample scope for government to structure the intelligence driven narrative in a manner that is favourable to its case for war. Several inquiries have criticised how Parliament was treated vis-à-vis Iraq War intelligence in order to secure its support. They also showed that MPs were not given the proper amount of time to scrutinise the information, nor were they equipped with the tools required to do so.

D. Reforming the Intelligence Machinery: An Incomplete Solution

The political fallout over the treatment of intelligence[102] and human cost[103] of the Iraq War is difficult to overestimate. Parliament had somehow become irrevocably involved in armed conflict decisions (at least from the perspective of the public, if not the British Constitution). In addition to recommending scrutiny of intelligence by an independent committee such as the Parliamentary Intelligence and Security Committee (PISC), the Chilcot inquiry also recommended the 'need for clear separation of the responsibility for analysis and assessment of intelligence from the responsibility for making the argument for a policy'.[104] The close involvement of a small secretive groups of politicians in deciding how to publicly present intelligence to Parliament had resulted in the skewing of a nuanced expert judgement on the likelihood of Iraq's WMDs.

When the Conservative–Liberal Democrat Coalition assumed power in 2010, they were eager to ensure the separation of intelligence expertise from government policy so as to avoid a repeat of the Iraq War fiasco. Public confidence in this aspect of governance was also in need of a boost. In view of this, the Coalition Government sought to reform the Cabinet's internal intelligence machinery and to make national security policy more transparent on the whole. It is important to understand the nature of these reforms before we consider how they were used to justify the Government's presentation of intelligence during the debates in respect of the Syrian conflicts in 2013 and 2015.

The incoming Conservative–Liberal Democrat Coalition of 2010 were eager not to repeat the perceived mistakes of the Blair Government with respect to using intelligence in relation to armed conflicts. The 2010 Conservative Manifesto, 'Invitation to Join the Government of Britain', promised a slew of reforms to

---

[102] The Chilcot Inquiry was established on 30 July 2009 and held its final hearings in early 2011. It reported on 6 July 2016.

[103] An academic study estimates the total deaths from 2003–11 to be around 461,000 as a result of the conflict: A Hagopian, AD Flaxman, TK Takaro, SA Esa Al Shatari, and J Rajaratnam et al, 'Mortality in Iraq Associated with the 2003–2011 War and Occupation: Findings from a National Cluster Sample Survey by the University Collaborative Iraq Mortality Study' (2010) 10 *PLoS Med*: e1001533, <journals. plos.org/plosmedicine/article?id=10.1371/journal.pmed.1001533> accessed 06 December 2016.

[104] Chilcot Report (n 11), Vol 4.2: Iraq WMD Assessments, July to September 2002, para 900.

Parliament, including 'making the use of the Royal Prerogative subject to greater democratic control so that Parliament is properly involved in all big national decisions'.[105] In the same year, the Coalition Government published the first ever public 'National Security Strategy: A Strong Britain in an Age of Uncertainty', which sought to reform the Cabinet intelligence committees to avoid the perceived follies of their predecessors.

The 2010 National Security Strategy placed the threat from international terrorism and the prospect of an international military crises among the first tier of threats to British national security. For the purpose of this discussion the key reform set out by the document was the establishment of a National Security Council (NSC), using prerogative powers,[106] on the first day of the new Coalition Government. The National Security Council, according to the document, 'brings together key Ministers, and military and intelligence chiefs. It meets weekly and is driving a culture of change in Whitehall, placing a powerful structure right at the heart of Government to make sure our limited resources are deployed to best effect'.[107] The concept of a National Security Council was imported from the United States where such an institution has existed since 1947.[108] During the debate on proposed military action in Syria in 2013, David Cameron implied that the addition of the NSC significantly strengthened the rigour of decision-making and was a bulwark against the types of perceived errors made in respect of Iraq: 'Let me conclude. This is not 2003. We must not use past mistakes as an excuse for indifference or inaction … We face a clear threat … We have discussed our proposed actions extensively at meetings of the National Security Council and the Cabinet'.[109] The formal role of the NSC is to act in an advisory capacity to the Prime Minister; it has no Executive function. On four occasions, members of the Opposition (both of whom were also Privy Councillors) have been entitled to attend meetings of the NSC: Harriet Harman attended in 2010 and 2015, and Ed Milliband attended in 2011 to discuss Libya and 2013 to discuss Syria.[110]

The NSC now sits above the JIC in the intelligence hierarchy, and JIC reports no longer contain a section headed 'policy implications'.[111] The NSC 'institutionalises the relationship between intelligence and policy'.[112] The Prime Minister begins each meeting of the NSC with a briefing from the Chairman of the JIC.[113]

---

[105] The Conservative Party, 'Invitation to join the Government of Britain: the Conservative Manifesto 2010' 67, < www.conservatives.com/~/media/Files/Manifesto2010> accessed 17 September 2017.

[106] J Lunn, L Brooke-Holland and C Mills, 'The UK National Security Council' House of Commons Library, SN/PC 7456, 11 January 2016, 4.

[107] HM Government, 'A Strong Britain in an Age of Uncertainty: The National Security Strategy' Cm 7953 (2010) 5.

[108] US National Security Act 1947, s 101 and RA Best Jr, 'The National Security Council: An Organizational Assessment', CRS Report No 7-5700, RL30840) (Washington DC, Congressional Research Service, 2011).

[109] HC Deb 2 December 2015, vol 603, col 339.

[110] Lunn, Brooke-Holland and Mills, 'The UK National Security Council' (n 106) 10.

[111] Aldrich, et al *Spying on the World* (n 71) 413.

[112] ibid, 409.

[113] ibid, 7.

In his evidence to the Foreign Affairs Select Committee, Lord Hennessy reflected upon the benefits brought by the reorganisation of Cabinet and the creation of the NSC:

> [It] is one of the emblems of the restoration of a much more alive form of collective Cabinet Government ... The National Security Council is properly collective and it is serviced in the old collective way, with proper sessions from the Departments ... I think that, so far, it's a beneficial change. I think that mitigates against excessive prime ministerialism.[114]

However, the forthcoming discussion demonstrates that these reforms neither guarded against excessive prime ministerialism, nor fully restored parliamentary confidence in the Government's intelligence assessment machinery.

Whilst there has been a broadening of transparency in relation to the overarching governmental approach to national security this has not been replicated by similar parliamentary involvement in matters of acute detail. Purposely separating intelligence assessment and the formation of policy is to be welcomed. The JIC is now responsible for producing agreed intelligence, and the NSC is responsible for ensuring that, within a policy framework, JIC intelligence passes the '"so what" test'.[115] The new committee structure has provided the heads of the intelligence agencies 'greater opportunity to talk to Ministers and the Prime Minister'.[116] However, there remains genuine debate about the utility of the new arrangements. Its critics caution that the 'NSC direction can potentially skew intelligence towards myopic short-termism'.[117] Furthermore, the FAC expressed concerns about the extent to which the wishes of the Prime Minister continue to dominate what should be a primarily technocratic policy making exercise.

There is of course no constitutional compulsion to make intelligence-based claims in public sessions of Parliament. Government still controls if, when, and how intelligence is to be disclosed, and can use this to their strategic advantage to secure parliamentary approval for a policy of armed conflict. However, the decision not to rely publicly on intelligence in respect of the Libyan crisis speaks volumes about the limitations of the post-2010 reforms. The decision not to present any intelligence-based claims to Parliament in respect of the Libyan conflict in 2011 is in step with tradition. Our constitutional mechanisms appear to be insufficiently robust to prevent the pursuit of an armed conflict which the Prime Minister is personally invested in, despite compelling evidence that it would amount to the pursuit of a flawed policy. However, despite Cameron's reforms to the internal intelligence machinery of government, the problems with interrogation of intelligence seem to have persisted. The House of Commons FAC revealed activity

---

[114] Foreign Affairs Committee, 'The Role of the FCO in UK Government: Volume I Report, together with formal minutes, oral and written evidence' 7th Report, HC 2010–12, 665, Lord Hennessy Oral Evidence (8 December 2010), Q8.

[115] Aldrich, et al *Spying on the World* (n 71) 413.

[116] ibid, 412.

[117] ibid, 412.

which is emblematic of groupthink in respect of the Libyan conflict which began in 2011. In an excoriating report, published in 2016, the Committee revealed that the decision to initiate armed conflict in Libya 'was not informed by accurate intelligence'.[118]

The Libyan crisis was the first test of the new depoliticised, expert-driven Cabinet intelligence machinery. David Cameron's reforms had been designed to mitigate the risk of another groupthink-driven crisis in respect of the use of intelligence. However, the FAC Report revealed that the wishes of the Prime Minister continued to overshadow the technocratic aspects of the new National Security Council. Concern was expressed that former Prime Minister David Cameron had a 'decisive role when the National Security Council discussed intervention in Libya'.[119] In the aftermath of the decision to enter armed conflict in Libya, it emerged that some members of the NSC did not view the conflict as being in the British national interest.[120] The operation of NSC therefore did not prevent prime ministerial decision-making and groupthink. As a consequence, the relevant section of the report concluded with a call for an independent review into the operation of the National Security Council in order to examine whether the 'weaknesses in governmental decision-making in relation to the Iraq intervention in 2003 have been addressed by the introduction of the NSC'.[121] The Government still has the option of leaving intelligence out of the public case for war if that intelligence does not support their view of the correct policy. At present, Parliament has no effective means by which to contest decisions of this nature. In 2016 the Chairman of the Public Administration and Constitutional Affairs Committee put it to the Cabinet Secretary that the treatment of intelligence in respect of Libya 'read horribly like a repeat—albeit, on a much smaller scale—of all the mistakes that were made in Iraq'.[122]

Further evidence of persistent problems with information asymmetry and the perpetuation of groupthink can be seen with respect to the debates on Syria in 2013 and 2015. In both of these debates the Government made public intelligence-based claims which drew upon the conclusions of the JIC. In the forthcoming analysis of these debates, we shall see that whilst the internal intelligence machinery may now theoretically be capable of producing more independent and impartial results, the subsequent public presentation of intelligence-based arguments to Parliament still suffers from a lack of context and nuance. Although there has been an overall improvement in the quality of parliamentary debate and the scrutiny of intelligence-based claims, the way in which JIC intelligence is presented to Parliament by government is still problematic, as it limits scrutiny

---

[118] Foreign Affairs Committee, 'Libya: Examination of intervention and collapse and the UK's future policy options' 3rd Report, HC 2016–17, 119, summary.

[119] ibid, para 66.

[120] ibid, paras 62–66.

[121] ibid, para 66.

[122] House of Commons Public Administration and Constitutional Affairs Committee, 'Chilcot Inquiry: Lessons for the Machinery of Government', 14 September 2016, HC 656), Examination of witness Sir Jeremy Heywood (Cabinet Secretary and Head of the Civil Service), Q45.

and continues to facilitate information asymmetry. This is clearly illustrated by the debates and votes relating to the Syrian conflicts of 12 August 2013,[123] 26 November 2015[124] and 2 December 2015.[125] Moreover, the reform of the internal intelligence machinery with the aim of separating expertise from policy is to be welcomed, but it is insufficient to mitigate the risks of groupthink and information asymmetry. This has led to two further problems; first, the Government defeat in Syria in 2013, which can be largely attributed to parliamentarian's lack of trust in the Government's public presentation of the intelligence-based case. The consequences of this range beyond the specific problem at hand, and impact upon the wider constitutional settlement. As a result of this, the Conservative Government could not risk the embarrassment of another defeat on Syria in 2015. As discussed in Chapter 3, the privilege of a debate and vote on Syria in 2015 was explicitly exchanged for the guarantee of parliamentary support for war against ISIS/ISIL. Cameron made clear that he would not allow a debate under the War Powers Convention unless Parliament would support the initiation of armed conflict.

In 2013 David Cameron publicly released a letter from the head of the JIC which concluded that the Syrian Government had used chemical weapons against its own citizens. The letter stated, inter alia, that: 'This judgement was made with the highest possible level of certainty following an exhaustive review by the Joint Intelligence Organisation of intelligence reports plus diplomatic and open sources ... *Some of this intelligence is highly sensitive but you have had access to it all.*'[126]

Despite the increase in transparency represented by the disclosure of a politically unadulterated letter from the JIC, the Government lost the vote on military action against Assad's regime in 2013. The case for war was rejected by 332 votes to 220. Although intelligence remained central to the Government's case, Cameron maintained that, 'I do not want to raise, as perhaps happened in the Iraq debate, the status of individuals or groups or pieces of intelligence into some sort of quasi-religious cult.'[127] It is undoubtedly the case that the presentation of intelligence was handled better in this instance than in 2002–03. In the first place, the intelligence conclusions were clearly presented as an *assessment* from the JIC, as opposed to a Government-authored dossier. The conclusions of the JIC, based partly upon secret intelligence, were also balanced against references to open-source information. David Cameron told parliamentarians that, 'I have told the House that there is an enormous amount of open-source reporting, including videos that we can all see.'[128] It seems as if the availability, for the first time,

[123] HC Deb 12 August 2013, vol 566, col 1425.
[124] HC Deb 27 November 2015, vol 602, col 1489.
[125] HC Deb 02 December 2015, vol 603, col 323.
[126] Letter from the Chairman of the Joint Intelligence Committee, 'Syria: Reported Chemical Weapons Use' (29 August 2013) <www.gov.uk/government/uploads/system/uploads/attachment_data/file/235094/Jp_115_JD_PM_Syria_Reported_Chemical_Weapon_Use_with_annex.pdf> accessed 17 September 2017, [emphasis added].
[127] HC Deb 29 August 2013, vol 566, col 1437.
[128] ibid, col 1437.

of information directly from the JIC really did influence parliamentarians.[129] However, despite its expert source, it did not compel the uncritical acceptance which characterised the debate on the September Dossier. Richard Ottoway, a Conservative backbencher, summed up the scepticism of many parliamentarians about the level of disclosure: 'those of us who were here in 2003, at the time of the Iraq War, felt they had their fingers burnt ... *A summary of the intelligence has been published, but it is the bare bones, and I urge the Government in the following days to consider how more intelligence can be provided.*'[130]

An issue of trust lay at the core of disconnect between government and Parliament over the issue of intelligence. Leading current affairs magazine *The Economist* reported that the result amounted to a 'vote of shame' because it considered military intervention as necessary to protect Syrian civilians. That is, of course, for history to judge. What was particularly clear, though, was that parliamentarians viewed the approach to the presentation of intelligence to be insufficient. Commentators were of the view that the Government could and should have done more to assure Parliament that 'any parallels between what he was proposing and Tony Blair's use of the "dodgy dossier" to take Britain to war in Iraq were wholly and contemptibly specious'.[131] Despite the wording of the JIC letter to the Prime Minister stating that 'there are no plausible alternative scenarios to regime responsibility' for use of chemical weapons against the Syrian people,[132] Parliament remained unconvinced. Gaskarth regards the reasons for Government's failure to convince Parliament of the need for action against Assad to be driven by the Government's failure to adequately address the concerns of key policy actors before the vote. These concerns included a failure to convince parliamentarians of the integrity of the intelligence case in the JIC letter released prior to the debate. There was a 'continual questioning of the premise that there was a solid intelligence basis to action'.[133]

In 2015 the Prime Minister once again put JIC assessments front and centre in making the case for military action against ISIS in Syria. The core of the intelligence-based claim was that the proposed campaign of British airstrikes would succeed because there were around 70,000 moderate forces on the ground who were receptive to Western intervention. In an attempt to assuage any fears that intelligence had been in any way politicised, Cameron assured parliamentarians that the claim was based upon the work of experts, as opposed to politicians, commenting that 'it is the considered opinion of the Joint Intelligence Committee, a Committee that was set up and given independence to avoid any of the mistakes we had in the past of the potential misuse of intelligence and other information'.[134]

---

[129] Aldrich, et al *Spying on the World* (n 71), 420.
[130] HC Deb 29 August 2013, vol 566, col 1460.
[131] MJS, 'Britain and Syria: the Vote of Shame' *The Economist* (30 August 2013).
[132] Letter from the Chairman of the Joint Intelligence Committee (n 126).
[133] J Gaskarth, 'The fiasco of the 2013 Syria votes: decline and denial in British foreign policy' (2016) 23 *Journal of European Public Policy* 718, 724.
[134] HC Deb 26 November 2015, vol 602, cols 1501–02.

Before the 2015 debate on Syria the Leaders of the Opposition were given access to a briefing on 'Privy Council terms' by the Prime Minister's National Security Advisor, Mark Lyall Grant.[135] The role of the National Security Advisor, who is appointed directly by the Prime Minister, is to advise on issues of national security, to chair meetings of the National Security Council, and to head up the National Security Secretariat, which has around 200 staff members.[136] Although Cameron facilitated the provision of direct access to the Government's National Security Advisor, prominent parliamentarians remained concerned about the relatively low level of disclosure of intelligence information. Following the debate on 26 November 2015 Yvette Cooper MP wrote to the Prime Minister expressing the following concerns:

> [V]ery few MPs have been given detailed briefing by the Foreign Office and Ministry of Defence (MoD) on this, and even fewer have had access to full security sessions. That makes it very difficult for MPs to contribute to the Government consideration of what form any motion should take, as well as to respond to the motion.[137]

Cooper's letter highlights, in real terms, the persistent problems created by sharing information both through selective public disclosure and on Privy Council terms, which we have discussed above.

However, perhaps because of consciousness of the 2013 parliamentary defeat, the Government held two debates in relation to the 2015 engagement. The first was on 26 November.[138] This debate was wholly devoted to allowing backbenchers to speak, and 103 such MPs took the opportunity to participate.[139] During this debate, in addition to the claim regarding the presence of '70,000 moderate troops' being on the ground and willing to assist the coalition in fighting ISIL/Daesh, the Government made two additional intelligence-based claims, based upon JIC assessments, to assist their case. First, the case for intervention was framed in terms of the JIC assessing that there was a *direct threat* posed by ISIL to British national security.[140] Secondly, the Prime Minister set out that in the last year 'our police and security services have disrupted no fewer than seven terrorist plots to attack the UK, every one of which was either linked to ISIL or inspired by its

---

[135] HC Deb 2 December 2015, vol 603, col 328, David Cameron: 'Privy Counsellors across the House have had a briefing from the Chair of the independent Joint Intelligence Committee. Obviously, I cannot share all the classified material, but I can say this: Paris was different not just because it was so close to us or because it was so horrific in scale, but because it showed the extent of terror planning from Daesh in Syria and the approach of sending people back from Syria to Europe. This was the head of the snake in Raqqa in action, so it is not surprising that the judgement of the Chair of the Joint Intelligence Committee and of the director general of the Security Service is that the risk of a similar attack in the UK is real, and that the UK is already in the top tier of countries on ISIL's target list.'

[136] Joint Committee on National Security Strategy, 'Work of the National Security Adviser' HC 644, 1 February 2016.

[137] Letter from Yvette Cooper to Prime Minister David Cameron, <www.yvettecooper.com/letter_to_pm> accessed 17 September 2017.

[138] HC Deb 26 November 2015, vol 602, cols 1489–1537.

[139] ibid, col 1537, Mr Speaker.

[140] ibid, col 1489: 'The reason for acting is the very direct threat that ISIL poses to our country and to our way of life'.

propaganda'.[141] The Prime Minister repeatedly emphasised that these claims were the considered opinion of an independent body of experts, free from the influence of policy-makers.[142] In both debates parliamentarians interrogated these claims. There were five serious interventions on the subject of the Government's intelligence-based claims.[143] When the Prime Minister was asked for more detail about the specific nature of the alleged 'seven foiled plots' against the United Kingdom, the answer supplied was as full as could reasonably be expected in a wholly public forum. The Prime Minister cautioned the House that 'I must be careful in what I say. From time to time, the Home Affairs Committee interviews the director general of our Security Service, and he may be able to give more detail.'[144]

The substantive motion put forward by the Government on 2 December 2015 noted specifically that 'this House notes that ISIL poses a direct threat to the United Kingdom'[145] but made no other reference to information sourced from JIC reports. Before this debate, there was the usual briefing on Privy Council terms for the select few members holding that title. In his opening statements the Prime Minister alluded to the fact that there was a briefing by a security expert available to all members of the House prior to the debate and vote. However, this was less detailed in nature than the Privy Council briefing.[146] In addition to reiterating that the action against ISIL/Daesh in Syria was 'legal, necessary and the right thing to do',[147] the Prime Minister reiterated to the House that 'This is about our national security'[148] and that the House should 'see all of this through the prism of national security'.[149]

The debates were also set against the backdrop of a report by the FAC, which had been broadly critical of the Government's proposed policy of airstrikes.[150] The report had concluded that 'there should be no extension of British military action into Syria unless there is a coherent international strategy that has a realistic chance of defeating ISIL and of ending the civil war in Syria'.[151] There was no indication that the Committee had access to a briefing by any members of the intelligence or security services prior to the publication of their report.[152] As already stated, there were three central intelligence-based claims made by the Government on the Floor of the House. These were, of course, that 70,000 friendly troops were present to

---

[141] ibid.
[142] ibid, cols 1496, 1501, 1502, 1506, 1511, 1514, 1525, 1530.
[143] Nigel Dodds, col 1506; Derek Twigg, col 1511; Craig Whittaker, col 1524; Kristin Oswald, col 1526; Ian Paisley, col 1536.
[144] ibid, col 1536.
[145] HC Deb 2 December 2015, vol 603, col 323, text of substantive motion.
[146] ibid, col 326.
[147] ibid, col 325.
[148] ibid, col 327.
[149] ibid, col 339.
[150] Foreign Affairs Committee, 'The extension of offensive British military operations to Syria', 2nd Report 2015–16, HC 547.
[151] ibid, para 2.
[152] ibid, paras 26–27.

resist ISIL/Daesh as a ground force, thus making a campaign of air strikes worthwhile[153] and that the actions of ISIL/Daesh in Syria represented a direct threat to the national security of mainland Britain.[154] Finally, there had already been seven terrorism plots against the United Kingdom which had been foiled by the Security Services, and their origin and inspiration could be traced to ISIL/Daesh-held territory in Syria.[155] In view of this, the Government's presentation of the intelligence-based case to the House was a crucial element in shifting opinion towards support for military intervention, along with arguments related to international legality, morality, and overall necessity.

The House divided: Ayes 211, Noes 390 in favour of the Government, which meant approximately 65 per cent of MPs supported the airstrikes. However, during the debate the Government's national security claims were subjected to intensive scrutiny. Around 20 per cent of members expressed some doubt as to the content of the JIC Report (as presented by the Prime Minister).[156] It would be impossible (not to mention unwieldy) to reproduce all interventions of interest here. However, concerns expressed by parliamentarians clustered clearly around three inter-related issues. These issues highlight the serious epistemic problems with holding a debate of this nature in a purely public forum.

First, there appeared to be a disparity between the views of the FAC and the JIC regarding the number of ground forces willing to support air strikes. This was highlighted several times in the debate, including by a member of the FAC, who was of the opinion (after visiting the region and consulting relevant military and counterterrorism experts) that 'There are about 10,000 to 15,000 [friendly troops], and that was the answer given by everyone there'.[157] One member reiterated that 'Every single expert witness to the [Foreign Affairs] Select Committee said that there are "thousands" of disparate groups; allegiances are like shifting sands, and there are few moderates left'.[158]

Secondly, as successive interventions by Privy Counsellors (ie those with access to additional confidential sessions) mounted up, the concreteness of the claim relating to the presence of 70,000 ground troops and the directness of the threat from ISIL/Daesh in Syria were further called into question. For example, Privy Counsellor Keith Simpson was of the view that 'there is no direct threat as far as intelligence is concerned'.[159] Another Privy Counsellor, who had consulted with the Former leader of the United States' Joint Special Operations Command, was of the opinion that the 70,000 troops forecasted by the Prime Minister were

---

[153] HC Deb 2 December 2015, vol 603, col 333.
[154] ibid, cols 329, 331.
[155] ibid, col 328.
[156] ibid. This refers to 31 of the 157 parliamentarians (19.7%) who spoke during the debate either querying or expressing some other form of misgivings about the government claims based upon the JIC report.
[157] ibid, col 354, Yasmin Qureshi (Lab).
[158] ibid, col 435, Barry Gardiner (Lab).
[159] ibid, col 377.

'not useful, even as target spotters'.[160] Other parliamentarians speculated that the 70,000 troops numbered as many as 56 separate factions and included Islamist extremists such as Al Qaeda who were considered hostile to the United Kingdom. The number of Islamists described in the security briefing was as many as 30,000.[161]

Finally, (and perhaps inevitably given the twin catalysts of party politics and information asymmetry) there were general concerns about the presentation of the claim regarding the 70,000 friendly troops as a central element of the case for airstrikes, and comparisons were drawn with the Iraq intervention in 2003. Members from both sides of the House drew parallels with the ill-fated claims relating to WMDs.[162] In the end, Conservative backbencher Dr Julian Lewis made the acerbic remark which sums up the problem underlying selective publicity, namely that classified intelligence is deprived of its proper context in a public forum: 'instead of having dodgy dossiers we now have bogus battalions'.[163]

E. Towards a New Nomenclature of Secrecy

The various roles of information asymmetries, presented above, amount to the amplification of secrecy across the constitutional arrangements engaged by war powers decisions. These arrangements potentially allow for groupthink to remain ever present. Legitimate national security secrecy is not a problem in and of itself; in fact, it is to be expected. However, the above examples show secrecy operating in a range of ways to the detriment of parliamentary discourse. Whilst we may expect a decline in information asymmetry to be concomitant with increased disclosure, this has not proven to be the case in the present context. Secrecy may have become shallower, to revisit Pozen's rubric, but information asymmetries persist, varying only in degree as opposed to in nature. Shallow secrets do not eliminate the obstacles to democratic good governance in the context of the war prerogative, which the mechanism of the War Powers Convention is supposed to help facilitate.

The figure below illustrates the real and imagined consequences of the narrative of moving from blanket secrecy to progressive disclosure of information based upon classified information to parliamentarians. The x axis shows the progress in disclosure, from blanket secrecy at point (A), progressing along sharing information on Privy Council Terms (B), and to selective disclosure of intelligence in the Iraq War (C), through to continued selective disclosure after the reform of the Government's intelligence machinery (D). On the y axis information asymmetry is maximal where a blanket policy of secrecy is adopted (A), and lessens as we shift through the various phases and type of Government disclosure.

---

[160] ibid, cols 388–89, David Davis (Con).
[161] ibid, col 459, Barbara Keeley (Lab).
[162] ibid, col 422, Paul Flynn (Lab).
[163] ibid, col 370, Dr Julian Lewis (L Dem).

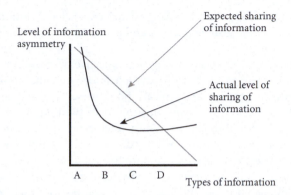

Figure 4.1: **The relationship between information asymmetry and disclosure: expected and actual**

However, the relationship between the types of disclosure on the *x* axis and the reduction of information asymmetry between government and Parliament (*y*) is by no means directly proportional. A quick glance at the loose historical trajectory of information sharing might lead to the conclusion that the relationship is best represented by the grey line, but this is not the case. The relationship indicated by the black line is a more accurate representation of the ongoing relationship between information asymmetry and disclosures of sensitive information from government to Parliament. Government's selective use of information has maintained a level of information asymmetry which is reduced, but nonetheless highly significant in its consequences.

In light of this we can draw the following conclusions about the real impact of secrecy across all of the above examples. The common theme to be found along the spectrum of uses of secrecy: from blanket refusal to inform Parliament, through sharing limited sensitive information on Privy Council Terms, through to the selective disclosure of information based upon classified intelligence, is the *exclusionary* nature of secrecy. That is to say, secrecy in the various guises described herein is used to deprive parliamentarians of access to a level playing field from which to assess the Government's case for war. There is of course a spectrum ranging from full exclusion of parliamentarians towards partial inclusion of a privileged class (Privy Counsellors), who are then deprived of the right to publicly interrogate governments' confidential assertions. However, along the spectrum, the role of secrecy as exclusionary (ie secrecy which puts parliamentarians at a disadvantage in terms of participation) holds true. At its core, the use of secrecy as an exclusionary tool (even when masquerading as a form of publicity) serves to perpetuate the problem of groupthink, as secrecy can be used to effectively negate any real possibility of Parliament effectively contesting the Government's narrative or perspective on armed conflict. At the furthest end of the spectrum—where claims based upon classified information are publicly disclosed with the assurance that they are apolitical and expert-driven—Select Committee inquiries have still revealed ideological dominance and groupthink to be the driving factors in decision-making.

The move away from deep secrecy towards selective disclosure of claims based on secret intelligence has created a trust deficit between the Government and Parliament. Parliamentarians are cynical about these claims. The fallout over the selective disclosure of intelligence in support of the Iraq War has penetrated deep into British political discourse. Whilst intelligence information should not dominate the domestic discourse on armed conflict, it is unlikely to disappear from the agenda. Chilcot recognised that both the public and parliamentarians will make increased demands for an evidence base for the use of force. But, without a radical solution, references 'to intelligence and attempts to present documentary proof inevitably recall earlier influence attempts by the New Labour Government to put intelligence material in the public domain to serve their policy ends'.[164] Successive governments have not as yet overcome this credibility problem. There exists 'a paradox at work in which the more the Government seeks to justify its actions, the more suspicion it arouses about the strength of its case'.[165] In the end, therefore, shallow secrets are no better: the problems of groupthink and information asymmetry persist among different actors. Parliament remains excluded from exercising meaningful democratic control. In the end we must ask ourselves: 'What is national security, if not the vitality of its democratic institutions that would be hobbled by secrecy?'[166] There is, however, another way to utilise secrecy to remove the information asymmetry which plagues this aspect of the relationship between government and Parliament, and to in turn potentially challenge groupthink. This is a re-conception of the purpose of secrecy as *inclusive* by allowing a highly limited role for closed sessions of the whole House of Commons, to allow for the scrutiny and debate of JIC Reports by all Members. This is intended to redress the deficit in participation demonstrated in this chapter. A proposal for closed intelligence sessions of the whole House of Commons as a means to foster inclusive secrecy will be discussed in chapter six.

---

[164] Gaskarth, 'The fiasco of the 2013 Syria votes (n 133) 729.
[165] ibid.
[166] Aftergood, 'Reducing Government Secrecy' (n 5) 401.

5

Re-arming Parliament: Fostering Politics

VERONIKA FIKFAK AND HAYLEY J HOOPER

The preceding chapters focused upon the various problems encountered in the relationship between governments and Parliament in the context of armed conflict decisions. We uncovered the core elements of the 'secret war' that parliamentarians have been fighting to exert some form of democratic control. Now we propose possible solutions to these problems. Our over-arching aim is to foster a 'culture of challenge'[1] and a 'culture of justification'[2] between not only government and Parliament, but also between Parliament and the electorate. Our solutions put parliamentarians at centre stage. They are not easy solutions, as they demand significant efforts from politicians individually and collectively, as well as candour from government. The pages that follow are intended to provide a blueprint for parliamentarians. Our aim is to move the debate in Parliament beyond its current state of binary imperatives; ie beyond legal or not, beyond military force or non-intervention, and beyond the rhetoric of 'good' or 'evil' which often characterises debates. We seek to empower MPs to construe their role in debates more broadly, and to assert their power more forcefully vis-à-vis governments in relation to war. Solutions are addressed in two parts: as they relate to debates in Parliament on the one hand, and in relation to voting in Parliament on the other.

This is of course not the first proposal for parliamentary reform in this context. Since the Iraq War there have been a number of proposals for either a parliamentary resolution governing war powers, or indeed a War Powers Act. Part A of our discussion explains why neither of these alternatives would solve the problems we identify in the first half of this book. Part B addresses the substance of our argument in relation to parliamentary debates. Here we seek to redefine the relationship

---

[1] House of Commons Public Administration and Constitutional Affairs Committee, 'Lessons still to be learned from the Chilcot Inquiry' 10th Report 2016–17, HC 656, para 58. The Committee discusses a 'culture of challenge' in respect of Cabinet intelligence reform. We believe such a culture must also exist during debates on the floor of the House of Commons.

[2] E Murenik, 'A bridge to where? Introducing the interim Bill of Rights' (1994) 10 *South African Journal on Human Rights* 31.

parliamentarians have with international legality, by reducing its influence on debates, and tasking politicians with probing government on a broader range of issues in relation to the legitimacy of any armed conflict. In short, in the course of our argument in Part B we reject a continuation of the legalisation of parliamentary discourse evident in previous conflict discussions, and seek to provide an appropriately constrained role for legality in such debates. The considerations of legitimacy we argue for represent a broad church: these relate to concerns both on the international plane, and to questions relevant to domestic politics. Displacing legality—which has been the dominant discourse—creates a vacuum for parliamentarians. In legality's absence, politicians require a new set of tools. We argue MPs should focus upon the legitimacy of any conflict and press the Government to search for, and discuss a spectrum of, political options as alternatives to military action. All of our proposals are aimed at reinvigorating the neglected domestic political discourse relating to war. The central purpose of these proposals is to help foster a 'culture of challenge' on the Floor of the House of Commons.[3]

Part C deals with the constitutional role of voting in these debates. Here we argue that MPs are faced with conflicting constitutional demands; including the demands of their own conscience, and potentially competing loyalties to party politics and the wishes of their constituents. This is a paradox we outline and acknowledge, but do not seek to resolve. Instead, we argue that the electorate is best served when MPs are entitled to a free vote, but parties adopt a non-enforceable but publicly clear party line. Overall, we propose these reforms in order to create a 'culture of justification' in relation to how Parliament debates and votes in relation to armed conflict. The central premise behind such a culture is that the legitimacy of every exercise of power (whether it is governmental power to wage war, or parliamentary power to affirm or withhold support from government) rests upon the 'cogency of the case offered in defence of [the] decision'.[4]

A. Moving Beyond the Standard Solutions

I. Reform Proposals to Date

From early in the twenty-first century some parliamentarians have been anxious to play a greater role in controlling the Government's exercise of war powers. On several occasions since the Iraq War, MPs from all major political parties have sought to formalise and enhance Parliament's role in relation to the use of force through either a Parliamentary Resolution or a Bill promoting a War Powers Act (ie primary legislation). Several Private Members Bills as well as drafts of parliamentary

---

[3] 'Lessons still to be learned from the Chilcot Inquiry' (n 1) para 58.
[4] Murenik, 'A bridge to where?' (n 2) 32.

resolutions have been put forward in government consultations and Select Committee Reports. At the time of writing, no draft resolution has been adopted and no Bill has progressed beyond a second reading.[5]

The history of attempts to formalise Parliament's war powers is as follows: The first Bill was introduced by New Labour MP Claire Short in 2005, who proposed legislation in response to the Blair Government's pursuit of the Iraq War. Short, who resigned from her Cabinet position over the Iraq War, insisted that in future the Prime Minister should lay a report before each House indicating the reasons for proposed participation by the British armed forces in conflict.[6] These reasons were to include any information the Government thought appropriate to make public, including the geographical extent and duration of the conflict, and the legal basis of the proposed action.[7] Once the report had been made available and debated by both Houses of Parliament, a resolution would be passed to approve military action. If prior approval for an armed conflict proved impossible, the Bill allowed for retrospective approval by Parliament.[8] This Bill failed to gain the support of enough Commons' Members to progress to the next reading.[9]

The issue was revisited in 2007.[10] Whilst in Opposition, Conservative MP William Hague put forward a motion which asked the Government to bring forward proposals to give effect to 'the principle that parliamentary approval should be required for any substantial deployment of British Armed Forces into situations of war or international armed conflict'.[11] In an opinion piece for *The Guardian* Hague argued that legislation must compel the Government to 'explain to Parliament the reasons for deployment, its objectives, the size of the deployment and in as much as is possible, its duration. If, in the case of an emergency, this was not possible, Parliament should be provided with retrospective information'.[12] But when presented with the opportunity as a Government Minister, Hague failed to introduce a Bill. Nevertheless, he publicly reiterated his desire to put Parliament's role on a statutory footing in 2011.[13] Ultimately, however, the Coalition Government decided against a statute and codified the War Powers

---

[5] Three Private Members Bills were introduced in the period 2003–07, and a further Bill was introduced in the 2015–16 session. See C Mills, 'Parliamentary Approval for Military Action', House of Commons Library Briefing 7166, 12 May 2015, 14.

[6] Armed Forces (Parliamentary Approval for Participation in Armed Conflict) Bill, cl 2.

[7] C Taylor, 'Armed Forces (Parliamentary Approval for Participation in Armed Conflict) Bill', House of Commons Library Research Paper 05/56, 8 August 2005, 18.

[8] Armed Forces (Parliamentary Approval for Participation in Armed Conflict) Bill, cls 4–6.

[9] HC Hansard Deb 21 October 2005, vol 437, col 1085.

[10] A draft Parliamentary Resolution was produced by Gordon Brown's Labour Government as part of the consultation paper 'War Powers and Treaties' in 2007. See Ministry of Justice et al, 'The Governance of Britain War Powers and Treaties: Limiting Executive Powers' Cm 7239, October 2007, Annex A.

[11] HC Hansard Deb 15 May 2007, vol 460, col 481.

[12] W Hague, 'The seal of approval' *The Guardian*, 15 May 2007.

[13] HC Deb 21 March 2011, vol 677, col 799, William Hague: 'We will also enshrine in law for the future the necessity of consulting Parliament on military action.'

Convention in the 2011 Cabinet Manual. By the end of the 2010–15 Parliament, during which Hague served as Foreign Secretary, the issue of putting the convention on statutory footing had faded from the political agenda.[14]

Since 2011 several Select Committee reports investigated the operation of war powers and prime ministerial power.[15] These reports have doubtless been catalysed by the problems experienced in implementing the War Powers Convention, discussed in chapter three. Most notably, in March 2014, the Commons Political and Constitutional Reform Committee issued a report entitled 'Parliament's Role in Conflict Decisions: a way forward'. It described the War Powers Convention as guaranteeing Parliament's right to a debate in the absence of countervailing considerations of emergency or the public interest.[16] In the course of evidence, however, the Committee found that there were serious concerns regarding the scope and operation of the convention. Lord Wallace (a Liberal Democrat Peer) informed the Committee that 'The definition of armed conflict and the deployment of forces has all sorts of ragged edges, questions of urgency and secrecy come in',[17] all of which pose interpretive problems for the relationship between the Government and Parliament. The Committee's concluding recommendations were that the War Powers Convention be strengthened by being captured in a parliamentary resolution.[18] The consequence of such a resolution, in theory at least, would be that the involvement of Parliament would no longer depend on the strategic decisions of government (dictating timing and quality of engagement). Instead, the relationship would be formalised as part of the rules of Parliament. This would mean that MPs themselves—rather than government—would theoretically be in charge of the resolution's application and operation.

In May 2016 Liberal Democrat Peer Baroness Falkner introduced the Armed Forces Deployment (Royal Prerogative) Bill into the House of Lords, in a further attempt to put war powers on a statutory footing. During the Second Reading Debate the legacy of Iraq still loomed large in the Baroness's mind. She argued that the electorate 'need to know that one lesson of the Iraq war has been heeded and that never again should the country shed blood … on the basis of sofa government and inadequate, hurried information and processes'.[19] The Bill provided that: 'The prior approval of the House of Commons shall be obtained for any

---

[14] C Mills, 'Parliamentary Approval for Military Action', House of Common Library Briefing Paper 7166, 12 May 2015, 5.

[15] House of Commons Political and Constitutional Reform Committee, 'Parliament's Role in Conflict Decisions: a way forward' 12th Report of 2013–14, HC 892 [18]. See also House of Commons Political and Constitutional Reform Committee, 'The Role and Powers of the Prime Minister' 1st Report 2014–15, HC 351, 42.

[16] ibid, para [3].

[17] ibid, para. [18]; see also House of Commons Political and Constitutional Reform Committee, 'The Role and Powers of the Prime Minister' 1st Report 2014–15, HC 351, 42.

[18] The report was the subject of a Westminster Hall debate on 19 June 2014, in which divided views were expressed in respect of the Committee's recommendation that the convention should be formalised. HC Deb 19 June 2014, vol 582, col 129WH.

[19] HL Deb 8 July 2016, vol 773, col 2262.

conflict decision following the passing of this Act'.[20] To address concerns over MPs being 'misled or ... given inadequate information or inadequate time to reflect on the most serious decision they will ever take',[21] the Bill required that the Prime Minister provides information about objectives, locations, and legal matters before the vote is taken.

II. Issues Common to Both Proposals

Capturing the War Powers Convention in a parliamentary resolution or an Act of Parliament would not essentially change the character of the activities currently undertaken by governments or Parliament pursuant to the convention. Both the draft parliamentary resolutions and the Bills in pursuit of a War Powers Act would continue to vest the balance of power in the hands of government. All of the proposals to date allow the Government to 'define' what constitutes an 'international armed conflict'. Although these are usually referred to as overseas military interventions to which the Geneva Conventions, or the law of armed conflict more broadly, apply, this would necessarily exclude internal armed conflict, and actions by special forces or the use of drones. All documents except Short's Bill exempt the deployment of special forces from the reporting requirement. This potentially means that not only would the Government control the process of reporting, it would also dictate the terminology of the debate. The effect of this is that neither the proposed Bills nor the resolutions would place Parliament on a significantly stronger footing than the existing War Powers Convention.

In addition to this all the proposals—save Clare Short's Bill—provide exceptions for the disclosure of sensitive information to protect national security or the public interest. In each of the other proposals the Government is exempted from the reporting requirement where the decision to enter armed conflict would prejudice the effectiveness of the action, or the safety of British or allied armed forces. Where this is the case, these factors can simply be declared to Parliament as a reason for failure to seek prior approval. Moreover, there is no requirement to seek retrospective approval if national security would be prejudiced by subsequent disclosure of the relevant information. The interpretation of this exception is a matter for immediate concern. In general and historical terms, government answers to parliamentary questions on matters of national security are often deliberately vague.[22] If the Government were able to rely upon the security exception because a large part of the case for war was based upon classified information, it is difficult to envisage any meaningful scrutiny taking place under the terms proposed by either solution. This is a replication of an existing problem with

---

[20] Armed Forces Deployment (Royal Prerogative) Bill, cl 1(1).

[21] HL Deb 8 July 2016, vol 773, col 2257.

[22] H Wilson, *The Governance of Britain* (London, Weidenfield & Nicholson and Michael Joseph, 1976) 168.

parliamentary scrutiny, but would create specific problems of justiciability in the context of a War Powers Act, discussed below.

III. Parliamentary Resolution: Specific Issues

Parliamentary resolutions differ from constitutional conventions in one important respect: Resolutions form part of the parliamentary rulebook, and their implementation is policed not by government, but by the Speaker of the House. Yet neither of the draft Resolutions makes any provisions about their enforceability in the event of a perceived breach.[23] In practice, a breach of the resolution could be investigated by a specially constituted select committee, but would not be justiciable in a court of law. In that sense, a resolution could easily be overturned or amended, or could simply fall into disuse. Much like the breach of a constitutional convention, the sanctions for breach of a resolution would be purely political in nature and would depend on the presence of political will for their enforcement.

Another issue specific to the operation of a parliamentary resolution, the effect of which is decidedly political in nature, is its relationship to the domestic legal power to declare war pursuant to the Royal Prerogative. It is settled law that Parliament can displace the Royal Prerogative by enacting primary legislation in the same subject matter area.[24] However, it is unclear and unlikely that as a matter of constitutional law a parliamentary resolution would have the effect of displacing the legal power to declare war pursuant to the prerogative. In this regard, a resolution would not differ materially from the War Powers Convention in terms of enhancing Parliament's power to constrain government other than through the application of political pressure.

IV. War Powers Act: Specific Issues

It is equally unclear whether a new statute would considerably limit the Crown's legal power to deploy the armed forces abroad.[25] Baroness Falkner took the view that a War Powers Act would not be justiciable, and that justiciability of action taken pursuant to its statutory authority would be undesirable. We are inclined to agree with these conclusions. There are two broad categories of objections to

---

[23] C Taylor and R Kelly, *Parliamentary Approval for Deploying the Armed Forces: An Introduction to the Issues*, Research Paper 08/88, House of Commons Library, 27 November 2008, 24–29.

[24] *R v Secretary of State for the Home Department, ex parte Fire Brigades* Union [1995] 2 AC 513.

[25] The Political and Constitutional Reform Committee viewed a parliamentary resolution to be an interim step on the road to eventual primary legislation. House of Commons Political and Constitutional Reform Committee, 'Parliament's Role in Conflict Decisions: a way forward' 12th Report of 2013–14, HC 892, 28–29.

justiciability; one related to feasibility, and the other related to desirability. Some of these objections straddle both sides of the divide but they are separated here for analytical clarity. In terms of the feasibility of effective judicial review, the objections are based upon the attitude of courts to constitutional conventions, the role of parliamentary privilege, judicial deference in relation to foreign affairs and macro-political issues, and finally the unwillingness of the judiciary to issue declaratory opinions on matters of public international law. In terms of the desirability of judicial review, there are issues now familiar to the reader with 'legalising' the discourse on war, and creating a relationship of asymmetric or 'exclusionary' secrecy through conducting judicial review of security sensitive information.

Courts have been historically unwilling to rule on the precise scope of individual constitutional conventions. If any War Powers Act was simply viewed as a translation or 'recognition' of the War Powers Convention in statute law, then courts may be unwilling to conduct judicial review of activities taken pursuant to such an Act. This reading is suggested by the majority approach to the Sewel Convention in the *Miller* case.[26] In *Miller* a majority of eight Supreme Court Justices formed the view that the 'recognition' of a constitutional convention relating to devolution in a statutory provision did not imbue that provision with independent legal force.[27] Instead, although the convention in question was 'recognised' in primary legislation, the 'policing of its scope and the manner of its operation does not lie within the constitutional remit of the judiciary, which is to protect the rule of law'.[28] Or, more bluntly: 'Judges ... are neither the parents nor the guardians of political conventions; they are merely observers'.[29] This appears to suggest that statutory codification of political rules has little effect in practice. However, it is perhaps possible that a rule on war powers which was *not* simply a recognition of the War Powers Convention would be treated differently. For example, section 20 of the Constitutional Reform and Governance Act 2010 turns the constitutional convention that international treaties should be laid before Parliament (formerly known as the Ponsonby Rule) into a statutory obligation, without any explicit mention of the convention itself. This, in principle at least, is more likely to render a statutory provision justiciable under the ordinary common law rules of judicial review.

However, there are key differences between the content of the 2010 Act and the draft proposals for a War Powers Act. These speak directly to the nature and extent of the task for any court seized of judicial review proceedings. First of all, the 2010 Act merely places procedural requirements upon government towards Parliament vis-à-vis treaties. These include an obligation upon government to publish

---

[26] *R (Miller and Another) v Secretary of State for Exiting the European Union* [2017] UKSC 5, [2017] 1 All ER 593.
[27] Scotland Act 2016, s 2.
[28] *Miller* (n 26) [151].
[29] ibid, [145].

the treaty, to lay it before Parliament, to publish a Ministerial opinion explaining why the treaty should be ratified, and finally to allow for a consultation period of 21 sitting days of Parliament.[30] By contrast, the proposed War Powers Acts lay down requirements of substance. Although the Government is procedurally required to lay a report before Parliament prior to initiating armed conflict and to gain its approval (presumably through a vote in favour of the report), the proposals lay down rules about the required *content* of this report, discussed above. All of these are inherently contestable requirements (ie legality, the scope of the conflict, and the reasons for the proposed conflict). Questions could reasonably be raised by judicial review claimants regarding the *adequacy* of any governmental attempts to meet these statutory requirements. The extent to which these matters could be disclosed to Parliament sitting publicly without damage to the public interest is also highly contestable. As a result, the subject of any judicial review action is likely to centre upon the *quality* of either governmental reason giving or disclosure to Parliament (or some combination thereof). This would invariably raise issues pertaining to the constitutional protection of parliamentary privilege.

Parliamentary privilege, which includes the absolute protection of speech in Parliament, could be engaged if a claimant challenged the government's interpretation of its obligations in the statutory reporting procedure. For example, clause 2(2)(b) of the Armed Forces Deployment (Royal Prerogative) Bill requires government to place before Parliament information concerning the 'objectives, locations and legal matters that the Prime Minister thinks appropriate in the circumstances'. Whilst this clause vests discretion in the Prime Minister, any objection raised before a court would inevitably require the consideration of objections to the quality of the report made in the House of Commons so as to establish the reasonableness of the claimant's objection. The practicalities of determining the use of this statutory authority would inevitably lead to the questioning of proceedings in Parliament. This would be contrary to Article 9 of the Bill of Rights Act 1689, prohibiting the questioning of proceedings in Parliament. This type of judicial scrutiny is still considered a 'constitutional anathema' in the British Constitutional settlement.[31] A similar issue arose in *HS2* whereby the appellants invited the Supreme Court to consider the adequacy of parliamentary proceedings in order to argue that they did not meet the standards for the public consultation process required by the relevant European Union law.[32] The Supreme Court dismissed the appeal and emphasised the constitutional importance of the prohibition on questioning proceedings in Parliament. There was even an implicit suggestion that it may be among a category of constitutional principles which 'outranked' European Union law in the domestic hierarchy of norms in the joint judgment of Lord Neuberger and Lord Mance, despite the fact the supremacy of EU Law is

---

[30] Constitutional Reform and Governance Act 2010, s 20.

[31] S Briant, 'Dialogue, Diplomacy and Defiance: Prisoners' Voting Rights at Home and in Strasbourg' (2011) 3 *European Human Rights Law Review* 243, 248.

[32] *R (On the Application of HS2 Alliance) v Secretary of State for Transport and Another* [2014] UKSC 3, [2014] 1 WLR 324.

a recognised feature of the constitution.[33] This speaks directly to the force of the rule prohibiting the questioning of proceedings in Parliament. Moreover, it suggests that any claim regarding the quality of information provided to Parliament by government would not be amenable to judicial review.[34]

In addition to the issues of parliamentary privilege, courts are likely to be highly deferential to any assessment by government of the scope of the obligations towards Parliament under a War Powers Act. In general, English courts are highly deferential in the context of foreign policy or national security. There is a long tradition of case law reflecting this trend.[35] Courts seized of judicial review are especially unwilling to enter into the 'forbidden territory' of foreign affairs.[36] Taking the country to war can reasonably be considered to engage considerations of foreign affairs, and those higher order political considerations courts view as particularly unsuitable for judicial consideration.

The final reason which renders justiciability improbable is that any governmental (or parliamentary) conclusion on the legality of war would be based upon a reading of public international law, as opposed to English municipal law. When faced with this issue previously, the Administrative Court refused to issue a declaratory opinion on the legality of the Iraq War. The court held that it lacked jurisdiction to give an authoritative reading of the position in international law. In addition to this, it held that ruling in this sphere would be inappropriate as adjudication in this area was potentially damaging to the public interest because it engaged matters of national security, international relations, and defence.[37] It is highly likely that any case brought against the Government legal opinion as presented to Parliament under the proposals examined herein would suffer the same fate.

In terms of the desirability of judicial review, which is often constitutionally justified as a mechanism for promotion of values of good governance, there are two key objections. First of all, there is a risk of the promotion of asymmetric or exclusionary secrecy, as described in chapter four. Secondly, judicial review of the legality of the use of powers under any statute risks 'legalising' the political process from the perspective of the common law, as opposed to public international law. The damage to political discourse done by reference to public international law is explored in chapter two and in part B, below. It need not be revisited in detail here. The issue of secrecy, however, does merit attention.

---

[33] ibid, [207].

[34] Article 9 of the Bill of Rights 1689 would present a special obstacle in evaluating the quality of speech in Parliament: 'freedom of speech and debates or proceedings in Parliament ought not to be impeached or questioned in any court or place out of Parliament'. For a wider discussion on the legitimacy of judicial scrutiny of parliamentary proceedings see A Kavanagh, 'Proportionality and parliamentary debates: exploring some forbidden territory' (2014) 34 *Oxford Journal of Legal Studies* 443.

[35] C Turpin and A Tomkins, *British Government and the Constitution* (Cambridge, CUP, 2011) 771–89.

[36] *R (Abbassi) v Secretary of State for Foreign and Commonwealth Affairs* [2002] EWCA Civ 1598, [2002] All ER(D) 70.

[37] *Campaign for Nuclear Disarmament v Prime Minister of the United Kingdom* [2002] EWHC 2777 (Admin).

In chapter four we identified a category of 'exclusionary secrecy' which promoted damaging information asymmetries between government and Parliament, biased in favour of government. If government sought to claim that a situation was an emergency (so Parliament could not be involved) or that information about an armed conflict could not be disclosed to Parliament without damaging the public interest, then this could potentially be a catalyst for litigation. It is highly likely that any litigation on these matters, would motivate government to seek a closed material procedure (allowing information sensitive to national security to be insulated from the public gaze).[38] Recent judicial rulings suggest that an extremely wide definition is given to the category of materials considered to be 'sensitive to national security'.[39] In short, proceedings under the 2013 Act would create an information asymmetry between the Government, the applicants for judicial review, and the public at large. This risks compromising the values of accountability, transparency, and participation.

Finally, it should be remembered that a War Powers Act of sorts already exists on the statute book. Section 3 of The Act of Settlement 1700 mandates that 'this nation be not obliged to engage in any war for the defence of any dominions or territories which do not belong to the Crown of England without the consent of Parliament'. Yet, this provision, which still remains good law, has been dutifully ignored by successive governments throughout the twentieth and twenty-first centuries. This intentional disregard for existing legislative requirements has not been raised before domestic courts, and is rarely mentioned in parliamentary debate. This is perhaps indicative of a lack of political will on the part of governments to constrain the exercise of the war prerogative power, and a lack of political will in Parliament to demand observance of the Act. In light of the fate of this legislation, it is understandable that all attempts to put the War Powers Convention on a new statutory footing have been unsuccessful. The political will appears to favour the flexibility which the War Powers Convention in its current form permits. Reinvigorating Parliament's role will not come from the form the rules of procedure take. Instead, the role of politics and politicians must be reimagined.

B. Creating Space for Politics and Equipping Parliament for Deliberation

When the Government makes its case for war before Parliament, the discourse is often based on binary distinctions. By way of example, Tony Blair's novel argument for intervention in Kosovo to prevent a humanitarian disaster was presented as a choice between 'doing something' versus 'doing nothing'.[40]

---

[38] Justice and Security Act 2013, s 6.
[39] *R (Sarkani and Others) v Foreign Secretary* [2014] EWHC 2359 (Admin).
[40] HC Deb 23 March 1999, vol 328, col 168 (Tony Blair in relation to Kosovo).

In his lauded speech in favour of attacking ISIS/ISIL in Syria, Hilary Benn distinguished between 'good' and 'evil', arguing that the House of Commons previously 'stood up against Hitler and Mussolini' and 'against the denial of human rights', so MPs now had to 'confront this evil' in Syria.[41] The problem with the choices presented is that they are all false dichotomies.[42] The binary options give the impression that there is only one alternative: good has to conquer evil, and if faced with a choice, we cannot do nothing. Thus military option is the only choice. By excluding all other options, the narrative gives the impression that war is a choice between either/or, a move that insulates the Government from political scrutiny.

It is in this context that the need to show that the war is *legal* arises. It represents another dichotomy in relation to the legality or illegality of armed conflict. Since the Iraq War, parliamentary debates have focused heavily on the question of whether the proposed use of force is legal. MPs have been invited to discuss whether the situation in a particular country represents an 'international threat', whether measures of 'self-defence' are warranted, or indeed whether the Government can take 'all measures necessary' and begin military action. This is the language of public international law. Indeed, since the invasion of Iraq, a legal opinion or at least a legal explanation supporting the case for war has regularly been at the centre of the Government's arguments for the use of military action. Both arguments of self-defence and authorisation under the UN Charter are made, sometimes confusingly in relation to the same situation.[43] Yet, because the question of whether the war is *legal or illegal* is binary, only one right answer remains. Legality has to be established, the only question which remains is by whom. In this context, chapter two showed that when the Security Council has established the legality of intervention, this legal basis has been used to preclude the prior engagement of Parliament. In other situations, the Government has sought to persuade Parliament to provide its support on these binary terms.

In this book, we question the substance of the binary choices presented to Parliament, and the choice between the Security Council and Parliament as alternative forums. We wish to move away from either/or options and reconceptualise some of the dominant binaries that underpin conventional liberal thinking.[44] We therefore argue for nuance, ie for the blurring of lines as to who gets to be involved on decisions of armed conflict, in relation to the legality of military action. We also want debate in Parliament to move beyond the dichotomy between war or inaction. Instead, we seek a deeper and more searching inquiry of the available answers to these questions, and by mapping out a spectrum of options at every level of inquiry hope to reinvigorate the role of MPs in political debate relating to war.

---

[41] HC Deb 2 December 2015, vol 603, col 486.
[42] A Roberts, 'Legality vs Legitimacy: Can Uses of Force be illegal but Justified?' in P Alston, E Macdonald (eds) *Human Rights, Intervention, and the Use of Force* (Oxford, OUP, 2008) 179, 188.
[43] This was the case in relation to ISIS in Syria 2015.
[44] C Chinkin and M Kaldor, *International Law and New Wars* (Cambridge, CUP, 2017) 518.

Ultimately, our position is that MPs should push the debate in the House of Commons away from a binary choice between armed conflict versus non-intervention towards a spectrum of alternatives and available choices. By focusing the debate on whether military action *should* happen, rather than whether it *can*, MPs can maximise their political influence over the Government. More importantly, however, they can expand the scope and depth of discussion relating to military action. This is necessary to test the strength of the Government's case for armed conflict, and to represent the broader interests of constituents, who may not see the choice between war and peace in the binary terms which it is often presented. This form of political pressure may, in appropriate circumstances, lead governments to consider and pursue alternative means of action.

I. The Security Council and the House of Commons: Different Institutions, Different Roles

In this chapter we argue that Parliament should debate issues relating to war regardless of the position of the Security Council. This does not mean that MPs should not consider the Council's position, but we insist that the House has to be involved separately and independently of the discussion at the international level. Our argument, that Parliament should effectively re-examine the political case for war, stems from the characteristics of the House of Commons as an elected legislature but also from the flaws and democratic deficit inherent in the international system, and the Security Council in particular. Although the decision-making in the Security Council seeks to establish the legality of the international intervention, its functioning is inherently different from Parliament. The next sections make the case for Parliament's involvement on both questions of international legality and legitimacy of military intervention. In the course of discussion, we consider how debate in the House of Commons may redress some flaws inherent in the international system and bring the decision-making closer to the electorate, in whose name the Government takes political decisions. Even if the discussion of military action requires a domestic duplication of the debate held at the international level, such a debate *must* take place so that MPs can speak on behalf and to their constituents.

First, the task of the Security Council is to speak on behalf of and to the Member States. Since international law treats states as black boxes and remains ignorant of their internal arrangements, this means that the Security Council is specifically interested in the positions of Member States' governments as opposed to their electorates.[45] The UN Charter speaks of 'Governments'[46] and 'Members of the United Nations'. In the part relating to the establishment and functions of the Security Council it refers to 'members' and 'signatory states', as do resolutions

---

[45] This is because in domestic law governments as a rule hold the legal right to represent the state in international relations.

[46] The Preamble of the Charter of the United Nations 1945, 'The UN Charter'.

passed by the Council.[47] Even more, in the preamble, the Charter clearly reflects that 'our respective Governments' 'have agreed to the present Charter' and all obligations contained therein. It is therefore clear that the constituent power from which the Security Council as an institution draws its power is not 'the people' but states as members of the UN. In this sense, the Council's function is drastically different from that of Parliament. It represents and is accountable to states, and not to the people within those states. This remains the case even when real people may be impacted by the Council's decisions.

The extent of this focus on the state has been described by Carne Ross, a former Foreign Office diplomat, who served at the UN during the early 2000s. Ross argues that the Security Council (and more generally the United Nations) is an international organisation in which diplomats are 'encouraged and taught to see themselves as the embodiment of their state (not merely their government)'.[48] This 'identification between the diplomats and their state is a false and arbitrary one'. In fact, mandarins are not elected and their primary role is not to concern themselves with public opinion or the problems of the people on the ground.[49] Rather, it is their Government that they remain accountable to and it is their Government's policies that they have to implement. Ross insists that 'when a diplomat speaks as "we" that statement only very rarely has anything to do with the real collective wishes of the state concerned'.[50] When a diplomat in the Security Council who is acting as the Government representative speaks on behalf of 'the state' or uses 'we', he or she does not speak for the person on the street, or the troops going into battle. He or she does not represent any specific constituency and is not answerable to his or her electors. In fact, as Ross testifies, diplomats are often so distanced that, 'What we lacked in that nasty overheated little room was any sense of what was really going on'.[51] To hide this ignorance of the situation on the ground, of the domestic implications and cost of potential actions, and the disconnect from the 'people', diplomats talk about 'the world as it really is'. This stance is used to 'preserve their own role, and the belief—comforting to us as well to them—that governments are "in charge" of events' and must determine what is important and what is to be done, and make and enforce the rules'.[52] Ross insists that embedded in this process of secret deliberation was 'a deep sense that "we" are in the right'[53] and often, that 'what "we" were offering the world was good'.[54]

---

[47] See Chs V and VII of the UN Charter.

[48] Carne Ross explains that the idea of representation goes so far that 'when you become a diplomat, you are encouraged to submit yourself to the collective state: your individual "I" becomes "we"'. See C Ross, *Independent Diplomat: Dispatches from the Unaccountable Elite* (New York, Cornell University Press, 2007) 21.

[49] ibid, 21. This disconnect is strongly criticised by Carne Ross, who argues that civil servants in the Security Council talk about the world without considering the people on the ground.

[50] ibid, 21.

[51] ibid, 54.

[52] ibid, 103.

[53] ibid, 92.

[54] ibid.

But assigning a group of people 'the right to determine (or even invent) the wishes of the state' comes at a cost. As Ross argues, 'the creation of a separate polit-ical and moral identity for [this] group of people—the policymakers of foreign policy—must inevitably risk artifice, arbitrariness, and ... a lack of accountability'.[55] In fact, most often the real people who will be impacted by the Council's decisions are absent from the discussion. In the debates on the future of the sanctions regime in Iraq, the Iraqi people were entirely absent from the Council's discussions and were not represented in the decision-making process. Similarly, in other conflicts the concerns about the people on whose behalf military interventions will begin (the Syrians, the Yemeni, etc), and about the troops being sent into battle (British, American, and other), about the economic costs of waging war (impacting upon the GDPs of several countries) were put to one side. Instead, a secret and unac-countable elite of expert diplomats made decisions that would affect people on the ground without providing them a voice. Although diplomats speak of 'we', the concept of 'we, the people' does not exist in the Security Council.

As we can see, the deliberations in the Security Council suffer from a 'democratic deficit': there is a lack of transparency and a lack of accountability. Proceedings also suffer from a participation deficit: as the Security Council is staffed by technocratic diplomats, as opposed to democratic representatives, and these officials represent only few selected states. As Ross describes his time at the UN, he notes that most often negotiations and deals were made in small rooms, which can only accommodate a few people 'tightly squeezed together'.[56] Most often these negotiations were limited to the representatives of the five permanent members of the Security Council: 'After the first few days, some of the small non-permanent Council delegates stopped bothering to attend the negotiations at all, even though their countries would have to vote on the outcome'.[57] As Ross argues, 'these were small delegations ... and the truth was that they were irrelevant'. They were merely spectators at the main fight. 'We all knew that they would vote for whatever outcome the permanent members could agree to, and they knew it too.'[58]

In the end, Governments act out of self-interest, diplomats believe they are 'right', and people on the ground are both absent from and unrepresented in deliberations. The decisions reached by the Council are therefore often utterly divorced from domestic concerns and domestic politics. The disconnect between the governed and the governors (or the 'succouring and affirming officials' which enforce government policies) is apparent. As a consequence, arguments are increasingly being made that the work of this unaccountable elite of diplomats in the Security Council should be laid open to greater scrutiny and interrogation.[59]

---

[55] ibid, 85.
[56] ibid, 49, in relation to negotiations on the Oil-for-Food programme in Iraq and about easing sanctions in Iraq in 2001.
[57] ibid, 50. For a view on this and the decreased legitimacy of the Council, see J Cohen, *Globalization and Sovereignty* (Cambridge, CUP, 2012).
[58] ibid.
[59] ibid, 9; D Hovell, 'Due Process in the United Nations' (2016) 110 *American Journal of International Law* 1.

The only way to correct mistakes that are made is 'for the governed, through elections and other elements of the open society … to inform the governors that their policies [are] not working and to propose how they might be changed'. Yet, 'such feedback mechanisms only exist in scant form in the field of international policy'.[60] It is here that national parliaments can come in.

The purpose and workings of the Westminster Parliament are a world away from the UN Security Council. Domestic legislatures, like the House of Commons, can and do play an inherently different role than the Security Council and in that function, its members can potentially address some of the deficiencies of the UN system and give life to the values of transparency, accountability, and participation. The greatest advantage of parliamentary engagement is that MPs are elected to their post by the people and serve a limited term until re-election. Compared to members of the Security Council, which represent governments, MPs represent the people. They are accountable to the electorate and will spend extensive time in their constituency on constituents' business.[61] In this regard, MPs are not as far removed from the people on the ground as diplomats or government representatives. Indeed, their primary role is not to give effect to government's policies but to question and scrutinise these, and in so doing, to consider their constituents' position and needs. MPs' position is therefore different than that of diplomats in the Council. They do not represent the Government, but rather hold it to account. They enjoy a privileged position of having a close link with their constituents. And because of this link, they can, arguably, make more legitimate decisions than the Council.[62]

For these reasons we believe that Parliament should re-examine questions discussed by the Security Council from the perspective of their own constituents, and more generally, the electorate. Although MPs should not seek to replace the Security Council on the issue of the international legality of the use of force, they should address similar questions to the Council to question whether the state should intervene militarily. In this sense, Parliament plays a dual role—first,

---

[60] Ross, *Independent Diplomat* (n 48) 11; The lack of democratic accountability at the international level in relation to the use of force is extensively covered in C Ku and H Jacobson, *Democratic Accountability and the Use of Force in International Law* (Cambridge, CUP, 2003) 17. The issue of how the problems can be addressed has been debated extensively: E Benvenisti, 'Sovereignty as Trusteeship for Humanity—Historical Antecedents and Their Impact on International Law' (2013) 107 *American Journal of International Law* 295.

[61] House of Commons, Select Committee on Modernisation of the House of Commons, 'Revitalising the Chamber: the role of the back bench Member' 1st Report 2006–07, HC 337; Memorandum from the Hansard Society (M29). The Memorandum reports that MPs spend on average 49% of their time on constituency work, with one MP reporting he spent up to 97% constituency matters. <publications.parliament.uk/pa/cm200607/cmselect/cmmodern/337/7031408.htm> accessed 17 September 2017.

[62] J Alvarez, *International Organizations as Law-makers* (Oxford, OUP, 2005) 630, who talks about SC acting without 'the benefit of law-makers representative of the demos these rules purport to affect.' See also D Sontag, *Global Failures on a Haitian Epidemic*, New York Times, 1 April 2012, at A1, on the loss of local trust. Local trust has been described 'as the most important capital for any UN peacekeeper'. See sources cited in T Dannenbaum, *Translating the Standard of Effective Control into a System of Effective Accountability* (2010) 51 *Harvard International Law Journal* 113, 121.

it questions the Government's case for war, and second, it brings domestic concerns into consideration. Parliament therefore brings a distinctly different perspective to the questions addressed in the Security Council: it seeks to question the Government from the perspective of the electorate. In this sense, MPs can use proper domestic discourse to challenge the elite, technocratic discussion, in the international institution. More importantly, however, the involvement of the House of Commons supplements the work of the Council by bringing democratic constraints into the decision-making process.

II. The Parliamentary Role on Questions of Legality

Parliament plays no role in making a military intervention legal in either domestic or international law. This, of course, does not mean that the question of legality is irrelevant for the purposes of political debate in the House. The certainty with which international legality has been established is crucial for the political discourse in the House. We encourage MPs to consider the reputational costs for the United Kingdom (and Parliament itself) when deciding whether or not to lend political support for pursuing an illegal or legally uncertain war. In this context, we believe that legality can shift the debate in the House from a presumption in favour of action to one against, but it should not stop all discourse. Even when the Security Council has been clear in its authorisation of the use of force, and when no doubt exists that an intervention is legal, the debate in the House remains relevant.

a. Distinguishing Domestic and International Legality

In the Security Council, the adoption of a resolution authorising force is the end result of an extensive debate about whether and why the international community should intervene. It comes after an assessment of the situation and implications of intervention, following an analysis of alternative sanctions available to compel a state to comply with international law, and finally, after a thorough consideration of the utility of the use of force. Often, states will assess the situation from different angles, adopting first lesser sanctions under other chapters of the UN Charter before proceeding onto a discussion of allowing the use of force under Chapter VII. This means that often by the time military action is on the table, states will already be extensively familiar with the situation on the ground, they will have exhausted numerous diplomatic solutions, and will be aware of the improbability of the violating state complying with international law otherwise than if threatened with force. The gradual but constant involvement of the Security Council gives each state an opportunity to clarify its position, to gather the intelligence necessary to answer any unanswered questions, and a chance to persuade other states of the need to intervene. It is only when the threat posed by the violating state has escalated so much that there are no other options available, that force will be authorised. The legality in the Council is therefore the end-product of a lengthy and intense debate about whether and why the international community should intervene.

By contrast, debate in Parliament often begins after proceedings in the Security Council. MPs approach these questions anew. MPs can of course debate the same issues that states do in the Council: they can discuss the motives for intervention, explore different alternatives to military force, and they can question short and long-term strategy. Yet, it is important to state clearly that Parliament plays no role in making or rendering an intervention legal—either internationally or domestically. As chapter two showed, from an international perspective an intervention is legal when it is authorised by the Security Council or when the situation compels a state to respond to an armed attack in self-defence, with the Security Council acknowledging the attack and recognising a right to respond. Under the UN Charter only the Security Council has the authority to provide the legal basis for action. The Charter's intention to entrust the 'authorisation' of force to an international institution, rather than domestic legislatures or governments, is driven by the view that the issue of peace and security are the concerns of the international community, as opposed to lone states. In this context, a resolution of the Security Council authorising the use of force is a legal decision reached through international consensus. States can intervene in discussion at the Security Council to present their own position and make representations, but the actions of no one state are binding upon the Security Council. The recognition of the existence of the threat, the right to self-defence, or the authorisation to use 'all measures necessary' requires an agreement of the international community. A number of countries will therefore have to share a similar or even the same view of the situation and will have to agree on the measure to be adopted.

As a matter of public international law, the Westminster Parliament has no power to act instead of the Security Council, and thus plays no role in the process of 'legalising' military action in the international sphere. It cannot substitute its own view of public international law in the absence of a clear ruling from the Security Council. Therefore, even if Members of the Commons use terminology which mirrors the language and proceedings in the Security Council, this does not render subsequent military action legal. International law rejects unilateralism and requires that the use of force is decided on the international level.

Parliament's role is equally limited as a matter of domestic law. From a domestic, constitutional perspective, an intervention is legal whenever the Government decides to send troops into battle, authorise airstrikes, or to deploy drones. Regardless of whether the Government is acting pursuant to a Security Council Resolution or without it, the Royal Prerogative, which the Government exercises unilaterally, empowers it to decide when force should be used abroad. Ideally, the two types of legality—the international and the domestic—should overlap and the

Government should use force only where there is a sufficient basis in international law. Yet, if the Government decides to act without the presence of an international legal basis, as a matter of English public law it has the power to do so. Even if Parliament is asked to provide support and approval for government's decision, a move that happens most often when the international legality of intervention is not clearly established, this does not change the legal position of the Government. Whether Parliament votes for or against the deployment of troops, the Government is legally free to initiate armed conflict as a matter of British constitutional law.

It is important to add here that Parliament's lack of power to 'legalise' a military intervention does not mean that the House of Commons' involvement has no impact on decisions to go to war. Parliament's political endorsement of government's decision confers domestic constitutional legitimacy on the decision-making process. It gives the elected representatives of the people an opportunity to assess the Government's case for war. Although Parliament's support does not make the Government's action legal, the Commons' support is crucial. In a system of representative democracy, the function of government is contingent on the support of the people. In the British Constitution, the Government must command the support of a majority of the House of Commons.[63] As Mill argued, the people have a decisive say over how and by whom they are governed. They have 'a voice in their own destiny'.[64] In this context, the role of Parliament is to represent the people who elected them and make decisions on their behalf. Although there is usually no requirement for MPs to act consistently with the wishes of the people, there is a strong incentive to act in way that will please the majority of those represented thus leading to their re-election. The people—though indirectly—get to participate in the decision-making process by electing or re-electing their representatives. The fact that parliamentarians' power is contingent on the continued support of the people reveals the close link between representatives and the people. By involving Parliament on issues of war the Government can allow representatives of the people—and thus indirectly the people—a voice. The involvement of Parliament therefore has a direct domestic impact on the decision to go to war.

b. The Uncertainty of International Law and its Implications

Legality provides the answer to whether—as a matter of international law—the Government *can* go to war. The presence of this 'can' element, ie the international legal basis, is often a material component of the Government's case for war before Parliament and to the general public. Readers will recall from chapter two that

---

[63] A Tomkins, *Our Republican Constitution* (Oxford, Hart, 2005) 1.

[64] JS Mill, 'Considerations on Representative Government' in *On Liberty and other essays* (Oxford, OUP: Oxford World's Classics, 2008) ch 3.

Figure 5.1: The question of international legality before Parliament

when the legal basis is clear and the Security Council has been unambiguous, governments rely on international law as a basis for intervention. They phrase their action as interventions on behalf of and for the international community. In contrast, when the legal basis is ambiguous or unclear, governments often turn to Parliament in an effort to secure a political majority to diffuse political responsibility for a potentially illegal action. This practice raises questions about the extent to which MPs are bound to consider or follow international law when a legal position from the UN Security Council (1) is clear and supports the use of force, (2) when it is unclear or altogether absent, or (3) when it is clear and prohibits the use of force (see Figure 5.1 above).

In this section, we argue that although MPs are not bound by international law, they should consider how clear the international basis for intervention is. Although this should not preclude subsequent discussion of whether the state should use military force, the lack of a legal basis can shift the presumption in favour of intervention to the other side of the spectrum and thus place a greater burden on the Government to persuade MPs of the necessity and legitimacy of the proposed action.

According to the House of Commons Code of Conduct, MPs have a duty to uphold the law.[65] The Code references the law against discrimination, which appears to address MPs' conduct as employers, not as legislators. In contrast with the Ministerial Code, which provided until recently that Ministers were under a 'duty to comply with the law including international law and treaty obligations',[66] the MPs' Code of Conduct makes no mention of international law. MPs act as legislators in a sovereign Parliament, meaning the Constitution allows them to theoretically make or unmake any law whatsoever. The British Constitution does not obligate parliamentarians to abide by the rules of public international law. Therefore, as a matter of domestic constitutional law, even if the Security Council were to prohibit a military intervention in a specific situation, MPs could still vote in favour of such a deployment. They would not be in violation of international law

---

[65] House of Commons, 'The Code of Conduct: The Guide to the Rules relating to the Conduct of Members'(2012) HC 1076) 3, para III.5.

[66] Compare with the duties which Ministers have to fulfil under the Ministerial Code 2010 and in the 2015 edition, where the reference to international law was withdrawn; <www.gov.uk/government/publications/ministerial-code> accessed 17 September 2017.

for a vote supporting military action because a vote in favour of a substantive motion is only a vote conferring political support. It is not a legal decision. As stated above, the Government retains the power of independent legal choice, meaning it could still choose to ignore the House of Commons and not go to war. Even if the Government proceeded into battle, MPs enjoy parliamentary privilege for both their participation in the debate, and for their vote under Article IX of the Bill of Rights 1689. This means that they could not be prosecuted for a violation of international law—in particular the crime of aggression—in the exercise of their duties.[67]

Yet, although MPs may not be bound to inquire into international legality, we believe they should consider this issue. The nature of Parliament's inquiry into international law varies in accordance with the clarity of the position of the Security Council. For example, when the legal basis is provided clearly in a UN resolution and allows for the use of force, the position is straightforward: MPs should acknowledge that as a matter of international law the intervention can take place, and then proceed to consider the arguments as to why the intervention should occur. We discuss this aspect of the debate further in section III, below. The issue of legality, however, plays a more crucial role when no clear legal basis exists for military action or when military action would be clearly illegal.

Since the Charter prohibits the use of force generally in Article 2(4), in principle any action outside of the Charter should be prohibited. Yet, the Security Council does not issue resolutions prohibiting military action in advance of such action. Instead, condemnation of a particular use of force by the Security Council (or the General Assembly) or express findings of aggression which are 'conclusive or at least persuasive as to illegality' are issued ex post facto.[68] But the Commons cannot wait until such condemnations are made by the UN.[69] Prior to a vote Parliament is therefore unlikely to know for certain whether an intervention is clearly illegal. Even in the case of Iraq 2003, the Government asserted that the invasion was legal and produced an opinion which argued for a revival of the old Resolution 678 of 1990 in relation to the Gulf War, which authorised 'all necessary means' to be

---

[67] A recent judgment of the Supreme Court shows that privilege does not protect members of either House against prosecution for fraud committed against the House, and it would not protect against prosecution for other serious crimes merely because they happened to be committed while a member was using parliamentary resources. *R v Chaytor* [2010] UKSC 52 at 28 and 122. Aggression, however, is not a crime under English law (*R v Jones (Margaret)* [2007] 1 AC 136, HL; *R (Al Rabbat) v Westminster Magistrates' Court* [2017] EWHC 1969 (Admin) so there is unlikely to be a prosecution for this in any case.

[68] C Gray, *International Law and the Use of Force* (OUP, Oxford, 2008) 20 ff. Furthermore, 'condemnation of another state by a state with whom it normally has close relations … is exceptionally strong evidence of illegality'. Even rarer are express findings of aggression, which are reserved for states seen 'as outlaws', eg, Portugal when it refused to relinquish its colonial possessions, Southern Rhodesia after its unilateral declaration of independence, Israel after occupation of West Bank, Gaza.

[69] In fact, often states on the Security Council or the General Assembly may think that, although the legality of a particular use of force is open to question, the acts should not be condemned because they were morally or politically justified. The Entebbe raid where the Council failed to condemn Israel serves as an example.

taken if Iraq did not comply with international demands in previous resolutions. Read together with Resolution 1441, the report argued that the two sources allowed for the use of force. Although the then-Secretary General insisted that if the US and others were to proceed without a Security Council resolution 'and take military action, it would not be in conformity with the Charter'.[70] There was no advance warning of illegality or threat of condemnation from the Security Council or the General Assembly.

In practice, therefore, in advance of a deployment of troops the Commons is most often faced with a lack of clarity as to the existence of a legal basis for such action. Even when a UN resolution is passed, however, the legal basis for the use of force may be unclear and ambiguous. In 2015, a Resolution supposedly authorising force against ISIS/ISIL in Syria called upon

> Member States that have the capacity to do so to take all necessary measures, ... to redouble and coordinate their efforts to prevent and suppress terrorist acts committed specifically by ISIL also known as Da'esh ... and to eradicate the safe haven they have established over significant parts of Iraq and Syria.[71]

Although the paragraph does refer to 'all necessary measures', which is code for force, it does not rely on Chapter VII of the Charter, which gives the Council the power to authorise force. Nor does it 'actually authorize any actions against IS or ... provide a legal basis for the use of force against IS either in Syria or in Iraq'.[72] The Government made the case for legality before the House, but we argue that the Resolution was ambiguous.[73]

The constructive ambiguity of Security Council Resolutions and the potential inability to secure UN support for force leads states to invoke the only other legal basis upon which force can be used: self-defence.[74] As far as identification of the law of use of force is concerned, the practice relating to self-defence further complicates the picture. Namely, 'states have sought to bring almost any unilateral use of force within the legal ambit of self-defence'.[75] This means that the notion of self-defence, which traditionally was considered to apply to an (ongoing) armed attack by a state, has been redefined to include the pre-emptive use of force against non-state actors[76] and to justify the use of targeted killings. The notion of self-defence

---

[70] UN Secretary General Kofi Annan, Press Conference, The Hague, The Netherlands (10 March 2003) <www.hri.org/news/world/undh/2003/03-03-10.undh.html> accessed 17 September 2017.

[71] United Nations Security Council Resolution 2249 (2015).

[72] D Akande and M Milanović, 'The Constructive Ambiguity of the Security Council's ISIS Resolution', EJIL Talk, <www.ejiltalk.org/the-constructive-ambiguity-of-the-security-councils-isis-resolution> 17 September 2015.

[73] V Fikfak, 'Voting on Military Action in Syria' *UK Const L* blog (28 November 2015) <ukconstitutionallaw.org> accessed 17 September 2017.

[74] It therefore makes sense that in 2015 David Cameron made use of both the SC Resolution and self-defence as legal grounds on which intervention against ISIS in Syria was based.

[75] Chinkin and Kaldor, *International Law and New Wars* (n 44) 129.

[76] 'National Security Strategy', The White House (17 September 2002) 15, <www.state.gov/documents/organization/63562.pdf> accessed 17 September 2017, 6.

has thus been stretched not only to include self-defence against an attack that has not yet occurred, but also to respond to terrorist cells, rather than states.[77] The problem with these new interpretations is that they exploit the imprecise content of international law and create additional grey zones in international law and further uncertainty about the legality or illegality of a particular action.[78]

For Parliament, the inherent uncertainty of the international law on the use of force is critical. Political leaders who are contemplating unilateral military intervention may turn to MPs to seek support for action. In this situation MPs 'should not … encourage [the Government] to believe that international law is firmly on their side. It is not. At best, it is unclear'.[79] When MPs are therefore asked—or perhaps tempted—to fill the apparent gap with their own discussion of concepts such as 'threat', 'self-defence' and 'all measures necessary', they should instead acknowledge and recognise the limits of international law, the inherent uncertainty of the legal basis, and seek to compel the Government to accept this position as well. Only such honesty can enable and contribute to a better discussion on the question whether the state *should* go to war. The recognition of the uncertainty of the international legal basis can shift the presumption in favour of intervention to the other side of the spectrum and thus place a greater burden on the Government to persuade MPs of the necessity and legitimacy of the proposed action.

We believe that such honesty is crucial for two reasons: for its precedential value and for the reputational costs of fighting a potentially illegal war. Differing interpretations of international rules can incrementally carve out new exceptions to the prohibition of the use of force. Through consistent practice and belief about the scope of rules, state actions can change customary international law and effectuate a shift in the international law of the use of force.[80] State behaviour therefore has precedential value. If a state sets a precedent for other states to bypass the Security Council, and insists that its use of force qualifies as self-defence, this invites others to follow its lead. According to Chinkin and Kaldor, 'what is striking is that claims made by the liberal democracies for a more elastic interpretation of the permissibility of the use of force [under the self-defence

---

[77] As a consequence, some have argued that the prohibition of the use of force contained in Article 2(4) of the UN Charter is in a state of 'grave weakness' and is 'on the brink of clinical death or in intensive care'. J D'Aspremont, 'Mapping the Concepts behind the Contemporary Liberalization of the Use of Force in International Law' (2010) 31 *University of Pennsylvania Journal of International Law* 1089.

[78] Roberts, 'Legality vs Legitimacy' (n 42) 203. The self-defence exception has, for example, been invoked by states in bad faith. In 1968, the USSR's armed forces entered Czechoslovakia in order to replace Dubcek's liberalising regime with a hardline communist regime. The USSR argued that the intervention was necessary on the basis of collective self-defence against anti-communists. The justification was widely rejected though was not condemned by the Council because the USSR used its veto to block the Resolution. See S/8761 sponsored by Brazil, Canada, Denmark, France, Senegal, the United Kingdom and the United States.

[79] T Franck 'Conference Proceedings: Part II The Present' in RB Lillich (ed) *Humanitarian Intervention and the United Nations* (Charlottesville, University Press of Virginia, 1973) 64.

[80] *The North Sea Continental Shelf Case (Judgment)* [1969] ICJ 12 [15].

Figure 5.2: The question of international legality before Parliament

exception] are echoed by powerful, non-liberal states'.[81] Military operations by Russia in Georgia, Crimea, and Ukraine stand as examples.

For this reason, MPs should not be too quick to accept governmental arguments about the clarity of the legal basis. Clearly, MPs have no power to make the Government's decision internationally legal, but this fact alone does not alleviate the potential for problems. When parliamentarians affirm the Government's view and interpretation of international law, they may contribute to the development of public international law in a manner that they may not have intended or desired. This, in turn, has potentially unintended consequences for the reputation of Parliament on the international stage. Parliamentarians and the state as a whole may face rebuke and condemnation by the international community for contributing to the distortion of the rules of public international law by affirming the Government's viewpoint and contributing (unconsciously) to the development of state practice.

As Figure 5.2 (above) shows, the issue of whether a state can go to war is a valid question to begin a parliamentary debate in a domestic setting. Yet, international law almost always remains unclear and uncertain, especially in relation to the use of force. There is no one to enforce a specific interpretation of the law or to provide one.[82] The answer to such questions will crystallise only with time.[83]

---

[81] Chinkin and Kaldor, *International Law and New Wars* (n 44) 130, citing N Krisch 'Crimea and the Limits of International Law' *EJIL Talk* blog (10 March 2014) <www.ejiltalk.org> accessed 17 September 2017.

[82] Unless theoretically, recourse could be had to the International Court of Justice for an advisory opinion.

[83] Legitimacy of military action hinges on leader's powers' of persuasion and can be enhanced or diminished depending on whether the use of force enjoys some measure of collective support or not. Eg, Independent International Commission on Kosovo, Kosovo Report: 'Conflict, International Response, Lessons Learned' (2000) 194–95. Danish Institute of International Affairs, 'Humanitarian Intervention: Legal and Political Aspects' (1999) 24.

Precisely because of the inherent uncertainty of the state of international law and the reaction of the international community, it is often impossible to claim with any certainty that a legal basis exists or that it is clear. Of course, the extent of the ambiguity will be one of degree, this is precisely why we argue that MPs must recognise and be honest about the limits of international law, and in turn, proceed with healthy scepticism towards the Government's arguments. In this context, we would hope that MPs would seek out legal advice (discussed below). Most importantly of all, MPs should recognise and acknowledge on the Floor of the House the lack of clarity of international legal rules and the potential wide-reaching precedential impact and reputational costs their unconditional support could have.

III. Creating a Culture of Challenge: Interventions as Wars of Choice

Although we believe that the question of whether an intervention is legal should be asked in the House of Commons, we wish to underline that this issue should not overwhelm the debate in Parliament or preclude it altogether. In chapter two, we showed that if the Security Council is silent on a situation, MPs are drawn into discussion of legal concepts such as 'threat', 'self-defence' and 'all measures necessary'. The Government is partly responsible for framing the debate in this 'legal' language, seeking to use the House as a replacement for the silent international institution. But MPs themselves contribute to this discourse by prioritising interpretations of concepts associated with legality, and leaving concerns about the motivations for intervention and long-term plans only for secondary consideration. The House of Commons can therefore be constrained by legality at the expense of undertaking a wide-ranging debate that we might reasonably expect of a domestic representative body. The debate about whether the war is legal should not end up acting as a trump card. Instead, MPs should—having determined and acknowledged the scope or limits of the international legal basis—proceed towards other broader questions, specifically the question of whether the state should go to war. This question, we insist, should be asked always, even when the legality of intervention has been clearly established. Here we outline the elements of a 'culture of challenge' to equip MPs to enquire into the legitimacy of the Government's case for war in the widest possible sense.

a. From False Certainty to Distinguishing Legality and Legitimacy

Legal language provides the false certainty that interventions in certain conflicts are 'legal' and therefore legitimate, whilst others are 'illegal' and therefore should not be fought. This form of false dichotomy drives debates on war and presents them in binary terms. This makes recourse to law in difficult situations an ostensibly attractive proposition. But when we remove legal language from discussions of war, the questions of when and why we should go to war arise anew.

In this context, one of the first issues that arises is the distinction between the realms of legality and legitimacy. Even if legality has been clearly established at international level, we argue that MPs should proceed to inquire into and consider the legitimacy of military action. Even if the Security Council has therefore explicitly answered both questions, we insist that MPs re-examine these issues to establish the legitimacy of such an intervention in the domestic context.

The domestic importance of a broad discussion on legitimacy is acutely illustrated by the recent intervention in Libya. The 2016 Foreign Affairs Committee report on the intervention in Libya in 2011 reveals that the decision to use force against another state authorised by the Security Council may be made on a questionable basis, motivated by self-interest, and enabled by alliances and power dynamics between the permanent members. The report uncovered that whilst France insisted on the adoption of a resolution authorising force to protect civilians on the ground, the intelligence did not support the proposition that Gaddafi would have ordered the massacre of his own people. It is in fact doubtful whether the civilian population was in danger in 2011. Instead, the report found that French policy was motivated by other factors.[84] As the Foreign Affairs Committee reported, Libyan exiles based in France were influential in raising fears about the future of Libya and 'were anxious to push for a real change in Libya'.[85] The French motivations were further driven by a desire to gain a greater share of Libyan oil, to increase French influence in North Africa, and to improve the internal political situation in France. All of these reasons are hardly sufficient to legitimate a resolution authorising force for humanitarian reasons, especially one based on conjecture and without a clear long-term plan. Yet, the balance of power in the Security Council and the interests of Member States sitting on it allowed for a clear and unambiguous resolution from the Security Council to pass. The fact that ultimately the intervention was authorised on the international level—and was thus made legal—does not detract from the dubious reasons that motivated French policy. It also does not make the decision 'good' or 'correct', especially a decision that did not consider how the militant extremist groups would attempt to benefit from the intervention. So, an action can at once be legal (because of proceedings in the UN Security Council) but potentially also unnecessary or illegitimate because of the motivations of the actors involved.

The gap between the real reasons for military intervention and the humanitarian argument made by France before the Security Council should not surprise us. 'Governments will always prefer to make a moral case for war than one based purely on self-interest.'[86] Yet Libya shows clearly how the process of providing a legal basis for the use of force at the international level can be misused and how the functioning and effectiveness of the Security Council depends on the balance of

---

[84] House of Commons Foreign Affairs Committee 'Libya: Examination of intervention and collapse and the UK's future policy options' 3rd Report 2016–17, HC 119, 10.

[85] ibid, 10, citing George Joffe's testimony.

[86] L Freedman 'On War and Choice', 107 *The National Interest* 9, 15.

power and the interests of permanent members. It is the permanent members that prevented a UN-authorised invasion of Iraq and later interventions in Syria; but they enabled the intervention in Libya.

Yet, the Libya example also illustrates how legal authority can be secured for interventions which may not require such action, and how this alone can preclude a debate in Parliament or completely overwhelm parliamentary discussion. Once the Security Council authorised the intervention in Libya, the UK Parliament was silenced repeatedly. It was excluded by the UK Government, who only involved it in the discussion after troops had already been sent abroad and after airstrikes had started. Then, it was asked to reaffirm a clear but problematic Security Council Resolution, which MPs welcomed and commended the Government for securing before initiating military action. The legal basis which the Security Council Resolution provided was therefore the focus of debates in Parliament.

The Libya scenario illustrates why democratic scrutiny—even of an ostensibly legal conflict—remains vitally important. Democratic scrutiny can potentially redress imbalances in deliberation in the Security Council by bringing a wider range of perspectives to bear upon questions of legitimacy. Instead of focusing on the legality of the intervention, MPs should have questioned the British Government's motivation for seeking to intervene in Libya. As the Foreign Affairs Committee report showed, the UK's 'intervention was reactive and did not comprise action in pursuit of a strategic objective'.[87] As well as whether the UK should intervene in Libya, the report also notes that questions should have been raised about whether all political options available prior to military action had been explored.[88] The answer provided by the Foreign Affairs Committee was that they were not. It is clear from this that the international legal question completely overwhelmed the domestic debate. Instead of focusing on legality, it would have been beneficial to have a more intense domestic scrutiny of a purely political nature before Parliament approved the British Government's perspective. The question regarding whether we should go to war, the motives, and alternative options should have been explored.

The unquestioned legal authority and the automatic acceptance of the Resolution by the Government and by Parliament gave the intervention in Libya—as well as many other prior interventions—an 'outward appearance of virtue'.[89] It is precisely this façade that a UN Resolution accords to the decision to use force that we find problematic. The Westminster Parliament should not participate in the process of blindly following a UN resolution authorising force. If an answer to the question 'can we go to war?' is provided, this does not preclude a political discussion around whether the state *should* intervene with military force. To treat the legal question as conclusively establishing the need for intervention would

---

[87] House of Commons Foreign Affairs Committee, 'Libya' (n 84) 18.
[88] ibid.
[89] Plato, *The Republic*, [c.380BC] HDP Lee (trans.) (Harmondsworth, Penguin, 1955) quoted in M Loughlin, *Sword and Scales* (Oxford, Hart, 2000) 14.

unnecessarily and unwisely preclude a discussion of the legitimacy and necessity of such action. A decision to go to war is a complex combination of moral values and political strategy. There are hardly any objectively right or wrong answers. Yet, the legal language serves to simplify the debate and is used to present war as an obligation or a necessity and not as a complex moral and political choice.

In this context, to prioritise the traditional focus on legal questions to the exclusion of other, perhaps more apparently political questions, like legitimacy and necessity, undermines MPs' obligation to make political choices. It also leads to and reinforces cynicism about politics. But we are not cynical about politics: as Loughlin argues, 'law and politics are related, but also competing practices through which people aspire to settle their differences'.[90] When law acts as a trump over politics, it closes down the opportunity to see the differing viewpoints and puts a stop to a discussion that can lead to a more carefully balanced compromise to the extent that it 'no longer matters what are the outcomes of political deliberation'.[91] Law thus 'is not and cannot be a substitute for politics'.[92] Politics allows for the exchange of different opinions and disagreements and a contest between different visions of what ought to take place. In this regard, politicians are political animals who pursue political ends that are far more complex than abstractions such as a 'legal' war.[93] They balance and compromise and through the political process, and their decisions risk their reputation or position. It is this inherent vulnerability, but also the fact of having to be more attuned to the views of the people on the ground, and concerns of those who are directly impacted by their decisions that make politicians especially suitable to debate whether we should go to war.

We therefore believe that in domestic discussions of war, the issues of legality and legitimacy (together with necessity) should be treated as two distinct questions. Whilst the legality question may be debated by MPs, to either establish whether the Security Council has provided an unambiguous legal basis or to acknowledge that there is uncertainty in international law, we insist that establishing the legality of the use of force should not be the focus of MPs' deliberation. Instead, the debate in the House should focus on the legitimacy and necessity of such action, enabling inherently 'political decisions [to] be taken by politicians'.[94]

b. From False Dichotomies to Wars of Choice

In the absence of a legal framework, we wish to provide parliamentarians with a rubric by which to begin discussion and evaluate the Government's case for war.

---

[90] ibid, 217.
[91] GW Smith, *Liberalism—Critical concepts in political theory* (London, Routledge, 2002) 15.
[92] JAG Griffith, 'The Political Constitution' (1979) 42 *Modern Law Review* 1, 16.
[93] ibid.
[94] ibid.

Our proposal is that MPs must approach the issue of war in a manner that will facilitate political discussion and move the debate away from binary distinctions. In the vacuum created by the appropriate constraint of discussions on legality, parliamentarians must ask the Government three over-arching questions. In this regard, if interventions are perceived as wars of choice, the first question that MPs have to inquire into is the interests that are involved, and the dangers the situation represents to the United Kingdom. Although vital interests are likely to trigger a military response, this may not always be automatic. Equally, when vital interests are not engaged, military action is not excluded, but it is preserved for the moment in which other alternatives have been exhausted, and where benefits outweigh the costs of inaction. The second question Parliament must concentrate upon involves the identification of a spectrum of options available prior to considering military action. The final—third—question then focuses on the assessment between the benefits of using force versus the cost of using other alternatives. This ratio of benefits to costs 'must be superior to what would be expected from other policies'.[95] In essence, we therefore argue for a shift in perspective, from which the case for war no longer appears clear-cut. Instead, by presenting military action as a matter of choice, the outcome—and the subsequent deployment of troops—depend on the political debate in Parliament.

When governments make their case for war before domestic legislatures, the first question they seek to address concerns the interests involved. As a rule, governments portray interventions as involving important, even vital, national interests by underlining the considerable price of doing nothing. These wars are presented as wars of necessity, imposed on the British Government by others, and are conflicts which allow for no other alternatives to the use of force. On its face, a war of this nature is most likely to be a situation involving self-defence. As Maimonides argued, 'obligatory war does not start until one is actually attacked by an army'.[96] Yet, the war of necessity has been invoked also in situations where no attack has taken place. Governments will frequently package a case for war in terms of its necessity, however dubious history may eventually consider such claims. For example, when George W Bush was asked by a US media channel following the discovery that no weapons of mass destruction existed in Iraq, and whether he believed the 2003 Iraq War was one of choice or necessity, he responded, 'It's a war of necessity. In my judgment, we had *no choice* when we look

---

[95] RN Haass, *War of Necessity, War of Choice: A Tale of Two Iraq Wars*, 2nd edn (New York, Simon & Schuster, 2010) xviii. Haass's distinction between 'war of choice' and 'war of necessity' is not new. The great scholar Maimonides wrote more than eight centuries ago of wars he judged to be obligatory and those he termed optional. The distinction between choice and necessity was also drawn by the late Israeli Prime Minister Menachem Begin in 1982, where he described the Israeli invasion of Lebanon to push Palestinian Liberation Organisation forces out of the country as one of choice. He contrasted this decision with a war 'of no alternative' in 1973, when the country had been attacked by Egypt and Syria.

[96] See Maimonides' commentary to Sotah 8:7 quoted in J Patout Burns (ed), *War and Its Discontents: Pacifism and Quietism in the Abrahamic Traditions* (Washington DC, Georgetown University Press, 1996) 5.

at the intelligence I looked at that says the [Saddam Hussein] was a threat'.[97] This assessment contradicts those who acted as Bush's advisors at the time: 'We did not have to go to war against Iraq, certainly not when we did. There were other options: to rely on other policy tools, to delay attacking, or both'.[98]

The Bush example shows how even in situations when a choice exists, there is an 'addiction to selling all wars as vital'.[99] This pressure to present war as 'necessary', 'unavoidable', and as having 'no alternative' predetermines the outcome and acts as a trump in a similar manner as questions of public international law. An unchallenged claim of war-as-necessity presents a significant barrier to worthwhile deliberation in Parliament. As Sir Lawrence Freedman argues 'because of the strong legal and ethical presumptions against war, it is not surprising that when committing to combat, governments like to assert that they are following some unassailable strategic logic that permits no alternative'. In this context, 'talking of a war of choice opens up debate; asserting a war of necessity closes it down. Choices can be good or bad; necessity chooses for you'.[100] It is worth repeating this: thinking of war as a matter of choice facilitates debate, whilst referring to war as a 'necessity' closes it down.

In this book, we seek to facilitate and invigorate the deliberating space in Parliament. Instead of accepting the idea that all wars are potentially wars of necessity, we therefore think it is crucial that MPs assume that today most wars are *wars of choice*. We make this argument for several reasons. First, whether an intervention is a matter of choice or necessity is rarely apparent at the time the decisions are made. As Freedman, an expert in the area of war studies, comments on the necessity–choice distinction between the Gulf and Iraq Wars in 1990 and 2003: 'the truth is these decisions are never quite so obvious at the time, and they always depend on the political circumstances'.[101] Furthermore, in relation to the Gulf War, a number of choices were open at the time of decision-making. It was open to governments to concentrate on defending Saudi Arabia or on liberating Kuwait. Questions arose as to whether efforts should be undertaken through the United Nations or a coalition of the willing, or whether a response should have focused upon economic sanctions, or primarily the use of military force. Finally, if military force was used, a decision about whether this should include ground troops or be

---

[97] T Russert, 'Meet the Press', 7 February 2004, interview with George W Bush; <www.nbcnews.com/id/4209295/ns/meet_the_press/t/pres-george-w-bushinterview-highlights> accessed 17 September 2017. In more detail, Tim Russert asks: 'In light of not finding the weapons of mass destruction, do you believe the war in Iraq is a war of choice or a war of necessity?' President Bush responds: 'I think that's an interesting question. Please elaborate on that a little bit. A war of choice or a war of necessity? It's a war of necessity. In my judgment, we had no choice when we look at the intelligence I looked at that says the man was a threat.'

[98] RN Haass, *War of Necessity, War of Choice: A Tale of Two Iraq Wars*, 1st edn (New York, Simon & Schuster, 2010) 15 (emphasis added). Haass is currently the President of the Council on Foreign Relations but at the time acted as Bush's former US Director of Policy Planning.

[99] J Record, 'Back to the Weinberger-Powell Doctrine?' (2007) *Strategic Studies Quarterly* 79, 90.

[100] 'On War and Choice' (n 86) 11.

[101] ibid.

limited to attacks from the air was required. Put simply, a choice was available at each stage. Describing the Gulf War as one of no alternative only obscured these choices. What was described as a 'war of necessity', ie a conflict touching upon a country's vital interests, is much more accurately described as a 'war of choice' that requires that a decision be made promptly and allows for no delays.[102]

Secondly, experts in strategic studies argue that today 'war is more a matter of choice than necessity'.[103] The nature of warfare has changed. Although in certain circumstances, the UK may be attacked and thus a need may arise for immediate defence of the country from military invasion (eg in a manner similar to the protection of the Falkland Islands), the expert consensus is that these situations are increasingly rare.[104] Situations similar to the World Wars in which major military powers faced off are now less likely.[105] Instead, since the 1990s, regular instances in which force is needed for humanitarian purposes when dysfunctional countries turn on their own people, and civil wars leading to inter-communal violence (Kosovo, Bosnia, Somalia, Rwanda, and today in Libya and Syria, and other neglected areas like Yemen) are the most common paradigm. As Freedman continues, 'these humanitarian interventions became the archetypal "wars of choice"'.[106] In addition, new adversaries have come to the fore. The threat of terrorism from failed or rogue states has become more acute, rendering the choices that governments have to make more complex:[107] 'When you are clearly at risk … then a decision of some sort is required'.[108] But it is often unclear what this decision should include when threats are unspecific or general (ie a threat of a terrorist attack anywhere in the world), and interventions appear to require pre-emptive action. In these circumstances, we believe a country always has a choice— if not *whether* to intervene, then regarding *how* it intervenes.[109]

Finally, a decision to go to war is bound to lead to the loss of many lives and 'ought to be taken with a heavy heart'.[110] As a consequence, any choice that is made to put lives in danger, has to satisfy a number of requirements. As Haass argues, all wars of choice have to go through a two-prong test. On one side, governments have to show that the benefits outweigh the costs and that the overall or net results of employing force will be positive. On the other side, other alternatives have to be seriously considered and exhausted before force can be employed. This is because 'Wars of choice place added burdens on decision-makers because of the

---

[102] ibid.

[103] ibid, 12 citing letter from Gerry Segal.

[104] From our perspective, the phrase 'war of necessity' is narrower than the international practice relating to self-defence. We link it to the traditional realist-based model under which self-defence applies only to an (ongoing) armed attack by a state.

[105] 'On War and Choice' (n 86) 10.

[106] ibid, 11.

[107] ibid, 12.

[108] ibid, 14.

[109] In *A (FC) and Others (FC) v Secretary of State for the Home Department* [2004] UKHL 56, paras 96–97 (Lord Hoffmann).

[110] 'On War and Choice' (n 86) 14.

often-considerable human, military, and economic costs associated with going to war. Such wars should be fought only after the most rigorous assessments of the likely costs and benefits of action—as well as of the likely costs and benefits of implementing other policies'.[111]

We therefore encourage MPs to internalise the assumption that all wars are wars of choice, and adopt these tests in order to perform their function of scrutinising government proposals for action. The conception of a war as a 'war of choice' will help structure domestic political discourse in Parliament. It will provide a template for discussion that was previously (and erroneously) provided by legality. In this context, the initial perception of military action as an action of choice can automatically lead MPs to focus on two crucial tasks: the identification of a range of options available prior to considering military action; and the conduct of a cost–benefit assessment between using force *versus* using other alternatives.

Our claim is that when the question whether we should go to war is asked in the House of Commons, the choices available are most likely numerous. They exist at two levels: whether to take some action or not; and what that action should be. This exercise requires MPs to disaggregate a necessity to intervene from the necessity to intervene through the use of force. A necessity to intervene does not equate to a war of necessity. Although the Government may present its case in stark terms, it is rare that no alternatives to force exist. For example, we opened this chapter by explaining that in the case of bombing of Kosovo in 1999, Tony Blair presented it as a choice between doing something and doing nothing. However, the reality of this conflict was that states could have used more flexible diplomacy in negotiating with the Former Republic of Yugoslavia before the bombings. They also could have avoided excluding Russian diplomats from the negotiations. Finally, states could have avoided offering terms to which the Federal Republic of Yugoslavia would clearly never agree.[112] Furthermore in relation to Iraq, the Chilcot Report concluded, all alternatives were not identified or explored.[113]

Taking the starting position that intervention is always optional is crucial to creating opportunities to allow for a political discussion. As Chilcot concluded: 'Above all, the lesson is that all aspects of any intervention need to be calculated, debated and challenged with the utmost rigour'.[114] We believe a large part of this responsibility falls upon the House of Commons. The war of choice rubric allows

---

[111] R Haass, 'The Necessary and the Chosen' *Foreign Affairs* (July/August 2008) <www.foreignaffairs.com/articles/iraq/2009-04-23/necessary-and-chosen> accessed 17 September 2017.

[112] R Falk, 'Kosovo, World Order, and the Future of International Law' (1999) 93 *AJIL* 847 at 850. Others argue that greater pressure might have been placed on China and Russia to abstain from voting instead of vetoing an authorisation to use force, and that Russia and China could have made statements to the effect that their abstentions did not amount to approval of the action and did not form a precedent for future humanitarian interventions. D Joyner, 'The Kosovo Intervention: Legal Analysis and a More Persuasive Paradigm' (2002) 13 *European Journal of International Law* 597, 608.

[113] Sir John Chilcot, 'Sir John Chilcot's Public Statement' (6 July 2016) <www.iraqinquiry.org.uk/the-inquiry/sir-john-chilcots-public-statement> accessed 17 September 2017.

[114] ibid.

MPs to question the Government as to whether viable alternative policies, like diplomacy, inaction, delay, or economic or other sanctions are possible, and to assess whether the case for war is sound. The nature of the cost–benefit test may further compel more open Government through requiring more access to information, and ease restrictions on the subject matter under debate.

Our proposals ask a lot of MPs. If the discussion of legality allowed both Government and Parliament to avoid many of the underlying issues relating to war, our approach asks both institutions to put the fundamental assumption that war is a necessary and viable option squarely under the microscope. In this context, we would expect MPs to consider—as Rodin has asked—whether it can be right to use the methods of war to protect people when this also involves the killing of, and injury to, other non-combatants; whether it can be right to kill civilians to save other civilians; and whether collective enforcement could ever be an appropriate tool against brutal oppressors, since it also involves attacking the victims of those oppressors.[115] These are difficult questions, but a decision to wage war should not be 'easier … because it's about other people's countries'.[116] In this context, we subscribe to the view of Chinkin and Kaldor who propose a new 'strategy of resistance … as an alternative to the War on Terror' and a new 'right to be protected'. This strategy rejects the use of force as a viable alternative and instead involves and empowers local actors to 'resist and ultimately reshape peace initiatives through interactions with international actors and institutions'.[117] The move—both in scholarship and in practice on the ground—is therefore away from either/or options towards a reconceptualisation of some of the dominant binaries that underpin conventional liberal thinking in relation to war.[118] From this perspective, military intervention becomes more of an exception rather than the rule.[119] And in every case, it has to be accompanied by 'a culture of challenge'.[120]

The tools of a 'culture of challenge' are offered to parliamentarians to better equip them to fulfil their constitutional duty of effective scrutiny of the Government's case for war. In the table below, we summarise the role Parliament should play in relation to the different issues raised in discussion of armed conflict. In relation to whether the state *can* go to war, Parliament should consider the legality and acknowledge the problems of uncertainty of international law where applicable.

---

[115] D Rodin, *War and Self-Defense* (Oxford, OUP, 2002).

[116] Rory Stewart, MP and the Minister of State at the Department for International Development states that 'waging war is oddly an easier thing to do because it's about other people's countries.' In C Ross, *Accidental Anarchist: Life Without Government* (2017) <www.imdb.com/title/tt6130010> accessed 17 September 2017.

[117] OP Richmond and A Mitchell, 'Introduction—Towards a Post-liberal Peace: Exploring Hybridity via Everyday Forms of Resistance, Agency and Autonomy' in OP Richmond and A Mitchell (eds), *Hybrid Forms of Peace: From Everyday Agency to Post-Liberalism* (Basingstoke, Palgrave Macmilllan, 2012) 1–38, 11.

[118] Chinkin and Kaldor, *International Law and New Wars* (n 44) 518.

[119] Sir John Chilcot, Public Statement (n 113), noting implicitly that war should be a last resort.

[120] 'Lessons still to be learned from the Chilcot Inquiry' (n 1) para 58.

	Issue	Who is the initiator?	What is the role of Parliament and MPs?
Can	International legality	Security Council/ Government	Consider legality, uncertainty of international law, implications for international reputation
Should (Government's case for war)	All or nothing, good or evil	Government	Seek to push debate from binary options to a spectrum of options
Should (domestic concerns)	Domestic political questions	Parliament	Bring into debate public opinion, consider constituents' views, resources and GDP

Figure 5.3: The role of Parliament in relation to the different issues that arise in the discussion of armed conflict

This should, in turn, lead to a discussion of the broader implications a decision to intervene could have for the state's international reputation, and development of international law more generally (including encouraging other states to fight their own wars elsewhere). On the question of whether the country *should* go to war we encourage Parliament to think about wars as wars of choice, and to seek to shift the debate from binary options to a spectrum of alternatives and a cost–benefit analysis in which military action is presented and considered to be the last available option.

Conceptualising conflicts as *wars of choice* is a crucial step towards fostering better quality deliberation and debate in the House. If it becomes clear during debate that the vital interests of the state are involved, the balancing act required by the cost–benefit analysis will be easier to satisfy than when these are not involved. We do not seek to have Parliament exert political pressure on the Government to prevent *necessary* military action. 'When a country has been attacked and the choice is between resistance and surrender, there may only seem to be one honourable decision its leaders can make. There may have been a choice but not much of one.' Or, 'it may seem self-evident that the costs of inaction far outweigh those of action'.[121] The right approach is therefore 'not to rule out' fighting, but to minimise it so 'as

---

[121] It is this quasi-obvious outcome that has led Haass (and others) to define a situation involving vital interest as a 'war of necessity', a war that has to be fought.

to ensure that there is still the adequate will and ability to fight wars' when vital interests are engaged.[122]

The approach we propose here allows for fluidity between the international and the domestic questions—we propose that MPs consider international legality and then move to re-examine the legitimacy of military action from an international and domestic perspective. In this latter context, we believe that the MPs have to take into account the public opinion, constituents' views, and the available resources, etc. These domestic questions have to supplement the international questions of legality and legitimacy and domestic concerns have to be addressed.

IV. An Informed Parliament

Our next proposals are aimed at Parliamentarians specifically. From an MP's perspective a discussion about military action has to start with an awareness and understanding of the available information. Having accurate information is key for a proper perception of the threat, and to assess whether the approach chosen by the Government is needed. It is only if MPs are willing to bring their own perspective to the legitimacy of any proposed intervention that a move away from the 'all or nothing' presentation of armed conflict is possible. This requires MPs to act on their own initiative.

In relation to Libya, the 2011 intervention was labelled as aiming to protect civilians. But the Foreign Affairs Committee inquiry on Libya, discussed above, uncovered clearly that the available information did not support the claim that Gaddafi represented a threat. Instead, what the final report reveals is that the UK Government did not have 'reliable intelligence on what was happening on the ground in Libya in February 2011 to inform its new policy'.[123] In testimony to the Committee, former Ambassador to Libya Sir Dominic Asquith acknowledged that 'the database of knowledge in terms of people, actors and the tribal structure—the modern database, not the inherited historical knowledge—might well have been less than ideal'. Academic experts on the issue highlighted 'the relatively limited understanding of events' and the fact that 'people had not really bothered to monitor closely what was happening'.[124] More importantly, some expressed shock 'at the lack of awareness in Whitehall of the "history and regional complexities" of Libya'.[125] This 'lack of insight led to the failure to ask the key question why the rebellion was happening in Benghazi but not in Tripoli and to consider the significance of regional and tribal factors'.[126]

---

[122] RN Haass, 'The Necessary and the Chosen' (n 111).
[123] House of Commons Foreign Affairs Committee, 'Libya' (n 84) 12.
[124] ibid.
[125] ibid, citing Alison Pargeter's testimony.
[126] ibid.

This lack of understanding of Libya before February 2011, however, does not mean that no information was in fact publicly available prior to the March intervention. An investigation by Amnesty International showed that it was not possible to corroborate allegations of mass human rights violations by Gaddafi regime troops. It criticised 'a very one-sided view of the logic of events, portraying the protest movement as entirely peaceful and repeatedly suggesting that the regime's security forces were unaccountably massacring unarmed demonstrators who presented no security challenge'.[127] Instead, academics testified that there was 'no real evidence at that time that Gaddafi was preparing to launch a massacre against his own civilians'.[128] Equally, journalists cited intelligence officials as describing the intervention as 'an intelligence-light decision' and talking of Libya as 'Hilary Clinton's WMD moment'.[129]

We are not arguing here that it is the task of MPs to assess the threat and seek out the best policy to address this threat. Those are the tasks of government. However, the first step for parliamentarians tasked with evaluating the Government's case under the war of choice rubric must involve gaining an understanding of the situation on the ground. This should include where possible the relevant history and its complexities, the motivations of the key players, and of the needs and realities on the ground. This is essential for parliamentarians if they are to perform their scrutiny function. Rory Stewart, a Conservative MP and Minister for International Development, argues in his book on intervention that 'It is not a question of what we ought to do but what we can'.[130] Stewart further insists in particular that 'International attempts to impose foreign will through overwhelming force ... tend to make the situation worse not better'.[131] This is because 'the foreigners who comprise "the international community" ... are inevitably isolated from local society, ignorant of local culture and context, and prey to misleading abstract theories'. Even more, the 'international community' rarely counts on the resilience of local institutions and local political leaders who are often 'far more competent and powerful than the foreigners think'.[132] As Stewart insists, 'local and regional factors tend to be far more important determinants of success than foreign analysts acknowledge'.[133] If MPs were more

---

[127] P Cockburn, 'Amnesty questions claim that Gaddafi ordered rape as weapon of war', *The Independent* (23 June 2011).

[128] House of Commons Foreign Affairs Committee, 'Libya' (n 84) 14, citing Alison Pargeter's testimony.

[129] K Riddell and JS Shapiro, 'Hillary Clinton's 'WMD moment: US intelligence saw false narrative in Libya', *The Washington Times* (29 January 2015).

[130] R Stewart and G Knaus, *Can Intervention Work?* (New York, Norton: Global Ethics Series, 2012) 102 (Kindle location) citing WJ Clinton, 'US Support for Implementing the Bosnian Peace Agreement,' address to the nation, 27 November 1995.

[131] ibid, 194.

[132] ibid, 192.

[133] ibid, 193.

aware of the perils of intervention in general and the local specifics of any planned intervention, they would be better placed to participate in debates.

From our perspective, scrutiny of government's proposals has to facilitate pragmatic solutions—those that are well informed and realistic because they take into account the history, decisions, and individuals involved.[134] In this context, MPs need to make sure to elicit as much information as they can from governmental sources. Yet, as we have shown, successive governments have been reluctant to provide MPs sufficient access to information. This selective presentation of the case for war has led to poor decision-making and perpetuated groupthink. As Sir John Chilcot summarised the lessons on Iraq, the need for 'frank and informed debate and challenge'[135] and 'honest disagreement' about the case for any armed conflict is necessary to improve the decision-making process.[136]

In this context, we believe that it is the responsibility of individual parliamentarians to equip themselves with available knowledge from sources beyond the Government. In order to understand the situation on the ground, MPs should seek publicly available information from the media, reports from NGOs, and testimony and advice from academics knowledgeable of the area. They should keep abreast of select committee reports and maintain their awareness of the issues raised in specialised inquiries, like the Foreign Affairs Committee reports on Libya and Syria, and the 2016 Chilcot report on Iraq. On Libya, for example, MPs could have refused to automatically support military action and questioned the scant information provided and the motivations behind intervention. They could have relied on Amnesty's report, journal articles and academic opinion pieces, which were publicly available at the time of the debate to dispute the claim that Gaddafi was a threat to his own people. This may have led first to a potential admission that Gaddafi was not a danger to civilians, and that therefore the basis for intervention was not humanitarian but rather 'regime change'. Such an endeavour may have prompted some parliamentarians to table amendments to the Government's motion to include alternatives other than military action.

Currently reliance on such additional information is rare, perhaps because in the words of one Member of the Commons: 'it's just not humanely possible to know about everything you're voting for'.[137] For example, in 2015, in relation to Syria, only 13 MPs referred to the Foreign Affairs Committee Report, which was critical of the Government's favoured policy of military intervention. Four of these 13 were FAC Members.[138] Out of a total of 601 MPs who voted in the debate

---

[134] ibid.

[135] Sir John Chilcot, Public Statement (n 113).

[136] ibid.

[137] P Cowley, *The Rebels* (London, Politico, 2005) 28, citing Jeremy Corbyn. We recognise that parliamentarians do face some, but not insurmountable, constraints on both time and available resources.

[138] HC Deb 2 December 2015, vol 603, cols 341–42, 347, (Jeremy Corbyn), cols 352–54 (Angus Robertson), col 354 (Yasmin Qureshi), col 360 (Crispin Blunt), col 365 (John Baron), col 368 (Alan Johnson), col 376 (Derek Twigg), col 404 (Caroline Lucas), col 409 (Angus Brendan McNeil), col 424 (Stephen Gethins), col 426 (Adam Holloway), col 435 (Barry Gardiner), col 475 (Brendan O'Hara). Note that amongst these MPs, four were members of the Foreign Affairs Committee: Qureshi, Blunt, Gethins and Holloway.

and 157 MPs who had applied to speak in the debate, this is a very small fraction indeed.[139] Although more may have, of course, read the report, this is not clear from their interventions and the report appears not to have affected the end result.

As discussed above, MPs who lack sufficient knowledge to make an informed decision, sometimes seek to justify their position through rhetoric.[140] This distorts the quality of debate. In relation to Libya, Jim Dowd, for example, cited a former editor of *The Sun* as saying that 'all the lives in Libya were not worth one ounce of British blood'.[141] This 'brutal' position was quickly dismissed both by him and by the leader of the opposition Ed Miliband, who insisted that the UK had the responsibility to protect the Libyan people. '[W]e have to make a judgment about our role in the world and our duty to others. Where there is just cause, where feasible action can be taken, and where there is international consent, are we really saying that we should be a country that stands by and does nothing?'[142] As the FAC report on Libya revealed, MPs hearing the 'humanitarian intervention' argument immediately turned to 'a fear of ... another Srebrenica on our hands'. This 'was very much a driving factor in the decision-making at the time'.[143] Lord Richards talked about Srebrenica weighing on members as a 'stain on our conscience',[144] whilst others—including Lord Hague and Tobias Ellwood—admitted to being influenced by 'the horrific examples of Srebrenica, and Rwanda before'.[145] The individual and collective memories of the massacres were 'formative' for many in the Government and the House and—given the perceived lack of reliable intelligence on which to build policy—they were attached undue weight. Libya—and before it Iraq—show the dangers of having no information provided to or sought by MPs. When a void is created by a lack of information, it is filled with other (often invalid) concerns.

In a more general sense, the gravity of the decision to pursue armed conflict is so great that MPs also need to be informed of the wider national security and defence strategies surrounding any one decision. Information of this nature is also available from Select Committee Reports. For example, the Report of the Joint Committee on the National Security Strategy for 2015 includes a specific section on the capabilities and readiness of the British armed forces. In particular, this report concluded that despite increased investment, the Committee remained 'concerned about military manpower'.[146] In another report in 2016, the Defence

---

[139] HC Deb 2 December 2015, vol 603, col 340.

[140] Hilary Benn, for example, used rhetoric as a way to conceal how little power MPs actually have; see HC Deb 2 December 2015, vol 603, col 486.

[141] HC Deb 21 March 2011, vol 525, col 729.

[142] ibid, vol 525, col 718; Jim Dowd agreed, vol 525, col 729.

[143] House of Commons Foreign Affairs Committee, 'Libya (n 84) 15–16, citing Secretary of State Fox.

[144] ibid, 16, citing Lord Richards' testimony.

[145] ibid, citing the Parliamentary Under-Secretary of State for Foreign and Commonwealth Affairs, Tobias Ellwood MP.

[146] Joint Committee on the National Security Strategy, 'National Security Strategy and Strategic Defence and Security Review 2015', 1st Report 2016–17, HL Paper 18, HC 153, para 58.

Select Committee raised concerns that spending 'barely 2% of GDP on defence'[147] meant that 'the fleet is way below the critical mass required for the many tasks which could confront it'.[148] These facts may of course vary from time to time, and reports cannot always be available immediately prior to any one conflict. However, given the wealth of specific, well-resourced information produced by Parliament on matters of defence and national security that MPs can engage with directly, an increased volume of direct references to, and reliance on, these materials over and above emotive or abstract moral arguments would be highly welcomed.

By educating themselves about the situation on the ground, the international and domestic motivations for action, the long-term strategy and the economic investment as well as capability of the British armed forces, MPs can ensure better transparency and accountability of governmental decision-making. But more importantly, they can confidently assert their constitutional role within the deliberation space we have attempted to create for them. In the end, the fuller the inclusion of the House of Commons, the higher the number and diversity of challengers of the 'case for war' and the more nuanced the ultimate decision.

C. Voting Within a Culture of Justification

The solutions we propose in this chapter aim to reinvigorate discussion of domestic political discourse relating to the war prerogative in the House of Commons. First, we have sought to liberate the debate in the House from international law and pre-deterministic legalese. Secondly, we argued that only an informed and knowledgeable Parliament can provide a strong counterweight to government. Both these elements can contribute to upholding the values which motivated this book. Yet, there is another element that seems key to us in decisions to go to war—the question of how MPs can consider and best reflect their constituents' positions, concerns, and opinions through the act of voting for or against the Government's motion in support of armed conflict.

MPs face pressure from their constituents and their party, and carry the burden of their individual judgement. As a result of the complex position MPs find themselves in, we propose that any decision on armed conflict should be the subject of a free vote. However, given that there is a public interest in the electorate knowing broadly which parties support a given course of action, we recommend that each party should adopt a non-enforceable political position on the matter.

---

[147] House of Commons Defence Committee, 'Restoring the Fleet: Naval Procurement and the National Shipbuilding Strategy', 3rd Report 2016–17, HC 221, 42.

[148] ibid, summary. See also: K Rawlinson, 'Royal Navy risks having 'pathetically low total' of ships, warn MPs', *The Guardian* (21 November 2016).

This middle ground solution—a free vote with a public party line—would allow (but also implicitly require) individual MPs to voice not only their own reasons for voting on the motion, but also who they see themselves as representing with their vote. An unenforced party line would help inform the public and allow them to gauge the positions of MPs who voted on the motion but did not speak in the debate. This, we argue, would lead to the emergence and realisation of a culture of justification, in which parliamentarians would have to explain and justify their vote. Providing reasons for your vote, we believe, is a crucial step to the realisation of the three good governance values of accountability, transparency, and participation.

I. The Competing Demands of Representation on Parliamentarians

Various theories of representation have been created in an attempt to explain and justify how elected representatives should vote. The forthcoming discussion sets out the various positions in representation theory, but does not attempt to solve the dilemma itself. In the theory of representation, the competing pressures of loyalty to constituents and the burden of individual judgement gives rise to the 'mandate-independence' controversy.[149] The controversy asks whether a representative should always do what his or her constituents want (the mandate theory), or alternatively, whether he or she should be free to act in pursuit of constituents' welfare using his or her own judgement (the agency theory).[150] This dichotomy sees the mandate theory as reducing the representative to the role of a servant, whereas the agency theory sees the representative as a free agent. The Electoral College of the United States is an example of one organisation which obeys a mandate from the electorate.[151]

An extreme example of the agency theory was presented by Edmund Burke in his *Speech to the Electors at Bristol* in 1774. He argued against any form of constraining mandate for parliamentarians, emphasising instead that: 'Parliament is not a—*congress*—of ambassadors from different and hostile interests; which interests each must maintain, as an agent and advocate, against other agents and advocates; but parliament is a—*deliberative*—assembly of—*one*—nation, with—*one*—interest'.[152] There have been equally vociferous critics of the agency theory, who argue that representatives should not be wholly free to reject the wishes of

---

[149] HF Pitkin, *The Concept of Representation* (Berkeley, University of California Press, 1967) ch 7.
[150] ibid, 145.
[151] ibid, 149.
[152] E Burke, 'Speech to the electors at Bristol' (3 November 1774) <press-pubs.uchicago.edu/founders/documents/v1ch13s7.html> accessed 17 September 2017.

their constituents, branding those who do as 'merely an oligarch'.[153] John Stuart Mill also rejected the notion that representatives should undertake a pledge to carry out the will of constituents. He rejected this notion as contrary to 'constitutional morality, or the ethics of representative government'.[154]

Resurrecting Burke in 2017 may seem archaic, but he featured in discussions on the floor of the House of Commons in the same year. In the context of a Bill authorising the Government to initiate Brexit negotiations, Conservative MP Kenneth Clarke reminded his fellow parliamentarians that:

> Most Members, I trust, are familiar with Burke's address to the electors of Bristol. I have always firmly believed that every MP should vote on an issue of this importance according to their view of the best national interest. I never quote Burke, but I shall paraphrase him. He said to his constituents, 'If I no longer give you the benefit of my judgment and simply follow your orders, I am not serving you; I am betraying you.' I personally shall be voting with my conscience content.[155]

The debate on the Brexit Bill illustrates various theories of representation. In direct contrast with Kenneth Clarke, who voted against the Bill, it was clear that some MPs felt directly bound by the result of the 2016 referendum in which 52 per cent of the public voted in favour of leaving the European Union. The Secretary of State for Exiting the European Union, David Davis MP, considered the referendum to be a 'democratic mandate' from the electorate.[156] The two extremes of representation theory seem prima facie irreconcilable. In an attempt to reconcile these competing demands Pitkin argues that if a representative is either wholly free to ignore constituents, or wholly bound to exercise their will, he or she cannot truly be executing a representative function.[157] She suggests two ways to mediate these seemingly incompatible positions. The first is achieved by focusing upon the interests of the constituents. If a representative takes account of the interests of constituents, yet continues to retain independent judgement as to the public good in any given situation, then, the competing demands of representation can be reconciled in any given situation. So, MPs are required to consider—as opposed to obey—constituents' wishes.[158]

There is a third dimension to the competing demands placed on representatives: loyalty to political parties. Parliamentary parties generally expect their members to be loyal to the 'party line' in their voting records. Although we defend the notion of armed conflict being seen as an 'issue of conscience', it would be unwise, for reason of damaging the values of transparency, participation, and accountability, to altogether marginalise or eliminate the party system in the current context.

---

[153] H Belloc and C Chesterton, *The Party System* (London, Steven Swift, 1911) 2.
[154] JS Mill, 'Considerations on Representative Government' in *On Liberty and other essays* (Oxford, OUP: Oxford World's Classics, 2008) 373.
[155] HC Deb 31 January 2017, vol 620, col 831.
[156] ibid, col 818.
[157] Pitkin, *The Concept of Representation* (n 149) 153.
[158] ibid, 162.

At the turn of the twentieth century Belloc and Chesterton castigated the party system for its corruption of the concept of representation. This was particularly so in respect of the war prerogative, whereby the authors took the view that 'something alien has intervened between the electors and the elected ... something that deflects the working of representative institutions. That thing is the Party System'.[159] The authors point further to the 'progressive emasculation' of the House of Commons as an 'instrument of government' in the context of war powers by comparing the relative influence of the Commons in respect of the Crimean War one the one hand, which was fought when 'Parliament was relatively free', compared with the later South African War, during which popular unrest over the Government's action was apparently commonplace but 'within the walls of Parliament scarcely a voice was heard, and it certainly never entered the head of any Conservative member (or Liberal member either for that matter) to take the strong step of driving out the men in power'.[160]

Whilst this analysis may be of its time, the party system has been subject to strong contemporary criticism. In the twenty-first century, Tomkins claimed that party loyalty damaged the chances of creating a 'deliberative, contestatory style of democracy' because it inevitably eats away at the necessary separation of interests between Ministers and parliamentarians.[161] On this view, what is required is 'the removal of party and party loyalty from the working of Parliament'.[162] This, for Tomkins, compels the conclusion that 'whips should be prohibited'.[163] But this overlooks the reality acknowledged by many representatives that most are elected due to their party label, as opposed to on their individual merits.[164] Criticism of the utility of political parties is based upon two flawed assumptions: first, that the system of whips stifles the independent judgement of parliamentarians; and secondly that the public good in any democracy is non-partisan, and capable of discovery through deliberation. Prejudice against party and the party whip is also founded upon the 'caricature of whip as bully'.[165] However, Labour's most rebellious MP (and, at the time of writing, the Party Leader) Jeremy Corbyn, viewed the concept of the party whip as a bully to be a distant memory:

> Whips have long been the pantomime villains of Westminster politics ... The reality, though, is usually much less salacious or exiting, and most academic accounts of Parliament have tried to stress the more prosaic functions of the whips as party managers ... providing a channel of communication from leaders to led and vice versa.[166]

---

[159] Belloc and Chesterton, *The Party System* (n 153) 36.
[160] ibid.
[161] Tomkins, *Our Republican Constitution* (n 63) 136–37.
[162] ibid, 138.
[163] ibid, 138.
[164] J Corbyn and S Simon, 'It's a bit more complicated than that' in P Cowley (ed), *The Rebels: How Blair mislaid his majority* (London, Politico's, 2005) 26.
[165] D Nicol, 'Professor Tomkins' House of Mavericks' (2006) *Public Law* (Autumn) 467, 467.
[166] Corbyn and Simon, 'It's a bit more complicated than that' (n 164) 37.

Moreover, rebellions, including rebellions in armed conflict votes, are relatively common. Neither is the strength of party leadership so great that it displaces conscience or independent judgement. Most MPs say that they will do what they think is right, even if this means contradicting the wishes of voters.[167] The rebellion against the New Labour Government in respect of the Iraq conflict was in fact the largest recorded rebellion in 150 years.[168] In one sense it was 'the mother of all rebellions' as it occurred in a context where Blair had put his leadership on the line. Many MPs were aware that the balance of public opinion lay against the war and many parliamentarians did not understand either the rationale or justification for further conflict in the region. These concerns were compounded by the lack of planning of an exit strategy, and a strong dislike of President Bush, as well as scepticism over United States' foreign policy.[169] At the time polls showed that the public was against the war in Iraq by 54 per cent to 38 per cent.[170] The most significant contemporary indication of public opinion, however, was the so-called 'largest protest event in human history'[171] on 15 February 2003, where an estimated one million people across Britain took place in a series of marches against the war as part of a coordinated effort in many cities across the globe.

Finally, political parties remain necessary in a representative democracy to allow citizens to promote their preferred vision of the public good, which will always be partisan. If such an objective concept of the public good were to exist, it is more feasible that parliamentarians exercising their own judgement in a deliberative democracy would be capable of reaching a consensus on that common good without any form of guidance from a 'party line'. Critics of this perspective cite the interest in breathing clean air as the classic example of a universally agreed public good. The explanation for this is that it is assumed that nobody imbued with reason could doubt the public interest in the existence of clean air to breathe. However, the common or public good is a relative concept, as opposed to an objective one. Interested actors will 'disagree over the extent to which the common good will require air purity to be "traded off" in favour of other policies'.[172] To this end, political parties are necessary because they allow individuals to identify a position closest to their own conception of the common good in respect of any issue, including war. This enhances transparency, particularly in respect of the actions of parliamentarians who vote on a motion, but do not contribute to the debate. The presence of a public party line allows citizens to judge whether or not a given parliamentarian has voted in respect of a transparent position.

---

[167] ibid, 47.
[168] Nicol, 'Professor Tomkins' House of Mavericks' (n 165) 468.
[169] J Ennis and J Grogan, 'The mother of all rebellions' in P Cowley (ed), *The Rebels: How Blair mislaid his majority* (n 164) 109.
[170] <https://yougov.co.uk/news/2015/06/03/remembering-iraq> accessed 17 September 2017.
[171] S Walgrave and D Rucht, *The World Says No to War: Demonstrations against the War on Iraq* (Minneapolis, University of Minnesota Press, 2010) xiii.
[172] 'Professor Tomkins' House of Mavericks' (n 165) 470.

In short, removing the presence of party politics from any given issue risks severing the 'fundamental cord of accountability that links British governments to the electorate'.[173] The party system has therefore rightly been called the 'indispensable foundation of British democracy'.[174] So, it is not feasible for MPs to abandon either party loyalty or sensitivity to constituents' will entirely. Some middle ground is therefore necessary.

II. Armed Conflict Votes as Votes of Conscience

A decision to wage war is, at its core, a moral issue. Jeremy Corbyn recognised that 'decisions to send British forces to war are the most serious, solemn and morally challenging of any that we have to take as Members of Parliament'.[175] In common with many other MPs across a number of votes on substantive motions, James Gray (Conservative) described the matter as 'truly a conscience vote—a vote based on our instincts, on the balance of probabilities, on our feeling for things'.[176] The prevalence of such moral language suggests that voting on initiating armed conflict should be a conscience vote, or a free vote as they are commonly known. In view of this, freedom from the party whip may allow parliamentarians to be more sensitive to constituents' opinion without fear of sanction. The absence of a party line, however, can create confusion in the situation where an MP votes, but does not speak in the debate (or the media thereafter). In this situation, his or her constituents are given no information upon which to evaluate their representative's conduct. To mitigate this scenario, a clear party line is desirable. However, the pull of party loyalty risks compromising the other facets of representation (judgement and constituent sensitivity). In view of this, we argue for the adoption of a compromise position which mirrors the approach of the Labour Party in respect of Syria 2015. Before the vote, Jeremy Corbyn (Leader of the Opposition) stated that there was a party line, namely, to vote against war, but that the vote would not be whipped.[177] Therefore, in the case of Labour MPs who voted but did not speak, their conduct could be evaluated according to the party line. Transparency, accountability and participation are not compromised by this mid-way approach: they are enhanced.

The easiest way to identify whether or not something is an 'issue of conscience' subject to a free vote is to identify it as a moral issue.[178] However, circular reasoning takes us little further. Most of the public bills in which free votes have been

---

[173] ibid, 471.

[174] ibid, 467.

[175] HC Deb 2 December 2015, vol 603, col 340.

[176] ibid, col 408.

[177] P Wintour and R Mason, 'Syria airstrikes: Jeremy Corbyn gives Labour MPs free vote' *The Guardian* (30 November 2015).

[178] P Jones 'Members of Parliament and Issues of Conscience' in P Jones (ed), *Party Parliament and Personality: Essays Presented to Hugh Berrington* (London, Routledge, 2002) 143.

permitted share moral underpinnings. It is easier to list these issues than to truly determine what makes them distinctly moral.[179] Since 1997 free votes have been held on matters such as hunting with animals, the age of sexual consent, euthanasia, smoking in public places, stem cell research, House of Lords reform, prisoner voting, same-sex marriage, and termination of pregnancy on the grounds of a foetus's sex.[180] There is undoubtedly room for disagreement as to what makes any given issue an issue of conscience, and many whipped votes will involve difficult moral issues. Jones notes that 'Defence and foreign policy notoriously raises questions of a conscientious character'.[181] Among the most famous examples are the debate on the Medical Termination of Pregnancy Bill from 1966, authorising abortion. Waldron described this as 'a fine an example of a political institution grappling with moral issues as you could hope to find ... One remarkable thing was that everyone who participated in that debate ... paid tribute to the respectfulness with which their positions had been listened to and heard'.[182] Part of the appeal of a free vote is that debates on matters of conscience are likely to be somewhat removed from the 'Punch and Judy politics' which has contaminated much of the House of Commons' activities, including question time, where party loyalty is most prevalent.

The commonsense objection to free votes is that they create an accountability gap: as the electorate cannot attribute the result of any vote to a particular party political perspective. Given that the British electoral system is dominated by party politics, a vote of conscience makes it difficult for the electorate to evaluate the performance of their representative, particularly when the voting records of individuals are not widely known. However, in the context of recent votes pursuant to the War Powers Convention, this issue has been mitigated. Prominent news outlets including the BBC have made MPs voting records public.[183] After the 2015 vote, a leading Conservative Party blog identified the seven members of the parliamentary party who had rebelled against the whip.[184] Moreover, research on the House of Commons indicates that even during free votes, MPs tend to split roughly along party lines on issues. This is perhaps unsurprising, as 'there are considerably more factors contributing to unity amongst British parliamentarians than there are to disunity'.[185] This factor might call into question the purpose

---

[179] P Cowley, 'Unbridled Passions? Free Votes, Issues of Conscience and the Accountability of British Members of Parliament' (1998) 4 *Journal of Legislative Studies* 70, 70.

[180] S Pridy, 'Free votes in the House of Commons', House of Commons Library Briefing No 04793 (2016).

[181] P Jones 'Members of Parliament and Issues of Conscience' (n 178) 151.

[182] J Waldron, 'The core of the case against judicial review' (2006) 115 *The Yale Law Journal* 1384–85, 1346.

[183] Iraq 2003: <news.bbc.co.uk/1/hi/uk_politics/2802819.stm>; Libya 2011: <www.bbc.co.uk/news/uk-politics-12816279; Syria 2015: <www.bbc.co.uk/news/uk-politics-34987921> accessed 17 September 2017.

[184] <www.conservativehome.com/parliament/2015/12/the-list-of-the-seven-conservative-mps-who-voted-against-air-strikes-on-isis-in-syria.html> accessed 17 September 2017.

[185] Corbyn and Simon, 'It's a bit more complicated than that' (n 164) 22.

of arguing for freedom of conscience and a free vote in respect of the war prerogative. The justification, however, is rooted in the vision of representation we have for parliamentarians. Recalling the above discussion, the three competing tensions upon parliamentarians stem from party loyalty (which free votes seek to remove), personal judgement (the Burkean vision), and a duty to constituents (the principal-agent thesis). Votes of conscience liberate parliamentarians from the constraints of party, as they will face no sanction for taking a different viewpoint from the party leadership. This may allow greater sensitivity to the opinions of constituents. Public opinion and parliamentary voting have generally but not necessarily always gone hand in hand with regard to votes taken under the War Powers Convention. The most recent polls in relation to Syria in 2013 and 2015 reflected how MPs eventually voted.[186]

There may still be doubts remaining about the utility of free votes in the presence of an unenforced party line. In this monograph, we do not seek to solve all of the dilemmas of representation theory. We simply argue that politicians must be transparent as to which position underpins their voting choice. There is also a further objection vis-à-vis moral issues (including war), namely that parliamentarians are not necessarily better at moral reasoning than their constituents. They possess no special moral resources. This is undoubtedly true. However, what potentially sets them apart, is being better informed than those they represent. Being better informed and having formulated a position, however, requires also that debates under the War Powers Convention take place against the wider backdrop of a 'culture of justification'. Of course, MPs require time to process these complex arguments, and to mediate between public opinion, the party position, and their own judgement on matters. This is yet another reason why votes should occur prior to the deployment of troops, and sufficient notice of the intention to hold such a debate should be given by the Government.

III. Realising a Culture of Justification

The decision to go to war is the ultimate exercise of power. Lives may be lost, states may be destroyed, and lifelong trauma may result on both sides. In view of the gravity of the decision, our final proposal in this chapter requires a deeper shift in constitutional practice. We think this shift is necessary in order to require

---

[186] Polls in relation to Libya in 2011 did not square parliamentary and public opinion. A YouGov poll suggested that people supported the military action against Libya by 45% to 36%. Meanwhile, a ComRes poll for ITV news found almost the exact opposite: 35% supported the action, but 43% opposed it. The polls fared better in respect of the 2014 airstrikes against ISIS in Iraq, which the public supported by 57%, compared with 24% against action. When Parliament refused to politically authorise action against Syria in 2013, this reflected strong public opposition to intervention. In respect of Syria 2015, a minority of the public approved (48%), and in the period of a week, disapproval ratings climbed to 31%, which translated to a shift in the opinion of five million people in the course of one month: <yougov.co.uk/news/2014/09/26/isis-how-majority-came-favour-air-strikes> accessed 17 September 2017; <yougov.co.uk/news/2013/08/30/public-opinion-syria-policy> accessed 17 September 2017.

Parliament and the Government to deliberate and vote in a manner which does justice to the gravity of deciding to wage war (or not). Therefore, in order to fully realise the values of accountability, transparency and participation, both government and Parliament must be forthcoming in providing information and explanation for their positions and their votes. We argue that to best realise these values both government and Parliament must commit to a 'culture of justification', ie to subject the case for armed conflict to a process of debate and voting which compels government to be as transparent as possible about the case for war, and to offer a reasoned justification of its proposed course of action. But counting on government to provide sufficient information and to allow for meaningful discussion is only half of the story. In this chapter, we have argued that MPs play a crucial role in giving life to the three governance values. This section will focus on how MPs can best undertake explanation and justification of their votes, before turning to consider the wider constitutional impact of a culture of justification.

If—as we propose—MPs should be free to vote on military intervention with the party making its position public but without the intervention of the Whips, then this will generate a need for MPs to explain and justify their positions. Voting on armed conflict is, as we showed above, capable of being seen as an issue of conscience, as well as a party political issue, and one on which public opinion should be influential. MPs must therefore explain their specific reasons for voting in a particular way, and they must also explain who or whose interests they are representing when they vote for or against a government motion. In this regard, voting is a two-stage process. MPs must articulate both the specific reasons for their votes and whether or not these accord primacy to their own judgement, constituents' views, or the demands of party loyalty. Parliamentarians must provide detailed explanations for their vote, ones which show clearly to the electorate that the decision-maker has considered all the serious objections to the decision taken and provided answers which are plausible. In addition, a 'rational connection between ... the evidence and argument' before the decision has been taken has to be established.[187] It may well be that public opinion sways some parliamentarians. In a representative democracy this is perfectly proper, provided that an MP explains that this is the central reason for his or her decision.

For some MPs, these requirements have already been met, as best illustrated by example. Although she did not speak in Parliament, Stella Creasy MP (Labour) gave an explanation to a local newspaper which amply conformed to the requirements of a culture of justification. She explains, first, that despite the views of many constituents, her judgement was swayed by the Government's case for war, and secondly, she presented her own evaluation of the pertinent facts:

> So why did I on balance decide to vote yes? Firstly, because I am convinced there is a clear and present threat to the UK from Daesh and it is a danger to all citizens. From the emails I received many of you said you feared any extension of air strikes against Daesh

---

[187] Murenik, 'A bridge to where?' (n 2) 41.

targets in Syria could lead to radicalization, and a greater risk level for Britain. Britain is already taking military action against Daesh in Iraq (and has been since October 2014) and we are in the top tier of countries for them to attack, so we are already considered to be at the highest level of risk. With at least seven attempts to attack UK citizens recorded already this year here in our country. We also know this year Daesh were implicated in the killing of 30 British tourists in Tunisia, 224 Russian holidaymakers on a plane, 178 people in suicide bombings in Beirut, Ankara and Suruc and 130 people in Paris. There is also intelligence that they are plotting more attacks on the UK and other countries from their headquarters in Raqqa, Syria.[188]

It is clear that Creasy's explanation is compatible with the requirements of acting in a culture of justification. She has clearly considered objections to her chosen course of action and provided a plausible explanation for her vote. Moreover, she has been explicit that she used her own judgement about the situation when rejecting the requests of her constituents that she vote in the opposite direction. However brief this may seem, it is the core of the culture of justification. Evaluation is privileged over rhetoric, the decision to vote is explained, and the approach to representation is disclosed.

As discussed above, the competing demands of constituency, conscience, and party which MPs face does not readily lend itself to a solution. It will vary between circumstances and subject matter. Representatives will often find themselves in situations where their constituents' wishes are unknown to them, or they opt to reject the views of their constituents in favour of their own judgement. In alternate circumstances, they may feel their vote is best served by towing the party political line. No matter which way a politician decides to vote in the context of an armed conflict decision, commentators tend to agree on the importance of one matter: that the representative should be transparent in their reasoning, so as to preserve constituents' ability to hold them to account. The representative must explain their choice in any given situation. Moreover, 'it is necessary that the choice be justifiable … And not just anything the representative says will be satisfactory'.[189] In short, the emphasis is upon justification by explanation of any vindication of (or departure from) constituents' views. Creasy's explanation manages to mediate between these competing demands to satisfy the requirements of a culture of justification.

Although there is undoubtedly some evidence of the willingness of MPs to explain and justify their votes, the realisation of a culture of justification requires a shift in the aims and approach of both *government and Parliament*. The purpose of the culture of justification in the present context is not necessarily to compel government to be more forthcoming about the motives, strategy and evidence which exists within the realm of 'genuine national security secrecy'.[190]

---

[188] D Patient, 'Stella Creasy MP explains why she voted for Syria airstrikes' *The Guardian* (4 December 2015) <www.guardian-series.co.uk/news/14124885.Stella_Creasy_MP_explains_why_she_voted_for_Syria_airstrikes/?ref=rss> accessed 17 September 2017.

[189] Pitkin, *The Concept of Representation* (n 149) 164.

[190] S Aftergood, 'Reducing Government Secrecy: Finding What Works' (2009) 27 *Yale Law and Policy Review* 399, 401.

Instead, a culture of justification calls for the integration of more transparency and information in general into debates on the floor of the Commons. This is what we propose to do. Therefore, politicians should be under a constitutional obligation to explain not only the specific reasons for their vote, but also whose interests they are representing.

However, the endeavour of explanation does not need to occupy column after column of Hansard. Although the ideal would see as many MPs as possible participating in the Commons' debate, such events are time-limited. In view of this, there is room for the culture of justification to be realised and supported by the media. Despite the concerns expressed in this book, there are steps being taken by both parliamentarians and the media to make the justifications for voting more easily accessible to the public at large. This is to be welcomed. In the wake of the Syria 2015 vote, a number of national newspapers and political blogs published explanations by a range of MPs on their votes, not all of which were drawn from the pages of Hansard.[191] Some MPs wrote blogs[192] or opinion pieces in the national press to explain their views.[193] Among the most cogent of these came from Conservative Rory Stewart, who made no speech in Parliament. Instead, on his personal website, he explained that: 'The Royal Air Force can join these strikes legally, in a broad coalition, without endangering the lives of our troops, and in a way that protects some of the most vulnerable refugees in the world. This is worthwhile'. There are many others, including explanations from Labour MPs using their free vote to go against the party policy.[194]

The purpose of arguing that both Parliament and government should commit to a culture of justification in the context of debates and votes on armed conflict is to effect a cultural change in this aspect of the Constitution. In fact, changing the culture of a constitution is at the very core of the idea of a culture of justification. South African lawyer Etienne Murenik coined the term 'culture of justification' during his country's transition from Apartheid to constitutional democracy. The notion is captured in Murenik's supposition that South Africa's transition from the Apartheid regime to a liberal democracy represented a bridge away from a 'culture of authority' towards a 'culture of justification'.[195] In some senses the shift from absolute power over armed conflict being vested solely in Prime Ministerial control at the outset of the twentieth century, towards the greater political influence of the House of Commons symbolically represents a similar trajectory.

---

[191] <www.mirror.co.uk/news/uk-news/23-labour-mps-explain-theyre-6935035>; <www.independent.co.uk/news/uk/politics/five-labour-mps-explain-why-they-are-voting-to-bomb-isis-in-syria-a6757271.html>;<www.libdemvoice.org/liberal-democrat-mps-explain-syria-vote-48489.html> accessed 17 September 2017.

[192] <www.rorystewart.co.uk/rory-stewart-mp-on-syria> accessed 17 September 2017.

[193] John Baron (Basildon and Billericay): <www.theguardian.com/commentisfree/2015/dec/01/vote-syria-airstrikes-david-cameron-libya> accessed 17 September 2017.

[194] J Stone, 'Five Labour MPs explain why they are voting to bomb ISIS in Syria' *The Independent* (2 March 2016).

[195] Murenik, 'A bridge to where?' (n 2) 31–32.

To this end, we believe that strengthening the elements of a culture of justification will serve to strengthen the political control of Parliament.

A culture of justification as 'a culture in which every exercise of power is expected to be justified; in which the leadership given by government rests on the cogency of the case offered in defence of its decisions, not the fear inspired by the force at its command. The new order must be a community built on persuasion, not coercion'.[196] Throughout the first half of this book, we have demonstrated at length that since World War I successive governments have dominated Parliament almost to the extent that it is coerced into approving armed conflict. With these proposals we argue the default position must shift to that of reasoned persuasion. Commitment by both the Government and Parliament to a culture of justification is the way to achieve this. A culture, after all, reflects not just one or two norms, but refers to the 'distinctive ideas, customs, social behaviour, products, or way of life of a particular nation, society, people, or period'.[197] Murenik initially invoked the term to justify judicial review under a Bill of Rights, but we feel it is equally applicable to the appropriate relationship between government and Parliament in the context of war powers. Just as with conflicts under a Bills of Rights, political decisions in the context of armed conflicts require the decision-maker (or voting MP) to consider objections, provide rational explanations for his or her decision, and to consider all viable alternatives. Commitment to a culture of justification imposes demanding requirements upon parliamentarians and governments alike. This is an inescapable fact. Justification is a burden: it is a hurdle to be cleared. But without recourse to a culture of challenge during debate and deliberation and a culture of justification in respect voting we are left with the potential continuation of the unsatisfactory state of affairs described in chapters two, three, and four.

[196] ibid, 32.
[197] 'culture, n'. OED Online (OUP, December 2016), <www.oed.com/view/Entry/45746> accessed 17 September 2017.

6

Closed Intelligence Sessions

HAYLEY J HOOPER

In chapter five, we outlined how parliamentarians should engage with and vote upon the Government's public case for war. The aim was to 're-arm' Parliament with the tools to reorient its relationship with government. This chapter deals with a subset of considerations within that theme, namely, how to equip parliamentarians to debate and evaluate the Government's intelligence-based claims (ie those claims based upon classified information) fully and in their proper context. The goal of the forthcoming analysis is to outline the adjustments that ought to be made to parliamentary proceedings where the Government bases its case for armed conflict partly upon classified material (secret intelligence). Readers will recall that this has been a feature of debates in relation to the Iraq War in 2003 and in relation to Syria in 2013 and 2015. Chapter four explained that the presentation of these arguments in public abstracted them from their essential context, and rendered parliamentary scrutiny difficult, if not impossible. It concluded by explaining that the use of secrecy in governments' interactions with Parliament across the twentieth and twenty-first centuries was best described as exclusionary secrecy. This was because, regardless of its depth (ie how intense the veil of secrecy government projected over aspects of the war prerogative), secrecy created an information asymmetry which in turn amplified the risk of groupthink. This effectively meant that the Government could use secrecy and partial publicity to dominate important aspects of war powers decision-making at the expense of parliamentary deliberation.

This chapter responds to the current misuse of secrecy in order to avoid the pitfalls of the public presentation of intelligence described in chapter four. It proposes a solution to ameliorate the issues to date with the public reliance upon classified intelligence-based claims by government. It does so using secrecy. In short, it proposes that the whole House of Commons should scrutinise and debate reports of the Joint Intelligence Committee (JIC) in closed session. There has been some tentative suggestion in existing literature that secrecy is a constitutional value.[1] This form of secrecy promoted in this chapter, which we might call inclusive

---

[1] P Cane, 'Theory and values in public law' in P Craig and R Rawlings (eds), *Law and Administration in Europe: Essays in Honour of Carol Harlow* (Oxford, OUP, 2003) 16.

secrecy, works for the benefit, as opposed to the detriment, of the Constitution. It recognises that our elected representatives must see classified information or secret intelligence in the context of war powers because the secrets kept therein are in some sense '"our" secrets'.[2] Secrets kept by the British state ostensibly for the wider public interest must be subject to some form of democratic check by elected representatives. This is especially so when the Government is relying upon secrets to advance its case for the ultimate use of force. The importance of representative engagement with such material is compounded by the fact that the contents of JIC reports are, like the contents of any committee report, essentially a judgement call which is part of a wider factual matrix. It is for these overarching reasons, the following analysis argues in favour of holding limited closed intelligence sessions on the floor of the House of Commons between otherwise entirely public debates. The sole purpose of these sessions would be to allow all members of the House of Commons to consider and debate the reports of the JIC upon which government bases its public intelligence-based claims. This procedural innovation would dramatically reduce the information asymmetry between Parliament and government in respect of intelligence-based claims. Moreover, the real function of closed intelligence sessions would be to allow parliamentarians the opportunity to interrogate the Government's intelligence-based claims in their proper context. These sessions would allow all Members of the Commons to provide dissenting views on the relative weight of these claims when measured against other competing, public sources of information. This proposal builds upon the notion of creating a 'culture of challenge' that we outlined in the previous chapter.

Unsurprisingly, since the fallout from the Iraq War, several calls to reconceive Parliament's relationship with classified information have been made. Reforming Parliament's relationship with intelligence in the wake of the Iraq War has been considered in the Chilcot Report, and by other scholars. Chilcot's proposal takes the form of bestowing an increased responsibility upon the Intelligence and Security Committee for evaluating intelligence in camera and reporting to Parliament on the status of intelligence claims ex post facto. Part A considers Chilcot's proposal (and other similar suggestions) and explains why they risk perpetuating the information asymmetry and groupthink which beget the current and historical arrangements.

Discussion then moves to the idea of closed intelligence sessions in the broader context. The idea of the closed intelligence sessions argued for in this chapter is not without precedent. Part B lays out the specifics of the proposal for closed intelligence sessions of the whole House of Commons. The remainder of the chapter is devoted to understanding and explaining the precedents for this proposal. These are to be found in the wartime practices of the Westminster Parliament, the contemporary practices of the United States' Congress, and to a lesser, but nonetheless interesting, degree in the practices for scrutiny of classified information of the European Parliament.

---

[2] J Chafetz, 'Whose Secrets?' (2013–14) 127 *Harvard Law Review* 86, 87.

Part C looks at each of the three systems' approaches to allowing elected representatives access to classified information in camera. This comparative analysis draws out two main principles. First, there is a strong sense in each legislature of the need for a clear normative justification for departing from the principle that representative democracy should be conducted in public. This is clear regardless of the specific reasons put forward in any given case for holding a closed session. This is to be welcomed, and should be retained in respect of any future proposal. Secondly, a pattern emerges in respect of the strength of the legislatures' position relative to their decision-making power and the need to engage with classified information. In effect, the more involved a legislature is in making decisions which engage classified information, the greater its need to not only see the information, but to be able to question and debate it on equal terms with the Executive. The argument taken from these experiences is as follows: because the House of Commons is and increasingly involved in armed conflict decisions it is ostensibly moving towards a position where it requires equal access to and the ability to debate JIC reports in the context of armed conflict. Given the nature of the information in these reports, this can only occur in a closed session.

The idea of closed sessions in a representative institution will inevitably perturb some readers. To meet these concerns Part D looks to the three legislatures to consider ways of reducing the potential for abuse of closed sessions. In doing so the analysis makes clear that secrecy in the context of a representative assembly has limits which should not be transgressed. Finally, Part E considers the security implications of letting politicians access classified information. The overall picture painted illustrates that a system of closed intelligence sessions is both possible in a legislature, and potentially able to enhance the scrutiny of war powers.

At its core, the proposal for closed intelligence sessions is underpinned by a desire to empower Parliament to its fullest possible extent, by allowing it access to the broadest range of information before making its decision. Obviously, if this information is sensitive to national security, or other aspects of the public interest, Parliament cannot see this information in public proceedings. Therefore, empowering Parliament in this context must be achieved by temporarily trading some publicity to increase the evidence base available to parliamentarians, and to allow questioning or dissent over the value of that evidence. Parliament should not be forced to uncritically accept the Government's perspective on intelligence as it has been since the Iraq War. Taking this step, however counterintuitive, will help parliamentarians realise the values of participation, and accountability in a realm where representatives have hitherto been misled or entirely excluded. As chapter five made clear, both authors favour increased disclosure of information to promote greater transparency, participation, and accountability within a culture of justification. This chapter suggests sacrificing some amount of transparency in favour of increased participation which would allow parliamentarians to make a more informed decision on the case for armed conflict. The mass majority of information in relation to any case for war will be suitable for public discussion, and rightly so. But secret intelligence remains a democratic blind spot that demands its own set of solutions.

A. Chilcot's Proposal for Parliamentary Scrutiny of Intelligence Material

Before commencing the argument for closed intelligence sessions, the recommendations of the Chilcot Report for dealing with the presentation of classified information must be considered. The report recommended that: 'When assessed intelligence is explicitly and publicly used to support a policy decision, there would be benefit in subjecting that assessment and the underpinning intelligence to *subsequent* scrutiny, by a suitable, independent body, such as the Intelligence and Security Committee'.[3] Chilcot's proposal is not the first of its kind in relation to solving the conundrum of parliamentary treatment of secret intelligence. In 2006 the House of Lords Constitution Committee noted that one possible solution was to create a Committee similar to the German Standing Committee of Defence which would scrutinise secret intelligence on behalf of the whole Parliament. According to the report the 'German Defence Committee works in co-operation with the Foreign Affairs Committee and has access to relevant security information'.[4] A similar suggestion was made by Rosara Joseph in her treatment of the history of war powers. Joseph proposed a Joint Committee on National Security (JCNS). This Committee would 'scrutinize the information relevant to the Government's case for war and it would be able to report to the Commons on its assessment of this information'.[5] It would also 'ensure that the Government publishes as much information as possible' for disclosure to the House of Commons.[6]

These proposals are driven by a desire to limit and circumscribe secrecy in democratic institutions. However desirable this limitation is, proposals of this nature are short-sighted for a number of reasons. First of all, limiting access to classified information to a select group perpetuates the information asymmetries and increases exclusionary secrecy in the manner described in chapter four. This is effectively what happens when information is shared on Privy Council terms. It is crucial as a matter of principle for the whole House of Commons as an institution, rather than for some smaller sub-committee, to be the institution in

---

[3] Sir John Chilcot, Report of the Iraq Inquiry, 6 July 2016, HC 264, Vol 4.2: Iraq WMD Assessments, July to September 2002, para 901, emphasis added.
[4] House of Lords Constitution Committee, 'Waging War: Parliament's Role and Responsibility' 15th Report, HL Paper 236-I, 2005–06, para 76.
[5] R Joseph, *The War Prerogative: History, Reform, and Constitutional Design* (Oxford, OUP, 2013) 197.
[6] ibid, 198.

respect of which the information asymmetry is removed (or at least tangibly reduced). Moreover, Chilcot's emphasis on subsequent as opposed to prior scrutiny would leave judgement on sensitive information until after the decision, which would not necessarily enhance the quality of parliamentary scrutiny under the War Powers Convention in any meaningful sense.

The choice of the Intelligence and Security Committee as a model is of general concern, too. Despite the reform of the Intelligence and Security Committee by Part 1 of the Justice and Security Act 2013, its credibility as a real and effective select committee remains the subject of considerable doubt. Although the 2013 Act reforms were designed to strengthen the parliamentary accountability of the intelligence community, key shortcomings remain a feature of the new regime. The former Intelligence and Security Committee was 'often referred to by the media as a "select committee" or a "parliamentary committee" but in fact it is neither'.[7] In reality, the 2013 Act reforms are minor and do not render this committee a suitable forum for scrutinising intelligence-based claims on behalf of the whole House of Commons.[8] The reformulated Parliamentary Intelligence and Security Committee created by the 2013 Act still differs from a regular parliamentary committee (despite its name) because its power is sourced in legislation, as opposed to the Standing Orders of Parliament. This affects 'the appointment of its members, the procedure it adopts, its powers over witnesses and hearings, and the publication of its reports'.[9] Under the new slightly adjusted Parliamentary Intelligence and Security Committee regime, Parliament appoints its membership, subject to the approval of the Prime Minister and the Leader of the Opposition. Also, Select Committees are usually staffed by backbenchers, whereas the Parliamentary Intelligence and Security Committee and its predecessor have always been dominated by former Government Ministers. So, unlike an ordinary Select Committee, the Government has significant control over the composition of this Committee. As a result, this may affect its ability to deliver robust scrutiny to policies or intelligence received. Therefore, Parliament has: 'Assume[d] formal ownership—but certainly not full control—of the oversight arrangements' relating to national security.[10] At the time of writing all but one of the current members of the Parliamentary Intelligence and Security Committee was a Privy Counsellor.

The weakened status of this new committee, in terms of its lack of independence from government, compared with other parliamentary committees has attracted high-profile concern. For example, the Joint Committee on Human Rights has openly criticised the former Intelligence and Security Committee, calling for it to be turned into a 'proper' parliamentary committee with its own independent

---

[7] R Rogers and R Walters, *How Parliament Works*, 6th edn (London, Pearson Longman, 2006) 356.
[8] I Leigh, 'Rebalancing Rights and National Security: Reforming UK Intelligence Oversight a Decade After 9/11' (2012) 27 *Intelligence and National Security* 722, 725.
[9] ibid, 725.
[10] ibid, 726.

secretariat, legal advice, and investigatory mechanisms.[11] These concerns still remain relevant to the post-2013 Parliamentary Intelligence and Security Committee upon which Chilcot based his recommendations. All of these concerns mean that a Committee of this nature is unlikely to provide the robust forum for deliberation and dissent in respect of intelligence that would be necessary to make parliamentary engagement with such material worthwhile.

However, even if these issues were rectified, there remains a fundamental issue of principle at stake. If the Commons is required to make a political decision authorising the use of lethal force, and in turn endangering the lives of British military personnel, foreign combatants and civilians, then it cannot rely upon the judgement of others, even if some of those others come from within its own membership. As previously stated, classified information may go to the heart of whether a proposed conflict is an appropriate course of action. In such a potentially grave situation, every voting Member of the Commons must have parity of access to intelligence information. To rely upon a subset of parliamentarians in a Committee simply replicates existing problems, including the fact that the majority of MPs will be required to take the judgement of any sub-committee at face value.

Secrecy which creates information asymmetries is problematic because of the abstract worth that those outside the 'circle of trust' assign to it. Research in the context of foreign policy and national security demonstrates that the worth of information which is secret may well become artificially inflated in the minds of MPs charged with making vital decisions on armed conflict. Although there is 'no more truth to be found in classified records than there is to be found in unclassified records'[12] it has been demonstrated by experiment that people inflate the value of secret information. In one study, participants considered a document from the US National Security Council to be a more important source of information when it was presented as a secret or classified document, as opposed to when it was described as publicly available or unclassified information. This phenomenon is known as the 'secrecy heuristic', as secrecy compels people to attach more weight to information simply because it is secret, regardless of whether it really is of greater quality than publicly available information.[13] This compels the conclusion that it is unwise for small groups (be it government or a parliamentary committee) to present inferences based upon secret information to the Commons in public. This is because those parliamentarians who are unable to examine or contest that information for themselves risk artificially inflating its worth in their own decision-making process.

---

[11] Joint Committee on Human Rights, 'Counter-Terrorism Policy and Human Rights: Bringing Human Rights Back In' 16th Report, 2009–10, HL 86/HC 111, paras 108–12. See also, N Bamforth, 'Accountability of and to the Legislature' in P Leyland and N Bamforth (eds), *Accountability in the Contemporary Constitution* (Oxford, OUP, 2013) 286.

[12] S Aftergood (interview 26 October 2010) quoted in M Travers, L Van Boven and C Judd, 'The secrecy heuristic: inferring quality from secrecy in foreign policy contexts' (2014) 35 *Political Psychology* 97, 97.

[13] ibid.

B. The Alternative: Closed Intelligence Sessions of the Whole House of Commons

There is an alternative solution to the information asymmetry and hierarchy of parliamentarians which begets Chilcot's proposal and other similar proposals. This proposal for closed intelligence sessions—bounded on either side by public sessions—advanced here surrounds secrecy with publicity in order to enhance the values of transparency, participation and accountability which both authors argue lie at the core of democratic control of war powers. The over-arching purpose of these closed intelligence sessions is to allow MPs to better determine if the Government's case for armed conflict is a sound one, or if alternative non-military means are preferable. A closed session of the House of Commons would only be necessary where government attempts to base its case for war on the findings of the JIC. There would be no other reason to move from public to closed session. Closed sessions of this nature would give parliamentarians the hitherto unprecedented power to 'call the bluff' of Government in relation to intelligence claims. There may well be other applications for a proposal of this sort, but these are not considered herein.

There is already a contemporary power to hold closed sessions of the House of Commons, found in Standing Order No 163.[14] The motion 'that the House sit in private' is the subject of some confusion; as it is frequently used to test whether the House is quorate, or to postpone business until the next sitting. The procedure committee reviewed the rule in 2014 and recommended reform. The main reforms the committee suggested were that the purpose of the rule be clarified, so as it is only used when an actual private sitting is necessary, as opposed to for reasons of procedure or as a protest motion. Secondly, the Committee recommended that the decision to sit in private should be capable of debate, rather than being exclusively the prerogative of the Speaker. The current procedure for sitting in private does not allow for a debate before the motion is put, which is unsatisfactory, because MPs cannot voice their concerns about (or support for) the course of action about to be taken. So, the public will not have any basis upon which to evaluate MPs conduct save the vote itself. Debate and free vote before entering a closed session (even after the Speaker's independent judgement that it is necessary) is required. Parliament, after all, should reflect seriously on the decision to depart from the principle of public debate—it must be clear that there is something to be gained in a closed session which would not otherwise be available in public discourse.[15]

After a closed session, debate should resume immediately in open session regarding whether or not to support the Government's case for armed conflict.

---

[14] Standing Order No 163. See also House of Commons Procedure Committee, Motions 'that the House sit in private' 2nd Report, 2014–15, HC 753.

[15] ibid, para 22.

In addition to the absence of debates before a closed session, Standing Order No 163 does not allow fluid transitions between open and closed sessions on the same subject matter. Under the current rules, closed sessions (also known as 'private sittings') are ended via a motion to adjourn. Thereafter, the House of Commons may well resume a public sitting, but this will inevitably be on an unrelated topic. Erskine May notes that during wartime it 'was also a frequent practice to devote part of a sitting only to secret matters, and then resume in a public sitting'.[16] The example given is from 13 November 1940; however, and this reflects a transition from a closed session to an open session on a fundamentally different subject matter, namely a message from the House of Lords regarding compensation for injured workers.[17] It is therefore misleading to think that there was fluidity between open and closed deliberations in the context of wartime closed sessions. A properly functioning Parliament concerned with war powers must know how to balance expert deliberation (in secret) alongside populist involvement (in the open chamber), the optimal process is 'fluid with a back and forth between closed bargaining and open public debate'.[18] The Speaker made one ruling on raising a matter decided upon in secret session in an open session on 3 August 1944:

> A matter which has been decided in Secret Session cannot be discussed again, whether in Secret Session or in open Session. It is, in fact, the ordinary Rule which prohibits re-opening in the same Session a question which has once been decided. A matter which has been *debated but not decided* in Secret Session *may be debated again in open Session, provided there is no allusion to proceedings in Secret Session, and no disclosure of information acquired in Secret Session* ... A question which has thus been debated in Secret Session is not, thereby, what may be called permanently sterilised, but, obviously, much depends on the nature and scope of the question.[19]

In short, the formula to provide for fluidity between open and closed sessions, and to maximise the quality of deliberation by transitioning between public and private fora is clearly present. However, whether it was appropriately taken advantage of in wartime is of course extremely difficult to quantify. In the present proposal, the Speaker would be placed under an obligation to assess when a closed session should begin and end, and a public session should resume. This would be kept under review by the Speaker as a closed session progressed, with the aim of ensuring that secrecy did not continue unnecessarily. When a public session resumed, discussion of the merits and demerits of the armed conflict being considered could resume, without explicit reference to the sensitive material seen and debated in closed session. By contrast, any time a closed session is under consideration, both government and the Speaker would have to consider the reputations of the Executive and Parliament vis-à-vis the public.

---

[16] CJ Boulton, *Erskine May: Parliamentary Practice*, 21st edn (London, Butterworths, 1989) 252.
[17] The headings in Hansard are respectively 'secret session' followed by 'message from the Lords' HC Deb 13 November 1940, vol 365, cols 1714–15.
[18] ibid.
[19] HC Deb 3 August 1944, vol 402, cols 1608–09, emphasis added.

The present proposal seeks to build upon the existing contemporary provision for closed sittings. Closed intelligence sessions are necessary to protect sensitive information in JIC reports from being shared in a manner damaging to national security. There are four further reasons which render this procedural innovation necessary. The first and strongest reason for advocating that all parliamentarians should have an opportunity to consider and debate relevant reports of the JIC and to form their own view of their worth is that this may promote better-quality decisions about armed conflict. This is because the conclusions of the JIC are essentially a judgement call. Reports of the JIC are not based upon objective facts, but on educated assessments. In her statement to the Chilcot Inquiry, Baroness Manningham-Buller, the former head of MI5 (the Security Service) stated that treatment of JIC Reports in the lead up to Iraq as somehow special perpetuated a culture of groupthink.[20] According to the Baroness, this was unwise as '[the JIC] is another Whitehall committee. It is fallible. It produces some excellent things; it produces some less good things. Reflecting back, with the wisdom of hindsight, *there was an inadequate challenge*'.[21] Furthermore, 'it is always recognised and others must recognise that its judgments may be fallible'.[22] Like any policy issue to be discussed in a parliamentary setting, deliberation about the weight to be accorded to these intelligence judgments would benefit from input from a diverse range of individuals.[23] A wider range of views on the worth of any intelligence judgment may also prevent the dangers of groupthink and 'group polarisation'; the phenomenon which occurs when like-minded individuals develop more extreme views as a result of exposure to an echo chamber.[24] In addition to the reduction of the potential for group polarisation, direct access to and scrutiny of JIC reports may compel additional pressure to ensure the accuracy of these reports, because they will be the subject of wider scrutiny. In turn, such scrutiny may lead to the removal of the veneer of 'secrecy' which leads consumers of information to over-inflate its worth.[25]

The second reason compelling closed intelligence sessions is the presence of a clear desire on the part of parliamentarians to engage substantively with intelligence-based claims when the Government presents them. Chapter four explained that there has been a clear growth in MPs' interventions related to intelligence where the Government bases its case for war on JIC reports. The contemporary constitutional arrangements of both the United States' Congress and the European Parliament make provisions for elected officials to view (and in some cases debate) classified information. In short, the House of Commons is at a disadvantage when compared with these institutions.

---

[20] Baroness E Manningham Butler, Statement to the Iraq Inquiry, 43, line 11, (20 July 2010) <www.iraqinquiry.org.uk/media/95374/2010-07-20-Transcript-Manningham-BullerS1.pdf> accessed 28 February 2017.

[21] ibid, 43, lines 6–9, emphasis added.

[22] ibid, 43, lines 15–16.

[23] J Waldron, 'Legislating with Integrity' (2003–04) 72 *Fordham Law Review* 373, 383–85.

[24] CR Sunstein, *Why Societies Need Dissent* (Cambridge MA, Harvard University Press, 2003) ch 6.

[25] Travers, Van Boven and Judd, 'The secrecy heuristic' (n 12).

Thirdly, intelligence-based claims will most likely persist before Parliament in relation to armed conflict. Additionally, for 'intelligence to have value the reader must trust the author, without being clear on the identities of sources, the methods of collection or the integrity of the process'.[26] Giving all MPs access to reports of the JIC is a method of providing this trust. Closed sessions are essential for fully informed decision-making in this context. As noted above, Chilcot was of the view that successive governments would continue to use intelligence-led arguments before Parliament, and that reform of the process of scrutiny was required. The alternative is to continue with the present arrangements in full cognisance of presenting 'sanitised' intelligence briefings in the public domain. Chapter four explained that this practice deprives classified information of its essential context, and potentially leads to the over-estimation of its importance in the minds of parliamentarians.

Fourthly and finally, the nature of the disadvantage parliamentarians face in relation to their peer institutions is becoming clear in the context of the Brexit negotiations, if not in the context of armed conflict. Members of the European Parliament can access classified briefings from the European Union Council and Commission in relation to the Brexit negotiations under the rules for information sharing between EU institutions.[27] Parliamentarians in Westminster are at a comparative disadvantage during Brexit negotiations, as they will not have access to similar material under the current constitutional arrangements. Members of the United States' Congress can also see and debate classified material by virtue of their position as an elected official. At the time of writing the House of Lords European Union Committee had considered a similar proposal of secure rooms to allow parliamentarians in Westminster access to confidential diplomatic material related to the Brexit negotiations.[28] However, amendments tabled to the European Union (Notification of Withdrawal) Bill which would have allowed MPs sight of confidential information relating to the negotiations were defeated by 284 to 333 votes.[29] The purported purpose of the amendment was to give Westminster parliamentarians the same access to information as their EU counterparts. The amendment was intended to act as a 'means of ensuring robust parliamentary oversight throughout the formal negotiation period … and a meaningful debate and vote in Parliament on the proposed [Brexit] deal'.[30] There were some concerns

---

[26] A Snell, 'How to Read the Trump Dossier' (2017) *London Review of Books* (online exclusive) <www.lrb.co.uk/2017/01/17/arthur-snell/how-to-read-the-trump-dossier> accessed 17 September 2017.

[27] 'Framework Agreement on relations between the European Parliament and the European Commission', Annex II, 1: Forwarding of confidential information to Parliament' OJ L 304/56 (20 November 2010); General Secretariat of the Council of Europe, 'Access by the European Parliament to classified information in the area of the Common Foreign and Security Policy' (23 October 2012) 15343/12; and European Parliament, 'Security Briefing', <www.guengl.eu/uploads/publications-documents/ERNST2.doc> accessed 3 February 2017.

[28] House of Lords Select Committee on the European Union, 'Brexit: Parliamentary Scrutiny' 4th Report, 2016–17, HL Paper 50, para 52; see also HL Deb 22 November 2016, vol 776, col 1902, Lord Bridges of Headley.

[29] See Committee Stage of the Bill, 6–9 February 2017; HC Deb 6 February 2017, vol 621, col 123.

[30] HC Deb 6 February 2017, vol 621, col 58, Matthew Pennycook (Lab).

about preventing leaks of information,[31] but no objections to the proposal were based upon the idea that MPs receiving confidential information would undermine either public trust or transparency. According to Armstrong the defeat of amendments aimed at enhancing Parliament's role at this stage can be attributed to the fact that 'MPs found themselves caught between ... their own preferences about whether the UK should remain in the EU and, [the] demands of party discipline ... as well as the expectations of their constituents'.[32] As such, MPs' rejection of such a step appears to be driven not by concerns about the tensions between publicity and secrecy, but instead by the potential fallout of appearing to be 'anti-Brexit' or insufficiently attentive to the outcome of the referendum. In light of Parliament's larger political role in relation to war, the need for not only mere access to, but the ability to actively contest the worth of classified information is clearly necessary.

The relationship between publicity and secrecy in the context of deliberation is complex. Far from being entirely in opposition to secrecy, representative democracy 'contains a presumption in favor of publicity although it in no way denies the necessity of secrecy'.[33] This chapter argues that secrecy is valuable in a representative democracy only where it can remove information asymmetries, enhance the quality of deliberation by providing greater information to deliberators, promote unencumbered discussion, reduce groupthink and promote dissent. There is the need for a level of secrecy which is necessary and proportionate to the need to protect vital national security interests. To ensure attention is paid to the concepts of necessity and proportionality, authority to initiate a closed session would be vested in the politically independent officer of the Commons: the Speaker. If the Speaker, having heard the Government's perspective in camera decides that a closed session is necessary to inform Parliament, a debate and free vote on the value of entering a closed session should also be held in the House of Commons. This would allow individual MPs to explain their position to the public on the matter and also to reject the possibility of a session if they considered it too damaging to Parliament's reputation.

Leaders of the Opposition should also be entitled to request that Parliament receive a closed intelligence session where none has been offered. The Speaker, on viewing the JIC report, would have to be convinced a closed session was necessary, and would be responsible for ending the session when national security information was no longer in danger of being compromised. The sitting would then resume in public. The value of vesting this responsibility in the Speaker of the Commons is that he or she is the highest official in the Commons, and is constitutionally bound to be politically impartial. His or her responsibilities include representing the House of Commons in its relations with the Crown, presiding over debates, and enforcing rules for preserving order during Commons'

---

[31] ibid, col 76, Sir William Cash (Con).
[32] KA Armstrong, *Brexit Time: Leaving the EU—why, how and when?* (Cambridge, CUP, 2017) 248.
[33] S Chambers, 'Behind Closed Doors: Publicity, Secrecy, and the Quality of Deliberation' (2004) 4 *Journal of Political Philosophy* 389–410, 389.

proceedings.[34] The chief characteristics of the Office of Speaker are summed up as 'authority and impartiality'.[35] The Speaker also takes political (and occasionally legal) responsibility for guardianship of the privileges of Parliament. This independent check would prevent government from over-reliance upon closed sessions, and, it would in turn help protect the reputation of Parliament as a public and representative assembly. In respect of national security matters, there is also precedent for sharing information on Privy Council terms with the Speaker to allow him or her to consider national security information held by the Government. By convention the Speaker of the House of Commons is a Privy Counsellor. However, like most of the 600 or so Privy Counsellors, he or she is not a regular participant in Privy Council briefings which are held at the discretion of the Prime Minister. In the late 1980s the Speaker of the House of Commons was invited to a meeting on Privy Council terms so that he could have sight of classified information to assist in his decision-making about banning the screening of the Zircon film on the parliamentary estate.[36] It was believed that the Zircon documentary contained information potentially sensitive to national security. A similar process could be reinstituted, allowing the Speaker to apply a threshold test of necessity after seeing the JIC report on a confidential basis.

It is crucial that no voting on matters of substance should take place in a closed session. In chapter five we explained that given the complex demands on parliamentarians in a representative democracy, it is imperative that voting records are public. In addition to the need for a public voting record, we argued that parliamentarians must try wherever possible to present explanations for their votes which conform to the requirements of a culture of justification. This is a difficult burden for individual parliamentarians to discharge, as it involves a fairly detailed explanation of the factors the MP took into account, as well as an indication of whether he or she was swayed by her own conscience, the party line, or the views of constituents. These requirements are clearly incompatible with secrecy. In view of this, permitting voting on matters of substance in secret would entirely undermine the culture of justification both authors seek to realise through the argument in this monograph.

Closed intelligence sessions would demand the complete integrity of government Ministers. The Cabinet Manual (and the British Constitution) obligates Ministers to 'give accurate and truthful information to Parliament'.[37] Moreover, Ministers who 'knowingly mislead' Parliament are expected to resign.[38] Historically, there appears to be only two clear exceptions to the rule that a Minister who misleads Parliament must resign; these arise in the instance of currency devaluation,

---

[34] M Jack (ed), *Erskine May Parliamentary Practice*, 24th ed (London, LexisNexis, 2011), 59.

[35] ibid, 61.

[36] House of Commons Committee of Privileges, 'Speaker's Order of 22 January 1987 on a Matter of National Security', 1st Report, 1986–87, HC 365, para 5.

[37] HM Government, 'The Cabinet Manual: A guide to laws, conventions and rules on the operation of government' (London, The Stationary Office, 2015) para [5.6].

[38] ibid.

or (crucially) in 'times of war or other emergency threatening national security'.[39] Yet, this is not the end of the matter. There may well be other informal exceptions. Former senior civil servant Sir Robin Butler (in)famously stated in his 1994 evidence to a Select Committee that 'lying and misleading is always unequivocally wrong ... but there are very rare occasions ... when a greater wrong is done by not lying than by lying'.[40] This sentiment was pushed further still by William Waldegrave. He took the view that not only were there such exceptional cases when Parliament could be deliberately misled, Parliament itself 'understands that and has always accepted it'.[41] It is time to abandon such ambiguities favouring the Executive. Considerations limiting access to sensitive information may be appropriate for the House of Commons in public session, but failure on the part of the Government to present information accurately in closed session would severely undermine the reputation of both the Government and Parliament. Effective closed intelligence sessions would require the rigorous enforcement of the prohibition on misleading Parliament.

The object of allowing these limited closed sessions (circumscribed on both sides by public debate) may paradoxically also promote transparency. Neither the Government nor Parliament would wish to be perceived as resorting to secrecy excessively, due to the risk of damaging public confidence in both institutions. Government would be compelled to think carefully about what information to keep classified in order to preserve its reputation as acting above board with the electorate. The result may be that more information is pushed into the public domain, which is ultimately the most desirable outcome. Not all of the contents of JIC reports are actually classified. In the United States, there is relative parity vis-à-vis access to 'finished' intelligence reports[42] between Congress and the Executive. As a consequence of this arrangement, the US Government, it is thought, uses intelligence more wisely in policy formulation, as it can be scrutinised by parliamentarians. By analogy, it might be expected that a similar phenomenon would be observed were Parliament to adopt closed intelligence sessions. To fully realise the benefits of allowing all parliamentarians access to intelligence there would have to be recourse to some training. Such a system already operates in Congress, and the argument herein is that a similar initiative should be recommended for Members of the House of Commons.[43] In England and Wales,

---

[39] A Tomkins, *The Constitutions After Scott: Government Unwrapped* (Oxford, Clarendon: OUP, 1998) 43.

[40] House of Commons Treasury and Civil Service Committee, 'The Role of the Civil Service', Minutes of Evidence, 26 April 1994, HC 1993–94, 27(vii). See also A Tomkins, 'A right to mislead Parliament?' (1996) 16(1) *Legal Studies* 63.

[41] Treasury and Civil Service Committee, 'The Role of the Civil Service', Minutes of Evidence, 8 March 1994, HC 1993–94, 27(vi).

[42] The term 'finished intelligence' refers to intelligence reports of a similar status to JIC reports, as opposed to 'raw' intelligence from single sources (ie surveillance tapes or the reports of individual officers).

[43] FM Kaiser, 'Protection of Classified Information by Congress: Practices and Proposals' (Washington DC, Congressional Research Service, 2006) 8.

judges having sight of national security evidence in judicial review proceedings receive training from the intelligence agencies. It therefore seems incongruous that judges who are unelected officials can have sight of material sensitive to national security by virtue of their position, but our elected representatives are precluded from doing so.

Security provisions to prevent the leaks of classified information during or after closed intelligence sessions also would be required. Much of the groundwork for this already exists. The doctrine of parliamentary privilege means that none of the Official Secrets Acts are applicable to disclosures of classified information made in the course of parliamentary proceedings.[44] Instead, disclosure by a parliamentarian is considered a breach of privilege. During wartime, the Westminster Parliament had a procedure for investigating allegations of disclosure of the content of closed sessions. The Committee on Privileges would meet to determine whether or not a leak had taken place, and in turn, whether or not a punishable breach of privilege had occurred. The scope of parliamentary privilege has clearly been narrowed since wartime, and its position with respect to the criminal law clarified by the highest judicial authority. In view of this, an unauthorised leak or disclosure not made on the floor of the House may well result in a Member incurring criminal liability under section 1 of the Official Secrets Act 1989, upon the consent of the Attorney General to prosecution. The twin safeguards of parliamentary privilege and the possibility of criminal sanctions should act as a sufficient deterrent to the leaking of classified information by parliamentarians. However, as discussion below progresses, it will be demonstrated that in the three systems considered, the arrangements for sharing intelligence with parliaments has developed by mutual agreement over time. Therefore, it is in the interests of parliamentarians to protect information in order to guarantee future access to it.

Defenders of openness may yet retort that the more valuable approach would be to omit intelligence from the discussion altogether, thus obviating the need for any 'secret' proceedings. There have been situations post-2003 where the Government has made no intelligence-based claims before Parliament. The debate on a substantive motion in support of military action in Libya held on 21 March 2011 was one such instance.[45] The Government's public case turned only on questions of international legality, morality, and necessity of the intervention. To sum up, the question for parliamentarians was whether: 'Action to protect Libyan civilians struggling for democracy is internationally supported, legally justified and morally right'.[46] However, the Foreign Affairs Committee expressed grave concerns about the overall use of intelligence in policy making, discussed in chapter four.

---

[44] House of Commons Select Committee on the Official Secrets Acts, 'Report together with the proceedings of the committee, minutes of evidence, and index', 1938–39, HC 101, para 10.

[45] Which was commenced after the outset of the conflict presumably due to the 'perceived urgency of the crisis' C Walker and A Horne, 'Parliament and National Security' in A Horne and A Le Sueur (eds), *Parliament: Legislation and Accountability* (Oxford, Hart, 2016) 214.

[46] HC Deb 21 March 2011, vol 525, col 746.

The issue of intelligence split the 40 or so MPs on the National Security Council. The report explained that 'Given the lack of reliable intelligence on which to build policy, British politicians and policy-makers may have attached undue weight to their individual and collective memories of the appalling events at Srebrenica'.[47] Once again, parliamentary discourse was driven by emotion as opposed to information, and this led to a decision which has been the subject of severe criticism.

Where intelligence is highly divisive, it must form part of the discussion and be presented in its proper context. The need for diversity of input and dissent on the value of JIC reports is as great as in any other area of parliamentary debate about armed conflict. This can only be undertaken in closed session. A closed intelligence session is the only way in which Parliament would be able to effectively scrutinise the Government's secret intelligence-based case. As a matter of constitutional principle this opportunity should be afforded to all elected representatives, not simply a chosen few. Without proper access to closed intelligence sessions for all parliamentarians, discourse on the Government's intelligence-based claims will take the form of either uncritical acceptance or ill-informed scepticism.

C. Justifications for Initiating a Closed Intelligence Session

Publicity (or transparency) is a core requirement of a functioning representative democracy. In any deliberative forum, such as the House of Commons, publicity has a potentially transformative power, as it is capable of subjecting the private interests of political actors to the rigours of public discourse.[48] In view of this, any decision to depart from the principle of publicity in a legislature seems counterintuitive, and subject to a high burden of justification. Any measures involving secrecy must be aimed at enhancing the constitutional functions of a legislature by providing access to information in a manner that simply would not be possible in the course of a public session. The examples considered in this section, namely the Westminster Parliament in wartime, the contemporary practice of the United States' Congress, and the European Parliament in the context of the Common Foreign and Security Policy all indicate that there are circumstances in which the ability of a representative legislature to conduct scrutiny of an Executive

---

[47] Foreign Affairs Committee, 'Libya: Examination of intervention and collapse and the UK's future policy options', 3rd Report, HC 2016–17, 119, para 40.

[48] A Gosseries, 'Publicity' in EN Zalta (ed), *The Stanford Encyclopaedia of Philosophy* (Stanford, Stanford University, 2010) para 2.2 'Deliberation', <plato.stanford.edu/archives/fall2010/entries/publicity> accessed 17 September 2017. See also M James, C Blamires and C Pease-Watkin (eds), *The Collected Works of Jeremy Bentham, Political Tactics (1791)* in M James, C Blamires, and C Pease-Watkin (eds) (Oxford, Oxford Scholarly Editions Online, 2015), ch II, 34.

policy based on classified materials in closed session can enhance the ability of politicians to check Executive power. Where classified material is the basis of a decision a compromise in transparency is necessary to promote participation and accountability.

However, the nature and extent of access to classified information, and the role played by parliamentarians across the three legislatures examined is varied, even though the subject matter area in each case concerns matters of defence and security. This is to be expected. The relationship between the Executive and the Legislature in relation to war powers and national security varies according to the constitutional tradition in which the legislature exists. Nonetheless a useful pattern emerges. It is as follows: the greater the role played by the legislature in respect of war or defence powers (ie the greater the extent to which there is an obligation for debate and decision by the legislature) the greater the need for members to have equal access to classified material, and the ability to debate this fully in closed session. By contrast, there is also a constant in play. The nature of that constant is the need to have a strong over-arching normative justification for departing from the standards of public deliberation. In each of the jurisdictions surveyed, a sense of striking a balance between the need to inform parliamentarians and the need to preserve the legitimacy of the legislature emerges. These tests form the overarching justifications for departing from the principle of publicity.

I. The Westminster Parliament During Wartime

The important features of the operation of wartime closed sessions fall into three categories: (1) the opportunity for enhanced disclosures to parliamentarians; (2) the presence of debates and free votes on whether to sit in private prior to commencing some sittings; and (3) the search for a genuine balance of interests between open and closed debate. Although the wartime context is unique and might even be considered exceptional,[49] these features can be abstracted to form the basis of a contemporary proposal.

The first closed session of Parliament was held in the House of Lords on 25–26 April 1916 after the beginning of World War I. In World War II the first closed session was held in the Commons on 12 December 1939, the war having started on 1 September 1939. In total, Parliament held 46 secret sessions: seven during World War I; 37 during War II; and a further two during 'peacetime', occurring in 1958 and 2001 respectively.[50] The initial impetus for a closed session was to

---

[49] H McD Clockie, 'Parliamentary Government in Wartime' (1940) 6 *The Canadian Journal of Economics and Political Science* 359, 359.

[50] C Bryant, *Parliament: The Biography Volume 2: Reform* (London, Doubleday, 2014) ch 5, fn 1 and HC Deb 18 November 1958, vol 595, col 1116 and HC Deb 4 December 2001, vol 376, col 314. See also House of Commons Procedure Committee, 'Motions "that the House sit in private"' 2nd Report, 2014–15, HC 753.

discuss the need for the military conscription of adult males to fight in World War I. In an open debate on 14 March 1916 the Under-Secretary for War first raised the possibility of a closed session. The principle of equality between all parliamentarians as a matter of principle was firmly evident in his proposal. Eschewing the possibility of a secret committee system used in France, where individual Ministers became responsible to separate secret parliamentary committees, because it 'weakens the Executive and divides the responsibility',[51] the Under Secretary for War instead pointed out that:

> [The] German Reichstag meets in secret Session ... the members of the Reichstag are made acquainted with all that goes on, and yet there is not any leakage of information ... What is the reason why the representatives of the people here are to be less trusted than the representatives of the people in France and Germany?[52]

Demands for a closed session on various aspects of the Military Service Bill and Military Service (Review of Exceptions) Bill continued as parliamentarians perceived the French and German legislatures, who already utilised closed sessions, to be better informed of their respective governments' prosecution of the war.[53] The Military Service Bill was also the subject of open sessions, on 27 April 1916, where members were deeply critical of the two-day closed session which had been held on the conscription issue, with one Member suggesting that 'if this expedient is tried again we shall have some kind of Secret Session in which Members do really get information'.[54]

Despite these concerns, it was the Opposition, as opposed to the Government, who demanded a return to the practice during World War II.[55] Closed Sessions could take place in either the House of Commons or the House of Lords. There has only ever been one comprehensive academic treatment of the impact and purpose of these sessions, which was published by Clive Parry in 1954.[56] He considered the innovation to be largely successful. Parry's conclusion was that the temporary sacrifice of transparency in Parliament was a reasonable price to pay in order to secure political accountability: 'If democracy is not to destroy itself in the process of ensuring its salvation, some technique other than that of non-information must be developed in order to ensure the continual democratic check upon Executive arbitrariness'. This meant that 'Serious consideration should therefore be given to an alternative to non-information: that of the Executive's taking the legislature into its confidence'.[57] The reappraisal of wartime practice in this chapter, conducted over 60 years later, builds upon Parry's perspective by examining relevant Hansard and archival material which would have been unavailable to him at the time.

---

[51] HC Deb 14 March 1916, vol 80, col 1960.
[52] ibid, col 1960.
[53] HC Deb 20 March 1917, vol 92, cols 707–08.
[54] HC Deb 27 April 1916, vol 81, cols 2525–82.
[55] C Parry, 'Legislatures and Secrecy' (1954) 67 *Harvard Law Review* 737, 740.
[56] ibid, 741.
[57] ibid, 741.

The investigation largely squares with Parry's conclusions, but imports additional nuance. Whilst closed sessions were in many ways imperfect, and may even have been abused (see Part D, below), they provided valuable information to Parliament on many occasions. Thus, they constituted a check on government which was not incompatible with the general commitment to public discourse, due to the operation of the mechanisms for adopting closed sessions.

The power to hold closed sessions, or, more accurately to exclude the public and control the reporting of debates, appears to be routed in the doctrine of parliamentary privilege. Historically, Parliament has always had the power to control the reporting of its own proceedings.[58] However, during World War I, the power to conduct closed sessions was thought to be sourced in the Royal Prerogative, and exercisable by the Prime Minister on behalf of the monarch.[59] Despite the presence of prerogative power, it seems that during World War II the Government made greater efforts to convince Parliament of the need for a closed session; ie the need for an 'abrupt departure from established traditions and practice' of openness.[60] There appears to have been two ways in which closed sessions were initiated: they could either occur as the result of a free vote in either House, or they could be initiated by the Government upon agreement at a Cabinet meeting. However, as the process developed it appears clear that the Government (as controllers of the relevant information) retained the unilateral power to both initiate closed sessions, and to refuse requests from the Opposition to hold them.

Parry noted that in 1940 parliamentarians remained divided about the nature and purpose of closed sessions; there 'was still a division of opinion as to whether the purpose of a secret session was to inform Parliament or enable Parliament to instruct the Government'.[61] On 9 July 1942, the Lord Privy Seal, then Clement Atlee (also Deputy Leader of the Commons) outlined the factors to be considered before commencing a secret session on the floor of the House. The subject matter of the planned secret session concerned British naval capabilities. The test put forward was expressed in the following terms:

> [The] Government wish to take this opportunity of putting before hon. Members a frank review of the shipping situation, both from the point of view of losses and of construction. In order that this may be done with safety to the people of this island and to our very gallant merchant seamen, it will be *necessary* to hold the Session in secret … The *sole factor* actuating the Government in their decision is their *paramount duty to protect the food and the lives of our people*, and of our seamen in particular … I feel certain that the House will agree that, *however valuable publicity may be for our Debates, it must not be allowed in so vital a matter to endanger the lives of our people*, especially of those who are already running such constant and grave risks as our merchant seamen.[62]

---

[58] Jack, *Erskine May* (n 34) 223.
[59] HL Deb 25 April 1916, vol 21, col 813.
[60] ibid, col 811, Marquess of Crewe.
[61] Parry, 'Legislatures and Secrecy' (n 55) 754.
[62] HC Deb 9 July 1942, vol 381, col 951, emphasis added.

The points to note about the proposed justification include the necessity based test, balancing publicity against the protection of other vital interests, and the desire to avoid the provision of misleading or inaccurate information in open debate. The latter has of course been a problem in twenty-first century debates on armed conflict. It is difficult to state with any certainty whether these test factors were rigorously applied throughout the wartime period, and there are some suggestions to the contrary in archival and declassified material which is available in the National Archives and the Westminster Parliamentary Archives. However, the threshold test represents an encouraging template. The other issue worthy of note here is that the specific reasons for initiating a closed session during wartime were often much broader in scope than proposed in this chapter. Instead, what is important about these examples is the fact that both parliamentarians and the Government felt that there was a heavy burden of justification to be met before departing from public discourse.

Before the development of the above test, there was some strong evidence that the requirement of publicity should not be lightly departed from, and that government felt it was their duty to justify calling a closed session to MPs in a prior open session. There was a debate and free vote prior to the first secret session of the House of Lords.[63] It will be recalled from chapter five that during a free vote each parliamentarian is permitted to vote according to his or her conscience, as opposed to being compelled to follow a particular party line. In this debate, steps were immediately taken to satisfy the need for publicity, namely, the publication of 'a considered description of the proposals which the Government in due course will make to Parliament and the country, though without that description of the reasons which induce us to make the particular proposals'.[64]

On 30 July 1940 there was another free vote in the House of Commons prior to the initiation of a closed session.[65] The request for the session on this occasion came from parliamentarians, as opposed to the Government. The purpose of the proposed session, according to Churchill, was

> to have a Debate about foreign affairs, and that it was the wish of the House for it to take place in secret, so that Members of all parties could say what they really felt about foreign countries without any danger of adding to the number of those countries with which we are at present at war.[66]

The motion that the House sit in private was debateable, and the vote was the subject of Members' individual conscience.[67] The Foreign Secretary had prepared two speeches—one for public consumption, and one for the closed session—which were different in content. As the debate on the motion progressed the nature of the

[63] HL Deb 25 April 1916, vol 21, cols 811–80.
[64] ibid, col 812.
[65] HC Deb 30 July 1940, vol 363, col 1166.
[66] ibid, col 1166.
[67] ibid, col 1166.

dilemma facing parliamentarians became clearer: prioritise openness and be kept in the dark, or sacrifice some publicity in order to be more accurately informed and to have the ability to make franker contributions and ask more searching questions. Earl Winterton explained that the request for the session came entirely from Parliament as 'it was not the Government's desire to express any opinion upon the subject' but there was recognition that the majority of the House favoured a closed session in order to gain information on the Executive's policies in the area.[68] From the debate it is clear that the two countries under discussion were in Europe and Asia, respectively.[69] There were some objections amongst the MPs, however, as one Member remarked that the House was 'contributing to secret diplomacy'[70] whilst another expressed scepticism that anything of a genuinely secret nature would actually be revealed.[71] In the end, the House divided 200:109 in favour of the closed session, after the Speaker put the question 'that strangers be ordered to withdraw'.

Various specific reasons were put forward by the Executive to explain why closed sessions were necessary, and in practice, the Cabinet minutes and other records reveal that the relevant parties paid clear attention to concepts such as the public interest and necessity in these discussions.[72] However, the common thread amongst all the justifications for initiating a closed session was to furnish Parliament with information it could not otherwise receive in public. For example, in the debate immediately prior to the closed session of the Commons on 12 December 1917 the Prime Minister advised that in open session 'if, after hearing my statement, the House desires a public discussion, we would be ready to give it, but the Government could not take the responsibility of giving the public figures which it would not be in the public interest to give'.[73] Immediately thereafter the House entered a closed session. At the same time, however, it retained the power to unilaterally refuse Opposition requests for closed sessions.[74] Furthermore, the Cabinet Minutes of 13 July 1950 reveal a refusal to hold a closed session to discuss the country's preparedness for a possible war with Korea. This request had been made by the Leader of the Conservative Opposition.[75]

In short, entry into closed sessions was not taken lightly by the Government. In many instances ample steps were taken to explain publicly on the floor of the House that a closed session was indeed a necessity. Closed sessions allowed

[68]   ibid, col 1194.
[69]   ibid, col 1197.
[70]   ibid, col 1201.
[71]   ibid, Col Josiah Wedgwood (Lab, Newcastle-under-Lyme).
[72]   HC Deb 12 December 1917, vol 27, cols 1483–88. Note this Hansard is available in the records on Secret Sessions held in the Westminster Parliamentary Archives.
[73]   ibid.
[74]   British National Archives Reference CAB 128/18/5.
[75]   British National Archives Reference CAB 128/18/5 'Declassified Cabinet Minutes' (13 July 1950): The minutes of the Cabinet Secretary recorded that there was concern about using a 'wartime power in Parliament' and that: 'It was the general conclusion of the Cabinet that the balance of the arguments lay against conceding this request for a debate in secret session'.

information to be given to parliamentarians that would have undoubtedly caused populist alarm. For example, the Speaker's Report of 1917 gave totals on shipping losses on a month-to-month basis.[76] Other such instances of this include closed session debates in World War II relating to food shortages and agriculture strategy on the British Isles, and the possibility of a German invasion of Britain.[77] The private papers of Lloyd George (held in the Westminster Parliamentary Archives) also demonstrate the need for closed sessions to promote candid policy-making. The Prime Minister's handwritten notes reveal a 'Government dilemma' regarding how to address the public in relation to food supplies. Making a 'reassuring statement' to the public risked the public becoming 'indifferent' and would render any attempt at rationing ineffective. The notes continue by stating that if a public statement is made, there is a risk of sounding 'alarmist ... then there is a panic [and] demands are made upon the Government for unnecessarily drastic action'.[78] The viable solution was a closed session because: 'At a secret session *real facts can be given and [the] House can judge*'.[79]

The first records regarding closed sessions, with particular reference to Cabinet Secretary's minutes, in the British National and Westminster Parliamentary Archives, suggest a variety of specific motivations on the part of Government for holding closed sessions. On 9 July 1917, during a debate in the House of Commons[80] the then Prime Minister (David Lloyd George) made clear that: 'If the House wishes full information it will be impossible for me to give it except in Secret Session ... I could make a statement, but *it would be a truncated and an incomplete statement if it were made in Public Session*'.[81] Further evidence of the balancing of interests in search of a justification for departing from sitting in public is evident in the Cabinet records from 4 June 1940, in which the Cabinet considered the request of the Lord Privy Seal for a closed session to discuss British defences against invasion. The minutes suggest that parliamentarians 'felt the need of an occasion on which they could state openly their views as to the situation of this country in regard to defence against invasion, and to point out what appeared to them to be weaknesses, without ... disclosing information to the enemy.'[82]

In the Speaker of the House of Commons' accounts of the closed session which followed (which is publicly available in Hansard)[83] we can see that there was discussion of matters which were intensely sensitive to national security, defence, and international relations. Setty notes that this system allowed the Executive to

[76] HC Deb 11 May 1917, vol 93, cols 1291–93, Speaker's report of secret session.

[77] Cabinet Minutes, 'Memoranda prepared for a secret session of the House of Commons on Home Defence 1940' 1 January 1940, British National Archives Record CAB 106/1202.

[78] David Lloyd George, 'Personal and Political Papers: Notes and Briefs for Speeches' LG/F/232 (1917).

[79] ibid, emphasis added.

[80] HC Deb 9 July 1917, vol 95, cols 1701–08.

[81] ibid, col 1703, emphasis added.

[82] ibid.

[83] ibid, cols 1704–08.

'share security related information with the Parliament and maintain a high level of secrecy within Parliament to minimize the leak of intelligence to enemy forces'.[84] Churchill's 'Secret Session Speeches',[85] published after the war, demonstrate that he addressed Parliament on subjects as sensitive and diverse as the prospect of a German invasion as a consequence of the fall of the French resistance, the effects of air raids on both the safety of parliamentarians and the general public, and specific intelligence information relating to the number of German warships poised to invade Britain.[86]

Churchill himself explained that parliamentary engagement was capable of being substantively better in the context of a closed session, because it allowed Members of the House to be frank with government, without damaging national morale.[87] On balance, Parry is correct that closed sessions allowed Government to take between six and 1,400 persons into its confidence, despite the fact that the vast majority of parliamentarians lacked relevant experience.[88] This is a highly inclusive form of secrecy, and it seems to have functioned substantively better than the selective publicity we have uncovered in recent parliamentary engagement. On 19 December 1945, after the end of the Second World War, it was moved in the Commons 'that no proceeding in this House during the last Parliament held in Secret Session be any longer secret'.[89] This motion applied to the Speaker's reports of the secret sessions, whereas publishing anything that went beyond this remained a breach of privilege.[90] The motion was actually moved by government who required the consent of Parliament on this matter. The fate of the Speaker's reports was a parliamentary, as opposed to an Executive, decision.

II. The United States' Congress

Whilst the role of the House of Commons in relation to control of war powers has ostensibly developed and grown since World Wars I and II, the role of Congress in this domain has always been clearly enshrined in the United States Constitution. The US Congress is constitutionally entrusted with the mandate to declare war pursuant to Article 1, Section 8 of the Constitution.[91] The nature of this obligation has resulted in a heightened desire for intelligence sessions in relation

---

[84] S Setty, 'The Rise of National Security Secrets' (2012) 44 *Connecticut Law Review* 1563–83, 1575.
[85] HC Deb 5 March 1917, vol 91, col 89–90, Winston Churchill.
[86] W Churchill (author) and C Eade (ed), *Secret Session Speeches by Churchill* (London, Cassell and Co, 1946).
[87] HC Deb 5 March 1917, vol 91, cols 89–90, Winston Churchill.
[88] Parry, 'Legislatures and Secrecy' (n 55) 741.
[89] HC Deb 19 December 1945, vol 417, cols 1407–36.
[90] ibid, col 1409.
[91] Constitution of the United States of America, Article 1, Section 8, Clause 11.

to armed conflicts.[92] Article One, Section 5 of the US Constitution mandates that: 'Each House shall keep a Journal of its Proceedings, and from time to time publish the same, *exception such Parts as may in their Judgment require Secrecy*.'[93] Whilst the United States' position might well be thought constitutionally unique (and therefore an inappropriate comparator), it is argued that the comparison is apt as the flow of intelligence information from the Executive to Congress has been developed largely through a process of political 'conventions' over time. Comparison is undertaken with a view to showing that this can be done successfully with minimal concerns about leaks or damage to the public trust in Congress. The inference which follows, is of course, that it would be possible to implement a similar system in the House of Commons to allow MPs to scrutinise JIC reports. Moreover, it illustrates that as the role of the legislatures grows, so does the demand to consult classified information in camera.

Since 1947, the United States Government has also been under a statutory obligation to 'ensure that the congressional intelligence committees are kept fully and currently informed of the intelligence activities of the United States, including any significant anticipated intelligence activity as required by this title'.[94] There has never been litigation which has settled the meaning of either 'fully and currently informed' or 'significant anticipated intelligence activity' under this statute. Instead, as there are 'no written rules, agreed to by both branches, governing what intelligence will be shared with the Hill or how it will be handled. ... [the] current system is entirely the product of experience, shaped by the needs and concerns of both branches over the last 20 years'.[95] The evolution of these circumstances as a product of convention mirrors the developments in increased parliamentary involvement and increased intelligence disclosure in the British Constitution.

The increase in demand for classified intelligence sessions by Members of Congress post-Vietnam was partly prompted by the fact that many of Congress's constitutional responsibilities are in fact intelligence-driven. Members of Congress can access intelligence information by virtue of their elected position, they do not require to be security vetted or cleared. That is to say, that in order for Congress to fulfil its function of scrutiny judiciously it will at least need to be aware of, if not

---

[92] ibid, Article 1, Section 8: ('The Congress shall have Power ... [t]o declare War'). There is also an ongoing controversy regarding the exact relationship between Congress and the President in relation to the War Powers Resolution of 1973, which empowers the President to introduce US armed forces into conflict subject to certain procedural requirements. The interaction between the War Powers Resolution and the Constitution is the subject of ongoing controversy and scholarly debate, but this does not detract from the argument pursued in this chapter. For further discussion, see: M Zeisberg, *War Powers: The Politics of Constitutional Authority* (New Jersey, Princeton University Press, 2013), RF Grimmett, 'The War Powers Resolution: After Thirty-four Years' (2010, Congressional Research Service, Paper RL32267), and S Prakash, 'Unleashing the Dogs of War: What the Constitution means by "declare war"' (2007–09) 93 *Cornell Law Review* 45.

[93] Constitution of the United States of America, Article 1, Section 5, emphasis added.

[94] National Security Act 1947, SEC 501 Ø 50 USC 413 (a)(1).

[95] L Britt Snider, *Sharing Secrets with Lawmakers: Congress as a User of Intelligence* (Washington, DC, Central Intelligence Agency: Centre for the Study of Intelligence, Library of Congress, 1997) 23.

actually able to interrogate, the full range of claims made by the Government in a policy area including those based upon classified material. The fallout of the Chilcot Inquiry means that if successive governments continue to make arguments for conflict based upon intelligence British parliamentarians effectively are in a similar position vis-à-vis intelligence to Member of Congress.

The Congressional Research Service points out that there are a number of types of intelligence which Congress is precluded from accessing. These restrictions apply to the identities of intelligence sources, and the methods of collection employed by the Intelligence Community in collecting and analysing intelligence. Furthermore, there is no direct access to 'human' intelligence sources, single-source intelligence or signals intelligence, and 'certain written intelligence products tailored to the specific needs of the President and other high-level Executive branch policymakers. Included is the President's Daily Brief (PDB), a written intelligence product which is briefed daily to the President'.[96] In short, Congress has routine access to what is known as 'finished intelligence'. This term refers to any report in which 'an analyst evaluates, interprets, integrates and places into context raw intelligence'.[97] The broad equivalent product from the British intelligence community would of course be a report of the JIC. As discussed in chapter four, this is also 'finished' intelligence as it reflects a consensus within the intelligence community and the considered judgment of experts. In view of this it is the most suitable product to be discussed by British parliamentarians in a closed intelligence session. One unnamed source interviewed for a CIA manual on the relationship between the Executive and Congress in the context of intelligence sharing explained that: 'None of our customers has a right to all of the intelligence that is produced, not even the Congress … they cannot see everything that is produced. The President has the right, if not the responsibility, to control it'.[98] Furthermore, a study carried out on behalf of the Central Intelligence Agency (CIA) found that: 'Most [members of staff interviewed] believed that Congressional needs were satisfied by access to finished intelligence intended for general circulation'.[99] One of the other reasons which drove Congressional requests for intelligence was 'when votes are scheduled on issues … on which intelligence has a significant bearing—such as, *a vote to send US troops into hostilities* … Members look to intelligence analysis' as a source of guidance in their own decision-making process.[100]

Intelligence is generally shared with Congress on a hierarchical basis, that is to say in the following specific order: first, the Leadership in both Houses of Congress, secondly, the Intelligence Committees of Congress, thirdly the National Security Committees, and finally, the rest of Congress.[101] However, in July 1969 the

---

[96] A Cumming, 'Congress as a Consumer of Intelligence Information' Congressional Research Service Washington DC, 7-5700, R40136, 2010, 5.

[97] ibid, 9.

[98] Britt Snider, *Sharing Secrets with Lawmakers* (n 95) 17.

[99] ibid, 26.

[100] ibid, 31, emphasis added.

[101] ibid, 27.

Senate debated funding the 'Safeguard Anti-Ballistic Missile System'. Its adoption was approved and for this occasion the Senate met in a full closed session and the CIA prepared a classified briefing paper on the matter for use by each and every Senator.[102] There may continue to be some hierarchical structure for general intelligence sharing in Westminster. This is effectively how sharing information on Privy Council terms works. However, the issue of deciding upon an armed conflict under the War Powers Convention is, much like the issue of ballistic missiles, simply too important an issue to risk partially informing the House of Commons.

Concerns about the unnecessary spread of closed sessions jeopardizing democracy seem to be unfounded. In the twentieth and twenty-first centuries, there has been a total of 57 closed sessions of the Senate, whereas the House of Representatives have held only four closed sessions.[103] There appears to be no widespread secrecy as a result of the process, and much like Westminster during wartime, there is a burden of justification before a closed session occurs. The procedure for meeting in camera is permitted in order for either Chamber to receive and discuss classified information, matters of national security, and confidential communications from the President. The authority to conduct these closed sessions (also known as Executive sessions) is vested in the respective rules of each Chamber.[104] The procedures for initiating a closed session differ slightly in both Chambers. In the House of Representatives a closed session is generally initiated pursuant to special rule or motion.[105] On one occasion the House resolved into closed session by way of unanimous consent.[106] Generally, the procedure is initiated by a Member declaring that he or she has classified information that he or she wishes to share with the House. Thereafter, a vote takes place, and a simple majority will be enough to initiate a closed session. However, a motion of this sort is not debatable. To return to open session the Speaker can dissolve the session.[107] In the Senate a closed session can be initiated by a motion from any Senator, and is required to be seconded by another Senator. If this occurs the Presiding Officer cannot exercise discretion about entering such a session.[108] The Senate may resolve from closed session into open session by way of a simple majority vote.[109] Neither the motion to enter the closed session, nor to revolve into open session are debatable. However, Members may register an objection to the motion, and that results in some discussion of the matters. Thereafter the Member can choose to sustain or withdraw his or her objection.

---

[102] ibid, 5.

[103] CM Davis, 'Secret Sessions of the House and Senate: Authority, Confidentiality, and Frequency' Congressional Research Service 2014, R42106, 7-5700, 3. For a full list see Tables 1 and 2 at 4–6.

[104] Rules of the United States' House of Representatives, Rule XVII, cl 9, Rules of the United States' Senate, Rules XXIX and XXXI.

[105] US Congress, House, 'Constitution, Jefferson's Manual, and Rules of the House of Representatives', H Doc 112–61, 112th Congress, 2nd Session (Washington, GPO, 2013) §969, 774 in Davis, n 103, 1.

[106] ibid.

[107] 'Secret Sessions' (n 103) 1; see also House of Representatives 13 March 2008, 110th Congress, 2nd Session Issue, Vol 154, No 43, H1690.

[108] Secret Sessions' (n 103) 2.

[109] ibid, 1.

A more formalised process of debate and division of the sort proposed in Part B (above) would lend more legitimacy to the process, as it represents a clearer indication of parliamentarian's choices on the Congressional Record. Moreover, the absence of a discretion vested in either the Speaker or the Chair of the respective Chambers may also contribute to a perceived bias, as closed sessions can be initiated by a politically partisan figure. Despite these concerns each Chamber retains the right to publish the contents of a secret session by way of a vote. If the vote to release the proceedings is affirmed, proceedings in closed session become part of the Congressional Record.[110] So, unlike wartime closed sessions in the United Kingdom, the equivalent of Hansard records continue to be kept when Congress sits in private.

In addition to the benefits of intelligence sharing with Members of Congress on a much broader scope than experienced in Westminster, the next positive insight to be drawn from the US experience is the ability of sessions to transition fluidly between open and closed debate. Space precludes an exhaustive treatment of this process, but the following example is taken from the one-hour closed debate in the House of Representatives on the Foreign Intelligence Surveillance Act on 13 March 2008. The House initiated a closed session by a process of unanimous consent. During the closed session the time for debate was allotted equally between the majority leader and the minority whip. It was requested not by the Democratic Party majority, but by the Chief Whip of the Republican Minority. According to Democrat Steny Hoyer: 'The minority whip ... thought the Members ought to have knowledge ... that ... could not be divulged in public debate ... [We] did not want to ... preclude that from being offered, because we want no indication that any information is being withheld.'[111] Discussion on the matter covers several pages of the Congressional Record.

Much like the examples from Westminster in wartime, there are also clear indications that members of Congress feel the burden of justifying any decision to depart from a public session. And rightly so. Before the unanimous consent motion was moved, there was a focused discussion in the House so as to ensure that a closed session would not result in 'doing the public's business in secret'.[112] Lloyd Doggett, in a masterclass on good parliamentarianism, pressed the Congressman proposing the motion to agree that: 'the only reason for convening the House tonight in secret is because there are classified matters that you feel would jeopardize the security of our country if we discussed them in public'.[113] A necessity requirement of this nature should undoubtedly form part of the litmus test for initiating any closed intelligence session. After securing an affirmative answer Doggett withdrew his objection to the closed session. It is this type of narrow focus that British wartime closed sessions often seemed to lack.

---

[110] ibid, 2.
[111] House of Representatives 13 March 2008, 110th Congress, 2nd Session Issue Vol 154, No 43, H1690, Hoyer.
[112] ibid, H1691, Doggett.
[113] ibid, Doggett.

The nature or level of the information to be shared in the debate was to be 'secret'.[114] Information of this nature is in the middle range of classified information in the United States (the higher level being 'top secret' and the lower level being 'confidential'). Disclosure of 'secret' information would be considered to cause 'serious damage' to national security. This was because the information was to be provided by Roy Blunt, who was then a member of the Permanent Select Committee on Intelligence. Although the Intelligence Committee had seen the information proposed to be discussed in closed session, Blunt made it clear that this 'does not preclude moving to secret session to share information with other members ... I think the information we will bring to the floor will not be confusing to the Members but enlightening to the Members'.[115] Over the course of the debate Hoyer consistently pressed Blunt to justify that he indeed had additional information, and that it was not sufficient for the Intelligence Committee alone to have sight of this information. It was agreed by both sides that calling for only the fifth closed session of the House in 182 years meant that 'a very high bar has been reached' in the decision to cross from public into temporary closed session.[116] In the end all objections were withdrawn, with one final note of caution being added that: 'We walk a very delicate balance this evening. Let us hope we walk it right'.[117]

Crucially, the debate on the Act did not end in closed session. A public debate did indeed take place the following day (14 March 2008) which included a division and vote.[118] This session was followed with further public debates relating to the Act on 14 and 31 March, and 20 June 2008. This reflects not only the desired fluidity between open and closed sessions, but also the desired ratio of open to closed deliberation: the bias is heavily weighted in favour of publicity. The historical record also indicates that secrecy has not metastasised through the legislature. There has been very low percentage of closed sessions in Congress. This undoubtedly comes as a result of their use being allowed only in respect of classified information. However, Snider's remark that written '"rules of the road" are needed to govern intelligence sharing with Congress' still ring true. Although he cautions that, given the ever-changing nature of intelligence and politics, 'these "rules of the road" should be put in the form of "understandings to be generally observed" rather than "absolutes from which there is never a deviation"'.[119]

III. The European Parliament

In terms of the size of the role played in relation to matters of defence, and the way in which classified information is accessed by elected officials, the contemporary

---

[114] ibid, H1695, Blunt.
[115] ibid, Blunt.
[116] ibid, H1696, Kucinic.
[117] ibid, H1696, Scott.
[118] ibid, H1707–H1719.
[119] Britt Snider, *Sharing Secrets* (n 95) 54.

practice of the European Parliament is the smallest of the three examples discussed in this chapter. There has long been talk of a general democratic deficit within the European Union.[120] This is especially true of matters relating to the Common Foreign and Security Policy, which is mostly conducted between diplomats on the intergovernmental level. Nonetheless, after a long struggle the European Parliament has managed to secure a mandate for itself to be consulted in respect of the activities of the Council and the Commission in this area. Compared with other areas of EU policy in which the European Parliament has attained the status of a co-equal legislature with the Council and the Commission, its role remains one of consultation as opposed to substantive decision.[121] This is because foreign policy and security matters are traditionally seen to be governmental prerogatives. However, that perception is changing gradually. Although the European Parliament can only ask questions and make representations in this area, there has still been recognition of strong normative reasons for some Members of the European Parliament (MEPs) to have access to classified information. As a result, the relationship between the Executive branches and the European Parliament has changed considerably since the turn of the twenty-first century.

In light of these changes it has also been recognised that the mandate to oversee the EU Executive's work is 'of limited use unless it is accompanied by access to the necessary information'.[122] According to Rosen, the European Parliament presented a 'coherent set of justifications for their demands' to access secret intelligence.[123] In order to secure more access to information, MEPs advanced arguments to the effect that access to classified information was necessary in order to facilitate democratic oversight and control. Parliamentarians also relied upon Article 21 TEU as implicitly creating a right of access to classified information. All in all, the European Parliament was able to 'activate the norm of parliamentary scrutiny' to enhance its role in this area.[124]

Unlike the US Congress or the House of Commons, the European Parliament has no general power to hold closed sessions, ie debates of the whole Parliament on matters of classified information. However, MEPs have access to classified documents in respect of certain areas and certain circumstances. The rules governing these arrangements are the product of both legal regulation and Inter-Institutional Agreements.[125] Article 21 of the Treaty on the European Union

---

[120] See inter alia J Weiler, *The Constitution of Europe: Do the new clothes have an emperor?* (Cambridge, CUP, 1999).

[121] P Craig and G De Burca, *EU Law: Text, Cases, and Materials*, 6th ed (Oxford, OUP, 2015) 54.

[122] European Parliament Directorate General for Internal Policies, 'Parliamentary oversight of security and intelligence agencies in the European Union' (Policy Department C: Citizen's Rights and Constitutional Affairs, 2011) 68, para 3.31.

[123] G Rosen, 'Can you keep a secret: How the European Parliament got access to sensitive documents in the area of security and defence' (RECON Online Working Paper 2011/2012) 9, <www.reconproject.eu> accessed 28 February 2017.

[124] ibid, 10.

[125] The European Parliament can access classified information in respect of other areas, but the Common Foreign and Security Policy provides the most direct parallel with the subject matter of this book. See also: 'Framework Agreement on relations between the European Parliament and the European Commission', Annex II, 1: Forwarding of confidential information to Parliament'

imposes an obligation upon the European Union's Executive bodies, namely the Council and the Commission, to consult the Parliament on the central aspects of and basic choices of the Common Foreign and Security Policy, and to take the views of the Parliament on board.

The first set of arrangements allowing the European Parliament access to classified information were concluded in 2002, as a result of a two-year bargaining process between parliamentarians and the Council.[126] There are four levels of classified information in the European Union, ranging from lowest to highest secrecy: restricted, confidential, secret, and top secret. After the completion of the 2002 Inter-Institutional Agreement, MEPs who were members of selected committees would be given access to classified information up to the level of 'classified' (but crucially not 'secret' or 'top secret'). This occurred either at the request of the President of the European Parliament, or in the event of a military or non-military crisis falling within the remit of the Common Foreign and Security Policy.[127] In addition to the President of the Parliament, access was limited to those MEPs chairing the Committee on Foreign Affairs, Human Rights, and the Common Security and Defence Policy Committee. Information must be consulted on the premises of the EU Executive authorities in a secure location. All in all, this amounts to access for around five of the 751 MEPs. The relevant committees may then discuss this information in closed session in secure premises, provided that no minutes are kept.

The 2002 Inter-Institutional Agreement also emphasises that any access to information may be circumscribed by the principle of Originator Control.[128] This principle states that permission must be sought from the generator or originator of classified information before it is shared with a third party. Born and Leigh describe the 'third party rule' or the 'originator control' rule as: 'the most jealously protected national security privilege of all'.[129] This is obviously a central concern where intelligence is being potentially shared with the national authorities of 28 EU Member States. In common with Westminster and the US Congress, access to classified information for these parliamentarians, although guided by rules in the Inter-institutional Agreements, has developed in an ad hoc manner as the general rules are subject to interpretation and are determined largely by the 'amount of trust and mutual confidence between the two institutions and the persons involved, and upon the EP's skill in dealing with this kind of sources'.[130]

OJ L 304/56 (20 November 2010); General Secretariat of the Council of Europe, 'Access by the European Parliament to classified information in the area of the Common Foreign and Security Policy' (23 October 2012) 15343/12; and European Parliament, 'Security Briefing', <www.guengl.eu/uploads/publications-documents/ERNST2.doc> accessed 3 February 2017.

[126] European Parliament and Council 'Interinstitutional Agreement of 20 November 2002 between the European Parliament and the Council concerning access by the European Parliament to sensitive information of the Council in the field of security and defence policy' OJ C 298/1 (30 November 2002).

[127] ibid, Arts 2.2 and 3.2.

[128] ibid, Art 1.2.

[129] H Born and I Leigh, *International Intelligence Cooperation and Accountability (Studies in Intelligence)*, (London, Routledge, 2012) 5.

[130] U Diedrichs, 'The European Parliament in CFSP: More than a marginal player?' (2004) 39 *The International Spectator* 31, 43.

Although there is a relatively low level of access to classified information for the European Parliament (which includes a clear information asymmetry) a broader set of lessons can be drawn from this. Even in the context of a purely consultative role the need for access to classified information is recognised. However, at present the War Powers Convention requires more of the House of Commons: it requires debate, and arguably, it includes the right to vote on a motion of support if precedents are taken into account. This is a more demanding and engaged role for parliamentarians; more akin to the parity of status between the US Congress and the US Executive. In light of this greater role for the Commons, there is a greater need for more access to relevant classified information such as JIC reports. The opportunity must not be limited to merely consulting these documents in a secure venue: it must extend to debate and discussion on the floor of the House. This can only be done in camera. Given that the vote of every MP counts equally, there cannot be a hierarchy of access. Each MP must be given equal access to secret intelligence in the context of the war prerogative.

D. Controlling Abuse of Closed Intelligence Sessions

Conducting democratic practices in secret amplifies the risk of abuse of power. There is evidence of potential abuse or erroneous use of the informal arrangements for conducting closed sessions and briefings in all of the examples considered in this chapter. Closed sessions have the potential to be abused, or to be called too often. Specific reasons for resort to closed sessions in Parliament during wartime were overly broad. In addition to this, some members of the United States Congress have, on occasion, struggled with the application of independent judgement to classified information. Finally, the European Union has struggled with coherent practices, and a lack of formal arrangements. By directly acknowledging the shortcomings in the examples, and by recognising the moral limits of secrecy in a representative legislature, the proposal for closed intelligence sessions in the House of Commons can be more strictly tailored to mitigate the risks of abuse.

I. The Westminster Parliament During Wartime

The closed sessions conducted during Wartime occurred in a broad range of contexts, and were not without controversy. Writing immediately after the Second World War, Jennings was of the view that by conducting representative government in closed session, the House of Commons had fallen victim to the erroneous notion that representative democracy could be conducted in secret.[131] He referred to the phenomenon of holding closed sessions as a 'strange unconstitutional

---

[131] WI Jennings, 'Parliament in Wartime: III' (1940) *The Political Quarterly* 351, 363.

idea'.[132] Closed sessions during wartime are conspicuous by their absence from the pages of most relevant texts, including recent reports on reform of the war prerogative.[133] The reticence of government and Parliament to return to similar practices (even in the wake of the Iraq War fiasco) may be driven by concerns about re-adopting an exceptional practice which stemmed from an exceptional situation. It has been pointed out that 'the standard volumes are careful to omit all reference to war-time devices except in an incidental and apologetic manner' and 'it seems axiomatic … that war-time parliamentary practices are so exceptional that they are not to be cited as precedents and are so irregular that they may be noted only as warnings of what is not good parliamentarianism'.[134] It is, perhaps, fair to say that they represent an imperfect solution to an intractable problem. This chapter does not take a Panglossian view of Parliament's wartime experiment. Closed sessions were called too often, for overbroad reasons, and lacked the ability to transition between public and closed sessions. Despite the Opposition's ability to request closed sessions, decision-making about closed sessions often fell to the Cabinet alone, although free votes were permitted on occasion.

Closed sessions were not universally well received by parliamentarians. Before a 1942 closed session regarding shipping capabilities and losses, MPs expressed discomfort about the Government's wish to inform Parliament behind closed doors. The argument in favour of a closed session was based upon the grounds that it was necessary for both the safety of British civilians on the mainland and naval personnel.[135] However, not all of the parliamentarians present were convinced of the need for this measure. As Aneurin Bevan commented: 'On more than one occasion Secret Sessions have been abused by the Government, and the things which have been told to the House at such Sessions could quite easily have been told in public'.[136] Bevan also commented that the American Government were 'much franker' on the same subject with both Congress and the press and public, and that shipping losses had been publicly reported.[137]

Another issue may have arisen with the level of disclosure to parliamentarians in closed session. The JIC slowly increased in prominence, and by 1943 had become 'an integral part of the war effort'.[138] However, it was not until September 2002 that any attempt was made to engage with the contents of these centralised intelligence assessments on the floor of either House. The minutes of Cabinet meetings suggest that full disclosure of intelligence materials or sources

---

[132] ibid.

[133] Ministry of Justice, 'The Governance of Britain—Analysis of Consultations (Part 3 of 3)' Cm 7342-III, 2008 [324]: 'One respondent suggested Parliament could if necessary go into secret session as it had done in the Second World War'.

[134] McD Clockie, 'Parliamentary Government in Wartime' (n 49) 359.

[135] HC Deb 9 July 1942, vol 381, col 951.

[136] ibid, col 954.

[137] ibid, col 954.

[138] RJ Aldrich, R Cormac and MS Goodman, *Spying on the World: The Declassified Documents of the Joint Intelligence Committee 1936–2013* (Edinburgh, Edinburgh University Press, 2014) 61.

was not made to the House in closed session. The minutes of a Cabinet meeting on 28 November 1939 state that:

> the object of a Secret Session was *not* to enable the Government to furnish very secret information. Indeed, the Minister … would have to *exercise great circumspection* … a Secret Session … would give Members an opportunity of bringing to the notice of the Government, without publicity, matters in regard to which they had grounds for believing that the position was not satisfactory.[139]

There appeared to be no minimum standard, nor litmus test for the threshold of disclosure, save the discretion of the individual Minister. Further concerns about the level of actual disclosure to parliamentarians was raised in the pamphlet written by Roy Townsend Leonard Day, a member of the British Union of Fascists. Day was the only individual convicted for publishing material purporting to relate to the content of a closed session.[140] He had allegedly received information on the content of a closed session from a parliamentarian (Captain Archibald Maule Ramsey, who was subject to internment under the Defence (General) Regulations 1939, 18B). The pamphlet, upon which the conviction was based, purported to describe the content of the closed session in the following terms:

> The Secret Session: Exclusive Information

> We have been fortunate in obtaining certain details regarding the Secret Session in Parliament Last Week. The debate was principally concerned with our diplomatic reserves in Rumania and Japan, and Ministers were anxious to learn what steps had been taken to protect British interests … The House adjourned in a state of great dissatisfaction and perturbation.[141]

In view of the source of the information its veracity is of course difficult to ascertain. However, it stands out as one of the key records of dissatisfaction with the content of closed sessions, despite the initial Opposition demands for the return to the practice.

The potential abuse of closed sessions may have been exacerbated by the nebulous criteria of 'public interest' used as a litmus test for their initiation. Even though the historical record shows reference to 'tighter' tests such as necessity being used alongside the public interest, this is insufficient to define the limits of a concept which has been described as a 'myth' which is not identified with 'concrete policies as such, but rather a particular kind of [democratic] process'.[142] The proposal advanced herein avoids engagement with this myth, and the cancerous spread of secrecy that its misinterpretation or subversion might facilitate. Centring the proposal on a specific document (the report of the JIC relevant to the conflict

---

[139] 'War Cabinet and Cabinet: Minutes 28 November 1939 (WM and CM Series). Cabinet Conclusions. (39) 67–(39) 123', the National Archives Ref: CAB 65/2/31, emphasis added.

[140] This was an offence under Regulation 3(2) of the Defence (General) Regulations 1939.

[141] R Townsend Leonard Day, 'Uncensored British News Bulletin' 7 August 1940 (available in British National Archives). See also HC Deb 17 September 1940, vol 365, col 121.

[142] HR Smith, *Democracy and the Public Interest* (Athens, GA, University of Georgia Press, 1960) 158–59.

at hand) would focus the aim of a closed briefing and reduce the concern that secrecy could be invoked for reasons of government self-interest. Concerns about secrecy would further be reduced by the framing of closed intelligence sessions with public debate on either side, or by permitting transition between open and closed sessions at the discretion of the Speaker.

II. United States' Congress

Sharing classified intelligence with Congress has not been without problems. Some members of Congress have demonstrated an unwillingness to form their own independent judgment on intelligence issues. For example, in December 1990 the Senate voted against sending troops to Iraq on the basis of intelligence sessions which suggested that the 'Iraqi military was the most advanced in that part of the world'.[143] This assumption was unseated when the coalition forces achieved almost immediate air superiority: '"In the end," said a former committee staffer, "it was apparent that the Intelligence Community didn't know squatola [sic] about the Iraqi military"'.[144] However, another analyst suggested that certain information may have been withheld from Congress for reasons of military operational safety.[145] Another concern in the late 1990s was the increasing requests by Congress Members for 'sanitized' intelligence sessions, ie those which could be discussed openly on the Floor of the Senate or House of Representatives.[146] It will be recalled that intelligence of a 'sanitized' (or more accurately intelligence without context) best describes the nature of what was presented to Parliament in September 2002 in the debate on the public 'September Dossier' in the approach to the Iraq conflict. Snider's answer to this dilemma is twofold. First, he views it as essential that intelligence sessions take place in closed session because they 'inherently involve the presentation of information derived from classified information'.[147] Another reason for sessions taking place in closed session is the need to provide information in its proper context. This is made even more pressing by the fact that political representatives are not 'experts in national security affairs, and fewer still have the time and energy outside their normal duties to become experts'.[148] Expertise of a special type, therefore, would not be required for viewing JIC reports. They do not require specialist knowledge, provided they are properly contextualised as opposed to publicly abstracted. Modern intelligence reports instead consist of a 'painstaking collection and analysis of fact, the exercise of judgment and clear and quick presentation'.[149]

---

[143] Britt Snider, *Sharing Secrets with Lawmakers* (n 95) 49.
[144] ibid, 49.
[145] ibid, 49.
[146] ibid, 61.
[147] ibid, 56.
[148] ibid, 59.
[149] *The Economist* (1 October 1966), 20 quoted in MS Goodman and D Omand, 'What Analysts Need to Understand: The King's Intelligence Studies Program' (2008) 52 *Studies in Intelligence* 1, 10.

III. The European Parliament

The major problem with the current EU system in terms of control of abuse, is of course, the lack of opportunity for plenary debates about classified information. The system overall is, at best, restricted to viewing documents in secure rooms within the European Parliament. There is also an explicit hierarchy (based on the classification of documents) which governs which categories of persons can access information. There are four categories of classified information within the European Union, ranging from lowest to highest security. The first is 'Restricted', disclosure of which would be 'disadvantageous' to the EU or one or more Member States. The next level is 'Confidential', disclosure of which would harm the 'essential interests' of the Union or one or more Member States. The third is 'Secret', and disclosure of information of this nature would 'seriously harm the essential interests of the Union or one or more Member States. The final category is 'Top Secret' which, if disclosed, would cause 'exceptionally grave prejudice to the essential interests' of the Union or of one or more Member States.

Evidence drawn from interviews also suggests that despite the presence of written rules in the Inter-Institutional Agreements, the processes for sharing classified information can be highly informal. Curtin's study revealed that one interviewee likened an oral briefing on classified information to being a character in a 'bad Le Carré novel'.[150] Part of the problem, as Curtin points out, is that 'at the European level a public debate is missing on when secrets must be kept' and 'as things stand at present it is a matter of total Executive prerogative and internal rule-making that is applied subsequently also to restrict national Parliaments'.[151] In addition to being informal and restricted to such a small percentage of MEPs, meetings regarding classified information are also infrequent. They take place approximately four times per year. Security cleared staff members assisting MEPs are also sometimes excluded from these meetings, which can amount to a mere oral briefing 'as one interviewee put it, 'a coffee with Solana [the High Representative for the Common Foreign and Security Policy]'.[152]

The nature of the European Union itself goes some way to explaining this. It involves cooperation between 28 governments each with extremely different attitudes to the security clearance of elected officials. Given this, establishing and agreeing an EU equivalent to the Official Secrets Acts, regulating penalties for unlawful disclosure, may well be an insurmountable hurdle. As information can

---

[150] A Rettman, 'Secret Documents Group was Like "Bad Le Carre Novel", MEP Says' (2012) EUobserver.com at <http://euobserver.com/institutional/31296> accessed 17 September 2017, quoted in D Curtin, 'Challenging Executive Dominance in European Democracy' (2014) 7 *Modern Law Review* 1, 28.

[151] D Curtin, 'Challenging Executive Dominance in European Democracy' (2014) 77 *Modern Law Review* 1, 31.

[152] European Parliament Directorate General for Internal Policies, 'Parliamentary oversight of security and intelligence agencies in the European Union' (Policy Department C: Citizen's Rights and Constitutional Affairs, 2011) 71.

potentially be leaked without a legal penalty, the Executive arms of the European Union will invariably be reluctant to share the more sensitive categories of information, and will also be restrictive and informal in their approach to politicians' access under the existing Inter-Institutional Agreements. The nature of the British Official Secrets Acts, which are broadly drawn and well established (as are the rules of parliamentary privilege), means that information is likely to be more secure.

IV. The Moral Limits of Secrecy in a Legislature

The notion of a representative democracy carrying out any of its functions in secret may still remain highly counterintuitive, or even draconian to some readers. The fatal role of secrecy in the history of democratic constitutionalism undoubtedly plays a part in fostering these views. After all, secrecy contributed to the collapse of a legislature (and in turn, democracy as a whole) in the Weimar Republic. What followed was the rise of the most brutal dictatorial regime in modern European history. However, the parallel between the collapse of Weimar and the proposal in this chapter is inapt. It bears mentioning only to illustrate the distance between them. In his study, *Constitutional Dictatorship*, Rossiter highlighted that at the height of the Weimar Republic's economic strife, the Reichstag (the German Parliament), fearing the threat of dissolution on the one hand, or resort to the emergency provisions in Article 48 of the Weimar Constitution on the other, felt compelled to act exceptionally in the name of self-preservation. To ensure its longevity in extreme circumstances it legislated on 8 December 1923 to the effect that 'all ordinances are to be discussed in secret session with committees chosen by the Reichstag and Reichsrat'.[153] During the 10 weeks which followed, 75 secret legislative decrees were issued.[154]

Several factors separate this example from the analysis of closed sessions of the Westminster Parliament proposed here. It should come as no surprise that legislation conceived of in secret is the antithesis of what is proposed here. First of all, the temporal extent of secrecy in Weimar was clearly greater than what occurred in the three legislatures examined in this chapter. In the Reichstag, legislating in secret lasted for a period of 10 weeks, and there were no public sessions of any kind. By contrast, closed intelligence sessions would last a matter of hours, and be sandwiched between open sessions during a full day of debate on the exercise of war powers. Secrecy which is not bounded by publicity will ultimately foster public mistrust and lack any form of accountability. Moreover, the situation in Weimar saw the Reichstag having secrecy forced upon it to ensure its own survival. Refusal would have been a suicide pact under the terms of the Weimar Constitution, which

---

[153] C Rossiter, *Constitutional Dictatorship: Crisis Government in Modern Democracies*, 5th edn (London, Transaction Publishers) 47–49.
[154] ibid, 47–49.

contained sweeping provisions for national emergencies, including dissolution of the legislature.[155] Moreover, if secret sittings were not agreed to, the Reichstag would almost certainly have been abolished under the emergency powers in the Constitution. This was not the case for Westminster in wartime, nor would it be the case for the contemporary Westminster Parliament. No vote should occur, nor substantive parliamentary decision be taken, behind closed doors. The proposal in this chapter falls vastly short of voting in secret, let alone legislating.

E. Security Considerations

Obviously, allowing all Members of the Commons equal access to JIC reports in closed sessions begs questions about security considerations and the possibility of damaging information leaks. For example, during a recent House of Lords debate on the need for a War Powers Act it was remarked that 'military intelligence … cannot be divulged to 650 Members of the House of Commons' without risking national security and the safety of troops.[156] Aside from the issues of principle at stake, some readers may still doubt that Members of the House could be trusted with classified information without prejudicing national security. However, in each of the legislatures considered in this chapter, security measures have successfully been put in place to mitigate risks of this nature. There are two broad categories of measures which are relevant: legislation concerning national security and rules of the legislature on the one hand; and specific arrangements about the physical security of debates and briefings themselves. Leaks are possible, and do occur. However, rules and secure rooms aside, the picture that emerges highlights the presence of developing relationships built on mutual trust between the Executive and the legislature.

In the British context, the doctrine of parliamentary privilege means that none of the Official Secrets Acts are applicable to disclosures of classified information made in the course of parliamentary proceedings.[157] Instead, disclosure by a parliamentarian is considered a breach of privilege. There were two such investigations for breach of privilege[158] in the course of the wartime closed sessions, and no breach was found in either case. One instance concerned an alleged disclosure of information relating to closed session proceedings at a dinner party, and the other to a disclosure in the course of a speech at a political rally in Cathcart, Glasgow. In the words of Parry, 'this, it may be hazarded, was

---

[155] ibid, 47–49.

[156] HL Deb 8 July 2016, vol 773, col 2266, Baroness Smith of Newnham (L Dem).

[157] 'Report together with the proceedings of the committee, minutes of evidence, and index' (n 44), para 10.

[158] House of Commons Committee of Privileges, 'Report from the Committee of Privileges on the matter of the complaint made to the house on 5th May, 1942' 1945–46, HC 47 and House of Commons Committee of Privileges, 'Report from the Committee of Privileges on the matter of the complaint made on 7 May 1942' 1941–42, HC 93.

[the result of] too liberal a construction' of the doctrine of parliamentary privilege.[159] However, in the wake of the *Chaytor* decision (regarding alleged fraudulent expenses claims by MPs), the Supreme Court clarified that the protections of privilege did not extend to criminal conduct which was not 'part of, nor is it incidental to, the core or essential business of Parliament, which consists of collective deliberation and decision making'.[160]

Parliamentary privilege has also been recently narrowed by the clarification of the Wilson Doctrine, following a ruling of the Investigatory Powers Tribunal (IPT).[161] The Wilson Doctrine, named after the former Labour Prime Minister Harold Wilson, was understood as a rule precluding the surveillance of Members of Parliament. However, the 2015 ruling of the IPT clarified that the Wilson Doctrine was never an absolute prohibition on surveillance of parliamentarians. The tribunal noted that whilst there was 'a need for caution and circumspection in respect of parliamentarians' communications … the Wilson Doctrine has no legal effect'.[162] In short, if a parliamentarian was suspected of attempting to leak or otherwise mishandling classified information outside of Parliament, he or she could be legally subjected to surveillance by the intelligence community in preparation for the pursuit of a criminal prosecution.[163] The scope of parliamentary privilege has clearly been narrowed since wartime, and its position with respect to the criminal law clarified by the highest judicial authority. In view of this, an unauthorised deliberate leak or disclosure made outside of the floor of the House may well result in a Member incurring criminal liability under section 1 of the Official Secrets Act 1989, upon the consent of the Attorney-General to prosecution. The twin safeguards of parliamentary privilege and the possibility of criminal sanctions should act as a sufficient deterrent to the leaking of classified information by parliamentarians.

In addition to criminal liability and sanctions for breach of privilege for deliberate disclosure, the British Government and the mainstream national media have a highly developed voluntary code aimed at preventing inadvertent disclosure of national security information. This originated in 1912 and is known as the D-Notice system. A D-Notice is a voluntary agreement between the Government and the media to 'to prevent inadvertent disclosure of information that would compromise UK military and intelligence operations and methods, or put at risk the safety of those involved in such operations, or lead to attacks that would damage the critical national infrastructure and/or endanger lives and is advisory in nature'.[164] D-Notice agreements are overseen by a Committee chaired by the

---

[159] Parry, 'Legislatures and Secrecy' (n 55) 748.
[160] *R v Chaytor* [2010] UKSC 52, [2011] AC 684, Lord Philips [62].
[161] *Caroline Lucas MP and Others v Security Service and Others* [2015] UKIP Trib 14_79-CH.
[162] ibid, [32]–[33].
[163] Regulation of Investigatory Powers Act 2000, s 5(3).
[164] HM Government, 'The Defence Advisory Notice System and the Defence Press and Broadcasting Advisory Committee: Report of the Review' (London, Stationary Office, 2015) para [4], <www.dnotice.org.uk/linkedfiles/dnotice/records/20150312-dpbacreviewreport-final-o.doc> accessed 5 May 2017. For the official history of the D-Notice system see N Wilkinson, *Secrecy and the Media: The Official History of the United Kingdom's D-Notice System: The Official History of the D-notice System* (London, Routledge, 2009).

Permanent Secretary of the Ministry of Defence. The Vice Chair of the Committee is a representative selected from the media outlets who have signed up to the D-Notice system. The Cabinet Office, which ultimately publishes JIC reports, is one of the branches of Government which participates in the D-Notice system. Ignoring a D-Notice has no inherent legal consequences, but the existence of such a notice can form the basis for obtaining a court injunction against the publication of material subject to such a notice.[165] A recent report on the operation of the system concluded that despite the proliferation of online media outlets, and the imperfect operation of the system in the past,[166] there was general support for the continuation of the system from respondents from within the media to the Government consultation.[167] It is important to note that the Review of the D-Notice system found 'national context and culture' were the key determinants of the D-Notice system's success.[168] Whilst there can never be a cast-iron guarantee against inadvertent leaks of information, the existence of such an informal voluntary arrangement between the mainstream media and Government for over 100 years is an encouraging sign. Under the current system the Cabinet Office could obtain an agreement from large parts of the British media with a view to preventing inadvertent disclosures of the content of JIC reports.

In respect of physical security of information within Parliament during a closed intelligence session, the Westminster Parliamentary Archives contains 'Secret Session Drill' papers,[169] revised in the approach to the Falklands War, which contain an extensive procedure designed by, inter alia, the Sergeant-at-Arms for securing Parliament in the event of a closed session. There are extensive procedures for the clearing of relevant spaces, locking doors, and increasing the presence of police outside key locations in the Palace of Westminster. The content of the Secret Session Drill rules (which may have been superseded by an updated version which is not currently archived) appear to have been the product of consideration by various Select Committees including the Joint Committee on Security (which makes recommendations to the Speaker of the Commons and the Lord Speaker on the security of the Parliamentary Estate), and the Select Committee on Broadcasting (now the Administration Committee) which administers services available in the Commons relating to the broadcasting of parliamentary proceedings, among other things. Of course, any updated version would need to take some account of technological developments, such as recommending the removal of mobile phones and tablet computers which have been permitted on the Floor of the House since 25 October 2007 to allow Members to 'to keep up to date with emails … provided that it causes no disturbance'.[170] However, concerns about

---

[165] ibid, para [7].

[166] The D-Notice System came to light as a result of revelations regarding surveillance during the Harold Wilson Government; see M Creevy, 'A Critical Review of the Wilson Government's Handling of the D-Notice Affair 1967' (1999) 14 *Intelligence and National Security* 209.

[167] 'The Defence Advisory Notice System' (n 164), para [16].

[168] ibid, para [19].

[169] Westminster Parliamentary Archives, 'Secret Session Drill' (1978–82) Ref: PWO/1/240.

[170] Resolution, based on report from the Select Committee on the Modernisation of the House of Commons, 'Revitalising the Chamber: the role of the back bencher' 1st Report, 2006–07, HC 337.

electronic surveillance of closed sessions had not escaped the relevant parties even in 1982. The archive contains a letter to *The Times* which, on anticipation of secret sessions in relation to the prosecution of the Falklands War (which never occurred), warns that Parliament 'must now take into account all the electronic equipment installed for the broadcasting of Parliament'.[171]

In the United States context, throughout the organic development of the relationship between the Executive and Congress, a number of methods have been developed for keeping information secure. There are, of course, occasional leaks of classified information, sometimes made for political gains. If made on the Floor of either House, these are constitutionally protected from prosecution by the Speech or Debate clause in the Constitution.[172] If Members of Congress make disclosures or leaks outside of the legislature, there is the theoretical possibility of prosecution upon the consent of the Attorney-General under the Espionage Act.[173] There is a history of Members of Congress leaking information on the floor of the House.[174] However, the most high-profile indiscriminate leaks of documents in recent US history, namely those by WikiLeaks and Edward Snowden, have been facilitated by sources in the Executive branch. These leaks were not made by elected representatives. This has caused Chafetz to argue that 'it is at least possible that, if members of Congress were more willing to evaluate and consider releasing classified information, future Mannings and Snowdens might be willing to leak to them rather than engaging in indiscriminate public releases'.[175] After all, the secrets of our governments are in some sense the secrets of the citizenry, so engagement by democratic representatives is necessary and should be welcomed.[176]

Furthermore, one Congressional staffer was of the view that having parity of access with the Executive to classified information actually discouraged Members of Congress from leaking information. This was because the willingness of the intelligence community to work with politicians to establish a publicly viable picture of intelligence meant that the perceived need to resort to leaks to inform constituents was significantly reduced.[177] Although the intelligence community will continue to provide intelligence sessions to Members of Congress whom they perceived to have 'handled intelligence irresponsibly' they will take 'more care than usual with what they say'.[178] Undoubtedly, misuse or unauthorised disclosure of

---

[171] Letter from Philip Nind to the editor of *The Times* (6 May 1982) in 'Secret Session Drill' (n 169).

[172] US CONST Art I, § 6, cl i ('[F]or any Speech or Debate in either House, [Senators and Representatives] shall not be questioned in any other Place').

[173] Espionage Act 1917, ch 106, §10(i), 40 Stat 422. For a general overview of US prohibitions on the publication of classified information see: JK Elsea, 'Criminal Prohibitions on the Publication of Classified Defense Information' (Washington DC, Congressional Research Service, 2013) and JK Elsea, 'The Protection of Classified Information: The Legal Framework (Washington DC, Congressional Research Service, 2013).

[174] Chafetz, 'Whose Secrets?' (n 2), 88–90.

[175] ibid, 91.

[176] ibid, 87.

[177] Britt Snider, *Sharing Secrets with Lawmakers* (n 95) 30.

[178] ibid, 39–40.

intelligence into the public domain by politicians would produce a 'chilling effect' on intelligence sharing: members of the legislature recognise that it may actually be counterproductive for accountability in the long run.

Where leaks and security breaches do occur, the Senate Ethics Committee is entrusted with adjudicating on whether an individual Member of Congress has breached the rules in either Chamber for handling classified information. Disclosing information heard in a closed session is punishable by each Chamber's respective disciplinary rules. According to Davis, a Member found in violation may be subject to a range of punishments 'including loss of seniority, fine, reprimand, censure, or expulsion'.[179] The House of Representatives has a committee which performs a similar function known as the Committee on Standards of Official Conduct.[180]

In practical terms, there are a variety of means for keeping intelligence information secure within the physical confines of Congress. In respect of the two main intelligence committees (the Permanent Select Committee on Intelligence and the US Senate Select Committee on Intelligence) specific rooms are located in 'vaulted' areas. These rooms are designed to meet standards set by the Director of National Intelligence (DNI) for the secure storage and discussion of 'information relating to intelligence sources and methods'.[181] The DNI is the official responsible for advising the President on matters relating to intelligence and national security.[182] In addition to this the DNI acts as Chairman of the National Security Council, which is the principal forum by which the President and his senior cabinet members consider national security and foreign policy matters. Both the Senate and the House of Representatives have additional procedures for protecting classified information. For example, both Chambers have security offices responsible for setting and implementing standards and safeguards for the protection of classified information.[183] Members of Congress are also required to swear a 'secrecy oath'.[184]

There is currently no requirement that Members of Congress be subject to security vetting themselves. The introduction of such a measure would mark a significant and unprecedented departure from current practice. Members of Congress (as with the President and Vice President, Justices of the Supreme Court, or other federal court judges) have never been required to hold security clearances.[185] Proponents of the proposal suggest that vetting would help ensure the 'trustworthiness' of Congressmen and provide a greater safeguard for classified information.[186] The perceived drawbacks of introducing a system of security

---

[179] Davis, 'Secret Sessions of the House and Senate' (n 103) 2.

[180] FM Kaiser, 'Protection of Classified Information by Congress: Practices and Proposals' (Washington DC, Congressional Research Service, 2006) 7.

[181] Britt Snider, *Sharing Secrets with Lawmakers* (n 95) 23–24.

[182] Office of the Director of National Intelligence, <www.dni.gov/index.php/about/mission> accessed 17 September 2017.

[183] Kaiser, 'Protection of Classified Information' (n 180) 1.

[184] ibid, 2.

[185] ibid, 8.

[186] ibid, 9.

clearance for Congressmen include the risk of compromising the independence of the legislature from the Executive. Other risks include a perceived bias or partisanship in the determination of security clearances, and the possibility of creating two classes of Congressmen (ie those who are vetted and those who are not).[187] This is precisely the issue with Privy Council sessions at present in the United Kingdom. Such a measure would only exacerbate the information asymmetry which the United States arrangements have worked so hard to overcome. However, staff working on behalf of Members of Congress are required to be security vetted if they wish to access classified information.[188] It is not proposed that closed intelligence sessions be extended to persons other than Members of the House of Commons. Physical security measures include stationing police officers at committee sites or outside either Chamber as appropriate, conducting sweeps of offices and other facilities to prevent surveillance, specific procedures for the transfer of information between individuals, and the requirement that foreign travel or contact with individuals overseas is reported to relevant officials.[189]

Finally, the European Union has no equivalent of the Official Secrets Act or the Espionage Act, and Member States have varying legal regimes relating to the security vetting of their elected representatives. A combination of the Inter-Institutional Agreements and ad hoc practices govern how MEPs see classified information. Nonetheless, the developing relationship between the European Parliament and the Council and Commission in respect of classified information has also led to innovations in the way in which information is transmitted and handled for security purposes. Before having sight of classified information, MEPs must undergo a security briefing.[190] They are advised on how to protect against espionage and leaks, and will only be given access if they are security vetted and have 'signed a solemn declaration on non-disclosure of the information'.[191] Parliamentarians can only view the classified information in secure premises. The building has been modified to include an extensive array of security measures including surveillance 'IT security measures, including training and awareness programmes, the establishment of classified and unclassified networks, secure telecom structures, secure internal voice, fax and e-mail networks'.[192] Classified documents must remain in approved storage containers at all times when not in use. MEPs may consult, but not distribute these documents in a secure room managed by the Classified Information Unit.[193]

---

[187] ibid, 9.
[188] ibid, 8–9.
[189] ibid, 2.
[190] Written Security Briefing for Members of European Parliament: <www.guengl.eu/uploads/publications-documents/ERNST2.doc> accessed 17 September 2017.
[191] ibid, 4.
[192] S Duke, 'Intelligence, security and information flows in CFSP' (2006) 21 *Intelligence and National Security* 604, 611.
[193] See further: COUNCIL DECISION of 23 September 2013 on the security rules for protecting EU classified information (2013/488/EU).

F. Inclusive Secrecy, Transparency, Participation and Accountability

In summary, this chapter proposes that where the Government makes a case for war based upon secret intelligence, the House of Commons should be entitled to see and debate the relevant report of the JIC in a closed session. Such closed sessions could be held only for this purpose, and would require the consent of the Speaker of the House (who must apply a threshold test of necessity before departing from a public sitting). Entering into such a session would also be the subject of a debate and free vote by all Members of the Commons. The leaders of opposition parties would also be permitted to request a closed session if they thought fit, but this would also remain subject to the necessity test and a debate and vote. A closed session would occur in the middle of an otherwise public debate on armed conflict, to ensure that secrecy is circumscribed on both sides by public discourse. No voting on matters of substance could occur during these sessions. It is important to note that where the Government did not base its case for armed conflict on classified information, no closed session would be required, and debates on armed conflict could be entirely public.

The core purpose of this book is to allow the reader to squarely confront the dilemmas posed by Parliament's increased participation in armed conflict decisions. Although both authors feel an instinctive moral inclination towards transparency, especially in the context of representative democracy, where it might be thought of as a *sine qua non*, this chapter has sought to caution the extent to which the maxim 'sunlight is ... the best of disinfectants'[194] is treated with almost religious fervour. The proposal for closed intelligence sessions advanced herein surrounds secrecy with publicity in order to enhance the values of participation, and accountability which both authors argue lie at the core of democratic control of war powers. In order to realise these values in the context of an intelligence-based claim, publicity must be traded off temporarily for access to relevant sensitive information. The underlying principle of representative government is that parliamentarians mediate between the interests of constituents (the people), party, and their own judgement. The argument which frequently follows from this is that a representative assembly which deliberates in private loses its representative qualities, and thus its legitimacy. These ideas, often presumed to be immutable truths, underestimate both the actual nature of the relationship between secrecy and publicity in a representative democracy and, in turn, the contribution made by certain forms of secrecy to the quality of deliberation. The foregoing discussion highlighted the difficulty in the assumption that 'there is a fairly straightforward

---

[194] LD Brandeis, 'What Publicity Can Do' (1932) *Other People's Money* 92. First published in *Harper's Weekly*, 20 December 1913.

positive correlation between openness and public legitimacy'.[195] Whilst there are rightful limits to secrecy in democracies, there are circumstances in which the quality of deliberation might be enhanced through a fluid relationship between secrecy and publicity. The ability of all MPs to engage on equal terms with secret intelligence, and to debate and contest its worth renders the proposal herein a form of inclusive secrecy. This is an essential element of the culture of challenge. What can be drawn from the examples across Westminster in wartime, Congress, and the European Parliament is that there is a clear burden of justification to be met when a legislature departs from publicity in favour of secrecy. Secondly, as a legislature becomes more deeply involved in war powers decisions, the need for parity of access to sensitive information becomes greater, and closed sessions become a more realistic prospect.

The argument in this chapter is that it is worth sacrificing transparency for increased participation in the secret intelligence context. It is a sacrifice that is required to allow parliamentarians to make better-informed decisions on armed conflict. Without closed intelligence sessions, we risk condemning Parliament to repeat after repeat of the Iraq War situation. The over-arching purpose of these closed intelligence sessions is to allow MPs to better determine if the Government's case for armed conflict is a sound one, or if alternative non-military means are preferable. Moreover, how to best integrate secret intelligence into democratic decisions about war powers is likely to remain an important issue. The desire of parliamentarians to engage substantively with intelligence-based claims when the Government presents them is now self-evident. In our constantly evolving and highly reactive Constitution, the position has been reached where closed sessions are neither strange, nor unconstitutional. Intelligence-based claims will persist before Parliament, and for 'intelligence to have value the reader must trust the author'.[196] Closed sessions are therefore essential to foster trust and understanding. The alternative is to continue with the present arrangements in full cognisance of the adverse consequences of presenting 'sanitised' intelligence briefings in the public domain. Secret intelligence which is central to the propriety of an armed conflict can neither be shielded from Parliament, nor divorced from its proper context. Parliamentarians are also required to bring diverse perspectives on the value of such material. After all, the worth of any intelligence is a matter of judgement not clinical expertise. Activities of this nature can only be conducted during a closed session of the type described herein. This proposal fosters the ideal that Parliament as a whole should be in a position to maximise the culture of justification in the context of war powers.

---

[195] J de Fine Licht and D Naurin, 'Open Decision-Making Procedures and Public Legitimacy: An Inventory of Causal Mechanisms' in J Elster (ed), *Secrecy and Publicity in Votes and Debates* (Cambridge, CUP, 2015) 147.

[196] Snell, 'How to Read the Trump Dossier' (n 26).

Conclusion

VERONIKA FIKFAK AND HAYLEY J HOOPER

Throughout this monograph we have sought to shine a light on the reality of the current political constitution in action, and to make prescriptions about its potential. This project for both authors, as public lawyers, was about honesty in several senses. First, we wished to create an honest account of how institutions (namely the Government and the House of Commons) work in the context of war powers. Secondly, we wished to paint an honest picture of how power is used (or potentially) misused in this context. Thirdly, we wished to be honest about the nature of the gap between the perception of democratisation caused by the recognition of the War Powers Convention in the Cabinet Manual, and the reality of the practice of parliamentary engagement in armed conflict decisions. It is this overarching contrast between perception and reality that has compelled this inquiry. The foregoing analysis revealed that both government and Parliament are complicit in the deception that the War Powers Convention has adequately democratised the war prerogative. The first part of the book explained the ways in which the political constitution falls short of fully realising the values of accountability, transparency, and participation in the context of war powers. Our analysis demonstrated that discussions of international legality suffocate other potential avenues of political discourse in the House of Commons. Next we unpacked the reality that the War Powers Convention was subject to a myriad of exceptions which are controlled by the Government. Finally, we revealed that information asymmetries and exclusionary secrecy continue to constrain parliamentarians' access to the full range of relevant information regarding the Government's case for war. In fact, the reality is much more complex than this. The picture that emerges demonstrates that the convention has at best achieved limited progress towards democratic control. The Government continues to hold the balance of power in this area. The struggle against these barriers by parliamentarians is the 'secret war' Parliament has been fighting since the early twentieth century: a war behind the democratic façade for more information and political control of the Government's power to wage war in the British electorate's name.

In light of this complex reality, chapters five and six put forward a package of solutions intended to bolster the governance values by reinvigorating political discourse, and securing a greater flow of information within Parliament. Our package of prescriptions for enhancing Parliament's political role wholeheartedly endorses Constant's aphorism that the 'only possible guarantee against useless or unjust wars is the energy of representative assemblies'.[1] An energised House of Commons is essential in realising both the culture of challenge and the culture of justification that we argue for in the latter half of this book. Re-energising the House of Commons in this sphere requires several things. Our proposed solutions sought to equip parliamentarians with the tools to move debates on armed conflict beyond the 'all or nothing' or binary light in which governments often present the case for armed conflict. This 'all or nothing' approach extends to the presentation of arguments relating to international legality, rhetoric relating to the 'good' or 'evil' of armed interventions, and to the case for intervention being presented as a choice between armed conflict or total inaction. We believe there can be no definitive 'right answer' to the question of war. Equally there can be no definite or categorical wrong answer. Instead of light and dark, there are infinite shades of grey.

However, if there is a central lesson to be drawn from the Chilcot Inquiry into the Iraq War it is that military action is a last resort to be considered after all possible alternatives have been exhausted.[2] The political constitution's discourse on war requires nuance. It is up to parliamentarians to push government to consider those alternatives. This requires us to be clear about the process of engagement of the House of Commons on questions of armed conflict. The only way in which MPs stand a realistic chance of achieving this or any other democratic objective is if they are engaged prior to any proposed military action on a substantive motion and are permitted to vote to approve or dismiss that motion and to propose amendments to the motion. Also, where the Government seeks to rely upon arguments based on secret intelligence, such as the content of a JIC report, the debate should proceed according to the process laid down in chapter six. Moving discussion and debate into this grey area, following the procedural requirements we argue for, are essential steps towards reinvigorating the good governance values we argue have been undermined throughout the twentieth and twenty-first centuries.

Pressing for greater fidelity to a culture of justification on the part of the relevant actors may also help create a greater trust in politics. The political fallout from the Iraq War still looms large in the public consciousness. But trust in government and politicians, even in developed Western democracies, is not commonplace. The Hansard Society's 2010 report 'What's Trust Got to do With It?',[3] published in the wake of the 2009 parliamentary expenses scandal, explained that Parliament has 'seen a marked decline in public confidence—only

---

[1] B Constant in B Fontana (ed), *Political Writings: Principles of politics applicable to all representative governments* (1815) (Cambridge, CUP, 1988) ch 13, 256.

[2] Sir John Chilcot, 'Sir John Chilcot's public statement, 6 July 2016', <www.iraqinquiry.org.uk> accessed 17 September 2017.

[3] R Fox, 'What's trust got to do with it? Public Trust in and Expectations of Politicians and Parliament (London, Hansard Society, 2010).

19 per cent see it as an influential institution on their everyday life'.[4] Similarly, in 2016 a YouGov poll measured trust in politicians at a mere 13 per cent, compared with other key constitutional actors, such as judges (78 per cent), and the unelected Members of the House of Lords (23 per cent). Trust in those who govern us (in the broadest sense) is perilously low.[5] This phenomenon is ubiquitous throughout history. Many people long for the return to a golden age of politics and parliamentary procedure, but no such age exists.[6] In many respects, Parliament is stronger vis-à-vis the Executive, in terms of the exercise of its scrutiny function, but it is not as highly regarded an institution as it once was.[7] The public relationship with Parliament and politics is best regarded as paradoxical: the public seem to long for more independently minded MPs, but at the same time they are suspicious of overtly divided parties.[8] At the same time, the more informed the public become regarding politics, the more it falls short of their expectations.[9] Such scepticism has a long lineage. In 1742 Hume was of the view that 'every man ought to be supposed a *knave*, and to have no other end, in all his actions, than private interest ... It is, therefore, a just *political* maxim, *that every man must be supposed a knave*'.[10] Hume's concern was that power had become overly concentrated in the House of Commons. Our concern is that government's power to wage war remains politically unchecked. The House of Commons should follow Hume's sentiment, by approaching Executive's case for war with scepticism. This is why the culture of justification is, at its core, a commitment to disclosure and reason-giving by all parties. Its goal is to make sure the explanation for any exercise of power crosses a threshold which is constitutionally acceptable. If government Ministers and MPs commit to striving towards the elements of a culture of justification in respect of debate and voting that we outline in this book, then, some increased public faith in the political process is at least possible.

We live in a particularly challenging era in which to make a case for engagement with, and ultimately faith in, the political constitution. This book opened with Junger's claim that, in respect of war, an 'evaluation, ongoing and unadulterated by politics, may be the one thing a country absolutely owes the soldiers who defend its borders'.[11] It might seem strange that we then proceed to argue for a need to repair the tools of the political constitution to counteract what we identified as the deficiencies in the current procedures. This may strike the reader as hypocritical, or even as absurd. But the practice of politics is an endeavour essential to

[4] ibid, para [4], executive summary.
[5] YouGov, 'Trust Tracker: November 2016', <www.yougov.co.uk> accessed 23 June 2017.
[6] Fox, 'What's trust got to do with it?' (n 3) 21.
[7] Fox, 'What's trust got to do with it?' ibid, para [16].
[8] ibid, para [17].
[9] ibid, para [13].
[10] D Hume, 'On the Independency of Parliament (1742)' (Adelaide, Blackmask Online, University of Adelaide, 2005) 1.
[11] S Junger, *War* (London, Harper Collins: Fourth Estate, 2011) 154.

democratic constitutionalism. However, the manner in which politics is practiced matters acutely. Recent events have seen the rise of a particularly problematic form of politics that we referred to in the preface. This is 'post-truth' politics.

Post-truth politics is a term which describes a corrosive political discourse which prioritises emotion and prejudice over facts and reason. Slogans such as 'Make America Great Again' in respect of the 2016 presidential election, and the Brexit campaign's 'Taking back control' represent the high watermarks (or perhaps the nadir) of politics in the post-truth era. The term 'post-truth politics' originated in a 1992 article by Steve Tesich in *The Nation*. Tesich argued that the American people, after enduring political scandals such as Watergate and the Iran-Contra Affair, had started to turn their back on the truth, rather than to confront the realities of failure in their cherished constitutional and governmental structures. The article concluded that: 'We, as a free people, have freely decided that we want to live in some post-truth world'.[12] But lies and spin are hardly novel features of democratic politics.[13] In 1946 Orwell was of the view that: 'Political language ... is designed to make lies sound truthful and murder respectable'.[14] This is perhaps an overly cynical view. However, the realistic view is that in the so-called post-truth era, there are wider threats to the health of the political constitution than we have previously witnessed. The present era is characterised by 'the democratising effect of the internet, the resultant decline in deference to experts, rising scorn for the political establishment, the tendency of social media to lock us in our echo chambers [and] the blurring of fact and fiction online'.[15] These are all direct threats to the realisation of a culture of justification and to the overall health of the political constitution. We acknowledged the onset of an era of post-truth politics in our preface, because we feel that it has real (but not insurmountable) consequences for the political constitution's ability to provide an appropriate check on the ultimate use of force. Creating a democratic culture of justification which vindicates good governance values requires effort from the Government, from Parliament, and perhaps most crucially from the electorate.

Honouring Junger's request for a debate about war that is 'unadulterated by politics' does not mean that it should be insulated from the political process. Nor does it mean that Parliament should reason in the same legalistic manner as courts. To wage war or not will always be a political choice; it has implications that cut across multiple dimensions in any polity. Removal from the political process would sever the relationship between war and democracy. Instead, we interpret

---

[12] S Tesich quoted in R Kreitner, 'Post-Truth and Its Consequences: What a 25-Year-Old Essay Tells Us About the Current Moment' *The Nation* (30 November 2016).

[13] M D'Ancona, *Post Truth: The New War on Truth and How to Fight Back* (London, Ebury Press, 2017) 26.

[14] G Orwell, 'Politics and the English Language' in S Orwell and I Angos (eds), *The Collected Essays, Journalism, and Letters of George Orwell* (New York, Harcourt, 1968) 139.

[15] S Jeffries, '"Bullshit is a greater enemy than lies"—lessons from three new books on the post-truth era' *The Guardian* (22 May 2017).

Junger's statement to mean that evaluation of the case for war requires discussion according to the norms of frank, adversarial politics underpinned by facts and reason that should be present in any healthy democracy. Politicians and citizens will always bring political biases to bear upon the question of a just war. This is healthy and normal in a democracy. We argue that parliamentarians are under a constitutional duty to push any government making an all-or-nothing case for war in a substantive motion into murkier waters to see if that case survives. This should be, however, as much as possible a politics of integrity. Lives at home and abroad are potentially at stake.

Counteracting post-truth politics requires us to realise that the relationship between the political constitution and the culture of justification works in two directions. It requires the Government to justify its case for war to Parliament, and it requires Parliament to justify its decision to the people, or the electorate. So, both the culture of justification and the primary locus of the political constitution may vary according to subject matter. The first wave of scholarship that sought to reorient and revive political constitutionalism within a tradition of civic republicanism erroneously concentrated exclusively on empowering Parliament as an institution.[16] This is despite the fact that before writing his seminal article, 'The Political Constitution', Griffith made clear that parliamentary democracy alone was not sufficient for politics to thrive. In describing government as the 'least masochistic of institutions' Griffith made clear that Parliament on its own was an insufficient check on Executive power; as government was unwilling to yield to structural parliamentary reforms which would limit either its power to legislate or to insulate itself from opprobrium.[17] More recent efforts, which build on Griffith's work, rightly caution that designating Parliament as the exclusive realm of the political constitution risks marginalising constituent power. It reminds us that 'where the latent but real power of the people is buried under the myth of Parliament's political omnipotence, the danger is that in their stupor those very people sleep walk through the degeneration of that constitution'.[18] We share these concerns: a well-functioning political constitution committed to fostering a culture of justification cannot be hermetically sealed within the parliamentary estate. Justification must exist in the first place from government to Parliament, and in turn from Parliament to the electorate. Ultimately, all Members of the Commons (including the Government) are accountable to the electorate via the ballot box, and the presence of debate and reasoned justification within Parliament is necessary to facilitate this broader public accountability.

---

[16] A Tomkins, *Our Republican Constitution* (Oxford, Hart, 2005); R Bellamy, *Political Constitutionalism: A Republican Defence of the Constitutionality of Democracy* (Cambridge, CUP, 2007).

[17] JAG Griffith, 'Why we need a revolution' (1969) *Political Quarterly* 383, 389.

[18] M Goldoni and C McCorkindale, 'Why we (still) need a revolution' (2013) 14 *German Law Journal* 2197, 2208.

Our argument asks a lot of Government Ministers and parliamentarians. But their efforts come with a reciprocal duty on members of the electorate, too, that is essential to the health of the political constitution. Constant was partially right when he argued for energised representative assemblies, but an energised, fact-checking, engaged electorate is also necessary. Spin and lies are nothing new in politics, but the unprecedented level public apathy that has let post-truth politics flourish certainly is. The present era is characterised as one where politicians are rewarded in the face of clear dishonesty. This malaise is potentially fatal to any attempt to democratise war powers. The duty of citizens to acquire knowledge to check the abuse of power in political institutions did not escape the constitutional architects of the eighteenth century. Thomas Jefferson, one of the Founding Fathers of the United States, considered an actively engaged electorate as necessary to prevent those who hold political power from 'pervert[ing] it into tyranny'. The most effective means of preventing such misuse of power is to equip the electorate with knowledge of the relevant facts.[19] Now, in the digital era, that duty falls on individual voters as much as any public institution. This need not be an onerous burden on the electorate, as the 'trivial tasks of research and information retrieval that used to consume days can now be accomplished in seconds on a smartphone or a tablet'.[20]

Secondly, if voters are dissatisfied with Parliament's choices on armed conflict, they must make this clear at the ballot box. Chapter five outlined how politicians should justify their votes; this information should help inform voters whether or not to re-entrust a politician with a seat in the House of Commons. Politics must be reconnected with electoral consequences. If the thresholds of justification are not met the electorate must make this clear when casting their votes at general elections. The culture of justification, in this sense, is very much in the eye of the beholder. What qualifies as an appropriate justification for armed conflict, or any of the options falling short of armed conflict will vary according to the politics of the voter. This is both usual and normal in a healthy democracy.

Finally, what became clear in the course of our argument is that cultivating rules which attempt to condition the behaviour of actors in this sphere, beyond the basic process requirements we outline, is an endeavour which is unlikely to alter the quality of discourse. Unlike municipal criminal law, where sanctions and a strong sense of public morality can be relied upon to compel certain courses of behaviour in the majority of people, the relationship between the Government and Parliament is not contingent upon these externally imposed rules. Instead, it evolves based on the morality, motivations, and ultimately the behaviours of the actors who occupy these institutions. In reality, this book is not about rules in the British Constitution; it is about people in the British Constitution.

---

[19] T Jefferson, Bill 79 of 1799 'A Bill for the More General Diffusion of Knowledge', <founders.archives.gov/documents/Jefferson> accessed 16 August 2017.

[20] D'Ancona, *Post Truth* (n 13) 124.

When Griffith delivered his seminal lecture, 'The Political Constitution', he was more than aware that the humans occupying institutions mattered more than the rules, forms and structures of those institutions.[21] In effect the research we undertook to write *Parliament's Secret War* confirmed the stark reality that 'who we are is all we have'.[22] The fact that the War Powers Convention, which enshrines a rule that is both easy to state and (in theory) to implement, could not appreciably influence the quality of debates and disclosures vindicates this argument. This is why neither the proposals for a parliamentary resolution, nor a War Powers Act could compel change in the behaviour of MPs or government as they currently stand. Rules in this domain are only valuable when the actors they affect commit to their implementation. Griffith's point in 'The Political Constitution' was that we get no more or no less than the constitution we as a polity deserve. Change in the political discourse on war powers must come from the ground up, it cannot be imposed from the top down. Realising a culture of justification requires all MPs and the Government of the day to act with candour. Politicians must press government to present its case with integrity. MPs must push the debate towards the exploration of other alternatives to war or non-intervention where this is considered appropriate. We acknowledge that this is an onerous obligation, particularly in the present political era. The energies of our democratic representatives are pulled in many different and competing directions. But these obligations must be taken seriously if the health of the political constitution in the context of war powers is to be maintained.

[21] JAG Griffith, 'The Political Constitution' (1979) 42 *Modern Law Review* 1, 20.
[22] AA Leff, 'Unspeakable ethics, unnatural law' (1979) 6 *Duke Law Journal* 1229, 1249.

BIBLIOGRAPHY

Aftergood, S, 'Reducing Government Secrecy' (2009) 27(2) *Yale Law and Policy Review* 399.

Aldrich, RJ, R Cormac, R, and Goodman, MS, *Spying on the World: The Declassified Documents of the Joint Intelligence Committee 1936–2013* (Edinburgh, Edinburgh University Press 2014).

Alston, P & MacDonald, E (eds), *Human Rights, Intervention, and the Use of Force* (Oxford, OUP, 2008).

Alvarez, J, *International Organizations as Law-makers* (Oxford, OUP, 2005).

Arend, AC, 'International Law and the Pre-emptive Use of Military Force' (2003) 26(2) *Washington Quarterly* 89.

Arendt, H (author) and Baehr, P (ed) H Arendt, *The Portable Hannah Arendt* (London Penguin Classics, 2003).

Armstrong, KA, *Brexit Time: Leaving the EU—why, how and when?* (Cambridge, CUP, 2017).

Bagehot, W, *The English Constitution* (Oxford, OUP: Oxford World's Classics, 2009).

Barnett, A, *Iron Britannia: Why Parliament Wages its Falklands War* (London, Allison and Busby 1982).

Belloc, H and Chesterton, C, *The Party System* (London, Steven Swift, 1911).

Benn, T, 'The Case for Constitutional Premiership' (1980) 33(1) *Parliamentary Affairs* 7.

Black, J, 'Parliament, the Press, and Foreign Policy' (2006) 25 *Parliamentary History* 9.

Black, J, *A System of Ambition? British Foreign Policy 1660–1793* (Longman, London, 1991).

Blick, A, 'Emergency powers and the withering of the Royal Prerogative' (2014) 18(2) *The International Journal of Human Rights* 195.

Blick, A, 'The Cabinet Manual and the Codification of Conventions' (2014) *Parliamentary Affairs* 191.

Blick, A, *The Codes of the Constitution* (Oxford, Hart, 2016).

Blomgren Bingham, L, Nabatchi, T, O'Leary, R, 'The New Governance: Practices and Processes for Stakeholder and Citizen Participation in the Work of Government' (2005) 65(5) *Public Administration Review* 547.

Bochel, H, Defty, A, and Kirkpatrick, J, *Watching the Watchers: Parliament and the Intelligence Services* (New York NY, Palgrave MacMillan, 2014).

Born H, and Leigh, I, *International Intelligence Cooperation and Accountability (Studies in Intelligence)*, (London, Routledge, 2012).

Born, H and Hanggi, H (eds) *The "Double Democratic Deficit": Parliamentary Accountability and the use of Force Under International Auspices* (Geneva, DCAF: Ashgate, 2004).

Born, H and Hanggi, H, 'The Use of Force under International Auspices: Strengthening Parliamentary Accountability' (Geneva, DCAF: Policy Paper No. 7, 2005).

Boulton, CJ, *Erskine May: Parliamentary Practice* (21st edn) (London, Butterworths, 1989).

Bovens, M, 'Analysing and Assessing Accountability: A Conceptual Framework' (2007) 13(4) *European Law Journal* 447.

Brazier, R, *Ministers of the Crown* (Oxford, Clarendon Press, 1997).

Briant, S, 'Dialogue, Diplomacy and Defiance: Prisoners' Voting Rights at Home and in Strasbourg' (2011) 3 *European Human Rights Law Review* 243.

Britt Snider, L, *Sharing Secrets with Lawmakers: Congress as a User of Intelligence* (Washington, DC, Central Intelligence Agency: Centre for the Study of Intelligence, Library of Congress, 1997).

Brownlie, I, International *Law and the Use of Force by States* (Oxford, OUP, 1963).

Bryant, C, *Parliament: The Biography Volume 2: Reform*, (London, Doubleday, 2014).

Burchill, R, White, ND and Morris, J (eds), *International Conflict and Security Law: Essays in Memory of Hilaire McCoubrey* (Cambridge, CUP, 2005).

Byrd, P (ed), *British Foreign Policy under Thatcher* (Oxford, Philip Allan, 1988).

Cane, P, McDonald, L and Rundle, K, *Principles of Administrative Law*, 3rd ed (Melbourne, OUP, 2018).

Chafetz, J, 'Whose Secrets?' (2013–2014) 127 *Harvard Law Review* 86.

Chambers, S, 'Behind Closed Doors: Publicity, Secrecy, and the Quality of Deliberation' (2004) 4 *Journal of Political Philosophy* 389.

Chester, DN and Bowring, N, *Questions in Parliament* (Oxford, OUP, 1962).

Chinkin, C and Kaldor, M, *International Law and New Wars* (Cambridge, CUP, 2017).

Churchill, W (author) and Eade, C (ed), *Secret Session Speeches by Churchill* (London, Cassell and Co., 1946).

Cook, R, *The Point of Departure* (London, Simon & Schuster Ltd, 2003).

Cowley, P (ed), *The Rebels: How Blair mislaid his majority* (London, Politico's, 2005).

Cowley, P, 'Unbridled Passions? Free Votes, Issues of Conscience and the Accountability of British Members of Parliament' (1998) 4(2) *Journal of Legislative Studies* 70.

Craig, P and De Burca, G, *EU Law: Text, Cases, and Materials*, 6th Edn (Oxford, OUP, 2015).

Craig, P and Rawlings, R (eds), *Law and Administration in Europe: Essays in Honour of Carol Harlow* (Oxford, OUP, 2003).

Creevy, M, 'A Critical Review of the Wilson Government's Handling of the D-Notice Affair 1967' (1999) 14(3) *Intelligence and National Security* 209.

Crick, B, *In Defence of Politics*, 5th edn (London, Continuum, 2005).

Cumming, A, 'Congress as a Consumer of Intelligence Information' (Washington DC, Congressional Research Service, 2010).

Curtin, D, 'Challenging Executive Dominance in European Democracy' (2014) 77(1) *Modern Law Review* 1.

D'Aspremont, J, 'Mapping the Concepts behind the Contemporary Liberalization of the Use of Force in International Law' *University of Pennsylvania Journal of International Law* 31.

Dale, HE, *The Higher Civil Service of Great Britain* (Oxford, OUP, 1941).

Dannenbaum, T, 'Translating the Standard of Effective Control into a System of Effective Accountability', (2010) 51 *Harvard International Law Journal* 113.

Davies, ACL, *Accountability: A Public Law Analysis of Government by Contract* (Oxford, OUP, 2001).

Davis, CM, 'Secret Sessions of the House and Senate: Authority, Confidentiality, and Frequency' (Washington DC, Congressional Research Service, 2014).

Davis, D, Richter, A and Saunders, C (eds), *An inquiry into the existence of global values* (Oxford, Hart: Studies in Comparative Public Law, 2015).

de Londras, F and Davis, FF, "Controlling the Executive in Times of Emergency: Competing perspectives on Effective Oversight Mechanisms" (2010) 30(1) *Oxford Journal of Legal Studies* 19.

Dicey, AV, *Introduction to the Study of the Law of the Constitution* (Indianapolis, Liberty/ Classics, 1982).

Diedrichs, U, 'The European Parliament in CFSP: More than a marginal player?' (2004) 39(2) *The International Spectator* 31.

Dieterich, S, Hummell, H, and Marschall, S, 'Strengthening Parliamentary "War Powers" in Europe: Lessons from 25 National Parliaments' (Geneva, DCAF, 2008).

Dillon, G.M., *The Falklands, Politics and War* (London, Palgrave MacMillan, 1989).

Dinstein, Y, *War, Aggression and Self-Defence*, 3rd ed (Cambridge, CUP, 2001).

Dinton, W, 'The Robustness of Conventions in a Time of Modernisation and Change' (2004) *Public Law* (Summer) 407.

Duke, S, 'Intelligence, security and information flows in CFSP' (2006) 21(4) *Intelligence and National Security* 604.

Elliott, M and Thomas, R, *Public Law*, 2nd edn (Oxford Oxford University Press, 2014).

Elsea, JK, 'Criminal Prohibitions on the Publication of Classified Defense Information' (Washington DC, Congressional Research Service, 2013).

Elsea, JK, 'The Protection of Classified Information: The Legal Framework (Washington DC, Congressional Research Service, 2013).

Elster, J (ed), *Secrecy and Publicity in Votes and Debates* (Cambridge, CUP, 2015).

Falk, R, 'Kosovo, World Order, and the Future of International Law' (1999) 93 *American Journal of International Law* 847.

Feldman, D (ed) *Law in Politics, Politics in Law* (Oxford, Hart, 2014).

Fisher, EC, 'Transparency and Administrative Law: A Critical Evaluation' (2010) 63(1) *Current Legal Problems* 272.

Freedman, L, 'On War and Choice', (2010) 107 *The National Interest* 9.

Freedman, L, *The Official History of the Falklands Campaign, Volume I* (London, Routledge, 2004).

Galligan, B and Brenton, S (eds) *Constitutional Conventions in Westminster Systems Controversies, Changes and Challenges* (Cambridge, CUP 2015).

Gaskarth, J, 'The fiasco of the 2013 Syria votes: decline and denial in British foreign policy' (2016) 23(5) *Journal of European Public Policy* 718.

Gee, G and Weber, G, 'What is a political constitution?' (2010) 30(2) *Oxford Journal of Legal Studies* 273.

Gibbs, GC, 'Parliament and Foreign Policy in the Age of Stanhope and Walpole' (1962) 77 *The English Historical Review* 18.

Goodman, MS and Omand, D, 'What Analysts Need to Understand: The King's Intelligence Studies Program' (2008) 52(4) *Studies in Intelligence* 1.

Gray, C, *International Law and the Use of Force*, 3rd edn (Oxford, OUP, 2008).

Gray, J, *Enlightenment's Wake: Politics and Culture at the Close of Modern Age* (London, Routledge, 1995).

Griffith, JAG, 'The Official Secrets Act 1989' (1989) 16(3) *Modern Law Review* 273.

Griffith, JAG, 'The Political Constitution' (1979) 42 *Modern Law Review* 1.

Grimmett, RF, 'The War Powers Resolution: After Thirty-four Years' (Washington DC, Congressional Research Service, 2010).

Gutmann, A, and Thomson, D, *Democracy and Disagreement: Why moral conflict cannot be avoided in politics and what should be done about it* (Cambridge MA, Harvard University Press, 1996).

Haass, RN, 'The Necessary and the Chosen' (2008) 88(4) *Foreign Affairs* 167.

Haass, RN, *War of Necessity, War of Choice: A Tale of Two Iraq Wars*, 2nd edn (New York, Simon & Schuster, New York, 2010).

Hagopian, A, *et al*, 'Mortality in Iraq Associated with the 2003–2011 War and Occupation: Findings from a National Cluster Sample Survey by the University Collaborative Iraq Mortality Study' (2010) 10(10) *PLoS Med*: e1001533.

Häkkinen, T, *The Royal Prerogative Redefined: Parliamentary Debate on the Role of the British Parliament in Large-scale Military Deployments, 1982–2003* (Helsinki, Jyväskylä Studies in Humanities 224).

Harlow, C, 'Global Administrative Law: The Quest for Principles and Values' (2006) 17(1) *The European Journal of International Law* 187.

Harlow, C, *Accountability in the European Union* (Oxford, OUP, 2002).

Hastings, M and Jenkins, S, *The Battle for the Falklands* (London, Book Club Associates, 1982).

Henkin, L, *International Law: Politics, Values and Functions:* vol. 78 Collected Courses of the Hague Academy of International Law (The Hague, Brill Nijhoff, 1990).

Hennessy, P, *The Prime Minister: The Office and Its Holders Since 1945* (London, Allen Lane, 2000).

Hood, P, 'Constitutional Conventions: Dicey's Predecessors' (1966) *Modern Law Review* 29.

Horne, A and Le Sueur, A (eds), *Parliament: Legislation and Accountability* (Oxford, Hart 2016).

Hough, B, 'Conventions and Democracy' 29 (2000) *Anglo-American Law Review* 368.

Hovell, D, 'Due Process in the United Nations' 110 *American Journal of International Law* 1.

Hughes-Wilson, J, 'Pre-war intelligence and Iraq's WMD threat: Intelligence blundering or intelligence laundering? (2004) 149(1) *Defence and International Security (The RUSI Journal)* 10.

Irvin, RA & Stansbury, J, 'Citizen Participation in Decision Making: Is It worth the Effort?' (2004) 64(1) *Public Administration Review* 55.

Jack, M (ed), *Erskine May Parliamentary Practice* (24th edn), (London, LexisNexis, 2011).

Jaconelli, J, 'The nature of constitutional conventions' (1999) 19 *Legal Studies* 24.

James, M, Blamires, C and Pease-Watkin, C (eds), *The Collected Works of Jeremy Bentham, Political Tactics (1791)* (Oxford, Oxford Scholarly Editions Online, 2015).

Jennings, WI, 'Parliament in Wartime: III' (1940) *The Political Quarterly* 351.

Jennings, WI, *The Law and the Constitution*, 5th edn (London, University of London Press, 1964).

Jessup, P, *A Modern Law of Nations: An Introduction* (Hamdon Conn, Archon Books 1968).

Johnstone, I, 'Security Council Deliberations: The Power of Better Argument' (2003) 14 *European Journal of International Law* 437.

Joseph, R, *The War Prerogative: History, Reform, and Constitutional Design* (Oxford, OUP, 2013).

Joyner, D, 'The Kosovo Intervention: Legal Analysis and a More Persuasive Paradigm' (2002) 13 *European Journal of International Law* 597.

Kaiser, FM, 'Protection of Classified Information by Congress: Practices and Proposals' (Washington DC, Congressional Research Service, 2006).

Kavanagh, A, 'Proportionality and parliamentary debates: exploring some forbidden territory' (2014) 34(3) *Oxford Journal of Legal Studies* 443.

Keir, DL, *The Constitutional History of Modern Britain 1485–1937* (London, Adam and Charles Black, 1938).

Kelsen, H, *The Law of the United Nations: A Critical Analysis of Its Fundamental Problems* (London, Stevens & Sons, 1950).

Kingsbury, B, Krisch, N, and Stewart, RB, 'The emergence of global administrative law' (2005) 68 (3/4) *Law and Contemporary Problems* 15.

Krisch, N, 'Unilateral Enforcement of the Collective Will: Kosovo, Iraq, and the Security Council' (1999) 3 *Max Planck Yearbook of United Nations Law* 59.

Ku, C and Jacobson, H, *Democratic Accountability and the Use of Force in International Law* (Cambridge, CUP, 2003).

Kuperman, AJ, *The Limits of Humanitarian Intervention: Genocide in Rwanda* (Washington DC, Brookings Institution, 2001).

Kyle, K, *Suez: Britain's end of Empire in the Middle East* (London, IB Tauris, 2011).

Leigh, I, 'Rebalancing Rights and National Security: Reforming UK Intelligence Oversight a Decade After 9/11' (2012) 27(5) *Intelligence and National Security* 722.

Leyland, P and Bamforth, N (eds), *Accountability in the Contemporary Constitution* (Oxford, OUP, 2013).

Lillich, RB (ed) *Humanitarian Intervention and the United Nations* (Charlottesville VA, University of Virginia Press, 1973).

Loughlin, M, 'The end of avoidance' 38(15) *London Review of Books* (28 July 2016).

Loughlin, M, *Sword and Scales: An examination of the relationship between law and politics* (Oxford, Hart, 2000).

Low, S, 'The Foreign Office Autocracy' (1912) 91 *Fortnightly Review* 1.

Mahapatra, D, 'The Mandate and the (In)Effectiveness of the United Nations Security Council and International Peace and Security: The Contexts of Syria and Mali' (2016) 21 *Geopolitcs* 43.

Marshall, G, *Constitutional Conventions: The Rules and Forms of Political Accountability* (Oxford, Clarendon Press, 1984).

Mayer, KR, 'Executive Power in the Obama Administration and the Decision to Seek Congressional Authorization for a Military Attack against Syria: Implications for Theories of Unilateral Action' (2014) *Utah Law Review* 821.

McD Clockie, H, 'Parliamentary Government in Wartime' (1940) 6(3) *The Canadian Journal of Economics and Political Science* 359.

McHarg, A, 'Reforming the United Kingdom Constitution: Law, Convention, Soft Law' (2008) 71(6) *Modern Law Review* 853.

Mill, JS (author) Gray J (ed), *On Liberty and other essays* (Oxford OUP: Oxford World's Classics, 2008).

Morton, P, 'Conventions of the British Constitution' (1991–1992) 15 *Holdsworth Law Review* 114.

Murenik, E, 'A bridge to where? Introducing the interim Bill of Rights' (1994) 10 *South African Journal on Human Rights* 31.

Murphy, R, 'Is the UN Security Council fit for purpose' (2015) 24(4) *Politics Review* 1.

Murphy, S, 'Assessing the legality of invading Iraq' (2004) 92 *Georgia Law Journal* 173.

Murphy, SD, 'The Doctrine of Pre-emptive Self-Defence' (2005) 50 *Villanova Law Review* 699.

Murray, C and O'Donoghue, A, 'Towards Unilateralism? House of Commons Oversight of the Use of Force', (2016) 65(5) *International and Comparative Law Quarterly* 305.

Nicol, D, 'Professor Tomkins' House of Mavericks' (2006) *Public Law* 467.

Omand, D, *Securing the State* (London, Hurst, 2010).

Oppenheim, L (author) and Lauterpacht, H (ed), *International Law vol2*, 7th ed (London, Longmans, Green and Co., 1952).

Parry, C, 'Legislatures and Secrecy' (1954) 67(5) *Harvard Law Review* 737, 740.

Patout Burns, J (ed), *War and Its Discontents: Pacifism and Quietism in the Abrahamic Traditions* (Washington DC, Georgetown University Press, 1996).

Payne, S, 'War Powers: The War Prerogative and Constitutional Change' (2008) 153(3) *The RUSI Journal* 28.

Pearce, E, Campbell, E and Harding, E, *Australian Law Schools: A Discipline Assessment for the Commonwealth Tertiary Education Commission* (Canberra, Australian Government Publication Service, 1987).

Phillips, H, 'A Constitutional Myth: Separation of Powers' (1977) 93 *Law Quarterly Review* 11.

Pitkin, HF, *The Concept of Representation* (Berkeley CA, University of California Press, 1967).

Pozen, DE, 'Deep Secrecy' (2010) 62(2) *Stanford Law Review* 257.

Prakash, S, 'Unleashing the Dogs of War: What the Constitution means by "declare war"' (2007–2009) 93 *Cornell Law Review* 45.

Qvortrup, M (ed), *The British Constitution: Continuity and Change: A Festschrift for Vernon Bogdanor* (Oxford, Hart, 2013).

Rawlings, R, 'Concordats of the Constitution' (2000) *Law Quarterly Review* 257.

Raz, J, *The Morality of Freedom* (Oxford, OUP: Clarendon Press, 1986).

Record, J, 'Back to the Weinberger-Powell Doctrine?' (2007) *Strategic Studies Quarterly* 79.

Reisman, WM, 'Unilateral Actions and the Transformations of the World Constitutive Process: The Special Problem of Humanitarian Intervention' (2000) 11 *European Journal of International Law* 3.

Richards, J, *A Guide to National Security* (Oxford, OUP, 2012).

Richmond, OP and Mitchell, A (eds), *Hybrid Forms of Peace: From Everyday Agency to Post-Liberalism* (Basingstoke, Palgrave Macmilllan, 2012).

Rodgers, D, *By Royal Appointment: Tales from the Privy Council—The Unknown Arm of Government* (London, Biteback Publishing 2015).

Rodin, D, *War and Self-Defense* (Oxford, OUP, 2002).

Rogers, R, and Walters, R, *How Parliament Works*, 6th edn, (London, Pearson Longman, 2006).

Rosen, G, 'Can you keep a secret: How the European Parliament got access to sensitive documents in the area of security and defence' (RECON Online Working Paper 2011/2012).

Ross, C, *Independent Diplomat: Dispatches from the Unaccountable Elite* (Ithaca NY, Cornell University Press, 2007).

Rossiter, C, *Constitutional Dictatorship: Crisis Government in Modern Democracies*, 5th edn (London, Transaction Publishers, 1948).

Saunders, EN, *Leaders at War: How Presidents Shape Military Interventions* (Ithaca NY, Cornell University Press, 2011).

Schmitt, C (author) and Schwab, G (trans), *The Concept of the Political* (Chicago, University of Chicago Press, 1995).

Setty, S, 'The Rise of National Security Secrets' (2012) 44(5) *Connecticut Law Review* 1563.

Smith, D, 'The Separation of Powers in New Dress' (1966-67) 12 *McGill Law Journal* 491.

Smith, GW, *Liberalism—Critical Concepts in Political Theory* (London, Routledge, 2002).

Smith, HR, *Democracy and the Public Interest* (Athens, GA, University of Georgia Press, 1960).

Snell, A, 'How to Read the Trump Dossier' (2017) *London Review of Books* (17 January 2017).

Stahn, C, 'Between Law-Breaking and Law-Making: Syria, Humanitarian Intervention and "What the Law Ought to Be"' (2014) 19 *Journal of Conflict and Security Law* 25.

Steiner, ZS, *Britain and the Origins of the First World War* (London, MacMillan, 1977).

Stewart, R and Knaus, G, *Can Intervention Work?* (Norton: Global Ethics Series, New York, 2012).

Strong, J, 'Why Parliament Now Decides on War: Tracing the Growth of the Parliamentary Prerogative through Syria, Libya and Iraq' (2015) 17(4) *The British Journal of Politics and International Relations* 604.

Sunstein, CR, *Why Societies Need Dissent* (Harvard University Press, Cambridge MA 2003).

T'Hart, P, *Groupthink in Government: A study of small groups and policy failure* (Baltimore, The Johns Hopkins University Press, 1990).

Taylor, RB, 'Foundational and regulatory conventions: exploring the constitutional significance of Britain's dependency upon conventions' (2015) *Public Law* 614.

Thatcher, M, *The Downing Street Years* (London, HarperCollins, 1995).

Thomas, C, 'The Use and Abuses of Legitimacy within International Law' (2014) 34 *Oxford Journal of Legal Studies* 729.

Tomkins, A, 'A right to mislead Parliament?' (1996) 16 *Legal Studies* 63.

Tomkins, A, 'In defence of the political constitution' (2002) 22(1) *Oxford Journal of Legal Studies* 157.

Tomkins, A, *The Constitution after Scott: Government Unwrapped* (Oxford, Clarendon Press, 1998).

Travers, M, Van Boven, L, and Judd, C, 'The secrecy heuristic: inferring quality from secrecy in foreign policy contexts' (2014) 35(1) *Political Psychology* 97.

Turpin, C and Tomkins, A, *British Government and the Constitution*, 7th edn (Cambridge, CUP, 2011).

United States Congress, House, *Constitution, Jefferson's Manual, and Rules of the House of Representatives*, H.Doc. 112–161, 112th Cong., 2nd sess. (Washington, GPO, 2013).

Utley, R (ed), *9/11 Ten Years After: Perspectives and Problems* (London, Routledge, 2012).

Von Clausewitz, C (author) and Heuser, B (ed), *On War*, (Oxford, Oxford World's Classics, 2008).

Waldron, J, 'Legislating with Integrity' (2003–2004) 72 *Fordham Law Review* 373.

Waldron, J, 'The core of the case against judicial review' (2006) 115(6) *The Yale Law Journal* 1346.

Walgrave, S and D Rucht, *The World Says No to War: Demonstrations against the War on Iraq* (Minneapolis, University of Minnesota Press 2010).

Warner, M, 'Wanted: A definition of "intelligence"' (2002) *Central Intelligence Agency* (Defence Technical Information Centre: Washington DC, 2002).

Watt, DC, 'Foreign Affairs, the Public Interest and the Right to Know' (1963) 34 *The Political Quarterly* 124.

Webber, G, 'Loyal Opposition and the political constitution' (2017) 37(2) *Oxford Journal of Legal Studies* 357.

Wehberg, H, *L'Interdiction du Recours à la Force: Le Principe et les Problèmes qui se Posent*, 78 Collected Courses of the Hague Academy of International Law (The Hague, Brill Nijhoff, 1951).

Weiler, J *The Constitution of Europe: Do the new clothes have an emperor?* (Cambridge, CUP, 1999).

Wheare, K. *Modern Constitutions* (Oxford, OUP, 1966).

White, N, *Democracy goes to War* (Oxford, OUP, 2009).

Wilkinson, N, *Secrecy and the Media: The Official History of the United Kingdom's D-Notice System: The Official History of the D-notice System* (London, Routledge, 2009).

Wilson, H, *The Governance of Britain*, (London, Weidenfield & Nicholson and Michael Joseph, 1976).

Wilson, W (author) Baker, RS and Dodd, WE (eds), *War and Peace* (New York, Harper and Brothers, 1927).

Young, A, 'Constitutional Implications of Brexit' (2017) *European Public Law*, forthcoming.

Zeisberg, M, *War Powers: The Politics of Constitutional Authority* (New Jersey, Princeton University Press, 2013).

INDEX